Problematic Behaviors
During Adolescence

McGraw-Hill Series in Developmental Psychology

Consulting Editor: Ross A. Thompson

Problematic Behaviors During Adolescence

Jeffrey J. Haugaard
Cornell University

Boston   Burr Ridge, IL   Dubuque, IA   Madison, WI
New York   San Francisco   St. Louis
Bangkok   Bogotá   Caracas   Lisbon   London   Madrid   Mexico City
Milan   New Delhi   Seoul   Singapore   Sydney   Taipei   Toronto

McGraw-Hill Higher Education

A Division of The **McGraw-Hill** Companies

PROBLEMATIC BEHAVIORS DURING ADOLESCENCE

Published by McGraw-Hill, an imprint of The McGraw-Hill Companies, Inc., 1221 Avenue of the Americas, New York, NY 10020. Copyright © 2001 by The McGraw-Hill Companies, Inc. All rights reserved. No part of this publication may be reproduced or distributed in any form or by any means, or stored in a database or retrieval system, without the prior written consent of The McGraw-Hill Companies, Inc., including, but not limited to, in any network or other electronic storage or transmission, or broadcast for distance learning.

Some ancillaries, including electronic and print components, may not be available to customers outside the United States.

This book is printed on acid-free paper.

2 3 4 5 6 7 8 9 0 DOC/DOC 0 9 8 7 6 5 4 3 2 1

ISBN 0–07–231685–3

Vice president and editor-in-chief: *Thalia Dorwick*
Editorial director: *Jane E. Vaicunas*
Senior sponsoring editor: *Rebecca H. Hope*
Developmental editor: *Rita Lombard*
Marketing manager: *Chris Hall*
Senior project manager: *Peggy J. Selle*
Lead media producer: *David Edwards*
Senior production supervisor: *Sandra Hahn*
Coordinator of freelance design: *David W. Hash*
Interior designer: *Jamie A. O'Neal*
Cover designer: *Joshua Van Drake*
Cover image: © *Stone Images, Mark Gervase*
Compositor: *GAC–Indianapolis*
Typeface: *10/12 Palatino*
Printer: *R. R. Donnelley & Sons Company/Crawfordsville, IN*

Library of Congress Cataloging-in-Publication Data

Haugaard, Jeffrey J., 1951–
    Problematic behaviors during adolescence / Jeffrey J. Haugaard. — 1st ed.
        p.   cm. — (McGraw-Hill series in developmental psychology)
    Includes bibliographical references (p.) and index.
    ISBN 0–07–231685–3
    1. Behavior disorders in adolescence.   2. Conduct disorders in adolescence.
3. Adolescent psychiatry.   4. Developmental psychology.   5. Health behavior in adolescence.
I. Title.   II. Series.

RJ506.B44 H28   2001
616.89'00835—dc21
                                                                        00–039428
                                                                        CIP

www.mhhe.com

For
N. Dickon Reppucci
and
Howard E. Nichols,
Whose Support and Guidance Have Made
Me a Better Teacher, Writer, and Person

About the Author

JEFFREY J. HAUGAARD is an associate professor of human development at Cornell University, where he has taught and conducted research for the past 10 years. He received his B.A. from the University of California at Santa Cruz in 1973, worked at a boarding and day school for elementary and junior high students for 10 years, returned to school full-time in 1984, and earned his Ph.D. in clinical psychology from the University of Virginia in 1990. Dr. Haugaard teaches in the areas of child and adolescent psychopathology and in family systems therapy. His research has been focused in the areas of child maltreatment, families that adopt school-age children, and problematic romantic and dating relationships among undergraduates.

Dr. Haugaard has been recognized several times for excellence in undergraduate teaching and advising while at Cornell. He was the founding president of the Section on Child Maltreatment (Division of Child, Youth, and Family Services) of the American Psychological Association, and he has served on several committees with the American Psychological Association. He is the chair of the Research Advisory Committee with the Donaldson Adoption Institute. Dr. Haugaard is the co-author of *The Sexual Abuse of Children* (with N. D. Reppucci) and the co-editor of books on community prevention programs and psychopathology. He has published many articles and book chapters on child maltreatment, adoption, and problematic behaviors in adolescence.

Brief Contents

Contents

Foreword

Rapid growth is often accompanied by vulnerability. This principle has long been recognized by developmental scientists. When an organism is changing in many significant ways during a brief period, harmful influences can have a greater impact than at other stages of development. During prenatal growth, for example, when physical structures and organ systems are maturing at an unparalleled rate, the fetus is highly vulnerable to damage from viral infection or drug exposure. Brain development during the early years of life likewise provides a foundation for life-long functioning, but the growing brain is more susceptible to damage owing to sensory deprivation or malnutrition than at any later age. Adolescence is also a period of rapid development, and the profound accomplishments of the teenage years provide insight into the vulnerability of young people during this stage of life.

Adolescence is, as everyone knows, a period of self-discovery and rapidly emerging self-understanding. Young people see themselves from a new, psychologically self-aware perspective, and identity and individuality take shape, yet for some adolescents the experience of self-discovery becomes distorted in the self-absorption of narcissism or the derogatory self-evaluations of depression. For others, eating disorders reflect conflicts over body image and self-worth. Adolescence is also a period of social discovery, as young people enter into a peer culture with its own structure, expectations, and rules. Teenagers become effective social actors outside of the protective milieu of the family and, in so doing, acquire greater self-confidence and become more independent individuals. For some, however, adolescence is a period of social turmoil, marked by painfully shy reserve or hostile, aggressive impulses. For others, social identity takes shape in the dysfunctional context of a gang or cult.

During adolescence, sexual maturation is part of self-understanding and social competence. Incorporating a sexual identity into a sense of self and learning how to relate psychosexually with others are among the most exciting—and challenging—features of the adolescent experience. For some young people, though, sexuality is not a friend but a foe when sexual victimization occurs through assault or coercion or when an unexpected (and undesired) pregnancy forces fundamental changes in life direction. Adolescence is also a time of rapidly growing independence and self-reliance as young people develop the skills of mature judgment. However, the reckless, risk-taking behavior of some adolescents reveals dangerous limitations in their decision-making capabilities.

Adolescence is, in short, a period of amazing growth and disturbing vulnerability. Teenagers who seem poised to master life's challenges often succumb to internal conflicts or external stressors. And, as the developmental principle previously stated suggests, these characteristics of the adolescent experience may be intrinsically united. The accomplishments that foreshadow adult functioning leave young people at risk because of the limitations in perspective, judgment, and experience that are part of their childhood legacy.

In *Problematic Behaviors During Adolescence,* Jeffrey Haugaard unfolds these issues with insight and sensitivity. Drawing on his extensive knowledge as a research scientist, his clinical practice with adolescent clients, and personal experience, the author weaves together the common themes of adolescent development with the uncommon challenges and stresses that lead some young people to depression, drug abuse, gang involvement, or even suicide. While reminding us that relatively few adolescents fall victim to serious problems, Haugaard also underscores how most young people will experience one or more of these difficulties, in some form, during their teenage years. The result is a book that offers fresh understanding of adolescence and a deepened appreciation of the origins of adolescent difficulty.

In his discussion of each of these "problematic behaviors," the author introduces the reader to the knowledge that guides researchers, therapists, program planners, and others who work with troubled youth. Each chapter opens with a definition of the problem, together with a discussion of different profiles or subtypes and their characteristics. This is followed by information concerning the prevalence of this problem in the adolescent population. The heart of each chapter, however, concerns influences on the development of the behavior: the internal (e.g., genetic, temperamental, cognitive) and external (e.g., familial, peer, cultural) influences that lead to problematic behavior in young people. As a gifted teacher, Haugaard interweaves hypothetical stories, first-person accounts, current events, and anecdotes into his narrative as a constant reminder of the people, not just the problems, that concern us.

Much of this is painful to read. It is difficult to hear of the pain of a depressed or suicidal adolescent, or the downward spiral of a young person with an eating disorder or drug addiction. Each chapter opens with a case study that provides human depth to the information that is subsequently presented, but each chapter closes with hope, as Haugaard discusses approaches to the treatment and prevention of these problematic behaviors. The author also offers practical advice to his readers, recognizing that many are adolescents or young adults. We learn, for example, what to do if we (or a friend or partner) have been sexually assaulted, how to apply "psychological first aid" to a suicidal friend, how to assist someone with a drug problem or an eating disorder, and how to respond tolerantly (but not unduly supportively) to a narcissistic roommate.

When readers reach the concluding chapter, they also better understand some of the broader lessons of adolescent development. Behaviors lie along a continuum—and, although relatively few young people succumb to serious problems with eating disorders, recklessness, depression, or substance abuse, most will experience some of the difficulties that contribute to these serious problems. Several problematic behaviors can go together, thus; one cannot consider any in isolation. Understanding the origins of suicide, for example, requires understanding the causes of depression and of anger in adolescents. Most important, Haugaard emphasizes that there are no simple explanations for problematic behaviors in adolescence and that simple answers are likely to be misleading. The complexity of human behavior is especially apparent in adolescence, and readers deterred by the ambiguity and uncertainty that are inherent in this field might wish to turn to simpler topics (Haugaard suggests theoretical physics or inorganic chemistry). These lessons of development remind us of how difficult it is to understand the challenges of the adolescent experience—whether as an adult or even as a teenager. They also underscore the importance of offering assistance to the young people who need our help.

This volume is part of the *McGraw-Hill Series in Developmental Psychology.* This series has been designed to enrich and expand our common knowledge of human development by providing a forum for theorists, researchers, and practitioners to present their insights to a broad audience. As a rapidly expanding scientific field, developmental psychology has important applications to parents, educators, students, clinicians, policymakers, and others who are concerned with promoting human welfare throughout the life course. Although the fruits of scholarly research into human development can be found on the pages of research journals, and students can become acquainted with this exciting field in introductory textbooks, this series of specialized, topical books is intended to provide insightful, in-depth examinations of selected issues from which undergraduates, graduate students, and academic colleagues can all benefit. As forums for highlighting important new ideas, research insights, theoretical syntheses, and applications of knowledge to practical problems, I hope that these volumes will find many uses: as one of several specialized texts for advanced coursework, as tutorials for scholars interested in learning about current knowledge on a topic of interest, and as sourcebooks for practitioners who wish to traverse the gap between knowledge and application. The authors who contribute to this series are committed to providing a state-of-the-art, accurate, and readable interpretation of current knowledge that will be interesting and accessible to a broad audience with many different goals and interests. I hope, too, that these volumes will inspire efforts to improve the lives of children, adolescents, and adults through research and practice, which are much needed in our world.

Problematic Behaviors During Adolescence reflects these goals by offering a view of the challenges, and the hopes, of the adolescent experience through the lens of a skilled clinician, developmental scientist, and thoughtful observer of human behavior.

Ross A. Thompson
Series Editor

Preface

Ten years ago, I taught my first course as a new assistant professor at Cornell University: Problematic Behaviors in Adolescence. To be honest, that first course was not very good. I was nervous; the list of topics was too constrained; and, since I had just finished my clinical internship, I had not had very much time to prepare my lectures. Based on comments from my students at the end of that semester, I made many changes to the content of the course, and I have continued to make some changes each year. Students encouraged me to add topics closely related to them and their lives, such as shyness, and topics that would help them understand the bothersome behaviors of peers, such as narcissism. They also pushed me continually to help them understand how problematic behaviors develop, rather than simply give them facts to regurgitate to me on an exam. They often wanted to know how to respond effectively to problematic behaviors in themselves and their friends: how to help someone with an eating disorder, how to respond if their roommate seemed suicidal, or how to deal with their own depression.

My course now enjoys a fair amount of popularity. This is partly because the topics we explore have meaning in most of the students' lives. Many of them have struggled with depression or an eating disorder; know someone who has been injured engaging in reckless behavior; wonder if their drug use is problematic; or have lived in a neighborhood that a gang considered its territory. The course is also popular because we struggle to explore how these problematic behaviors develop: to understand why an apparently successful high school student tries to kill herself, why someone might leave college to join a cult, or why someone who already is too thin continues to lose weight.

This text includes many of the topics discussed in my course and focuses on understanding how problematic behaviors develop. This is a difficult task because the development of problematic behaviors is very complex. As we will see throughout this text, there are many influences on the development of each problematic behavior. Each influence plays a role in the development of a problematic behavior in some adolescents but has little or no influence on other adolescents. In addition, several influences usually combine to create a problematic behavior in an adolescent, with the relative weight of each influence differing among individual adolescents. Consequently, in order to understand the development of a problematic behavior, we must know about the variety of influences on it and the many ways that these influences can combine to affect an individual's behavior.

The goals of this text are (a) to provide current, research-based knowledge about a variety of problematic behaviors during adolescence, (b) to provide guidance in applying this knowledge to understand how these behaviors develop in individual adolescents, and (c) to describe the ways in which an understanding of the development of problematic behaviors can be used to prevent them or to help adolescents engaged in them. We will focus on a broad range of adolescent problematic behaviors, from those that can result in death (e.g., suicide, eating disorders) to those that impede adolescents' abilities to live their lives as they would like (e.g., shyness). Some of the problematic behaviors we will explore affect many adolescents (e.g., depression), while others affect a small percentage of adolescents (e.g., joining a cult).

By the end of this text, you should have knowledge about several problematic behaviors and an understanding of how they develop. In addition, your increased knowledge about the range of influences on the problematic behaviors we explore should give you a strategy for thinking about the development of many other problematic and nonproblematic behaviors. This should help you think more expansively and more intelligently about the problematic behaviors you observe in others and experience in yourself.

ACKNOWLEDGMENTS

Thanks go to many people who have contributed to this text. Dick and Christine Reppucci gave me a place to live and lots of encouragement when I started this text during a sabbatical leave. My friends, including Rick Canfield, Cindy Hazan, Quan and Joan Howard, Ed and Laurie Mulvey, Todd and Nancy Tomlitz, and Patrick and Theresa Walsh, have all provided ongoing encouragement and support.

Ross Thompson, series editor, provided expert advice during this project. Thanks also to the many reviewers who shared their thoughts at different stages of this project, including Joseph P. Allen, *University of Virginia;* Jennifer Connolly, *York University;* Bonnie B. Dowdy, *Dickinson College;* Brad Donohue, *University of Nevada, Las Vegas;* Judith Dubas, *College of William and Mary;* Cynthia E. Erdley, *University of Maine;* Stephen M. Gavazzi, *The Ohio State University;* Helen Johnson, *Queen's College;* Bonnie Leadbeater, *University of Victoria;* Joseph Marrone, *Siena College;* Jerry A Martin, *University of North Florida;* Dennis R. Papini, *Western Illinois University;* Randall J. Russac, *University of North Florida;* and Denise Sloan, *University of Florida.* Erica Bates worked hard to find hundreds of lost references and type the reference section; the text would never have been completed without her help. Thanks also to Rosie O'Donnell, whose uplifting television program provided just the right break for me, every morning at 10:00.

Finally, thanks to 10 years of bright, inquisitive, thoughtful Cornell undergraduates who have taken my courses, challenged me to think more deeply about issues, and provided smiles and encouragement.

CHAPTER 1

Introduction

Many adolescents behave in ways that are troubling or bothersome to those around them, and often these behaviors are distressing or harmful to the adolescents themselves. These adolescents, their parents, and their peers often cannot understand why they behave as they do. Other adolescents experience burdensome emotions that sap their energy for living life the way they would like. Many hate having these emotions yet feel powerless against them.

Of course, not all adolescents experience high levels of problematic behavior or emotions, so it is not appropriate to think of adolescent development as consisting primarily of difficulties. However, most adolescents will experience one or more of the problematic behaviors discussed in this text, even if these problems arise during only part of their adolescence. Many adolescents feel depressed at one time or another, act in risky ways, worry that they are taking too many drugs, feel too shy to participate in social activities, or diet in unhealthy ways. Even adolescents who are highly successful in academics or sports; those who contribute to their family, school, and community; and those who are popular with their peers experience problematic behaviors. Consequently, knowing about a wide range of adolescent problem behaviors is important if we are to have a broad understanding of adolescent development and the adolescent experience.

This text focuses on understanding the development of some of the problematic behaviors and emotions experienced by adolescents. This introductory chapter discusses some fundamental principles found throughout this book, describes how each chapter is constructed, and describes how the book was created and its topics were chosen. This information should provide a foundation for understanding the problematic behaviors explored in this text.

ADOLESCENCE AS A LIKELY TIME FOR THE DEVELOPMENT OF PROBLEMATIC BEHAVIORS

Adolescence is a time when many problem behaviors and emotions begin or escalate. The biological, psychological, and social changes that occur during

1

adolescence can influence the development of such behaviors and emotions. For example, hormonal changes during puberty may exacerbate tendencies toward depression or sexual aggression in some adolescents, and changes in body shape and size may increase some adolescents' shyness or susceptibility to anorexia nervosa. Many young adolescents move to schools where they are surrounded by older adolescents, and the influence of this new environment can encourage them to drink or use other drugs, be aggressive, or take increased risks. Adolescence is also a time of new social activities, such as dating and having sex, and the stress and anxiety that often accompany these new activities can result in depression or aggression.

While these biological and social changes are occurring, most adolescents are moving away (psychologically or physically) from parents, other relatives, neighborhood friends, and others who supported and guided them as they struggled with the challenges of childhood. The consequent reduction of support and guidance can leave many adolescents more vulnerable to events that increase problematic behavior, reducing their ability to respond in a healthy way when faced with troubling circumstances or difficult decisions. In addition, adolescents are usually monitored less than children by parents, teachers, and other adults. This can give adolescents more opportunities to initiate problem behaviors and can make adults less available to notice behavioral or emotional changes and to intervene to stop them.

THE IMPORTANCE OF ADDRESSING PROBLEMATIC BEHAVIORS DURING ADOLESCENCE

Although most adolescents experience minor levels of problematic behaviors or emotions, some adolescents' lives are severely disrupted by them. For example, although most adolescents have times when they feel intensely sad, some develop a level of depression that interrupts their academic and social lives. Many adolescents who experience relatively minor forms of these problems are able to overcome them, through their own resources or with the help of those who give them support and guidance; however, adolescents with severe forms of a problematic behavior may need the intervention of mental health professionals, teachers, clergy, or other professionals.

There are many reasons for preventing the types of problematic behavior that disrupt the lives of adolescents and for intervening effectively with those whose lives have been disrupted:

- The most obvious reason is to reduce the suffering of the adolescents who are experiencing these problems. Their pain is sometimes intense and seemingly without end—as shown by those who attempt suicide. Even those not experiencing intense consequences may have their lives interrupted by these problems. In addition, problems experienced in adolescence can result in psychological or physical damage that can be carried throughout life—possibly influencing others who have contact with the adolescent, including parents and siblings, spouses, children, coworkers, and friends.

- Many adolescents' problematic behaviors cause pain and suffering for others. Every year, thousands of people are sexually assaulted by an adolescent, are involved in an automobile accident with an intoxicated adolescent, or are hit by a stray bullet from a gang shooting. Reducing such pain and suffering is another reason to reduce adolescent problematic behaviors.
- There are significant social costs of many adolescent problematic behaviors. Some social costs are obvious—for example, the monetary costs of arresting, trying, and incarcerating violent adolescents. Other costs are less apparent, however. Consider the potential costs to society of the suicide of a troubled adolescent who might someday have contributed to our understanding of quantum physics, medicine, or world peace, or of a shy adolescent who might have contributed to a new computer breakthrough or been an influential preschool teacher, but could not find the strength to attend a job interview. Although we may never know these specific costs, adolescent problems clearly result in many hidden costs to society.

To prevent problematic behaviors in adolescence, or to intervene effectively with those experiencing problems, we must understand the development of the problems. That is the purpose of this text. Learning facts about the problems and the adolescents who have them may be important in some ways, but it is only by understanding the forces that influence the development of problematic behaviors that we can deal with them effectively.

Our dilemma, however, is that we do not completely understand how problematic behaviors develop in adolescence, and we have only a rudimentary understanding of some of them. Consequently, this is not a book that contains all the answers about the development of problematic behaviors. The first professor for whom I served as a teaching assistant in graduate school put it succinctly: Know? No! Our understanding of the development of some of these problems is progressing, but we clearly are not there yet. By the end of this text, you should have a clearer understanding of the influences on the development of many problematic behaviors and of the many ways in which these influences can interact to drive an adolescent's behavior. However, you will not completely understand why certain adolescents have bulimia nervosa, why others are painfully shy, and why others sexually assault their peers. This is because no one completely understands these behaviors.

FUNDAMENTAL PRINCIPLES

Several fundamental principles are found throughout the chapters in this text.

There Are No Simple Answers

The most important principle to keep in mind when trying to understand the development of problem behaviors is that no simple explanation for them is correct. Simple explanations about problem behaviors abound, such as (1) eating disorders are the result of cultural pressure for girls to be thin, (2) adolescents join gangs because of social inequality in urban areas, and (3) sexual assault is caused by men's determination to dominate women. All these explanations are incomplete.

All the behaviors discussed in this text are too complex to be explained by simple answers. Cultural pressure for girls to be thin may contribute to the development of eating disorders, but only a small percentage of girls in our culture develop an eating disorder, so other influences must exist as well. Social inequality in urban areas may create an environment for the development of gangs, but gangs also develop in rural areas and in areas with less social inequality, so other issues must influence who joins gangs and who does not. Some men may use sexual assault to dominate women, but other men assault women for other reasons. To understand the development of problematic behaviors, we must be willing to struggle with their complexity.

Behaviors Are Influenced by Many Factors

Problematic behaviors are influenced by a wide range of issues. The culture in which an adolescent has been raised can influence the development of problematic behaviors. Some of these influences originate in racial, religious, and national cultures. Others originate in narrower cultures, such as the culture of a particular city or neighborhood. Many other influences on the development of problematic behavior are centered on the individual. Some individual influences are primarily biologically based—for example, a genetic influence on depression or reckless behavior. Some influences come primarily from a person's emotions, thoughts, and experiences. Other influences include those from families, peers, television and movies, political events, and natural disasters.

Trying to consider all these potential influences when thinking about the behavior of a certain adolescent can be overwhelming. However, keeping this complex web of influences in mind is essential when thinking about problem behaviors. Otherwise, one risks slipping into a situation in which simple, incomplete answers are the only ones considered.

Different Combinations of Influences Affect Different People in Different Ways

It is not just the multitude of possible influences that makes it difficult to understand problematic behaviors; it is also that these influences affect individuals in different ways. High levels of conflict in one adolescent's family may have a large influence on the development of her substance abuse problems, while the same level of conflict in another adolescent's family may have little or no influence on her substance abuse problem. A biologically based predisposition to depression may contribute to a suicide attempt by one adolescent but have no influence on a suicide attempt by another. The aggression of one adolescent may be affected largely by his family and to a lesser degree by his peers; the same level of aggression by another adolescent may be affected largely by his peers and to a lesser degree by his family. When thinking about the development of a problematic behavior in an adolescent, it is important to consider the relative importance of the many potential influences on that behavior.

Influences Interact with and Influence Each Other

Many of the influences on an adolescent's problem behavior do not operate independently. In some cases, one influence may affect the development of another influence. Consider a boy with a biologically based temperament that influences him to engage in much rough-and-tumble play. His interest in rough-and-tumble play influences his choice of friends, many of whom are also interested in rough-and-tumble play. When he becomes an adolescent, his level of aggression may be influenced by his temperament and the reinforcement he receives from his friends—with most of his friends being chosen because of his temperamental proclivity toward rough-and-tumble play.

Many people would describe the process of considering the ways in which some influences affect others as a developmental perspective. Factors present at any point in a person's life are influenced by factors present earlier in life, and they influence the way that the person develops in the future. These factors do not *determine* the person's ongoing development but, rather, *influence* it. For example, consider several preschool-age girls who are badly abused and neglected by their parents, and whose abuse influences the girls to believe that relationships are based on aggression and power. In elementary school, some of these girls may bully others, because other influences in their lives have resulted in their taking the role of aggressor. Other girls may become fearful of, and withdrawn from, people because other influences have resulted in their taking on the role of victim. In high school, some of the aggressive girls may join gangs, through which they can express their aggression and dominance over others. Other aggressive girls may express their aggression while on athletic teams; one might be the first girl on her school's wrestling team and be seen as a crusader for women's rights in her school. Some of the withdrawn girls may enter a series of relationships with boys in which they are victimized. Others may find work in a nursery school for abused children, where their quiet nature makes them effective teachers for frightened children. One thing leads to another, but the pathway from that one thing to the other is complex and is different for each of us.

Several Problematic Behaviors Can Occur Together

In this text, each problematic behavior is described separately. However, it should not be assumed that they always occur separately. Many adolescents experience more than one problematic behavior simultaneously, and others experience one problematic behavior after another. In some cases, two problematic behaviors may have a common cause—for example, a low sense of self-esteem may lead some adolescents to be shy and to develop problematic eating patterns. In other cases, one problematic behavior can lead to another. For example, some adolescents who are depressed may begin to smoke marijuana to relieve their depression, which could eventually lead to a dependence on marijuana. When two or more problems occur concurrently, simultaneous treatment for the problems may be needed, and failure to address one problem may make it more difficult to resolve others.

Behaviors Lie Along a Continuum

Each behavior discussed in this book can be thought of as lying along a continuum. Consider depression, for example. Milder forms of a depressed mood might result in someone's feeling sad for a day or so and having reduced energy for schoolwork or social activities. Moderate forms might mean more pronounced feelings of sadness lasting a longer time, with periodic withdrawal from work and social activities. More severe forms of depression might include ongoing strong feelings of sadness, a sense of hopelessness that the sadness will ever end, and minimal involvement in school, social, or family activities. Extreme forms of depression could involve such strong feelings of sadness and hopelessness that the person is unable to get out of bed. Shyness can be thought of in the same way. Some people feel shy in a few social situations, but their shyness does not affect their behavior; others experience stronger feelings of shyness that influence their behaviors in many social situations; and others feel such strong feelings of shyness that they are unable to attend social events at all. Even some behaviors that are often thought of as not lying along a continuum, such as joining a cult, actually do lie along a continuum. For example, some members of a cult are involved in cult activities only periodically, others are frequently involved, and cult activities are at the core of the lives of some members.

Three primary issues result from seeing problematic behaviors as points along a continuum. First, many people experience these behaviors at some level; many people have periodic sadness, thoughts of death, unhealthy dieting, and times when they act recklessly. You should not be alarmed, therefore, when you see some of your behaviors described in this text. Experiencing these behaviors in a mild way may help you understand those with more severe forms. Experiencing feelings of sadness, helplessness, and despair after breaking up with a boyfriend or girlfriend may provide a glimpse into the lives of depressed adolescents who experience sadness almost every day. Struggling with whether to have dinner when you are on a diet may provide a glimpse into the struggle that someone with anorexia nervosa faces several times every day for months or years at a time.

A second issue is that decisions must be made about where along this continuum a behavior is considered problematic. This requires that we divide the continuum of behavior at a certain point—with problematic levels of the behavior on one side and nonproblematic levels on the other side. This difficult, complex process is discussed in detail in chapter 2. It is important to note that values—such as cultural, neighborhood, or family values—can influence where on the continuum a behavior is considered problematic. A certain level of shyness may be considered problematic in one ethnic culture but not in another, or a certain level of risk-taking behavior might be considered problematic in some areas of the United States but not in others.

Third, interventions to prevent a problematic behavior or reduce its consequences do not have to have as their goal the complete elimination of the behavior. Keeping or returning a behavior to the level at which it does not have a pronounced negative effect on a person's life may be a more appropriate goal for preventive or therapeutic efforts. Interventions with adolescents who are depressed are not intended to eliminate sadness from their lives; similarly, efforts to prevent eating disorders do not have to eliminate dieting from the behavior of adolescents.

Most Behaviors Result from Decisions Made by an Adolescent

With a few exceptions, most of the problematic behaviors discussed in this book result from a series of decisions made by adolescents. Adolescents decide to join gangs or cults, to be sexually aggressive, or to take drugs. It is not just that adolescents make decisions that eventually result in a behavior; most often, they decide to engage in those behaviors each time they do.

These decisions are not made completely freely each time, however. A dieting adolescent experiences very strong physical cravings for food, and these cravings have a significant influence over decisions she makes about binge eating. Similarly, a young adolescent may face great pressure from members of a gang to join the gang, and this pressure may have immense power over his decision to join the gang. However, simply because a decision is not made completely freely does not mean that it is not a decision. For example, you probably experienced various pressures to make the decision to attend college. Imagine the reactions of your family and friends if you had decided not to attend college, and you can get a sense of the pressure you faced. Even if this pressure was not overt, it was still there. Decisions to engage in problematic behavior are often like your decision to attend college: they are influenced by many forces, but they are eventually made by the person engaging in the behavior. Just as you could have decided not to attend college despite the pressures to do so, aggressive adolescents can decide to stop being aggressive and adolescents taking drugs can decide to stop taking drugs, despite the pressures to continue.

Seeing problematic behaviors as resulting from a series of decisions made by adolescents is helpful in several ways. It encourages us to identify the influences on these decisions, and this is an important step toward understanding the development of problematic behaviors. For example, by understanding the influences on an adolescent's decision to eat in a binge/purge cycle, we can understand how he developed bulimia nervosa. Understanding the influences on an adolescent's decision to attempt suicide tells us a great deal about the development of her suicidal behavior.

Understanding the influences on adolescents' decisions to engage in problematic behaviors also provides essential information for those working to prevent these behaviors or to eliminate them once they develop. For example, understanding that a lack of economic resources in a community can influence an adolescent's decision to join a gang provides important information on ways the community can reduce gang membership. Understanding the influences of changes in brain functioning that occur after extended drug use can guide the development of interventions to reduce or eliminate drug abuse in an adolescent's life.

However, the development of some problematic behaviors is only remotely connected to decisions made by an adolescent. Of the behaviors explored in this text, depression, shyness, and narcissism seem to fall into this category. These behaviors appear to have the common features of either developing early in life and continuing into adolescence or developing primarily because of experiences or changes in biological functioning over which the adolescent has little or no control. Depression appears to occur largely because of biological changes over which a person has little control, because of stress imposed on an adolescent, or because of styles of thinking that develop early in life. The fundamental features of shyness and narcissism also appear to develop early in life. Although decisions seem to have less to do with the development of these three problematic behaviors than others, decisions can play an important role in reducing or eliminating these problems. For example, depressed adolescents can decide to think less about the depressing aspects of their lives and focus more on the positive aspects, and this decision can improve their mood. Shy adolescents can decide to change their style of interpersonal interaction (despite the difficulties of doing so) and, so, can reduce their feelings of shyness.

Considering Problematic Behaviors Involves the Use of Values

Values influence the way we decide that some behaviors are problematic, the ways we think about how they develop, and the importance that we assign to reducing or eliminating problematic behaviors. Even the scientific procedures used to investigate a problematic behavior involve the use of values. It is important that we acknowledge the role that values play in these processes, so that we can accurately recognize the extent to which our thinking is influenced by our values rather than by an objective understanding of the way the universe functions. Recognizing the role of values in our thinking about problematic behavior reduces the chance that we will criticize others' behavior simply because it does not conform to our own. We can use our values to conclude that a behavior is wrong, but it is important to understand that this conclusion is based on our own value system.

Being aware of the influence of our values is particularly important as we try to understand how a person could develop a pattern of behavior that we find objectionable. If we are too quick to condemn the person and the decisions that the person has made about a behavior, then we limit the extent to which we can comprehend the range of influences on the person and, consequently, our ability to understand the behavior and to intervene to reduce it. By working to understand the full range of influences on the behavior, we can come to a clearer understanding of it, even if we believe that it is wrong.

Many types of values can influence how we think about problematic behaviors. Some values come from the larger contexts in which we live. Most people in our culture, for example, believe that all people should be afforded the same basic rights. This is one reason that we consider sexual assault to be wrong—one person should not be able to damage another in pursuit of sex, because to do so says that one person is fundamentally more important than the other. This value has not always been present, however. Forcing sex on some members of a society has been acceptable in many cultures throughout history. Other values are based on racial or religious heritage. Some adolescent behaviors might be considered problematic in many Asian American families but not problematic in most European American families. A behavior considered wrong by many fundamentalist Christians might not be considered wrong by many Hindus.

Values can also come from smaller contexts, such as neighborhoods and families. For example, physical aggression in response to a verbal challenge might be perceived quite differently in many neighborhoods in large urban areas than in the surrounding suburbs—and these value differences might cut across races and religions. Also, values may differ among individual families in a neighborhood, with some families' passing along the value that physical aggression in response to a verbal challenge is wrong but others' communicating that such physical aggression is acceptable.

Our Ultimate Focus Is on People, Not on Problems

Although our emphasis in this text is on problematic behavior, it is essential to keep in mind that our ultimate focus is on people. As we try to understand an adolescent who attempts suicide, we must remember that we are discussing a person who is troubled and in pain. While we work to understand how a behavior develops, often using data gathered through scientific methods, we must not forget our humanity or lose sight of the individuals who are struggling with the behavior.

THE ORGANIZATION OF THE CHAPTERS

All of the following chapters are organized similarly. The first section of each chapter focuses on defining the problematic behavior discussed. This is an essential first step when thinking about or discussing a problematic behavior, a step that is often ignored. Before we can talk about rape, for example, we must define it clearly. Many definitions of rape exist, and your definition may be different from those others use. Consequently, if I were to discuss rape without defining it clearly, you might believe that I am discussing behavior quite different from the behavior that someone else believes I am discussing. This could lead to considerable confusion. Thus, at the beginning of each chapter, each behavior is defined as clearly as possible. Some definitions will be different from those preferred by others, but at least they are definitions on which the rest of the chapter can be understood.

The prevalence of each behavior is then described. Information about prevalence can influence the amount of attention paid to a behavior. Knowing, for example, that suicide is the third most common cause of death among adolescents can increase our attention to suicide and influence the extent to which we consider it an important social issue. Information about prevalence can also guide our thinking about the development of a behavior. For example, knowing that depression is more common among females points us in possible directions for understanding its development. Although knowing that more females than males are depressed does not tell us why this is true, it helps guide us to wonder about which biological differences between males and females, or which experiences females have more frequently than males, might influence the patterns of depression we observe.

The principal part of each chapter focuses on the development of the problematic behavior. The strategy for exploring the development of each behavior differs somewhat from chapter to chapter, based on the types and amount of available information about the behavior. However, all the strategies have some aspects in common: each strategy involves a description of the individual, family, and cultural influences on the behavior, as well as the characteristics or experiences associated with those who exhibit it. Then, ways in which these influences can combine to produce the behavior are described. Because of the many possible combinations of influences, many more pathways to the problem behavior exist than can be described in each chapter. You will need to think about other possible pathways yourself.

Most chapters end with a discussion of ways to prevent the development of the problematic behavior and of interventions for those experiencing the behavior. This discussion is always linked to the exploration of the behavior's development. Knowing the various pathways by which the behavior develops is essential for creating effective ways to prevent the behavior or reduce its occurrence. Knowing that many suicidal adolescents have little sense of the future, for example, points to the importance of helping them understand the ways in which they can create a positive future.

A FEW ADDITIONAL IMPORTANT POINTS

The Choice of Behaviors to Discuss

Limitations imposed by text length mean that not all adolescent problematic behaviors can be discussed in this text. Consequently, some problematic behaviors have been excluded. Decisions about which behaviors to include were influenced by several issues. First, I have tried to include a range of problematic behavior. For example, I have included some problems that are considered mental disorders (e.g., anorexia nervosa) and others that are not (e.g., risk taking). Also included are problems that have a range of consequences, from death to feelings of awkwardness and discomfort in social situations. Finally, many of the included behaviors are those that students in my courses on problematic behaviors have considered the most interesting or have requested be included in the course (e.g., shyness).

Some problematic behaviors are not included in this text because they receive extensive coverage in adolescent development textbooks, which may be assigned in a course along with this text. For example, adolescent pregnancy is an important issue for adolescents, their families, and society, but it is not included in this text because it receives extensive coverage in many adolescent development textbooks. Other problematic behaviors, such as juvenile delinquency, are partly dealt with in this text. For example, physical aggression and sexual assault, two types of delinquency, are covered here, but other forms of delinquency, such as shoplifting and vandalism, are not. Other important problematic behaviors (e.g., obesity, academic failure) have not been included simply because there was not space to include them.

Gender and Pronouns

All of the problematic behaviors discussed in this text affect males and females. Although some problems are more likely to be experienced by those of one gender (e.g., depression is more common among females and physical aggression is more common among males), it is essential that we not lose sight of the fact that both males and females experience every problem. In discussing these problems, however, using both the female and male form of each pronoun can be awkward. To avoid this awkwardness, each chapter opens with a vignette that features either a female or male. The chapter then uses the pronouns appropriate for the person in the vignette. This results in the use of male pronouns in some chapters and female pronouns in the others. This makes for easier reading while preserving the fundamental principle of considering all problematic behaviors as affecting both females and males.

Multicultural Issues

The culture in which an adolescent lives can have a significant influence on whether a particular behavior is considered problematic, how the behavior develops, and how best to prevent or reduce the problematic behavior. As noted already, in this sense, culture can be broadly defined—for example, by race or religion—or more narrowly defined—for example, by region of the country or by whether or not a person has a physical disability.

Whenever the research literature offers meaningful information on the influence of culture on a problematic behavior, that information is included in this text. There is little or no research information on the influence of culture and some of the problematic behaviors in this text, however, so some chapters have little mention of culture.

A FINAL THOUGHT

Neither struggling to understand the development of adolescent problematic behavior nor intervening with adolescents who exhibit these behaviors is for the faint of heart. The complex web of influences on these behaviors can make it difficult to understand them, and the challenges of intervening effectively with troubled adolescents can appear insurmountable. Those willing to struggle with the complexity and uncertainty of problematic behaviors among adolescents will find themselves in the middle of a fascinating and challenging enterprise.

CHAPTER 2

Designating Adolescent Behaviors as Problematic

Lisa is 14 and has been dieting continually for about a year. She is quite thin, but not thin enough to meet the criteria for anorexia nervosa. She has never binged and purged, so she does not meet the criteria for bulimia nervosa. She does well academically but has stopped participating in the three sports that she once played because of being too tired during practice. She spends many hours each week planning her diet. When Lisa's mother becomes concerned about her dieting, she asks their family physician to intervene. He talks with Lisa and raises the possibility of psychotherapy. Lisa says that she would refuse to go to psychotherapy. She points out that all her friends are thin, that she has to be thin to be popular, and that her diet contains healthy foods. She realizes that she is very thin, but she is proud of her thinness. She says that gaining weight just to please her parents would be terrible. She feels that her parents and her physician should just leave her alone.

Jon's parents are horrified when he tells them that he plans to leave college and join a religious movement, "The Chosen." He explains that he first learned about The Chosen a month ago and has been spending increasing amounts of time at their meetings. It was at the end of a recent weekend retreat, after being awake and in continuous meetings for 60 hours, that Jon made the decision to join the group. He talks extensively about the love that he feels in the group and about his commitment to its goal of bringing peace to the world. He has withdrawn his savings and plans to give it to the group, and he will be leaving the next week to live in its compound in a remote part of Arizona.

The school psychologist at Kennedy Middle School is asked to help a Vietnamese girl, Tran, who seems very shy. She seldom participates in class and usually eats alone during lunch. Her teachers are concerned that she is depressed. In conversations with Tran and her parents, the psychologist learns that Tran's grandmother, to whom Tran was very close, died about three months before. Tran says that she feels shy sometimes but points out that she gets good grades and got an *A* on an oral report the previous week. Tran's parents state that they do not believe that Tran is shy, that she behaves in ways that are consistent with how they have raised her, and that she seems about as outgoing as other Vietnamese girls they know. They do have some concerns about the amount of time she has spent in her room since her grandmother's death, however, they believe that she will eventually become less sad.

Are Lisa, Jon, and Tran engaged in problematic behaviors? Should Lisa's physician try to get her into psychotherapy? Should Jon's parents try to restrain him from leaving home? Should Tran's school psychologist help her become less shy or less depressed? What criteria or principles would you use to answer these questions?

The Plan: Before we can begin our exploration of problematic behaviors during adolescence, we must deal with two issues: who we are going to consider to be an adolescent and how we are going to determine whether a behavior is problematic. In this chapter, we will first discuss the characteristics that have been used to define adolescence. We will then turn to the process of designating a behavior as problematic. First, we will define problematic. Next we will look at several criteria for determining whether or not a specific behavior is problematic. Finally, we will explore the issue of who gets to use these criteria to designate a behavior as problematic. As we will see, no criterion is best for designating a behavior as problematic, and disagreement exists about who is best suited for making this designation. Consequently, by the end of the chapter we will not be able to conclude how a behavior should be designated as problematic, but we will know more about the ways in which these designations are made.

DETERMINING WHOSE PROBLEMATIC BEHAVIORS WE ARE DISCUSSING

Many people discuss issues related to adolescence without defining adolescence. It is often unclear, for example, whether sixth-graders are considered adolescents or whether undergraduates are considered adolescents. Much of the confusion about when adolescence occurs is due to the different strategies that can be used to define adolescence. For example, age can be used (e.g., adolescence begins at age 12 and ends at age 21), or educational status can be used (e.g., adolescence begins during middle school and ends when a person's formal education ends) (e.g., Santrock, 1998; Steinberg, 1999). Each strategy has some advantages but presents some ambiguities. For example, age provides well-defined beginnings and endpoints of adolescence. However, there is no general agreement on which age span is correct, and each can present some problems. For example, the use of ages 12–21 results in 20-year-old "adolescents" who are financially independent of their parents, married, and with a child of their own. Using educational status provides logical, socially based endpoints to adolescence but results in 16-year-old high school dropouts being considered adults, while those who continued on to graduate school are considered adolescents into their mid-twenties.

Although determining when adolescence begins and ends can be difficult, we will not be overly concerned with this difficulty in this text. The discussions in this text are relevant for understanding the problematic behaviors of those from the ages of about 12 to 21. While children and adults also experience many of these problematic behaviors, all of the behaviors discussed in this text are of importance to those from middle school to college age.

DEFINING THE TERM PROBLEMATIC

In the next section, we will explore several ways for determining whether a particular behavior is problematic. Before we can do that, we need to define problematic.

The term *problematic* is an adjective describing something that is a problem. Dictionaries provide two definitions of the term *problem:* (a) something that is perplexing and requires a solution, such as a mathematical problem, and (b) something that is difficult or troublesome, such as a problem child (e.g., Webster, 1999). At first glance, it seems that the second use of the term *problem* is the one best suited for our definition of problematic. The behaviors that we will focus on are troubling—sometimes to the adolescent engaging in them, sometimes to the adolescent's parents or peers, and sometimes to the society in which the adolescent lives. However, the first definition of the term *problem* is also appropriate. The behaviors that we will discuss are perplexing: it is often unclear why an adolescent engages in behaviors with many actual or potential negative outcomes. In addition, the behaviors often call for a solution. Many shy or depressed adolescents search for ways to end their shyness or depression, parents search for ways to end their children's association with gangs or cults, and society searches for ways to reduce physical and sexual aggression.

Given these meanings of the term *problem,* it seems reasonable to suggest that problematic behaviors are those that are perplexing and troublesome and that call for a solution. Many behaviors can be considered problematic, including those that are illegal (e.g., sexual assault, physical assault, and illicit drug use), those that are legal but dangerous (e.g., excessive risk taking and dieting), and those that cause emotional pain (e.g., shyness and narcissism). At their core, all these behaviors are troubling to adolescents or those around them, and all call for solutions to the trouble and pain that they bring.

DETERMINING WHICH BEHAVIORS ARE PROBLEMATIC

Although many might agree on the definition of problematic in an abstract sense, it can be difficult to decide whether specific behaviors are problematic. There is no universal standard that can be used to decide whether a behavior is problematic; rather, someone, or a group, must make a value judgment about the nature of the behavior. These judgments are always based on some criteria, even though these criteria are not always clearly specified. In this section, we will explore several of these criteria and the ways that they can be applied to judgments about adolescent behaviors.

Designating behaviors as problematic must be done cautiously, since doing so can have a meaningful influence on the lives of the adolescents who engage in them. In some cases, designating a behavior as problematic can help an adolescent, a family, or a community receive beneficial assistance. However, labeling behaviors as problematic can also have potential negative consequences. For example, designating a behavior as problematic can result in some adolescents being labeled as troubled or deviant, and this label may influence how peers, family members, or society deal with them. In addition, designating behaviors as problematic can open the way for various interventions. In some cases, everyone involved views these interventions as helpful, such as when an adolescent voluntarily joins a treatment program for drug abuse or a therapy group for shyness. However, in other cases, an intervention may be imposed on an unwilling adolescent and may significantly affect an adolescent's freedom. The thin adolescent who refuses to eat can be sent to a psychiatric hospital by her parents and the aggressive adolescent can be sent to prison by the courts.

Criteria for Determining Which Behaviors Are Problematic

As noted in chapter 1, the behaviors discussed in this text can be thought of as lying along a continuum. For example, there are low, moderate, high, and extreme levels of shyness, depression, aggression, and dieting. It is relatively easy to determine whether behaviors on both ends of a continuum are problematic. Low levels of most of these behaviors are often not considered problematic, especially if they occur only periodically, and high levels of the behaviors are often considered problematic. The problem comes with trying to determine where along the continuum to draw a line and say, "The behaviors on this side are not problematic and the behaviors on this side are problematic." Even if the continuum is divided into several groups, such as "not problematic," "somewhat problematic," and "very problematic," decisions must still be made about where on the continuum one group ends and the next begins. For example, most would agree that an overweight adolescent who diets in a sensible way is not engaging in problematic behavior and that a very thin adolescent who refuses to eat more than 700 calories a day is engaging in problematic behavior. But what of the many dieting adolescents somewhere between these points— the average-weight adolescent who is on a moderately strict diet or the thin adolescent who is trying to lose just a little more weight from her thighs? What criteria can be used to decide whether these adolescents are on the problematic or nonproblematic side of the dieting continuum?

Several criteria can be used for designating behaviors as problematic. None are generally accepted as superior to the others, and all are used at various times and in various circumstances. Two or more criteria are often used together. The use of each criterion has advantages and disadvantages, and the relative mix of advantages and disadvantages may change, depending on the circumstance in which the criterion is used. Being aware of the various criteria, and their advantages and disadvantages, may allow people to choose those that are best suited to a particular situation.

The use of one criterion may result in a determination that a certain behavior is problematic, while the use of another criterion may result in a determination that the behavior is not problematic. For example, the experimental use of marijuana might be considered problematic based on the illegal nature of marijuana use but not considered problematic based on the prevalence of adolescent experimentation with marijuana. It is often difficult to reconcile the different judgments about a behavior that can be reached when different criteria are used.

Specific Behaviors Are Problematic

One method for designating behaviors as problematic is simply to specify that a certain well-defined behavior is problematic. No concern is given to the context in which the behavior occurs or to the outcome of the behavior. This is similar to the way in which certain behaviors are designated as illegal, and many behaviors designated as problematic using this method are illegal. For example, driving with a certain blood-alcohol level is considered problematic and is illegal. It does not matter who the driver is or whether the driver has behaved recklessly or hurt anyone. A related method is to consider certain well-defined behaviors as problematic depending on the age of those engaged in them. For example, drinking one beer in a bar could be considered problematic for a 17-year-old but not for a 21-year-old.

A primary advantage of this strategy is that the problematic behaviors can be clearly specified, thus providing clear behavioral guidelines for avoiding problematic or illegal behaviors. In addition, the strategy can be applied equally to everyone: no one can have sexual intercourse with a 13-year-old; no one can take cocaine. The primary disadvantage of this strategy is that it does not take into account individual or cultural differences that may influence how the behavior is experienced by the individuals engaged in it and those around them. For example, people taking heroin to ease the pain of incurable cancer are treated similarly as those doing it simply to get high.

Behaviors That Deviate from Norms Are Problematic

A second method for designating behaviors as problematic is to use our knowledge about the prevalence and frequency of a behavior (the norms for the behavior) and to consider as problematic all behavior that deviates a certain amount from the norms. For example, one criterion for the diagnosis of anorexia nervosa is that the person must maintain a weight 15 percent or more below her expected body weight (APA, 1994).

One advantage of this method is that it takes a developmental perspective—some behaviors that might be considered problematic at one age are not considered problematic at another. For example, experimenting with alcohol might be seen as problematic when done by a 10-year-old but not problematic when done by a 16-year-old. This is because many 16-year-olds experiment with alcohol, but most 10-year-olds do not. This strategy also allows cultural and environmental contexts to be considered. Aggression in an environment where aggression is common may not be seen as problematic, while the same level of aggression in a nonaggressive environment could be seen as problematic.

One difficulty with using deviation from norms to designate behavior as problematic is that the reasons for choosing a particular deviation may not be clear. In addition, the size of the deviation may change over time. For example, 20 years ago, the weight criterion for anorexia nervosa was 20 percent below expected weight, but now it is 15 percent (APA, 1994). Determining which norms to consider when defining problematic behavior can also be difficult. When using norms to decide whether an adolescent's aggression is problematic, for example, should one use the norms for the section of the city in which the adolescent is being raised, the norms for the entire city, or the norms for adolescents throughout the country?

Behaviors That Are Harmful to the Adolescent Are Problematic

A third criterion for determining problematic behavior is whether the behavior is harmful to the individual engaging in it. Behaviors with a certain potential for long-term or short-term harm would be considered problematic, but those with little potential for harm would not be considered problematic. For example, smoking cigarettes or weighing 30 pounds less than your expected weight would be considered problematic because of the negative health consequences of these behaviors.

One advantage of using this criterion is that it focuses on an individual who may be in distress and who may need help coping with her problematic behavior. Adolescents may be more likely to acknowledge a need for help based on the criterion that they are harming themselves, rather than on criteria such as they are not a certain age or that society finds their behavior bothersome. This strategy also takes individual differences into account. Drinking four beers might be considered problematic for a 106-pound adolescent but not for a 250-pound adolescent, because the 250-pound adolescent can drink more before his judgment becomes impaired.

A primary disadvantage of this strategy is that actual harm to an individual may not occur for some time after a behavior begins. For example, harm from repeated smoking or drinking may not be apparent during adolescence, as it often takes many years of smoking or drinking for harm to be measured (O'Brien, 1996). It may be easy for adolescents to ignore the potential harm of a behavior when little actual harm occurs. Another disadvantage is that, while future harm may be easy to document for some behaviors, such as smoking a pack of cigarettes a day, it is more difficult to document for other behaviors, such as getting drunk occasionally.

Behaviors That Are Harmful to Others Are Problematic

This criterion is similar to the previous one but focuses on harm to others. For example, one reason that sexual assault is problematic is because of the harm caused those who are assaulted. This criterion also has many of the same advantages and disadvantages as the previous one. An additional disadvantage, however, is that apparent harm to another person may be primarily due to the other's sensitivity, and it may be unfair to designate an individual's behavior as problematic because others are sensitive to it. For example, consider a case in which an adolescent's family begins to fall apart because of the conflicts resulting from the adolescent's decision to join a cult. Does damage to the family constitute enough harm to others to consider the adolescent's behavior as problematic, or do we consider that the family's problems are due to family members' sensitivity rather than the adolescent's behavior?

The Context in Which the Behavior Occurs Determines Whether It Is Problematic

Another criterion for determining whether a behavior is problematic is the context in which it occurs. This context may be as broad as a cultural context. For example, what may appear to be painful shyness in one culture may be expected behavior for adolescents in another culture. High levels of aggressive play among adolescents may be accepted in some cultures but disdained in others.

Contexts other than cultural contexts can also influence whether a behavior is considered problematic. For example, it may not be considered problematic for a 19-year-old to have four beers at a party, but as soon as he changes the context of his behavior by starting to drive, his behavior is considered problematic. The behavior of another 19-year-old drinking at a party may not be considered problematic—unless she is pregnant.

Considering the contexts in which a behavior occurs allows us to be more flexible when determining whether a behavior is problematic. The behavioral expectations of one culture or group do not have to be imposed on all cultures or groups. Considering behaviors within their context can be a complicated process, however. The appropriate context to be considered is often not clear. For example, think about similar behavior by two boys of different races, living in the same low-income housing complex in an inner city. Are we to consider the broader racial or cultural groups from which the boys come, the fact that they live in an inner city, or the fact that they live in a particular housing complex when determining whether their behavior is problematic? In addition, it is debatable whether some behaviors that are relatively common in one context should be considered nonproblematic simply because they are relatively common. For example, it is not clear that we would consider physical or sexual aggression toward dating partners as nonproblematic in a social context where domestic or partner violence is commonplace.

Are Particular Criteria Used in This Text?

Most of the behaviors discussed in this text could be considered problematic because they result in harm, or potential harm, to the adolescent. Reckless behaviors and drug use, for example, can cause physical damage, and shyness and depression cause painful thoughts and emotions that can damage an adolescent's self-esteem. Narcissism may be more difficult to define as problematic using this strategy, because the narcissistic adolescent usually does not experience narcissism as painful (believing instead that those around her are acting incorrectly). However, people observing a narcissistic adolescent may see that her narcissism is harming her ability to interact successfully with others and to develop friendships with peers and others. The only two exceptions to the use of the "harm to the adolescent" strategy occur with physical and sexual aggression. Although both physical and sexual aggression can cause harm to the adolescent who initiates them, it is primarily because of the harm caused others that they are included in this text.

Criteria Can Be Combined

Each of these criteria can be combined with others to help us decide if a behavior is problematic. The use of two or more criteria often provides a more effective way of deciding whether a behavior is problematic than does reliance on only one criterion, because the advantages of one criterion can counteract the disadvantages of another. In some cases, a behavior can be considered problematic only if it meets two or more criteria. For example, shyness might be considered problematic only when a person's shyness interferes with her social life and when her shyness is uncommonly high for the cultural group in which she was raised. In other cases, behavior that meets any one of several criteria might be considered problematic. For example, a certain level of aggression might be considered problematic either when it deviates a certain amount from norms or when it causes harm to others.

Who Decides If a Behavior Is Problematic?

Not only are there different strategies for determining whether a behavior is problematic, but different individuals or groups of people can decide whether a behavior is problematic. In a broad sense, four categories of people can determine whether an adolescent's behaviors are problematic: society or its institutions, the adolescent's peers, the adolescent's family, or the adolescent. The category of people making these determinations can have a significant influence on the designation of behaviors as problematic. In addition, one group or individual might designate some behaviors as problematic while others would not see the behaviors as problematic.

Society or one of society's institutions (such as schools) can decide that a behavior is problematic, based on society's values or traditions. In some situations, these decisions can be influenced by professionals, such as physicians or psychologists, who present evidence that the behaviors lead to negative outcomes. These societal decisions are reflected in laws or regulations. Adolescents who engage in problematic behaviors can be punished or required to participate in therapy or another intervention.

An advantage of society or its institutions determining which behaviors are problematic is that society can draw on a wide range of knowledge and expertise about the behavior and its outcomes. In addition, once a determination is made, society can create clear prohibitions against the behaviors, which can help all members of the society understand which behaviors are not acceptable. However, these societal decisions can be based on biases rather than on evidence that a behavior results in negative outcomes and can be used by majority groups within society to impose their behavioral expectations on minority groups.

An adolescent's peer group can also determine that behaviors are problematic. These peer groups can be formal groups (e.g., a club or fraternity) or informal groups (e.g., an adolescent's close friends). These decisions are based on formal or informal behavioral expectations and may or may not be influenced by social institutions or adults. Adolescents who engage in problematic behaviors may be expelled from the group, or their standing in the group may be affected.

Peer group expectations may have a particularly strong influence on the behavior of many adolescents. However, peer group expectations may be based on the limited experiences of the adolescents in the group or may reflect the problems of a few influential adolescents in the group.

Whether a behavior is problematic can also be determined by an adolescent's parents or other caregivers, based on their own values, traditions, or beliefs. These beliefs may be influenced by evidence showing the negative outcomes of behaviors or by the family's experiences with the behaviors, and those beliefs are usually reflected in family rules. Adolescents who engage in problematic behaviors can be punished within the family or can be required to participate in a program to reduce the behaviors, such as individual or family therapy.

Family decisions can be more flexible than decisions made by society, because they can be based on specific knowledge about the adolescent, the family, and the social contexts in which the behaviors exist. For example, some families may conclude that allowing an adolescent to drink wine during dinner or drink during a party at home is appropriate, even though such behavior breaks society's laws. However, families usually have limited knowledge and experience on which to base these decisions. They may not understand, for example, the potential negative outcomes of certain behaviors. In addition, family rules may reflect the problems of the parents. For example, parents' decisions that drinking during parties is appropriate for their adolescent may be based on their own excessive drinking rather than on what is good for the adolescent.

Finally, the adolescent can determine that a behavior is problematic, based on his personal values or knowledge about the outcomes of the behavior. This decision is then reflected in the adolescent's self-image. The adolescent who engages in problematic behaviors may experience painful feelings, such as worry, guilt, or regret, and may attempt to change the behavior on his own or with the help of others.

Adolescents can have a much deeper knowledge of their own feelings and behaviors and thus may be in a better position to determine that a behavior is problematic. An adolescent may be the only one to realize, for example, that her level of depression is severe. In addition, allowing the adolescent to determine that a behavior is problematic, rather than having that determination imposed by society or parents, may enable the adolescent to seek help for the behavior more readily.

However, several factors can impede an adolescent's ability to judge whether her own behavior is problematic. An adolescent usually has limited knowledge of the behaviors of others and, consequently, may not be able to recognize whether her behavior is unusual. Because of this lack of knowledge, she may base an assessment of her behavior on the behaviors of people seen on television or in the movies, and this assessment can mislead her into thinking that certain behaviors are commonplace or generally accepted. In addition, some problematic behaviors themselves may inhibit the adolescents' ability to recognize their problematic nature. For example, the heavy use of alcohol or other drugs may inhibit an adolescent's ability to think clearly about her drug use.

What to Do with All This Uncertainty?

How do we deal with having different criteria for designating an adolescent behavior as problematic—with situations in which some criteria result in a behavior being designated as problematic and other criteria result in the behavior not being designated as problematic—and individuals or groups using these criteria in different ways—with value differences among the individuals or groups resulting in some of them considering some behaviors as problematic but others considering the behaviors not problematic? Three conclusions can be drawn from all this uncertainty:

- We must be willing to live with a certain degree of ambiguity when dealing with many adolescent problematic behaviors.
- We must be aware of the value judgments involved in designating adolescent behaviors as problematic. Not only may different groups or individuals use different criteria when designating a behavior as problematic, but they may use different values when applying the criteria in different circumstances. We must be cautious not to blindly apply individual, family, or cultural values to the behavior of others when determining whether their behaviors are problematic. It may be appropriate for us to apply our values, but we must be aware that this is what we are doing.
- When discussing problematic behaviors, it is important to be aware of the criteria we have used to designate a behavior as problematic and to

communicate this to others. When others are discussing problematic behaviors, it is important to ask how they have determined that the behaviors are problematic, without simply accepting their designation.

CHAPTER SUMMARY

Determining that a behavior is problematic can have important consequences for an adolescent. Despite this importance, no commonly accepted set of criteria exists for determining that a behavior is problematic. Frequently used criteria include declaring that a particular behavior is always problematic, using behavioral norms, basing the determination on whether a behavior is harmful to the adolescent or to others, and considering the context in which the behavior occurs. Each of these criteria has advantages and disadvantages. As a result, one criterion may be used regularly in some situations but rarely in others. The use of one criterion may result in a determination that the behavior is problematic, while the use of another criterion could result in a determination that the behavior is not problematic. Drinking at high school parties may be commonplace and thus not considered problematic from the perspective of behavioral norms, but it may cause harm to the adolescents who are drinking or to others and, consequently, may be considered problematic from those perspectives. Our inability to determine clearly and unequivocally that many behaviors are problematic can be frustrating.

An additional complication is that different individuals or groups have the ability to determine that a behavior is problematic. These include society or its institutions, the adolescent's peer group, the adolescent's family, and the adolescent. Each of these groups or individuals may have a different belief about the problematic nature of a behavior.

Because of these various ways in which adolescent behaviors can be determined to be problematic, no easy standard can be applied to these behaviors. It is important to keep in mind that a determination that an adolescent behavior is problematic is a judgment and that this judgment may differ between cultures, may differ between people within the same culture, and may change over time. When a behavior is described as problematic, it is important to know which criteria were used to make this determination and to remember that no criterion is infallible and that the use of other criteria might have resulted in a different determination.

Revisiting Lisa, Jon, and Tran

The behaviors of some adolescents are clearly problematic. However, it is less clear whether Lisa, Jon, and Tran are engaged in problematic behaviors. None of their behaviors are illegal. The behaviors of all of them deviate from the typical behaviors of all adolescents their age. However, when the cultures in which Lisa and Tran live are considered (Lisa's school culture and Tran's family or ethnic culture), their behaviors are more understandable.

All three adolescents are engaged in behavior that might be harmful to themselves—Lisa's undereating could develop into an eating disorder or have other health consequences, Jon could find himself unable to leave a dangerous cult, and Tran could develop a worsening sadness, leading to depression. However, none of their current behavior appears to be harmful to themselves or others. In short, there does not seem to be a clear answer as to whether Lisa, Jon, and Tran are engaged in problematic behaviors.

- If you had to decide about each of them, what criteria would you use? What determinations would you make and why?

CHAPTER 3

Shyness

Zach had felt uncomfortable in social situations for as long as he could remember. He preferred to sit by himself in the back of the room during most of his elementary school years. He did well academically but was often afraid to join games or other activities during recess or after school. He usually went home right after school and, if his one or two good friends were not available to play, he read in his room. His parents were not concerned about his tendency to be by himself—they seldom participated in social activities and could easily understand Zach's awkwardness in them. In high school, Zach seldom went to dances or parties. He hardly ever dated, even though girls almost always agreed to go out with him when he asked. Thoughts of kissing or making out with a girl were terrifying, as he was sure that he would be clumsy and his performance would be dreadful.

When Zach was a junior in high school, Rich moved next door. Rich was Zach's age and was friendly and easy to talk with. He and Zach quickly became friends. They rode on the school bus together, and Rich encouraged Zach to go out for the soccer team with him. Because of his outgoing and sociable nature, Rich soon became popular. He began asking Zach to double-date with him and pestered Zach until he agreed. Driving home after their first double-date, Rich asked, "How come you hardly ever talked? You just sat there like a lump the whole night." Zach answered that he never knew what to do on a date, hated dating, and went with Rich only because he had insisted. "I can see that I have a lot to teach you," Rich replied. Over the next few months, Rich took Zack to parties, dances, and sports events. They double-dated several times. After each event, Rich critiqued Zach's performance, and they even developed a set of signals that Rich could use to remind Zach how to behave when they were together. Although Rich was sympathetic when Zach complained about how difficult it still was for him to attend social activities, Rich insisted that Zach continue going. Over that school year, Zach found himself much less fearful in social situations and actually began to like them. He used his newfound social skills while working at a summer camp that next summer, where the other counselors considered him a fun person to be around.

Almost all adolescents feel shy occasionally, but some adolescents experience chronic shyness. Occasional shyness can be bothersome; however, chronic shyness can affect some adolescents' development and can be detrimental to the society in which they live. Shy children have higher anxiety and lower feelings of self-worth (Fordham & Stevenson-Hinde, 1999), and shy adolescents report low self-esteem and elevated feelings of loneliness and depression (Cheek & Busch, 1981). Shy students avoid participating in classroom discussions and avoid seeking help from teachers and counselors when they need it (Friedman, 1980). Shy high school students are less likely than their nonshy peers to seek out a suitable college or university, and shy college undergraduates are less likely to take the needed steps to be admitted to a graduate or professional school. It takes shy young adults several years longer than their nonshy peers to find a stable job, and this can interfere with their ability to advance in their careers (Azar, 1995). Shy adolescents and young adults marry several years later than those who are not shy. From a societal perspective, significant contributions that shy people could make may be lost.

The Plan: We will first define shyness. As with many of the problematic behaviors discussed in this text, we will find that shyness has not been defined unequivocally. In addition, it appears that there are different types of shyness. After a brief discussion of the prevalence of shyness, we will explore the thoughts, behaviors, and physical symptoms often experienced by shy adolescents, including the painful self-consciousness about their shyness and social awkwardness that they often endure. Using this understanding of the experience of shy adolescents, we will then focus on the development of shyness. We will examine two characteristics that form the foundation of shyness—sensitivity to the scrutiny of others and poor social skills—and we will examine several influences on the development of these characteristics. We will then explore interventions for shy adolescents.

THE DEFINITION OF SHYNESS

Although shyness has been studied on and off for several decades, no one has yet formulated a commonly accepted definition of shyness, and it is often vaguely defined. Most definitions of shyness include two components. First, shyness occurs in social or interpersonal situations. This distinguishes shyness from other types of anxiety. Second, shyness is characterized by three types of responses: (a) physiological changes and emotions indicating anxiety (e.g., blushing, fear), (b) negative thoughts about one's social self (e.g., "I am always a failure at parties"), and (c) awkward social behaviors (e.g., looking at the floor while talking to others) (Cheek et al., 1986; van der Molen, 1990). However, there is disagreement about whether all three of these responses must occur for shyness to be present.

In everyday language, the term *shy* is also used to describe or classify individuals (e.g., "He is a shy person"). It is often difficult for researchers who want to study shy people to determine who is shy, however, because almost everyone experiences shyness in some social situations (van der Molen, 1990). Researchers often get around this problem by simply asking people if they are shy and including everyone who says that they are (e.g., Cheek & Watson, 1989; Jones, Briggs, & Smith, 1986). While this may make it easier on the researchers, it makes the study of shyness difficult because each researcher may be studying people with different characteristics and experiences.

Distinguishing Shyness from Other Experiences

Shyness can be distinguished from several related experiences. While shyness and these other experiences may have some characteristics in common, they also have important differences. Understanding these differences can lead to a clearer picture of those who are shy and can lead to more effective interventions for them.

Introversion

Although shy people and introverted people are often withdrawn from others, they differ in fundamental ways. Introverted people prefer to be alone, are comfortable being alone, and have little difficulty interacting with others when necessary or desired (Eysenck & Eysenck, 1975). Shy people, on the other hand, often want to interact with others but have difficulty doing so successfully (Asendorpf, 1993). Consequently, shy people are often simultaneously pulled toward and repelled by social activities (Bradshaw, 1998).

Social Anxiety

Shyness is one type of social anxiety (Briggs, 1985; Buss, 1980). Social anxiety can occur in other forms, however, such as anxiety related to public speaking or other forms of public performance. Although some shy people experience high anxiety around public performances, others experience normal anxiety when performing in front of audiences. For example, some successful actors are shy in interpersonal situations, and some professors who have little difficulty lecturing to hundreds of students find it difficult to talk with a small group of students at a party. Alternately, some people who experience high anxiety during public speaking do not feel shy during interpersonal situations.

Embarrassment

Shy people often report feeling embarrassed after social interactions. However, nonshy people experience embarrassment as well. Miller (1995) found two important differences between embarrassment and shyness. First, shyness is felt in anticipation of a social interaction, while embarrassment is felt after a social interaction has gone badly. Second, shyness is linked to the effectiveness of social behaviors ("I never know what to say when I meet my girlfriend's parents"), and embarrassment is more closely linked to the appropriateness of social behaviors ("I should never have told that joke with her parents there"). Shyness occurs in anticipation of acting incompetently in social situations; embarrassment occurs after making a social gaffe.

Describing the Types of Shyness

Buss (1986) described two types of shyness: fearful shyness and self-conscious shyness. Fearful shyness begins during the first year of life, when an infant or a young child is confronted by an unfamiliar adult, resulting in wariness, retreat, and comfort seeking. A toddler screaming as he sits on Santa's lap in a department store is a classic example of fearful shyness. Self-conscious shyness usually begins during a child's fourth or fifth year, as he becomes aware of social evaluation by others. It typically occurs in social situations where a person feels conspicuousness and scrutinized by others, and it results in painful self-awareness, awkward behavior, and social withdrawal.

Kagan and his associates (e.g., Kagan & Reznick, 1986) have investigated an early developing type of shyness that they have labeled behavioral inhibition. It is found in about 10 to 15 percent of toddlers and young children and is characterized by cautiousness or timidity in situations involving new people or in risky or novel situations. Longitudinal research shows that behavioral inhibition is a stable character trait in most individuals, at least during childhood and early adolescence.

The focus of this chapter will be on the type of shyness characterized by Buss's concept of self-conscious shyness. However, you will want to keep fearful shyness (or behavioral inhibition) in mind, since there are substantial links between fearful and self-conscious shyness.

THE PREVALENCE AND COURSE OF SHYNESS

About 40 percent of children, adolescents, and adults consider themselves shy (e.g., Lazarus, 1982; Zimbardo, 1977; Zimbardo, Pilkonis, & Norwood, 1975). One study found that 54 percent of junior high school students rated themselves as shy, suggesting that shyness may peak during this time (Zimbardo, 1977).

Although research has not found consistent sex differences in the prevalence of shyness, when differences are found, more males than females consider themselves shy (Cheek et al., 1986; Ishiyama, 1984; Pilkonis, 1977; Porteus, 1979). In some ways, this may seem counterintuitive, since females in our culture are typically considered quieter and perhaps more socially withdrawn than males. However, shyness does not refer to the amount, loudness, or aggressiveness of a person's social interactions but, rather, to the person's experience in these interactions. Females may be quieter in social interactions, but it appears that they are at least as comfortable in them as males are.

As just noted, behavioral inhibition and fearful shyness appear very early in life. Self-conscious shyness begins to emerge at about age 4 or 5—about the time that children develop a sense of having a social self that can be scrutinized and evaluated by others (Buss, 1986). However, wide variation exists in the ages at which shy people say they first experience persistent self-conscious shyness: some people report that it began very early in their lives; others, that it began in adolescence or young adulthood. There are peak times when people first experience persistent shyness, and these are associated with significant social or physical changes: entry into school, the beginning of puberty, and entry into junior high (Bruch & Cheek, 1995).

Long-term longitudinal studies of shyness have not been completed, so the typical course of shyness over a lifetime is unknown. However, it does appear that levels of shyness are very stable in children and adolescents (e.g., Backteman & Magnusson, 1981; Coie & Dodge, 1983; Fordham & Stevenson-Hinde, 1999). Retrospective studies of undergraduates have shown that shyness is an enduring experience for many shy children. In one study, about 75 percent of the undergraduates who were shy in early childhood remained shy as undergraduates, and about 50 percent of those whose shyness first appeared in late childhood or early adolescence were still shy as undergraduates (Bruch & Cheek, 1995).

THE EXPERIENCE OF SHYNESS

Three Clusters of Shy Experiences

When shy people are asked to describe their shyness, three clusters of experiences emerge: physiological and emotional experiences, cognitive experiences, and behavioral experiences. Not all shy people experience all three clusters of experiences, however. Cheek and Watson (1989) found that 43 percent of a group of shy women experienced only one cluster, 37 percent experienced two clusters, and that only 12 percent experienced all three clusters.

The first cluster consists of physiological and emotional experiences (Cheek & Watson, 1989; van der Molen, 1990). Shy people report feeling anxious, tense,

BROADENING Perspectives

Shyness and Depression

There are important differences between shyness and depression, and most shy people are not depressed. However, the social withdrawal and negative thoughts that characterize shyness are also important components of depression. In some cases, what appears to be shyness is actually depression. Since interventions for shyness differ from those for depression, distinguishing between the two is important.

Shy people feel more anxiety than sadness. They are likely to find pleasure in much of their lives—it is just social activities that cause angst. Depressed people are more likely to feel sadness than anxiety and are more likely to feel sad consistently, rather than only in social situations.

and fearful in social situations. Their tenseness is often accompanied by troubling physiological responses, such as an elevated heart rate or nausea. Their hands or lips may tremble, they may feel the warmth in their neck and face that accompanies blushing, and they may stammer or have other speech difficulties.

The second cluster consists of cognitions (Cheek & Watson, 1989; Jackson, Towson, & Narduzzi, 1997; van der Molen, 1990). In social situations, shy people are self-conscious and have many self-critical thoughts. They monitor their social behaviors closely and usually believe that they are deficient and ineffective. They believe that others are also judging their social performance and are finding it deficient, and they worry that others are likely to reject them or embarrass them.

The third cluster consists of behaviors (Briggs, 1985; Pilkonis, 1977; Shepperd & Arkin, 1990). Shy people avoid social situations and are likely to withdraw from them if given the opportunity. Shy people are less adept in social situations than nonshy people. They speak less and more quietly when they do. They are less likely to initiate a conversation or restart a conversation during a period of silence. They tend to look away from people when speaking and may engage in frequent nervous gestures and self-touching. When in group interactions, shy people tend to migrate to the physical edge of the group. When a shy person's position on an issue is challenged, he is more likely than a nonshy person to moderate or change his position.

While shy children and adolescents may have difficulty in social situations, it is important to note that they are able to develop and enjoy close friendships (Fordham & Stevenson-Hinde, 1999). Some shy adolescents may ask friends to accompany them to anxiety-provoking social situations as a way of reducing their anxiety (Bradshaw, 1998).

Self-consciousness

Cheek and Melchior (Azar, 1995) have developed a model of shyness that includes two organizing categories above the three clusters of shy experiences. They suggest a metacognitive level associated with each of the clusters. *Metacognitive* refers to the process of thinking about thinking or behaviors. Here, the metacognitive level encompasses the ways in which shy people think about their symptoms of shyness. As shown in figure 3.1, shy people often reflect on their shy experiences and agonize over them. As they think more and more about their shyness, they develop a cognitive style dominated by a focus on their shyness when they are in social situations. Cheek and Melchior call this meta-self-consciousness: shy people become self-conscious about their self-consciousness. It is this level of persistent self-consciousness that distinguishes chronically shy people from those who experience only periodic shyness.

Self-consciousness about being shy can impair a shy person's ability to interact with others successfully and, thus, can reinforce and even increase self-consciousness. For example, when a shy person is interacting with others, he may be thinking, "I know I'm blushing," "I hate having to be places where others are going to see how shy I am," and "Am I standing the right way and

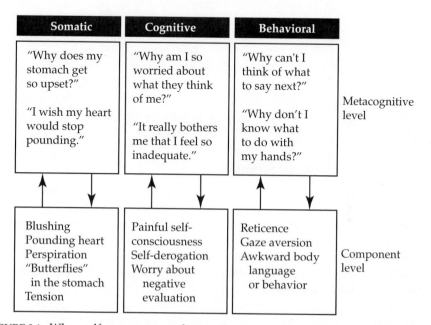

Meta-self-consciousness
Thoughts about being a shy person Focus on shyness symptoms Awareness of being self-aware Anxious self-preoccupation

Somatic	Cognitive	Behavioral	
"Why does my stomach get so upset?" "I wish my heart would stop pounding."	"Why am I so worried about what they think of me?" "It really bothers me that I feel so inadequate."	"Why can't I think of what to say next?" "Why don't I know what to do with my hands?"	Metacognitive level
Blushing Pounding heart Perspiration "Butterflies" in the stomach Tension	Painful self-consciousness Self-derogation Worry about negative evaluation	Reticence Gaze aversion Awkward body language or behavior	Component level

FIGURE 3.1. When self-awareness works overtime.
Source: Copyright © 1995 by the American Psychological Association. Reprinted with permission. Adapted from work by J. M. Cheek and L. A. Melchoir.

saying the right things?" As the shy person becomes more self-conscious, he focuses less on his social interactions. This increases his chance of acting ineptly: he may fail to follow the line of the conversation, mumble when he talks, or fail to notice that he is spilling the drink he is holding. As his inadequate attempts at conversation are met with silence or ridicule, or as he feels his spilled drink on his foot, his inability to perform socially is reinforced in his mind and in the minds of his companions. He is likely to focus even more on these failures in the future, ensuring an ongoing experience of social inadequacy and the physiological, cognitive, and behavioral responses to that inadequacy. In many ways, the shy person becomes his own worst social enemy, and it can seem as if there is no way that he can ever develop a sense of ease in social situations (although, as we will see in the upcoming section on interventions for shyness, this is not so).

THE DEVELOPMENT OF SHYNESS

As just described, chronically shy people are often caught in a vicious cycle. Their shyness causes them to feel uneasy and act awkwardly in social situations, and their uneasiness and awkwardness reinforces their shyness. Trying to determine the ways in which these types of cyclical behaviors begin is always difficult, because it is hard to identify where the cycle starts. Moreover, it is likely that the cycle starts in one place for some people but in another place for others. However, it is possible to explore the influences on the ongoing development of chronic shyness, even if the initiating event cannot be identified.

In this section, we will examine two primary building blocks of shyness—sensitivity to the scrutiny of others and poor social skills—and will look at the research supporting this hypothesis. We will then discuss a variety of influences on the building blocks of shyness. These influences can combine in many ways to increase the frequency and intensity of shyness.

The Building Blocks of Shyness

As described by Cheek and Melchior (Azar, 1995), shyness can be characterized as painful social self-consciousness, and as Buss (1986) points out, self-consciousness results from sensitivity to the scrutiny of others. Research has shown that shy people do have heightened sensitivity to the scrutiny of others and heightened fear of being rejected by others (e.g., Ishiyama, 1984; Jackson, Towson, & Narduzzi, 1997). Further, shy people have poorer social skills than nonshy people and are particularly sensitive about their poor social performance (Briggs, 1985; Jackson, Towson, & Narduzzi, 1997). Thus, it can be argued that sensitivity to the scrutiny of others and poor social skills are the building blocks of the painful social self-consciousness that is called shyness.

It is reasonable to hypothesize that either heightened levels of sensitivity to the scrutiny of others or poor social skills will increase a person's likelihood of being shy. To visualize this, consider a balance scale, with containers on one side representing sensitivity to the scrutiny of others and poor social skills and, on the other side, something representing a person's likelihood of being shy. As the level of either sensitivity or poor social skills increases (represented by more sand, water, or something else in the containers), a person's likelihood of being shy increases.

For example, think of someone who has moderate sensitivity to the scrutiny of others. If the person has consistently good social skills, he is less likely to experience shyness than is a person with the same level of sensitivity but only moderately good social skills. This is because the reactions that the person with good social skills receives are largely positive, while the person with moderate social skills receives reactions that are more negative. Since they both have the same sensitivity to these reactions, the person who experiences more negative scrutiny will be more socially self-conscious.

A Personal Experience

Although I am very outgoing with friends or when lecturing to a large class (some people would suggest that outgoing is too generous a description), I am quite shy around people I do not know. When I began graduate school, I decided to force myself to attend every social function to which I was invited for the first six months. By doing this, I became friendly with many people and soon found that I enjoyed many of my social interactions. If I had followed my natural inclination to avoid social situations with people I do not know, I probably would have been socially withdrawn throughout graduate school.

Alternately, consider a person who has moderate levels of social skills. If he is highly sensitive to the scrutiny of others, then even occasional negative feedback about his social skills will have a meaningful influence on his social self-consciousness. Alternately, a person with little sensitivity to the scrutiny of others will be nearly unaffected by periodic negative feedback from others.

This hypothesis assumes that a minimal level of sensitivity to the scrutiny of others and a less than perfect level of social skills are needed for shyness to exist. Someone who is unaffected by scrutiny from others will not experience painful self-consciousness, despite his level of social skills (e.g., consider the stereotyped movie version of a self-confident, unflappable hillbilly at an urban socialite party). Similarly, someone with perfect social skills would never have an opportunity to feel self-conscious in a social situation, despite his level of sensitivity to scrutiny, because he would never experience negative reactions from others. These people are probably very rare, however.

The Influences on the Building Blocks of Shyness

The personal characteristics of some adolescents can influence their sensitivity to the scrutiny of others or their social skills. In addition, a variety of experiences can increase sensitivity or negatively affect social skills. By influencing their sensitivity or social skills, these characteristics and experiences—genetic vulnerability, certain parenting practices, cognitions, and labeling—can have an impact on an adolescent's shyness.

Genetic Vulnerability

A moderately strong genetic influence on shyness exists (Plomin & Daniels, 1986). Levels of shyness are more similar between identical twins than between fraternal twins in toddlers (Plomin & Rowe, 1979) and high school students (Bruch & Cheek, 1995). Studies with twins have shown that there is a strong genetic component to behavioral inhibition (Robinson et al., 1992).

Genetic predispositions may influence the development of shyness by impeding the development of social skills. The innate inhibited style of some children can result in their engaging with peers and adults infrequently; thus, they may be slower to develop age-appropriate social skills. The combination of less well developed social skills at one age and a tendency toward inhibition may obstruct the development of social skills at later ages, resulting in a gradual worsening of the child's ability to interact successfully in social situations. By adolescence, an inhibited child may be considerably behind his peers in social-skills development, and the awkwardness from his lack of social skills may reinforce or increase his shyness.

Parenting Practices

Parenting practices can influence shyness in several ways. For example, parents who emphasize the importance of paying attention to social scrutiny and having flawless social skills may instill high sensitivity to social scrutiny in their children (Buss, 1986). In addition, parents who emphasize the shamefulness of behaviors such as being immodest or making a mistake in public may have children who are more fearful of participating in social situations and who consequently avoid them. This may limit the children's ability to learn about social interactions and may result in underdeveloped social skills.

Mills and Rubin (1993) suggested that higher levels of shyness are common in children who are genetically predisposed to shyness and who have parents who are not accepting of their inhibited social style. They found that shy children had mothers who are more likely to teach social behaviors in a coercive manner and that shy children's mothers are more embarrassed, angry, and disappointed than other mothers when their children's social performance is lacking. In other research, many adults with high levels of shyness recalled that their parents were very concerned with the opinions of others, that they went to fewer social activities as a family, and that their families were socially isolated (Bruch & Heimberg, 1994; Bruch et al., 1989). Although it is not clear from this research whether the child's shy behavior evoked a particular parenting style or the parenting style increased the child's shyness, it is possible that the parenting styles increased the child's sensitivity to social scrutiny or provided fewer opportunities to learn social skills.

Learning Theories

Several learning theories can help explain the development of higher levels of shyness. Operant conditioning theory suggests that a child who experiences negative reactions (e.g., punishment) to attempts at social interactions will be less likely to attempt future social interactions. For example, a child who is laughed at by his peers when he tries to enter a group activity will be less likely to try to enter group activities in the future. To the extent that a child experiences negative reactions in many social situations, he will engage in fewer and fewer social interactions. This could result in impaired development of social skills, which would likely lead to increasing negative evaluations in social interactions. This could lead to a spiral of social withdrawal, impaired development of social skills, and further social withdrawal.

Modeling, the process of one person's behavior being influenced by his observations of the consequences of others' behaviors, can also influence shyness

(Bandura, 1977). For example, if a child were to observe a parent acting anxiously during a social interaction and acting calmer only when away from the social interaction, then the child might avoid social interactions. Similarly, a child could be sensitized to the scrutiny of others by listening to a parent describe how terrible it was to be scrutinized by others when attending a social event.

Negative reinforcement can also maintain or increase shyness. A shy person often feels anxious when anticipating a social interaction (called anticipatory anxiety). If he decides not to engage in the social interaction, his anxiety usually ends or is diminished. The cessation of the painful experience of anxiety serves as a negative reinforcer for his social withdrawal—increasing the likelihood that he will withdraw in the face of future social situations. Ongoing withdrawal from social situations reduces the opportunities for learning and practicing social skills.

Cognitions

The thoughts of many shy people before and during social interactions can heighten their sensitivity to the scrutiny of others and reinforce their sense of social inadequacy. Shy adolescents are more likely to attribute their own behavior and the behavior of others to internal causes (e.g., their personality), whereas nonshy adolescents are more likely to attribute them to external causes (e.g., situational characteristics) (Alm & Lindberg, 1999). Thus, shy adolescents are more likely to explain their lack of social skills on personal failings. As mentioned previously, the thoughts of shy people tend to focus on their shyness and their ineptness when in social situations. They often believe that they are being evaluated negatively and that these negative evaluations will hamper their ability to interact with others (Azar, 1995; Glass & Shea, 1986). This ongoing focus on scrutiny from others is likely to keep shy adolescents' sensitivity to this scrutiny quite high. In addition, when a shy adolescent focuses on others' evaluation of his performance in a social situation, he will be less focused on the social interactions. This is likely to result in poorer social performance and an inability to learn better social skills by observing the social performance of others.

Labeling

Once a person is known as shy or socially awkward, the reactions that he receives from others may maintain and intensify his shyness. Others may give the impression that they expect social awkwardness and shyness, and these expectations may encourage shy behavior. Peers or others may insult or deride a shy or socially awkward person—increasing both the negative scrutiny he receives and his distress in social interactions (van der Molen, 1990).

Combinations of Influences

As we will see with many of the problematic behaviors discussed in this text, no one influence explains high levels of shyness. A mix of personal characteristics and experience influences shyness, with some characteristics and experiences having more influence over some people and less over others. For example, some children who have a genetic tendency toward shyness also have parents with the same tendency. These parents might model social anxiety for their children and give them fewer opportunities to develop good social skills. The child's innate tendency to avoid social situations and the parents' avoidance of the same situations may result in a shy child with poor social skills. In another situation, a parent who is so concerned about his social standing that he continually reminds his child of the shame associated with social gaffes, may have a child who is extremely sensitive to the scrutiny of others. The child may find social situations painful because of the negative evaluations that he believes he receives from others. He may discover that the anticipatory anxiety he feels before social engagements can be reduced by avoiding or withdrawing from these engagements, and his consequent withdrawal may interfere with his social-skills development.

A Summary of the Development Process of Shyness

The foundation of the painful social self-consciousness that characterizes shyness consists of heightened sensitivity to scrutiny from others and poor social skills. A variety of personal characteristics and experiences influence the development of poor social skills and high levels of sensitivity. Poor social skills result in poor performances in social situations, these poor performances lead to negative scrutiny from others, and those who are sensitive to this scrutiny feel painful self-consciousness (shyness) before and during social situations.

INTERVENTIONS FOR SHYNESS

If shyness is based on sensitivity to scrutiny from others and deficits in social skills, then interventions for shyness should address these issues. As it turns out, most interventions for shyness do address them. Deficits in social skills are primarily addressed through social-skills training. Decreasing sensitivity to the scrutiny of others is usually accomplished by changing shy peoples' thoughts about the importance of how others perceive them.

Most interventions for shy adolescents consist of group involvement. Groups might take place in high schools, colleges, or community mental health centers. Groups allow shy adolescents to share their shy experiences; recognize how their experiences are similar to the experiences of other shy adolescents; practice social skills; and receive empathy, encouragement, and feedback from others (Glass & Shea, 1986; van der Molen, 1990).

The development of effective interpersonal skills is a focal point of most interventions. Improved social skills are expected to lead to increasingly positive interpersonal interactions, thus encouraging shy adolescents to engage in more of them. The process of teaching these skills often involves (a) an explanation of the skill and a rationale for its importance; (b) a demonstration of the skill; (c) practice of the skill in the group, usually through role plays; (d) homework assignments for using the skill outside the group; and (e) a report back to the group on the homework, with feedback from the group (Gambrill, 1996).

Good listening skills are often emphasized in group work (van der Molen, 1990). Group members are taught how to listen carefully to the conversations of others (rather than focusing on their own discomfort or trying to formulate what they are going to say), as well as how to respond in an appropriate and timely way. Attending to nonverbal communication and communicating empathy and respect for the other person are also important components of good listening skills (Alden & Cappe, 1986). Group members are encouraged to express

HELPING
YOURSELF OR OTHERS

Reducing the Effects of Shyness in Your Life

Group interventions for shy people may be available at your college, high school, or community center. Get up your courage and join one. If groups are not available in your area, you can identify one or two friends who are shy or socially awkward and form your own self-help group, in which you can give and receive ongoing guidance and support. You can critique each other's social performances in a supportive way and perhaps attend social events together to provide mutual support and guidance.

Recognize that reducing your shyness will take a while. You cannot expect dramatic and sudden differences, but you may experience gradual changes that will eventually result in a meaningful reduction in your shyness. Also, expect some setbacks along the way—there will still be times when you feel extraordinarily shy. But remember that almost everyone feels shy periodically.

Monitor your thinking before social interactions. Notice your thoughts and work to decide which are irrational. Try to develop more accurate thoughts and substitute them for your irrational and inaccurate thoughts. Reward yourself when you are able to do this.

Observe people whose social behavior you admire. How do they behave? The answer to this question can guide your behavior in social situations. You *can* change your social behaviors. When talking with others, attend to what they are saying and how they are saying it. If your irrational thoughts get in the way, push them aside so that you can focus on the conversation. By becoming a good listener, you will be better able to participate effectively in conversations.

Practice your new skills. Take the opportunity to go to new places where people do not know that you are shy. Try joining or initiating conversations. At the end of each event, think about how you did. What worked and what did not? What modifications should you make the next time that you try this? Recognize that it will be frightening to try these new skills, but do what you must to get up your courage, and then reward yourself afterwards. The more you practice, the better you will become, and the more rewarding your social experiences will be.

their needs and opinions in an assertive way (van der Molen, 1990). Other specific skills that can be taught include how to join a group conversation and how to initiate or leave a conversation (Glass & Shea, 1986).

Several strategies are used to reduce the anxiety shy people feel in social situations. Most of these are based on classical conditioning theory: they encourage a socially anxious adolescent to experience social situations without feeling anxiety, thus reducing the association between social situations and anxiety. For example, Montgomery and Haemmerlie (1986) had shy adolescents interact for six 10-minute sessions with a confederate who was coached to be pleasant and warm. Gambrill (1996) found that providing shy people with good social skills, then requiring them to participate in social interactions until their anxiety decreases, helps break the association between anxiety and social situations. Teaching relaxation techniques that can be used before or during social events may also help reduce anxiety (van der Molen, 1990).

Many interventions focus on modifying the cognitions that shy adolescents have about themselves and their social performances (Glass & Shea, 1986). During these interventions, the ways in which cognitions can encourage shyness and impede effective social interactions are explained. Group members are encouraged to notice their cognitions as they anticipate or participate in social interactions and to share these with other group members. Cognitions that are inappropriately general and negative are challenged gently. For example, "I can never have a decent conversation with anyone" might be challenged by a group member pointing out that the person did have a good conversation with him on their way to the group meeting. Cognitions that are irrational are also challenged gently. For example, the belief that "everyone notices how shy I am when I'm at a party" might be challenged by asking, "Everyone? How do you know that everyone notices?" Group members are then encouraged to formulate more accurate cognitions and to substitute them for the inaccurate ones. For example, rather than "I can never have a decent conversation," a person could formulate the more accurate "I have a difficult time talking with people until I get to know them" or "When I listen carefully to the other person, I can have a decent conversation."

CHAPTER SUMMARY

Almost everyone experiences shyness at one time or another, and about 40 percent of all adolescents consider themselves to be shy much of the time. Although shyness can be only an occasional annoyance to some adolescents, it is a significant problem for others. People who are chronically shy tend to have low self-esteem and ongoing feelings of loneliness, they avoid seeking help in school when they need it, and they tend to get started in careers and marriages later than do nonshy people.

Shy people report three types of shyness experiences: (a) physiological and emotional experiences, such as blushing, elevated heart rate, anxiety, and fear; (b) cognitive experiences, such as being self-conscious and having many self-critical thoughts; and (c) behavioral experiences, such as avoiding social situations, looking away from people when speaking, and making nervous gestures while talking. People who are chronically shy tend to think about and focus on their shyness, leading to an ongoing experience of painful social self-consciousness.

Shyness appears to be based on two components: sensitivity to the scrutiny of others and poor social skills. As a person's level of sensitivity to the scrutiny of others increases or as his level of social skills lags behind that of others, the likelihood that he will experience shyness increases. Many personal characteristics and experiences influence sensitivity to scrutiny and poor social skills and, thus, shyness. Some children have a genetically influenced behavioral inhibition that makes them wary of new situations and unfamiliar people. Parenting practices can increase a child's sensitivity to being scrutinized by others and can also isolate a child so that he does not learn social skills. Negative feedback after social attempts can isolate a child from social situations, and negative reinforcement from the cessation of anticipatory anxiety can help maintain an adolescent's tendency to withdraw from social situations. Once a child or an adolescent gains a reputation for being shy, this reputation may influence how others interact with him, increasing the person's sense of social isolation and social failure.

Interventions for shyness focus on improving social skills and counteracting irrational, disparaging cognitions. Interventions usually occur in groups, so that shy adolescents can give each other support and help each other develop social skills.

Revisiting Zach

Many shy adolescents are like Zach, in that they have felt shy most of their lives. Zach's shyness appears similar to that experienced by his parents, suggesting that Zach and his parents may share a genetic tendency toward shyness, that the home environment in which Zach was raised may have influenced his shyness, or both. Many shy people feel that they will never be able to overcome their shyness and awkwardness in social situations. However, as Zach's story points out, there are ways for shy people to feel more comfortable socially. As shy people increase their social skills, they receive more positive feedback about their social performance. Over time, this can decease their sensitivity to scrutiny from others and their shyness.

- What qualities in Rich, or in the relationship between Rich and Zach, encouraged Zach to participate in social activities with Rich, even though he felt uncomfortable?
- Given their own shyness, how might Zach's parents' parenting style have increased Zach's shyness?

CHAPTER 4

Sensation-Seeking, Risk-Taking, and Reckless Behaviors

Ray was known among his friends as a wild guy. He drove fast, sky dived, bungee jumped, and almost never let a challenge go by. He was a great person to have at a party because he was so unpredictable. In addition, he was a genuinely nice person, and everyone enjoyed having him around.

One day after a fraternity party, Ray was missing. He had been drinking fairly heavily, but not more than usual and not enough to cause him, for example, to pass out in some remote place. Although he had been known to leave town at the spur of the moment if something exciting came up, he usually told someone or left a note. After several days, his friends became quite worried and contacted the police. A search for him was organized, but it was as if he had vanished without a trace.

About a week later, a bad smell developed in the fraternity house where the party had been held. Several searches of the house, however, failed to turn up the source of the smell. One member of the fraternity thought that maybe someone had thrown something down the chimney and, so, went on the roof and shined a light down the chimney. It was then that they found Ray. Although no one will ever know for certain, people came to believe that Ray probably thought that it would be great fun to drop down the chimney and emerge from the fireplace into the party. Unfortunately, though, the size of the chimney got smaller toward the fireplace; he became wedged in and suffocated.

Each year, communities across the country are shocked to learn that some of their high school students have been killed driving home, very intoxicated, from a prom or graduation. University students who have shown a lifetime of thoughtful, purposeful decisions find themselves unexpectedly pregnant. Adolescents attempting to increase sexual arousal by constricting their breathing during masturbation accidentally hang themselves (Sheehan & Garfinkel, 1988). Adolescents in Brazil "surf" on top of fast-moving trains, even though hundreds are killed and injured doing so each year, and adolescents in the South Pacific go spear fishing in areas frequented by large sharks (Arnett, 1995).

Considerable variation exists in the amount and type of risky behaviors that adolescents engage in; however, most people will engage in more risky behaviors during their adolescence than at other times in their lives (Steinberg & Belsky, 1996). In this chapter, we will explore what draws adolescents toward risky behaviors so frequently. By understanding why adolescents engage in risky behaviors, we may be able to decrease the number who engage in the most dangerous ones. We will explore risky behaviors in general, rather than focusing on any particular behavior. Several risky or reckless behaviors are explored more fully in other chapters in this text.

The Plan: We will first define sensation-seeking, risk-taking, and reckless behaviors. Precise definitions do not exist, but we will settle on definitions that are as clear as possible. We will then examine gender differences in risk taking. Next, we will explore why adolescents are more likely than those in other age groups to engage in risk-taking behaviors. As in other chapters, our exploration will be based on the premise that adolescents decide to engage in risky behaviors, and we will ask what influences them to make these decisions. First, we will examine research showing that adolescents tend to think primarily about the immediate and short-term positive outcomes of behaviors and tend to ignore long-term or negative outcomes. Next, we will explore the ways in which risk-taking behaviors have immediate benefits for adolescents. This will bring the argument full circle: adolescents are prone to focus on the immediate and positive consequences of behaviors, risk-taking behaviors often result in outcomes that are appealing to adolescents, and so adolescents engage in risk taking despite the potential negative consequences of doing so. At the end of the chapter we will use this knowledge to discuss interventions to reduce the frequency with which adolescents engage in reckless behaviors.

DEFINITIONS OF SENSATION-SEEKING , RISK-TAKING, AND RECKLESS BEHAVIORS

Sensation-seeking, risk-taking, and reckless behaviors have not been clearly defined in the research literature. Some authors use the terms interchangeably, while others distinguish them from each other. In this chapter, we will consider risk-taking behaviors as a subset of sensation-seeking behaviors and reckless behaviors as a subset of risk-taking behaviors.

Sensation-seeking behaviors: purposeful behaviors that result in physiological arousal and psychological excitement

Risk-taking behaviors: behaviors with a plausible likelihood of indentifiable negative outcomes

Reckless behaviors: behaviors with substantial personal and/or social costs; little personal control over outcome

Zuckerman (1979) proposed a definition of sensation-seeking as "the need for varied, novel, and complex sensations and experience, and the willingness to take physical and social risks for the sake of such experience" (p. 10). Many behaviors are considered sensation-seeking, based on their common outcome of heightened physiological arousal and psychological excitement. These include behaviors that are legal (e.g., rock climbing, sky diving, having sex), behaviors that are illegal but often tolerated by much of society (e.g., drag racing on the street, experimenting with alcohol, stealing mascots from rival high schools), and behaviors that are illegal and condemned by much of society (e.g., vandalizing property, driving while intoxicated, assaulting people). Risk-taking and reckless behaviors are subsets of sensation-seeking behaviors because one of the principal reasons for engaging in risky and reckless behaviors is the excitement of doing so (Pfefferbaum & Wood, 1994).

Igra and Irwin (1996) defined risk-taking behaviors as those "under-taken volitionally, whose outcomes remain uncertain with the possibility of an identifiable negative health outcome" (p. 35). These behaviors are distinguished from other sensation-seeking behaviors by an identifiable, plausible risk for short- or long-term negative outcomes. While riding a roller coaster or exerting oneself to achieve a "runner's high" are sensation-seeking behaviors, achieving the same level of arousal by sky diving or using drugs would be considered risk taking because of their relatively high chance of negative outcomes (admittedly, there is some risk to a roller coaster ride or extreme physical exertion—however, these risks are often not much more than we face living each day). Unfortunately, much research on risk taking has focused on a small subset of these behaviors—typically, illegal behaviors or high-risk sex behaviors. In this chapter, however, risk taking is defined more broadly to include other risky sensation-seeking behaviors, such as participation in potentially dangerous sports and other activities.

Following Arnett (1992), we will consider risk-taking behaviors that have substantial personal and social costs to be reckless behaviors. In addition, we will require that individuals have little control over possible outcomes for a behavior to be considered reckless. While sky diving is considered risk taking because much of the risk can be averted through careful training and preparation, taking large doses of LSD or engaging in unprotected sex is considered reckless because the individual has little control over the outcome. Drag racing on a track would be considered risk taking and driving while intoxicated would be considered reckless because intoxicated individuals have much less control over what happens to them while driving. The line between risk-taking and reckless behaviors is vague at times, with a substantial gray area between them. For example, one could argue about some behaviors such as robbery: some might consider robbery as reckless, while others would argue that robbery is risk taking because a carefully planned robbery has fewer risks. We will have to live with this amount of definitional ambiguity.

GENDER DIFFERENCES IN RISK TAKING

Males engage in more risk taking than females across all age ranges. Male children, adolescents, and adults are more likely than females to take risks in situations when it is clearly a bad idea to take the risk, and females are more likely than males to avoid risk taking, even in situations in which taking a risk is likely to result in a positive outcome (Byrnes, Miller, & Schafer, 1999; Morrongiello & Rennie, 1998). However, the extent of the gender difference varies from age to age. For example, smaller gender differences exist during early adolescence than during late adolescence. In addition, substantial gender differences exist for some risky behaviors (e.g., risky driving), with minor or no difference for others (e.g., smoking).

The reasons for gender differences in risk taking are not well understood, and they continue to be investigated. Wilson and Daly (1985) suggested that males have a greater genetic propensity toward risk taking because the environment of our early ancestors provided larger rewards for risk-taking males than for risk-taking females. Zuckerman (1990) suggested that naturally occurring lower levels of arousal in males encourage risk taking to raise their arousal levels. Arnett (1992) suggested that risk taking is largely influenced by the level of family, neighborhood, school, and cultural restrictions placed on risk taking and that males may take more risks because their behavior is less restricted than is the behavior of females.

RISK-TAKING DECISIONS DURING ADOLESCENCE

Furby and Beyth-Marom (1992) emphasized that, each time a person is presented with a behavioral choice, there is risk associated with engaging in the behavior and with not engaging in the behavior. For example, consider the choices presented to an adolescent asked to go driving with a friend who is intoxicated. There are identifiable negative and positive outcomes of going for the drive (e.g., being arrested or injured, being cool, having a good time) and there are identifiable negative and positive outcomes of not going for the drive (e.g., losing the friend, being considered a wimp;

avoiding trouble, remaining at the current activity). Therefore, thinking of risk taking as only deciding to engage in a potentially dangerous behavior is not appropriate. Risk taking also occurs when deciding not to engage in a dangerous behavior.

In this section, we will focus on several influences on adolescents' decisions about risk taking. The common feature of these influences is that they focus adolescents' attention on the potential short-term and positive outcomes of risky behaviors and reduce adolescents' attention on the potential long-term or negative outcomes. In the next section, we will explore what these potential short-term and positive consequences of risk taking are.

A Rational Choice Theory

In his rational choice theory, Gardner (1993) proposes that adolescents engage in more risk taking than adults because in adolescence the advantages of engaging in risk taking outweigh the disadvantages, while in adulthood the disadvantages of engaging in risk taking outweigh the advantages. It is not adolescents' faulty or immature decision-making abilities that lead them into taking risks. Rather, given their circumstances, it is often rational for adolescents to choose to engage in risk-taking behaviors. Gardner proposes the following:

> Imagine a society where the passage [from one life-stage to another] is marked by a dangerous but voluntary ordeal. Some of those who choose to undergo the ordeal will perish, but those who participate and survive will obtain a reward unavailable to nonparticipants. Those who forgo the ordeal miss the reward, but they are spared the risk of dying in the ordeal. (p. 72)

Of course, the percentage of people choosing the ordeal will depend on the likelihood of death and the size of the reward. However, given the same likelihood of successfully completing the ordeal and the same reward, Gardner asks whether the challenge would be taken by a greater percentage of rational-thinking adolescents entering adulthood or by a greater percentage of rational-thinking adults entering old age. One could argue that a higher percentage of adults would choose the ordeal, because they would be forfeiting much shorter lives if they were to fail. However, adults are less likely to engage in these types of risky behaviors.

Gardner asserts that adolescents would choose the ordeal more frequently than adults because of the relative uncertainty of their futures. Adolescents are in a transitional stage between childhood and adulthood, and many do not have clear expectations for their future. Even those with specific aspirations are uncertain about their ability to realize them, especially in a rapidly changing world. On the other hand, adults have a clearer sense of their future because of their years of experience and the general stability of their lives. When faced with uncertainty about one's future, Gardner argues, the rational response is to maximize immediate benefits at the risk of future and unpredictable benefits.

This is why adolescents are more likely than adults to engage in the ordeal. It is also why adolescents are more likely to decide to engage in risk-taking behavior: they are maximizing relatively predictable immediate gains (e.g., in excitement, peer respect, self-confidence) and risking a future that is largely uncertain.

Thinking Styles

Adolescents generally consider risks differently than do adults. Adolescents are more likely than adults to focus on the immediate and short-term benefits of risk taking and less likely to focus on potential negative, long-term consequences (Furby & Beyth-Marom, 1992). For example, Kegeles, Adler, and Irwin (1988) found that adolescents are less likely to consider the degree to which condoms would protect them from pregnancy or disease when deciding to use condoms and are more likely to consider whether they are easy to use, whether they facilitate spontaneous sex, and whether they are popular among their peers. Bauman (1980) found that adolescents are more likely to consider the immediate benefits of marijuana use, such as feeling less stress and feeling happier, than the potential negative, long-term consequences when deciding whether to smoke marijuana. Castle, Skinner, and Hampson (1999) found that knowledge about increased future risk of skin cancer from sunbathing does not reduce adolescents' sunbathing—possibly because of the perceived short-term advantages of being tan.

The degree to which an adolescent focuses on immediate or short-term benefits of risk taking may be influenced by several factors, and these factors may account for some of the variability in risk taking among adolescents. Parents,

BROADENING Perspectives

Everyday Risks

Although we often state that human life is priceless, at both a societal level and an individual level we regularly engage in behaviors that put our lives at increased peril, so that certain goals can be met (Gardner, 1993). Thousands of the people who are killed on our highways each year could be saved if we were to enforce a 30 mph speed limit on all highways. However, there would be significant costs of lowering the speed limit to 30 mph, such as the added time that people would have to spend commuting. As a society, we are willing to take the risks of a higher speed limit because of its benefits. At a more individual level, consider a person who speeds to make an appointment on time. The slight increase in the risk of injury is seen as acceptable because of the importance of being prompt. Thinking about the reasons that each of us engages in behaviors that increase risk even slightly may provide some insight into why some adolescents engage in blatantly reckless behaviors.

other important adults, and peers of some adolescents may have influenced them to consider long-term consequences, either through modeling or though reinforcement of behaviors that focus on long-term consequences. Adolescents who have experienced significant negative outcomes from risky behaviors, or who have observed others struggling with these outcomes, may see potential negative outcomes with more clarity. Adolescents with a more negative view of their future may be more likely to engage in risk-taking behavior because the potential value of any immediate gain would appear even stronger when compared with an unclear yet generally dismal future.

Adolescent Egocentrism

Elkind (1967) hypothesized that the normal development of egocentrism in adolescence results in a "personal fable," in which adolescents generally feel immune from harm or other negative consequences. He suggested that adolescents engage in more risky behaviors because of their greater sense of invulnerability.

The small amount of research in this area, however, suggests that adolescents feel no greater immunity from harm than do adults. Quadrel, Fischhoff, and Davis (1993) found that adolescents and their parents do not differ in the extent to which they think that the adolescents will encounter four health risks: having an alcohol dependency, being mugged, being in an auto accident, or having an unplanned pregnancy. Cohn et al. (1995) found that adolescents and their parents are both overly optimistic about the adolescents' likelihood of avoiding a variety of health risks and that the parents are even more optimistic than the adolescents themselves. In addition, Todesco and Hillman (1999) found that adolescents who take many risks rate their chance of experiencing negative events in their lives no differently than adolescents who take few risks. Thus, although a sense of invulnerability may influence risk-taking behavior, the research raises doubts about whether increased risk taking during adolescence is the result of a heightened sense of personal invulnerability during adolescence or among certain adolescents.

Adolescents' Influences on Each Other's Behavior

The behaviors of children and adolescents are increasingly influenced by peers as they get older (Rowe, 1994). Consequently, the natural tendencies of adolescents to consider the immediate benefits of risky behaviors are magnified by the influence of their friends, who are likely to be thinking the same way. Adults' focus on potentially negative and long-term outcomes is likely to have a relatively small influence on the behavioral choices made by adolescents.

Adolescents who are interested in risk taking may congregate and reinforce each other's risk taking. Attempts to avoid risks may be met with derision and loss of esteem in the group. Because of the benefits of risk taking in adolescence, groups of risk-taking adolescents may be admired by their peers. Other adolescents may take increasingly high risks in order to become part of such a group.

This peer pressure may be overwhelming, forcing many adolescents to decide to engage in risky and reckless behaviors even though they clearly see the potential negative consequences. The possibility of negative consequences may seem unimportant when compared with the relative certainty of the negative peer evaluation that would accompany avoiding the risky behavior.

The Influences of Alcohol and Other Drugs

Alcohol and drug use can encourage risky and reckless behaviors (Arnett, 1992). After drinking or using other drugs, adolescents may be particularly prone to focus on the immediate benefits of risky or reckless behaviors and may be strongly influenced by the encouragement of other adolescents who have been drinking or using drugs. Their ability to focus on the potential negative consequences of risky or reckless behaviors may be impaired. In addition, behaviors that could be considered risky under some circumstances are best described as reckless when alcohol or other drugs are involved, because of the decreased control over their circumstances that intoxicated adolescents experience.

THE BENEFITS OF RISK-TAKING AND RECKLESS BEHAVIORS

To this point, we have seen that adolescents are likely to focus on the short-term benefits of a behavior. What still needs to be investigated however, is why risk taking results in benefits that are attractive to adolescents. In this section, we will explore two ways in which risk taking results in immediate and positive consequences to adolescents: risk taking produces physiological arousal and psychological excitement and it helps adolescents meet important developmental goals.

Arousal and Excitement

An interesting discussion of sensation seeking is found in researcher Michael Apter's (1992) book *The Dangerous Edge*. He notes that many people—young and old—seek out and enjoy situations "on the dangerous edge of things":

> For example, from the moment the council of my hometown in Wales pronounced that the promenade along the seafront was in a dangerous condition, the crowds flocked not just to see it but to walk along it. The chance of the whole structure collapsing into the sea made it more popular than ever. Certainly the rope cordon intended to keep everyone out made not the slightest bit of difference. The young ducked under it, the old stepped over it, and those in wheelchairs—and even mothers pushing babies in prams—had it lifted for them. (p. 3)

When a person is confronted by a novel or dangerous situation, the sympathetic branch of the autonomic nervous system is activated (Carlson, 1986). The purpose of the sympathetic branch is to arouse an organism and, in some cases, to prepare it for "fight or flight." The physical sensations associated with novel or dangerous situations are a result of this activation. The heart beats faster to deliver more oxygen and nutrients to the organs and muscles. Perspiration appears to help cool the body. The feelings "in the pit of the stomach" result from a diversion of resources from the digestive system. Adrenaline is released to raise and maintain the body's level of arousal. The brain also becomes more alert and active, primarily through increased activation of the reticular activating system—with focused attention on the novel or dangerous situation.

Interestingly, this pattern of physiological arousal can be experienced psychologically in one of two very different ways: as excitement or as anxiety. Through a series of groundbreaking experiments, Schachter and Singer (1962) showed that it is the way in which a person thinks about an event that determines whether the physiological arousal it evokes is experienced as excitement or as anxiety. This helps explain how the same event (e.g., riding a roller coaster) evokes a thrill in some people but fear in others—they are thinking differently about the event.

The Safety, Danger, and Trauma Zones

Apter proposes the following conceptual model to represent a person's physiological response to a potentially dangerous activity. The safety zone represents an area where no risk exists. When in the safety zone, a person does not face any danger and, so, does not experience any physiological arousal. Once the person enters the danger zone, physiological arousal begins because of the automatic activation of the sympathetic nervous system. Arousal instinctively increases the closer one comes to the dangerous edge. Just over the dangerous edge is the trauma zone, or the zone in which a negative outcome occurs. A straightforward example of this concept is how you respond when being at the top of a tall cliff. When you are far back from the edge, you are in the safety zone. You feel safe and, so, experience no arousal. As you approach the cliff's edge, you enter the danger zone and physiological arousal begins. This arousal increases the closer you come to the edge of the cliff. The edge of the cliff is the dangerous edge, and just over the edge is the trauma zone, where a fall leads to injury or death. Driving a car can result in the same experience. As you drive on a deserted stretch of road at a low speed, you feel safe. If you decide to speed along the road, your level of arousal increases with your speed. As your speed increases to the point at which your control over the car starts to come into question, your arousal is very high. If your speed continues to increase, you may crash.

Trauma zone
_____

Dangerous edge -
Danger zone
_____

Safety zone

The Protective Frame

What determines whether the physiological arousal a person experiences in the danger zone results either in excitement or in anxiety? To answer this question, Apter introduces the concept of the protective frame. The protective frame represents the extent to which a person who is in the danger zone believes that he is protected from entering the trauma zone—in essence, the aroused person's cognitive appraisal of how safe from harm he is. When a person is in the danger zone and feels the protective frame, physiological arousal is experienced as excitement (or, when highly aroused, as ecstasy); when the person is in the danger zone without the protective frame, he experiences the physiological arousal as anxiety (or, when highly aroused, as terror). For example, standing near a cage containing an angry, roaring lion can be very exciting. However, the cage by itself is boring (because the person is not in the danger zone), and the lion without the cage is terrifying (because there is no protective frame).

The protective frame can exist in several different ways: as physical protection (e.g., a strong railing at the edge of a cliff), as expected assistance from others (e.g., a competent climber holding a rope as you approach the cliff's edge), and as one's own self-confidence (e.g., having successfully descended a cliff).

The Fallacious Frame

How is it that people are occasionally injured or killed while engaging in risk taking or sensation seeking? To explain, Apter introduces the concept of the fallacious frame. When in the fallacious frame, a person feels protected from trauma even though the protection does not really exist. As a result, people in the fallacious frame do not take the necessary precautions against entering the trauma zone. This increases the likelihood that they will inadvertently slip over the dangerous edge and become injured. People can be in the fallacious frame in two ways: (a) knowing that they are in the danger zone and having an unrealistic belief about the strength of the protective frame (e.g., overconfidence in one's ability) and (b) believing that they are in the safety zone when, in fact, they are in the danger zone (e.g., not understanding the danger associated with a particular behavior). Apter describes these people as "those who stupidly think that their lives are charmed" (p. 119).

Alcohol and Sensation Seeking

Apter's work on sensation seeking suggests two ways that the consumption of alcohol or other drugs may increase the likelihood of injury or death during risk taking. First, the depressing effects of alcohol on a person's physiology may require that the person experience higher levels of danger to achieve physiological arousal. This requires that the person move closer to the dangerous edge to achieve physiological arousal, and this can put the person at increased risk for entering the trauma zone. Second, the use of alcohol can increase a person's chance of experiencing the fallacious frame by impairing his judgments about the danger of a situation or his ability to handle it.

Adolescents may be particularly susceptible to experiencing the fallacious frame. They engage in many new experiences—the dangers of which may not be readily apparent to them. They are under less parental supervision than they were as children and, thus, have less input from people who have engaged in these experiences before. They are influenced to an increasing extent by peers who are also new to many of these experiences. Alcohol consumption may increase the likelihood that adolescents experience the fallacious frame. Further, the extent to which their judgment is being impaired by alcohol or other drugs may be less apparent to adolescents than to adults who have had more experience with these drugs.

The Promotion of Adolescent Development

Risk taking may be a component of normal adolescent development (Baumrind, 1987; Jessor, 1991). Just as the contrariness of 2-year-olds helps them differentiate from their parents, risk taking can help adolescents meet important developmental milestones. For example, risk taking may help adolescents build self confidence, show autonomy from parents and other adults, build an identity, and gain peer acceptance and respect.

In this section, we will explore two theories about the ways in which risk taking can benefit adolescent development. The first focuses on how our genetic heritage might make risk taking a normal part of adolescent life, and the second focuses on the ways in which risk taking can help adolescents meet important psychological goals. Unfortunately, little research exists to support these theories, but they do suggest interesting directions for future research.

An Evolutionary Perspective

Steinberg and Belsky (1996) argue that the processes of natural selection and sexual selection during humankind's early history may have resulted in increased risk taking in adolescence. The process of natural selection results in individuals with certain characteristics or behaviors having a greater chance for survival and, consequently, a greater opportunity to pass on the genes that influenced these characteristics. The process of sexual selection results in certain individuals having an increased likelihood of engaging in sexual reproduction, thus passing their genes along to future generations. Our behaviors may be influenced by the genes that were selected in our early ancestors and then passed on to us, even though these genes may have little benefit in today's society.

Steinberg and Belsky wonder if tendencies that result in behaviors considered risk taking today might not have been naturally selected because *not* engaging in them in the precarious world of our prehistoric ancestors would have resulted in decreased chance of survival. For example, running across a burning savannah, fording a swollen river, chasing a large animal from a cave, or attacking animals for food might have led to increased survival for those "risk-taking" enough to engage in them. Those who engaged in these behaviors after the pubertal growth spurt and before the relative feebleness of old age (which then came early in life) may have been the most likely to survive, which may be part of the reason that risk taking is so prevalent in adolescents. Risk taking is likely to have been more advantageous for males. Females during their early childbearing years may have been more likely to pass along their genes by focusing on childrearing and avoiding risk taking.

Similarly, male adolescents who engaged in dangerous and life-threatening activities may have been more attractive to eligible mates—possibly because of the esteem in which they were held by the social group. Thus, they would have had an advantage in sexual selection and would have passed on the genes that influenced this risk-taking style. Given the demands of life in those environments, it is difficult to imagine how an adolescent male who did not take regular risks would have been considered a desirable mate.

"Edgework" and the Development of the Autonomous Self

Lyng (1990) analyzes the value of risk-taking behavior through the concept of edgework, the process of "negotiating the boundary between chaos and order" (p. 855). It involves exploring one's personal limits or the limits of material forms, and it requires the ability to maintain control over a situation that verges on chaos and that is perceived by most people as uncontrollable. In short, edgework is extreme risk taking.

Lyng bases his analysis on years of observing and talking with skydivers and others who engage in risky hobbies and occupations (e.g., firefighting, bomb disposal). His descriptions of individuals' responses during edgework contain many of the same phrases that are used to describe important issues during adolescent development. For example, he states, "The experience [edgework] produces a sense of 'self-realization,' 'self-actualization,' or 'self-determination'" (p. 860). Although fear is often felt before engaging in edgework, "fear gives way to a sense of exhilaration and omnipotence" (p. 860). During edgework, a person's perceptual field becomes focused, which results in "a sense of cognitive control over the essential 'objects' in the environment" (p. 861). Finally, "edgework stimulates a heightened sense of self and a feeling of omnipotence" (p. 863).

Edgework provides a sense of freedom to a person who is "being pushed through daily life by unidentifiable forces that rob one of true individual choice" (Lyng, 1990, p. 870). Adolescents often complain that others constrain their behavior and that they are left with little self-direction. Even adolescents with a sense of control over their daily lives often feel constrained by constant pressure to behave in ways that will enable them to be accepted into a good college or will secure a personally or financially rewarding job. The value of edgework is that it allows the adolescent to break away from the demands of outsiders and focus completely on a pursuit he chooses. Emerging from these activities successfully gives the adolescent feelings of accomplishment, which can promote a sense of competence and self-determination. Thus, edgework helps the adolescent meet many normal developmental goals of adolescence. Less extreme forms of risk taking may accomplish the same goal.

A Summary of the Benefits of Risk-Taking and Reckless Behaviors

Apter's theories on sensation seeking and Lyng's theories on edgework help explain two potentially powerful influences on adolescent risk taking. The physiological and psychological arousal that accompanies behavior in the protective frame of the danger zone can provide periodic or ongoing excitement and pleasure. The sense of competence and self-directedness that can come from edgework and other risk-taking behavior can help adolescents meet important developmental goals. Both results of risk taking are positive and fairly immediate and, thus, may be a particular focus of adolescents.

INTERVENTIONS TO REDUCE RECKLESS BEHAVIOR

The short- and long-term negative consequences of reckless behaviors have made them the target of many interventions. Examples of these efforts include programs to reduce smoking, alcohol and other drug use, early-onset sexuality, unprotected sexual intercourse, involvement in gangs, and drinking and driving. Specific interventions for these behaviors are included in many chapters in this text. In this section, we will apply our knowledge of risk taking to hypothesize about general strategies that may be effective for reducing a wide range of reckless behaviors.

Strategies for Changing Adolescents' Thinking About Reckless Behaviors

Our knowledge of adolescents' tendencies to focus on immediate and positive consequences of behaviors suggests several strategies for reducing reckless behavior. The first is to help adolescents understand these natural tendencies and to give them techniques for also considering the negative or long-term consequences of their behaviors. The focus of these strategies is to give adolescents a better understanding of their own thinking processes—thus giving them more control over them. For example, a powerful component of the recent antismoking campaigns in some states describes the ways in which adolescents' thinking has been manipulated by tobacco advertisements. This can help adolescents

---

Knowledge Is Not Always Helpful

Knowledge about risk taking helps us understand why informing adolescents about the negative consequences of reckless behaviors has been largely ineffective in reducing their occurrence: it is because adolescents tend not to focus on these consequences when deciding how to behave, even when they are aware of what the consequences are.

resist this manipulation and may make them resent the manipulation and decrease their use of tobacco.

Other strategies use adolescents' tendency to focus on the immediate and positive consequences but stretch these tendencies to help the adolescents focus on the immediate and negative consequences of a behavior or on the positive and long-term consequences. For example, some antismoking advertisements have featured adolescents describing how disgusting it is to kiss someone who smokes (a negative immediate consequence). Some antidrug campaigns have focused on the long-term benefits of staying off drugs, such as becoming a better athlete. The slogan "Friends don't let friends drive drunk" takes advantage of peer influences on reckless behaviors by encouraging adolescents who are less likely to engage in reckless behaviors to encourage others to avoid recklessness.

Although some of these strategies appear simplistic, they can be powerful with some adolescents, primarily those who are occasionally reckless because they give little thought to their negative consequences. However, they may have less of an influence on adolescents who have a strong desire to engage in reckless behaviors.

Strategies to Increase the Attainment of Important Goals Without the Need to Act Recklessly

An entirely different set of strategies can be used to reduce reckless behaviors by giving adolescents alternate ways of attaining the goals that they could obtain through reckless behaviors. Even though these strategies may not appear to be aimed at reducing reckless behaviors, they can still be very effective in this regard. Involving adolescents in sports, academic, social, and other activities can give them a sense of accomplishment and individuality. Less dangerous risk taking can be encouraged to provide physiological arousal and psychological excitement—for example, participating in rope-challenge courses or climbing on an indoor artificial rock-climbing course. Not only do these activities provide excitement, but many of them allow adolescents to feel competent and to focus their energy and attention on activities that can increase their sense of identity.

CHAPTER SUMMARY

Although not all adolescents engage in frequent risky or reckless behaviors, most people engage in more risky and reckless behavior during their adolescence than during other times in their lives. Males engage in more risk taking than females across all ages, although the differences between males and females vary by age and type of risk.

Adolescents decide to take risks in some situations but not in others. They are more likely than adults to consider the positive and short-term consequences of potential risk taking when deciding to take risks and to ignore the negative or long-term consequences. This tendency may be enhanced by peer reinforcement, and the use of alcohol or other drugs may encourage risk taking. There are several short-term benefits of risk taking for adolescents. Physiological responses to dangerous behaviors and the sense of psychological excitement that comes from them can be very positive. The psychological benefits of feeling less like a protected child, less under the control of parents or other adults, and more a part of the adolescent culture can increase the attraction of risk taking for adolescents. In addition, the processes of natural and sexual selection in our ancestral environment may have resulted in a genetic predisposition toward risk taking during adolescence.

Adolescents can be taught to understand the ways in which their thinking processes and values can promote reckless behaviors; thus, they may be able to alter these processes when desired. In addition, helping adolescents attain the benefits of reckless behaviors in less dangerous ways can reduce their reliance on recklessness. While risk taking may remain a part of many adolescents' lives, it may be possible to help them protect themselves against the most dangerous consequences of risk taking.

Revisiting Ray

Ray's risk-taking and reckless behaviors fit with several of the theories discussed in this chapter. His risk taking likely resulted in high levels of excitement, and it appears that Ray's acceptance and popularity (important goals for many adolescents) were due in part to his daring exploits and willingness to "push the envelope" of excitement in many aspects of his life. His risk taking produced many benefits for Ray, and this is probably why he chose to continue taking risks. However, Ray's death is a reminder of the potential consequences of risky and reckless behaviors. Alcohol undoubtedly clouded Ray's judgment about climbing down the chimney, and the lure of impressing his many friends at the party may have eliminated any of Ray's misgivings about descending the chimney.

- What personal characteristics or experiences may have encouraged Ray to engage in risk taking more frequently than many of his peers?
- Is there anything that could have been done to reduce the types of incidents in which Ray was involved, or must we simply accept that terrible accidents like this are inevitable?

CHAPTER 5

Narcissism

Even as a young child, Mindy was often the center of attention. She became the darling of her parents' country club when she was just old enough to walk. While the other children ran around, Mindy sat quietly with her parents. Her parents' friends were envious of Mindy's parents and often commented to them that they must be wonderful parents to have such a well-behaved child. When Mindy occasionally squirmed or failed to be attentive to the adults around her, her parents would take her into another room, and soon they would return with Mindy again being the quiet, perfect child. The other parents saw this as another indication of Mindy's parents' ability to be perfect parents.

During her school-age years, Mindy had few friends and generally received only average grades. Her parents saw this as an indication that Mindy's teachers were unable to recognize her true talents and that her friends were jealous of Mindy's superiority. When Mindy was sad about her lack of friends, her parents told her to stop being sad—that sadness was not something that their daughter should feel. Their usual strategy was to stop speaking to Mindy until she could show that she was happy. Mindy did find one or two friends, and her parents often bought them lavish gifts and commented to them about how lucky they were to be smart enough to have Mindy as a friend.

By the time she entered high school, Mindy had surrounded herself with a small number of adoring friends. They always deferred to her when decisions were made and told her how smart and beautiful she was and how lucky they were to have her as a friend. To others in her school, it appeared that Mindy treated her friends with disdain and that she acted as if her friends were lucky to have her as a friend.

Mindy changed high schools at the end of her freshman and sophomore years, because she was not recognized as a leader in her class. Her parents often told Mindy how ashamed they were that she was not a leader—and that she should be working harder to pay them back for all their devotion to her. Now a senior, Mindy has applied to three highly regarded universities, despite her school counselor's concern that her grades are not good enough for her to be admitted. Mindy and her parents expect that these superior universities will recognize Mindy's talents, which have gone unrecognized in high school. However, if the universities are unable to recognize Mindy's talents, they plan that she will spend a year or two in Europe.

The term *narcissism* comes from a Greek myth and has traditionally referred to self-love and self-adoration. Most of us have some love for ourselves: we have positive regard for some of our abilities, we care for ourselves, and we see ourselves as important and worthy. Some people, however, have an excessive regard for themselves. They focus almost exclusively on themselves, believe that they are consistently entitled to special treatment, and show little regard for others. In addition, their relationships are often manipulative: they act friendly toward others when things are being done for them but turn hostile when others question their abilities or their special place in the world. Those with excessive regard for themselves have been described as having excessive or problematic levels of narcissism, and their style of relating to others has been labeled narcissistic.

In this chapter, we will explore this interesting, and often exasperating, style of interacting with others. As we will see, the grandiose, hostile, and selfish appearance of a highly narcissistic adolescent is often built on an unseen foundation of inferiority and shame. As with many problematic behaviors in adolescence, what you see is often only a small part of what is really there.

This chapter is different from others in this text because of the lack of research-based knowledge about narcissism. Much of the information about this style of interacting with others comes from clinical reports or from theory. Despite the problems presented by a lack of research foundation for understanding narcissism, it is included for several reasons:

- Many people would argue, including most parents, that adolescence is a time of excessive focus on the self.
- College students often complain about having to cope with narcissistic roommates, friends, or acquaintances from clubs or other social groups and want to learn how anyone could develop into such a manipulative, uncaring person.
- Narcissism is an interesting example of the ways in which outward behavior can mask inner feelings that are incompatible with the behavior. Understanding the ways in which this can happen in narcissism may expand our thinking about other problems and perhaps even increase our understanding and tolerance of those exhibiting problem behaviors.

The Plan: We will first explore the concept of narcissism—how it has been used in psychoanalytic theory and how it is used today—and will then explore the outward and inner experiences of narcissistic adolescents. Understanding these experiences, and how the outward experiences offer psychological protection from painful inner experiences, will provide a foundation for understanding the development of narcissistic behavior. Most theorists have suggested that narcissism is rooted in disturbed parent/child relationships. We will examine how these relationships can foster narcissism and will review one example of how this can occur. Finally, there will be a brief discussion of interventions that have been useful for some narcissistic adolescents.

THE CONCEPT OF NARCISSISM

Narcissism is a concept that has never been defined clearly; however, it has always referred to a focus on oneself (Pulver, 1986). As previously mentioned, the term *narcissism* comes from a Greek myth (Jacoby, 1990). Narcissus was the exceptionally beautiful son of a nymph and a river god. As an adolescent, he was pursued by many females. Echo, a nymph who could not initiate conversation but could only repeat the last few words spoken to her, fell in love with him. Although she threw herself at him, he rejected her. In her shame, she hid in the forest and eventually turned to stone—leaving only her voice to be heard. Because of Echo's plight, another woman rejected by Narcissus prayed that he, too, would fall in love with someone unwilling to return his love, and the god Nemesis answered her prayer. As Narcissus lay down by a pond to drink, he noticed his reflection. He believed that it was someone beneath the water, was enchanted by the person's beauty, and fell immediately in love. He could not take his eyes off the beauty of this person, and he gradually came to realize that it was his own reflection. He despaired yet could not pull himself away from his beloved reflection. Unable to leave the pond, he gradually wasted away until there was only a flower (a narcissus) left in his place.

Sigmund Freud made narcissism a central issue in psychoanalytic theory (Cooper, 1986; Kernberg, 1998). He regarded narcissism as a normal part of infant development. Infants are self-absorbed and relate to others only when others are necessary to meet their needs. Freud believed that, during childhood and adolescence, people develop the ability to form meaningful relationships with others—investing love and energy in these relationships. However, if severe problems or frustrations occur in these relationships, especially if they develop during early childhood, children may withdraw energy from relationships with others and reinvest it solely in their relationship with themselves. The result is a narcissistic style of relating to others that is similar to the style of infants: relating to others only when they are useful for meeting a personal need.

Some recent theorists view narcissism as a characteristic that promotes psychological health when it is present in moderate amounts. Moderate levels of self-focus and self-adulation are seen as necessary for a person to maintain a positive self-image (Davis, Claridge, & Cerullo, 1997). For example, Stone (1998) distinguishes between normal narcissism and pathological narcissism. Normal narcissism is a healthy sense of pride and self-regard; a person can recognize and appreciate her own talents and can use them positively when interacting with others. Lower than normal levels of narcissism result in deficient self-regard, depression, a need to defer constantly to the desires of others, and a failure to contribute to the efforts of others. Higher levels of narcissism result in excessive self-focus and ongoing denigration of the needs and accomplishments of others (Kernberg, 1998). High levels of narcissism interfere with the development of adolescents' social relationships and can anger, frustrate, and annoy those who must associate with them.

There is some controversy about the relationship between normal and problematic forms of narcissism. Some view problematic narcissism as an exaggeration of normal narcissism (Watson, Hickman, & Morris, 1996). Others believe that problematic narcissism consists of characteristics that are qualitatively different from those of normal narcissism, such as hostility and denigration of others (Davis, Claridge, & Cerullo, 1997). Although this controversy remains unresolved, those with problematic narcissism clearly have bothersome ways of interacting with others. It is this level of narcissism that will be our focus for the rest of this chapter, where problematic or pathological narcissism will be referred to as narcissism and those possessing this level of narcissism will be referred to as narcissistic (recognizing that some theorists and researchers consider that almost everyone is narcissistic to a point).

THE EXPERIENCE OF NARCISSISM

Narcissistic adolescents often possess two distinct, and often contradictory, sets of characteristics. Wink (1991) calls these characteristics the overt and covert aspects of narcissism. The overt characteristics are easily observed by others, and the narcissistic adolescent is aware of them (although she may interpret them differently than others do). The covert characteristics are generally unseen by those around a narcissistic adolescent, and the narcissistic adolescent is often unaware of them.

Therapists and researchers have come to believe in the existence of the covert characteristics of narcissism in two ways. First, much of the therapeutic work with narcissistic people has been done by psychoanalysts and therapists using other long-term therapies. They observed the emergence of the covert characteristics during therapy—characteristics of which the narcissistic person was often unaware on a conscious level. As the therapists became aware of

---

Controversy
Are Males or Females More Narcissistic?

Sufficient research has not been completed to show whether more males or females have problematic levels of narcissism. However, one interesting study had undergraduates rate their reactions to a videotaped performance of either a male or a female actor depicting either a sense of entitlement or high levels of self-absorption (Carroll, Hoenigmann-Stovall, & White-head, 1996). The male and female undergraduates rated the female actor more negatively than the male actor in both the entitlement and self-absorption scenes. This suggests that narcissistic behavior by females is reacted to more negatively and perhaps noticed more often. Why might the narcissistic female have been rated more negatively than the narcissistic male?

these covert characteristics, they came to believe that the covert characteristics formed the foundation on which the overt characteristics were based (Hulbert et al., 1994). Second, researchers found that people who exhibited the overt characteristics of narcissism often responded to questionnaires in ways that suggested the presence of the covert characteristics, even though the characteristics often were not apparent in their behavior. This was seen as evidence that the covert characteristics existed along with the overt characteristics (Raskin, Novacek, & Hogan, 1991; Rhodewalt & Morf, 1998).

Overt Characteristics of Narcissism

Overt characteristics are described in similar ways by many authors. The following information comes from APA (1994), Bleiberg (1994), Cooper (1986), Davis, Claridge, & Cerullo, (1997), Heiserman and Cook (1998), Kernberg (1975, 1998), and Millon (1998).

Self-centeredness

The overarching characteristic of narcissistic adolescents is their excessive self-focus. They think primarily about themselves and expect that others are thinking about them. When they focus on others, it is often to assess how much others are focused on them. They may initiate interactions with others, but the interactions revolve around them and their accomplishments or needs. They do not appear conscious of the needs of others, and they see even the most important needs of others as unimportant when compared with their own needs.

Grandiosity

Narcissistic people view themselves and their accomplishments more positively than is warranted. They exaggerate their accomplishments, and they expect to be recognized by others as superior and treated accordingly. They often treat others with disdain. Because of their self-perceived superiority, they often ignore the expectations of shared social living situations (e.g., doing the dishes). They may have grandiose fantasies in which they behold themselves as having unlimited success, intelligence, beauty, or other desired characteristics. They construct intricate rationalizations for any apparent failure—and these rationalizations usually involve the inability or unwillingness of others to recognize their own special talents. Because of their superiority, they believe that they should be expected to associate only with other superior people and institutions.

Entitlement

Narcissistic adolescents believe that they are entitled to special treatment. It is not just that special treatment would be pleasing; rather, it is owed to them because of their special status. They do not see disappointment as bothersome but as wrong. They believe that they should get what they want, when they want it. When they do get what they want, they seldom see a need to express gratitude, since they have merely been given what they deserve.

Exploitiveness

Because of their sense of entitlement, narcissistic adolescents often take advantage of others, and they expect others to do things for them without feeling the need to reciprocate. They often believe that others should feel honored to have a relationship with them because of their superior qualities.

Sensitivity to Criticism

Narcissistic adolescents are highly sensitive to criticism. They often perceive that others are criticizing them even when they are not being criticized, and they react very strongly to actual or perceived criticism.

Hostility

Narcissistic adolescents' sense of entitlement results in their being hostile toward those who do not treat them as special. They can quickly become angry with others, especially those closest to them, when their superiority is not acknowledged or their needs are not met.

Do You Recognize Yourself?

At this point, you may be questioning whether you have problematic levels of narcissism, because you are sometimes grandiose, sensitive to criticism, hostile, and entitled. Remember that the narcissistic characteristics lie along a continuum, and that most of us have these characteristics to some degree. It is only when they are consistently present or present in large amounts that narcissism can be considered problematic. Perhaps your willingness to seriously consider whether you are narcissistic is a sign that your self-worth is not very fragile and that your narcissism is not problematic.

Covert Characteristics of Narcissism

The covert characteristics of narcissism often are not seen by others, and the narcissistic adolescent is often unaware of them. The covert characteristics are often hidden by the overt characteristics, and the overt characteristics shield the narcissistic adolescent from the painful emotions that accompany them (Raskin, Novacek, & Hogan, 1991).

Shame

Narcissistic adolescents often have deep reservoirs of shame. When they experience this shame, they often feel much more pain than others do. Consequently, shame is a very painful and intense emotion for narcissistic adolescents.

Shame is often seen as the cause of narcissistic adolescents' hostility and sensitivity to criticism. They are vigilant toward any criticism that could trigger their shame. When they begin to feel shame, they shift blame onto other people and become angry with them. This anger protects narcissistic adolescents from their painful shame by absolving them of responsibility.

Fragile Sense of Self-Worth

Narcissistic adolescents often have a fragile sense of self-worth. At a deep level, they feel unsure of themselves. Despite what may be many successes, they often feel as if they are standing on the edge of failure.

Their grandiose behavior and sense of entitlement help narcissistic adolescents maintain their fragile sense of self-worth by allowing them to portray themselves as superior to others. In addition, grandiose behavior and sense of entitlement help the narcissistic adolescent avoid the pain that they experience when they question privately whether they have much worth at all.

Dependence on Others

Despite their outward disdain for others, narcissistic adolescents depend on others to give them the reassurance they need to maintain their fragile self-worth. They have so many deep doubts about themselves that they must have their self-worth repeatedly reinforced by others. Their reliance on others often results in anger and hostility when the others do not consistently provide the reinforcement they desperately need.

Increased Vulnerability to Narcissism in Adolescence

Descriptions of some common experiences during adolescence bear a strong resemblance to the covert features of narcissism: "a proneness to embarrassment and shame, acute self-consciousness and shyness, and painful questions about self-esteem and self-worth" (Bleiberg, 1994, p. 31). Changes in social, educational, and family demands result in many adolescents feeling inadequate and having little faith that they will be able to meet the challenges they face. Physical changes and heightened sexuality may create a sense of shame or embarrassment. In addition, support from family members may be reduced as the adolescent begins to disengage from parents as primary role models. Some adolescents meet these challenges with increases in the overt characteristics of narcissism: grandiosity, a sense of entitlement, hostility toward those evaluating them (e.g., parents and teachers), and sensitivity to criticism. As they become more comfortable in their changing world, many adolescents will be able to drop these defensive styles and be less narcissistic, although significant social changes, such as entry into a college or university, may exacerbate them temporarily.

A Summary of the Experience of Narcissism

Clinical reports from long-term psychotherapy and results from self-report measures of narcissism have shown that many narcissistic children, adolescents, and adults have private feelings and thoughts that are very different from the behaviors that they exhibit to others. Narcissistic people often have a very fragile sense of self-worth and depend on others to repeatedly reinforce a positive sense of self. Their efforts to distance themselves from feelings of shame and poor self-esteem result in grandiose and exploitive behaviors, as well as in anger and hostility directed at those who question their superiority.

THE DEVELOPMENT OF PROBLEMATIC NARCISSISM

Although many theories have been put forward about the development of narcissism, almost no research has focused on them. As a result, we can explore these theories but cannot evaluate their accuracy. Most theories about the development of narcissism emphasize the role of disturbed early parent/child relationships. These relationships often involve parents who repeatedly evaluate their children negatively and use shame to mold their children's behaviors (Fiscalini, 1993; Heiserman & Cook, 1998). As a result, the children develop a fragile sense of self-worth and a high level of shame. Some children cope with their shame and fragile sense of self-worth by developing a narcissistic style of interacting with others. This style protects them from painful feelings but interferes with their social and interpersonal development. As they continue to use narcissism, it comes to dominate their interpersonal behavior.

Raskin and colleagues (1991) described one example of this development. Their description starts with "stage parents," who expect their young child to behave in ways that show others that the parents are competent and wonderful. The child does this by being consistently "attractive, engaging, charming, and brilliant" (p. 912). The child receives love and approval when she is attractive, engaging, charming, and brilliant but scorn and punishment when she is not. As one might expect, these parents' expectations often conflict with the normal exploratory and play behaviors of young children. Despite this, the child is repeatedly required to behave in ways that benefit her parents, and her developmental needs are given little attention.

As this young child matures, she gradually realizes that she is not loved and admired by her parents, but that only her performances in social situations are admired. This can significantly influence the way that she views her parents and the way that she views herself. Anger, hostility, self-doubt, and a fragile sense of self-worth often develop from this new view of herself and her family. However, she cannot express these feelings because they are not part of the image that her parents expect her to maintain and because doing so will result in the withdrawal of her parents' affection and approval.

Children with this upbringing can develop in several ways. Some become primarily sad at the lack of love from their parents and may become depressed.

Others experience primarily anger and become aggressive. Still others develop a narcissistic style to shield themselves from their sadness and anger. In essence, these children develop a self-image based on their parents' expectations: they come to see themselves as attractive, engaging, charming, and brilliant. Their fragile sense of self-worth and their shame are hidden behind an ever increasing sense of superiority.

A child who develops a narcissistic style creates fantasies about her own power and superiority to counteract her fragile sense of self-worth. Since she receives little genuine adoration from her parents, she adores herself as a way to support her fantasized superiority (Cohen, 1997). As the child embraces these fantasies, she begins to see them as an accurate reflection of herself. As a result, her motivation to achieve is reduced because she already believes that she is achieving at a superior level. This can interfere with her development in many areas. For example, she may not ask for help when she does not understand her schoolwork and, so, may fall behind academically.

A narcissistic child enters adolescence with an interpersonal style that angers many peers and adults and that often results in ongoing rejection and ridicule (Bleiberg, 1994). She reacts to criticism with the type of anger and rage that increasingly alienates her from others. She is likely to see this alienation as the result of others' jealousy, which further fuels her sense of grandiosity. In short, throughout her adolescence and adulthood, she will live out the role imposed on her by her parents—being attractive, engaging, charming, and brilliant. It is the only role that she has ever known.

INTERVENTIONS FOR NARCISSISM

The primary obstacle to interventions for narcissistic adolescents is that they do not believe that they need any intervention. Their defensive superiority and grandiosity encourage them to believe that all the problems they encounter are the faults of others: they do not need therapy; rather, something needs to be done with the others who fail to appreciate their talents.

Some narcissistic adolescents do enter therapy, often at the insistence of their parents. They may do so with the goal of getting the therapist to understand their superiority and, thus, eventually helping them convince parents, teachers, and others to support them and their needs, or at least to leave them alone.

Clinical reports of therapy with narcissistic adolescents stress the importance of not challenging the adolescent's view of herself and the world (Masterson, 1990; Miller, 1992). Since the adolescent meets any challenge with defensive hostility, she is quick to ignore the therapist if she believes that the therapist cannot understand and appreciate her. Rather than challenging the narcissistic adolescent, the therapist gently explores the hurt and anger that the adolescent experiences at the hands of others. As therapy progresses, the therapist encourages the adolescent to explore her fears about her self-worth and the ways in which those fears have influenced her grandiose and superior attitudes. As the

HELPING
YOURSELF OR OTHERS

Interacting with Narcissistic Friends, Roommates, and Others

Unless you are willing to be dominated by narcissistic people, it can be very difficult to have a friendship, or even an acquaintanceship, with them. Remember, though, that underneath all of their bluster and sense of superiority is a person whose early experiences taught them to be unsure of themselves and to distrust others' ability to provide them with security and support. You cannot convince a narcissistic person that she is not superior to you and others, so it is not worth trying. Be genuinely kind and supportive when it is warranted—just as you would with anyone. Resist being blindly supportive, however. If you must criticize, it will be most effective if done gently and in private—this will reduce the narcissistic person's need to react with anger and hostility.

adolescent gains confidence in her ability to examine and tolerate her self-doubts, she can be encouraged to begin to see how they influence her interactions with others. As the adolescent continues to gain true self-confidence, she may be encouraged to relinquish her superior and grandiose attitudes. In short, the therapist recognizes and responds to the adolescent's underlying covert characteristics rather than doing what most people in her life do: respond to the overt characteristics. By reducing the strength of the adolescent's covert characteristics, the therapist can give her the strength to consider changing the overt characteristics that interfere with her ability to form relationships with others.

CHAPTER SUMMARY

Narcissism traditionally has referred to self-love and adoration. Most people love and adore themselves to some extent, but those considered narcissistic focus their adoration almost exclusively on themselves. In addition, they are often angry toward others and expect others to see them as superior and worthy of special treatment. The behaviors of narcissistic adolescents involve self-centeredness, grandiosity, a sense of entitlement, exploitiveness, sensitivity to criticism, and hostility. Several authors have suggested that these overt behaviors develop to compensate for covert narcissistic characteristics, such as a fragile sense of self-worth, severe feelings of shame, and dependence on others for reassurance about their fragile sense of self.

Several theorists have suggested that narcissism develops from disturbed parent/child relationships. One type of disturbed relationship involves parents who expect their young children to be consistently attractive, engaging, charming and brilliant—not because it is good for the children to be this way but because it meets the parents' need to appear to have raised perfect children. These parents use shame to mold their children's behavior and are quick to retract love and attention when the children do not act in ways that are beneficial for the parents. As these children develop, they recognize that they are not loved by their parents but, rather, are used by the parents for their own needs. One way these children can respond is to develop a self-image that reflects the expectations of the parents: attractive, engaging, charming, and brilliant. This self-image hides the shame and self-doubt instilled by the parents.

Revisiting Mindy

Some observers might have seen young Mindy and her parents as the ideal family. To most adults, Mindy often seemed perfectly behaved. In retrospect, however, Mindy's behavior appears to have been artificial and based on the need of her parents to be raising a perfect child rather than on what was good for her. One can imagine the continual pressure that Mindy must have been under to behave like an adult rather than a child. During childhood, Mindy probably began to incorporate her parents' expectations into her self-image—that of a girl (or perhaps the term "young lady" would be more appropriate) who is attractive, engaging, charming, and brilliant. This is who she had to be if she wanted to get any respect or praise from her parents.

Because she always had to be the best, Mindy surrounded herself with a small number of friends who were willing to acknowledge her superiority. She was hostile to those unwilling to treat her as special and blamed all her shortcomings on others. As a result, she distanced herself from everyone except her small circle of admirers. She has not achieved much in her academics—where performance is more valued than image. She may not go to college because of her inability to consider attending any college except for the most elite—again, the image of going to college is much more important to Mindy and her parents than the skills that she could attain there.

In short, Mindy's life as an adult is likely to mirror her early childhood. She will continue to seek a superior image as one who is attractive, engaging, charming, and brilliant. Her own children are likely to be an important part of this process, so they will consistently need to be attractive, engaging, charming, and brilliant as well—which may result in Mindy passing along her narcissistic style to another generation.

- What signs might have indicated that Mindy's childhood environment was troubled, even though she appeared to be the perfect child to others? How could one distinguish between Mindy's experience and well-behaved children growing up in a positive environment?
- Who would be friends with Mindy? Would you? What are the few people willing to be friends with Mindy getting out of the relationship?
- Are there things that Mindy's future spouse, or others in her adult life, might do to reduce the chance that Mindy's children will grow up to be narcissistic?

CHAPTER 6

Depression

Beginning in grade school, Elise had a difficult time making friends. She was overweight, and the other children teased her about being fat. She usually withdrew from the other children in response to the teasing. Her parents encouraged her to lose weight to stop the teasing, but they offered her little other advice on how to deal with her peers, believing that teasing was common and that all children had to endure some of it. Besides, her mother had been very quiet and withdrawn as a child. Elise's teachers saw her as a quiet girl who did well in class but never "lived up to her full potential." By high school, everyone knew Elise as a withdrawn, somber person. She had few acquaintances and no close friends. She went home after school and spent most afternoons and evenings in her room. Her parents were somewhat concerned about her lack of social interactions, but Elise claimed that she was studying and that she felt that doing well in school was more important than having friends.

Halfway through high school, Elise began to miss school once or twice a week. She often claimed that she did not feel well and would stay in bed for several days at a time. She lost weight and had little interest in eating. After several months of this, her family physician, who could find nothing physically wrong with Elise, referred her to a psychologist. The psychologist diagnosed Elise as having major depressive disorder and dysthymia. In consultation with a psychiatrist, antidepressant medication was prescribed. In addition, Elise began weekly cognitive-behavioral therapy. Elise's mood began to improve after about three weeks. Her school attendance improved, and she began to do better academically. After about six months, the antidepressant medication was ended on a trial basis. Since no relapse of Elise's depressed mood occurred, the medication was discontinued. Elise's therapist began to help her improve her social skills, and she became more socially adept, but her reputation as a withdrawn, awkward person continued to impede her ability to form supportive friendships. Elise chose a college far away from her home, knowing that no one from her high school was likely to choose that college. As she began college, she looked forward to applying all that she had learned in therapy over the past two years to starting a new life.

Depression is a common problem for adolescents, and the prevalence of adolescent depression seems to be increasing (Birmaher et al., 1996). The development of depressed adolescents is often disrupted, especially when the depression goes unrecognized and is seen instead as laziness or "growing pains." Depressed adolescents show deficits in social interactions with family members and peers, which often persist even after their depression has lifted. Depression is also associated with high levels of school drop out, substance abuse, conduct problems, suicide, and the development of bipolar disorder (depression interspersed with periods of mania) (Birmaher et al., 1996; Brent et al., 1993).

In this chapter, we will explore the growing body of research on the causes and consequences of depression in adolescents, as well as the best ways to prevent depression and treat adolescents who are experiencing it. As we will see, however, many fundamental questions about adolescent depression remain unanswered—for example, whether distinct depressive disorders exist in adolescence, why female adolescents exhibit more symptoms of depression than males, and why antidepressant medication is not as effective with adolescents as it is with adults.

The Plan: We will first define depression and the criteria for the diagnosis of depressive disorders and then will explore historical and current thinking about whether depression exists as a disorder in adolescents. We will see that beliefs about adolescent depression have vacillated and that there is currently disagreement about whether clearly demarcated depressive disorders exist in adolescence. We will next look at depression's prevalence and natural course. We will then explore various explanations of the development of depression in children and adolescents. As with the other problems described in this text, it will become clear that many pathways to depression exist, and we will explore the ways in which the explanations help us understand these pathways. Next, we will examine several explanations of the higher prevalence of depression among female adolescents than male adolescents. Finally, we will look at several interventions for depressed adolescents.

DEFINITIONS OF DEPRESSION AND DEPRESSIVE DISORDERS

Discussing depression is often difficult because the term *depression* is used in many ways (Cantwell & Baker, 1991; Nurcombe, 1994). It is used to describe transient feelings (e.g., "I was depressed when I got my grades") and prevailing moods (e.g., "She always seems depressed"). It is also used as a label for several mood disorders (e.g., major depressive disorder [MDD]). As a result, confusion can occur when the term is used but its meaning is not clarified. For example, it is not clear whether the statement "Twenty percent of high school students are depressed" means that 20 percent are feeling sad at any particular moment, have a few symptoms of depression, or have a depressive disorder. Consequently, it is important to clarify the meaning of the term whenever it is used.

The different uses of the term *depression* make it difficult to compare studies of depression. One type of research uses questionnaires on which people answer questions about their depressive symptoms (e.g., the Beck Depression Inventory). This research considers all those who score above a certain level as depressed (and this score can vary across studies). A second type of research uses structured interviews to determine whether a person meets the criteria for a depressive disorder, such as MDD. Typically, those who are considered depressed in the second type of study are also considered depressed in the first type of study, but the opposite is not true. As a result, these two types of studies typically report different findings.

In the Diagnostic and Statistical Manual of Mental Disorders-IV (DSM-IV; APA, 1994), depressive disorders are included in the mood disorder category (bipolar disorders are also included under mood disorders but are not covered in this chapter). Two depressive disorders are most commonly diagnosed in adolescents: dysthymia and MDD. In addition, adjustment disorder with depressed mood (found in the adjustment disorder category of the *DSM-IV*) is diagnosed in some cases.

Adjustment disorder occurs when a person experiences a stressful event and has a particularly difficult time adjusting to it. When the person's symptoms consist mainly of sadness, tearfulness, and hopelessness—and when no other depressive disorder, such as MDD, is present—then adjustment disorder with depressed mood can be diagnosed. According to the diagnostic criteria, an adjustment disorder can last for only six months. If a person's depressive symptoms last longer, some other disorder is said to be present. Thus, compared with the other depressive disorders, adjustment disorder with depressed mood is characterized by moderate symptoms that are of short duration.

Dysthymia is characterized by a long-term depressed mood that is not as severe as MDD. An adolescent must experience a depressed mood for at least half the days each week, for at least one year, for dysthymia to be diagnosed (adults must experience these symptoms for two years). Additional symptoms include eating disturbance, sleep disturbance, fatigue, low self-esteem, poor concentration, and feelings of hopelessness. Recovery from dysthymia is very gradual.

Major depressive disorder is characterized by a depressed mood that is severe but typically of shorter duration than dysthymia. In MDD, the depressed mood must be present most of the day, nearly every day, for at least two weeks. The depressed mood may be expressed in children and adolescents as an irritable mood or as an alternating depressed and irritable mood. Additional symptoms include loss of interest in previously pleasing interests, significant weight loss or failure to make expected weight gains, sleep disturbance nearly every day, daily psychomotor agitation or retardation that is sufficient to be observed by others, fatigue, feelings of worthlessness, diminished ability to concentrate, and recurrent thoughts of death or suicide. Adolescents with MDD may experience hallucinations or delusions.

HISTORICAL AND CURRENT PERSPECTIVES ON DEPRESSIVE DISORDERS IN ADOLESCENCE

Beliefs about whether adolescents experience depressive disorders have vacillated over the years. Little mention of child or adolescent depression was made in texts before the 1800s. In the mid-1800s, some physicians began to consider depression (referred to as melancholia) to be a childhood disorder. Explanations for melancholia included heredity, epilepsy and other seizure disorders, anxiety, bereavement, excessive study, religious excitement, and parental brutality (Parry-Jones, 1995).

In the early and mid-1900s, several researchers focused on depression in infants. Spitz (1949) coined the term *anaclitic depression* to describe the withdrawal of infants who were raised in institutions and had little human contact. Bowlby's (1950) work on attachment theory was influenced by his observations of similar infants. At the same time, however, psychoanalytic theory influenced many people to believe that children and early adolescents could not experience true depression (Munroe, 1955). It was believed that only those with a mature superego could experience depression and that it was not until late adolescence that the superego became mature enough to experience depression. As a result, the depressed mood seen in many children and early adolescents was viewed as a transitory, normal part of childhood.

Beginning in the 1960s, observations that many children and adolescents who had depressive symptoms also acted out and had symptoms of anxiety led to the concept of masked depression (Glaser, 1968; Toolan, 1962). It was hypothesized that depressive disorders did exist in children and adolescents but that they were expressed through hyperactivity, conduct problems, and learning disabilities, rather than through a depressed mood.

The theories that depression did not exist in childhood or that it occurred in masked form began to lose support in the face of a steadily increasing body of research showing that the depressive symptoms experienced by many children and adolescents were the same as those experienced by adults. In addition, research began to show that depression in adolescence often continued into adulthood in the same form. The Group for the Advancement of Psychiatry recognized depression as an adolescent disorder in 1966, and the *DSM-III* first listed depression as a disorder in children and adolescents in 1980. For two decades or so, depression in adults and depression in adolescents were seen as equivalent.

The issue of adolescent depression is currently being debated again (e.g., Angold & Costello, 1995; Nurcombe, 1994; Poznanski & Mokros, 1994). At issue is not whether adolescents exhibit symptoms of depression; undeniable evidence exists that they do. Rather, the question is whether these symptoms form a disorder—a categorically distinct syndrome—or whether the symptoms of depression intermingle with the symptoms of other disorders to form a more general adolescent unhappiness.

Those who question the existence of distinct depressive disorders in adolescence raise several issues. First, depressive symptoms are often present with symptoms of anxiety and conduct problems in adolescents, and these symptoms often wax and wane together (e.g., Angold & Costello, 1995; DuBois et al., 1995; Wilkinson & Walford, 1998). In addition, the cognitive style commonly found in depressed adults is found in adolescents who have depression, anxiety, and conduct problems in similar numbers (Gladstone & Kaslow, 1995; Marton et al., 1993). These findings suggest that depressive symptoms do not constitute a distinct disorder but, rather, are part of "general adolescent misery." Second, several biological abnormalities that are frequently present in adults with MDD are seldom present in children and adolescents with MDD (e.g., alterations of circadian rhythms, changes in REM sleep), and antidepressant medications that are often effective with adults are much less effective with adolescents (Birmaher et al., 1996; Brooks-Gunn, Petersen, & Compas, 1995). These findings suggest that the biological foundation for depression that appears common in adults is present infrequently in adolescents.

Where does the debate about adolescent depression stand? Rather than being able to give a "yes or no" answer to the question of whether adolescent depressive disorders exist, the most accurate answer appears to be "yes *and* no." It seems likely that adultlike depression is present in some adolescents, since certain characteristics of adult depression do occur in some depressed adolescents. However, it also seems likely that a more general mix of "misery" is experienced by other adolescents. Some of these adolescents may develop a distinct depressive disorder as adults, others will develop other disorders, and still others will not develop a disorder at all. At this point, identifying which adolescents will have each outcome is impossible.

THE PREVALENCE AND COURSE OF DEPRESSION

Depression is common among adolescents, and if left untreated it can recur and have many negative consequences. Most studies of depressive disorders in adolescents (which typically ask about depression for the six months preceding the study) show that the prevalence is about 3 to 4 percent (Angold & Costello, 1995). When the presence of a depressive disorder over a longer time is explored, the rates of depression increase. For example, Cooper and Goodyer (1993) found a rate of 8.9 percent over a one-year period among females, and Lewinsohn et al., (1994) found that 24 percent of 1,508 male and female high school students met the criteria for MDD at some point in their childhood or adolescence.

Studies of depressive symptoms have shown that many adolescents have symptoms of depression at any one time and that, over several years, a substantial number of adolescents will experience moderate to severe depressive symptoms. DuBois et al. (1995) reported that 10 percent of their sample of fourth- to tenth-grade students had moderate to severe symptoms of depression at one point in their lives and that an additional 11 percent had mild to moderate symptoms. Garber and colleagues (1993) reported that 12 percent of seventh- to twelfth-grade students had moderate to severe symptoms of depression at the time of their study and that an additional 28 percent showed signs of mild to moderate depression. Petersen, Sarigiani, and Kennedy (1991) reported that between grades 6 and 8, 28 percent of the females in their study and 25 percent of the males reported a depressive episode; between grades 9 and 12, 59 percent of the females and 40 percent of the males had a depressive episode.

As described in more detail later in this chapter, female adolescents have higher rates of depressive disorders and symptoms than do males (Nolen-Hoeksema & Girgus, 1994). Adolescents report more depressive disorders and symptoms than children, and older adolescents report more depressive disorders and symptoms than younger adolescents. Males and females differ in this regard, however. The prevalence of depression increases steadily for females during adolescence, while the pattern for males is less clear, with some studies showing a relatively small increase for males and other studies showing no increase (Angold & Costello, 1995).

In several studies, the average duration of MDD in children and adolescents ranged from 26 to 36 weeks (Keller et al., 1988; Lewinsohn et al., 1994;

BROADENING Perspectives

Experiencing the Feelings of Depression

Many people who have not experienced the severe symptoms of depression have difficulty imagining them. This may make it difficult for them to understand people who are severely depressed and may result in their minimizing the distress felt by those who are depressed. However, all of us have had flashes of the type of despair that depressed people feel most of the time:

- Perhaps toward the end of an exam you have come across a question that stymies you. You feel your emotions well up: "I hate this, I hate this, I HATE THIS!" You grip your pencil tightly, grind the point into the page, and feel so overwhelmed that your mind empties.
- Perhaps when a boyfriend or girlfriend broke up with you, you felt devastated. You thought only of this other person and how unhappy you were, you cried often, you were unresponsive to help from family and friends, and you were not able to do much of anything.

These are the feelings that severely depressed people feel much of the time. They are unable to refocus their thinking and emotions the way most nondepressed people can do. They continue to feel the depths of despair throughout most of their waking hours. Imagine what it would be like to live with those feelings continually.

McCauley et al., 1993; Strober et al., 1993). Some adolescents recover from MDD fairly quickly, while others may experience MDD for years. For example, Strober et al. (1993) reported that about one-third of those who recovered from MDD did so within 20 weeks, and DuBois et al. (1995) reported that one-third of a group of fourth- to tenth-grade students who had high levels of depressive symptoms continued to have those levels two years later.

Adolescents with MDD often experience more than one occurrence of MDD. Lewinsohn et al. (1994) reported that 5 percent of adolescents who recovered from MDD had a relapse within six months, 12 percent had a relapse within a year, and 33 percent had a relapse within four years. McCauley et al. (1993) reported a relapse rate of 54 percent over three years for adolescents who experienced MDD, and Rao et al. (1995) reported a relapse rate of 69 percent over seven years. The median number of relapses was two (with a range of one to six).

Depressed adolescents are likely to continue experiencing depression in adulthood. A 15-year follow-up of depressed adolescents showed high rates of MDD and suicidal behaviors (Weissman et al., 1999). Depression that develops during early adolescence is associated with greater ongoing problems in adulthood than is depression that develops late in adolescence (Rao, Hammen, & Daley, 1999).

THE DEVELOPMENT OF DEPRESSION

Several explanations for the development of depression in adolescence have been proposed. After examining the explanations that currently are influential and have research support, we will explore how they can be combined to provide a more complete picture of the development of depression in individual adolescents.

Biologically Based Explanations

Abnormal biological processes are often found in people who are depressed. Although these processes are found more frequently in adults than in adolescents, many depressed adolescents do exhibit the same biological processes as depressed adults, suggesting that these processes have an important influence on the development of depression in some adolescents.

Genetic Influences

The extent of genetic influences on adolescent depression continues to be debated. For example, Jacobson and Rowe (1999) found a significant genetic influence on adolescent depression. However, Fergusson, Horwood, and Lynskey (1995) found that, once social disadvantage, marital discord, and family adversity is considered, genetic heritability has little influence on the development of adolescent depression.

Rende et al. (1993) reported intriguing results in one of the few twin studies of depression in adolescents. They found that genes play a moderate role in the level of depressive symptoms and that the twins' shared family environment played an insignificant role. However, when they examined only those twins with high levels of depression (possibly similar to adolescents with MDD), they found an insignificant influence of genes and a significant influence of their shared family environment. This suggests that genes play a more important role than the environment in the development of moderate forms of adolescent depression and that genes have less influence on severe forms of adolescent depression.

Jacobson and Rowe (1999) found that genetic influences on depression are stronger among female adolescents than among males. They suggest that hormonal differences between the sexes may result in a greater behavioral expression of the relevant genes in females than in males.

Physiological Influences

Most of the research on physiological processes and depression has focused on the brain's limbic system, which is important in the regulation of emotion. However, most of this research has been with adults, and the results of studies with adolescents have been inconsistent.

Extensive research with adults has implicated the dysregulation of several neurotransmitters in depression, including norepinephrine, serotonin, acetylcholine (ACh), and γ-aminobutyric acid (GABA). However, only a small body of research with adolescents has been completed. One study found similar heightened sensitivity of ACh in adults and adolescents (McCracken, Poland, & Tondo, 1991). However, Birmaher and colleagues (Emslie et al., 1994) failed to find lower levels of serotonin in a group of depressed children and adolescents, as had been found in adults.

Neuroendocrine abnormalities also appear to play a role in depression. Abnormalities in the hypothalamic-pituitary-adrenal axis have been the most studied. Considerable evidence exists that baseline overactivity in this system (indicated by the hypersecretion of cortisol) is related to depression in adults (Emslie et al., 1994), although similar results have not been found consistently for children and adolescents (Birmaher et al., 1996). Several years ago, Carroll (1982) reported that an injection of dexamethasone suppressed cortisol secretion in many depressed adults but in few nondepressed adults, and similar results have been found among depressed adolescents and children, particularly when inpatients have been studied (Birmaher et al., 1996). Several other hormones, such as thyroid hormone and melatonin, have also been studied in adults. The few studies of these hormones completed with depressed adolescents have not shown the patterns observed in adults (Kurcher & Sokolov, 1995).

The secretion of growth hormone has also been studied in depressed adults and adolescents. The studies of baseline growth hormone secretion have been contradictory for both adults and adolescents, with some studies showing heightened secretion in people who are depressed, others showing reduced secretion, and still others showing no differences. However, depressed adults and adolescents show similar changes in growth hormone secretion when injected with several different substances (e.g., insulin, clonidine) (Kurcher & Sokolov, 1995).

Sleep has also been studied in depressed adults and adolescents. Sleep disturbances are consistently found in depressed adults (Dahl & Ryan, 1996). Although several differences have been found between the sleep of depressed and nondepressed adolescents, these differences are not in a consistent direction. For example, some studies have found increased REM latency but others have found decreased REM latency (Birmaher et al., 1996). The greatest divergence from normal sleep patterns has been found in depressed adolescents who are suicidal (Dahl et al., 1992b).

Cognitive Explanations

Several cognitive theories of depression have been put forward, and there is a significant body of research supporting them. In addition, the success of cognitive therapy with depressed adolescents supports the hypothesis that cognitions are an important influence on the development of depression. Two of the most influential theories are described in this section. Overall, cognitive theories do not directly address the ways in which depression develops; instead, they describe how dysfunctional styles of thinking predispose individuals to develop depression and maintain depressive moods (Beck et al., 1979).

Beck's Cognitive Theory

Beck's cognitive theory (Beck, 1976) states that the experiences of some children and adolescents result in their developing patterns of negative thinking that influence their views of themselves, their world, and their future. Through the lens of this negative thinking, they selectively notice and interpret experiences in ways that reinforce their negative views. Negative views of themselves lead to low self-esteem and derogatory self-evaluations. Negative views of the world encourage their ongoing negative perception of events. Negative views of the future lead to feelings of hopelessness. These thoughts about self, world, and future lead to the emotional experience of depression and to a withdrawal from the world and those in it. This withdrawal leaves depressed adolescents with few opportunities for positive experiences and a great deal of time to think about their failures and their unhappy lives.

Many types of experiences can lead to this style of negative thinking. For example, children who are abused or neglected or whose parents demean them repeatedly may come to see themselves as useless and incompetent and to see the world as hopelessly painful. Children whose attempts at accomplishment consistently lead to failure (either actual failure or failure because they can never meet others' expectations) may develop a negative view of themselves and their abilities. After years of these experiences, these children's patterns of negative thinking can become so ingrained that they are practically unable to view themselves or any of their experiences in a positive way. The negative thinking of many depressed adolescents appears to be firmly established by seventh grade (Garber, Weiss, & Shanley, 1993).

Research has shown that depressed adolescents have more negative cognitions than do nondepressed adolescents and that their level of negative thinking is correlated with the severity of their symptoms (Garber, Weiss, & Shanley, 1993; Leitenberg, Yost, & Carroll-Wilson, 1986). Depressed children and adolescents rate their performance on tasks more negatively than the performance of their peers, even in situations in which objective measures of task performance show no differences (Kaslow, Brown, & Mee, 1994).

It should be noted, however, that negative cognitions in children and adolescents are correlated not only with depression but also with anxiety (e.g., Garber, Weiss, & Shanley, 1993). This suggests that negative cognitions put adolescents at risk for a variety of disorders, not only depression. In addition, not all depressed adolescents have negative thinking patterns. Asarnow and Bates (1988) found that only about half the depressed inpatient adolescents in their study had negative thinking patterns.

Learned Helplessness

Seligman's learned helplessness model states that the early experiences of some adolescents result in the belief that they have no control over the events in their lives (Abramson, Metalsky, & Alloy, 1989; Seligman, 1975). This leads to the development of an attributional style (a way of understanding the causes of positive and negative events) that places them at risk for depression. The attributional style commonly seen in depressed individuals is one in which negative events are attributed to internal, global, and stable factors (e.g., "My mother hits me because I am bad, I'm bad at everything, and this will never change"). Positive events are attributed to external, specific, and unstable factors (e.g., "My teacher likes me because she has to, but soon she will see how bad I am, and then she will stop liking me"). When presented with a stressful event, this attributional style results in adolescents feeling a sense of hopelessness about their ability to influence, solve, or cope with the stressful event. This hopelessness results in the emotional experience of depression.

In a meta-analysis of 28 studies of attributions and depression in children and adolescents, Gladstone and Kaslow (1995) found strong evidence of correlations between attributional styles and depression. Weiss, Simson, and Simson (1989) found that depression in children and adolescents is associated with "personal helplessness," or their own perceived incompetence, rather than with attributions of universal helplessness (the inability of people in general to control outcomes).

The Influences of Stress and Social Support

High levels of stress are associated with depressive symptoms in adolescents (McFarlane, Bellissimo, & Norman, 1995; Rubin et al., 1992). For example, the death of a parent, long-term separation from parents during childhood, and the loss of a sibling or friend to suicide have been associated with depression (Brent et al., 1993; Goodyer, 1995). In addition, children and adolescents living in situations in which they experience ongoing stress, such as in poverty, public housing, or dysfunctional families, show increased symptoms of depression (DuRant et al., 1995; Fergusson, Horwood, & Lynskey, 1995; Warner, Mufson, & Weissman, 1995). However, only about 50 percent of all depressed adolescents have experienced significant stressors (Goodyer, 1995), and other depressed adolescents do not report high levels of stress. Thus, as with the other factors we have examined, stress is associated with some, but not all, cases of adolescent depression.

The ways in which stress influences depression are not clear, although several possibilities exist. High levels of stress are associated with changes in brain functioning, and these changes can produce a depressed mood (Carlson, 1986). In addition, significant life events and high levels of ongoing stress may result in a cognitive or an attributional style that can lead to depression.

Social and emotional support from others has been associated with reduced risk for depression, although family and peer support appear to have different influences on adolescent depression. For example, high levels of family support are associated with lower risk for depression for tenth-graders, but support from peers does not appear to reduce risk for depression (McFarlane, Bellissimo, & Norman, 1995). Rubin et al. (1992) found that family support is associated with reduced risk for depression in females but not in males and that peer support is associated with reduced risk for depression in males but not in females.

Interpersonal Relationships

Early Relationships

Early relationships in a young child's life can set the stage for the development of depression in childhood or adolescence (Cicchetti & Toth, 1998). Infants raised in unstable environments express more negative emotions and have a more difficult time developing the ability to modulate their emotional arousal. The interactions between depressed mothers and their infants and toddlers are often awkward, leading to withdrawal by both the mother and the child, and infants of depressed mothers often evoke depressive responses when interacting with strangers (Field, 1992).

The attachment to a child's primary caregiver (attachment typically develops during the second half of the first year of life) can influence the child's ability to regulate emotions and behaviors and can influence the child's relationships with adults and peers during childhood, adolescence, and adulthood (Hazan & Zeifman, 1999). Children of depressed mothers are at higher risk for having an insecure attachment to their mothers, and insecurely attached children have more difficulties with peer relationships and are at more at risk for developing depression in adolescence than are securely attached children (Cicchetti & Toth, 1998).

Relationships in Adolescence

Coyne (1976) suggested that an important influence on the maintenance of depression is the social interactions of depressed people. A growing body of research shows that others do perceive and interact with depressed adolescents more negatively than with nondepressed adolescents. For example, two studies examined the developing relationships between depressed and nondepressed undergraduates and their roommates. Hokanson and colleagues (1989) reported that the depressed undergraduates in their study had fewer social contacts with their roommates than did the nondepressed undergraduates and that the contact they had was less pleasant. The roommates of the depressed undergraduates reported low levels of enjoyment and high levels of aggression/competition in their interactions. Siegel and Alloy (1990) analyzed interactions separately for male and female roommates and found that the depressed men, but not the depressed women, received lower approval ratings from their roommates. However, both the depressed men and depressed women felt that they were viewed negatively by their roommates.

Negative interpersonal interactions can influence depression in several ways. They can reinforce a depressed person's negative thoughts about herself and her ability to interact with others, and they can strengthen her sense of hopelessness about developing positive relationships in the future. Further, as adolescents move away from the social support of their families, a lack of peer support may reduce depressed adolescents' abilities to cope with the stressors they experience. This heightened stress and their inability to cope with it may increase their feelings of depression.

Multiple Pathways to Depression

Each explanation for the development and maintenance of depression in adolescents has research support. However, the research in support of each explanation also shows it is applicable to only some cases of adolescent depression. Thus, we are left with several useful explanations—each of which appears valuable for explaining depression in some adolescents but not in others.

It is likely that combinations of these explanations will more successfully account for depression in most cases. Even when one explanation seems to account primarily for depression in an adolescent, attention to the influences described by the other explanations is important if a full picture of the development and maintenance of depression is to emerge. For example, a stressful early history of abuse or neglect could lead to a young child's developing a cognitive style that promotes depression. The stress could also result in biological changes in her brain, resulting in a depressed mood. This biologically and cognitively based depression could negatively influence her interactions with others as an adolescent—resulting in withdrawal, reinforced depressive cognitions, and increased stress. As another example, an infant might inherit genes predisposing her to depression but might live in a stable, supportive family, experiencing only normal and transitory sadness. As she leaves for college, however, the stress of college life and the reduction of consistent family support may result in a more significant depressed mood, and her depressed mood may inhibit her ability to form supportive friendships, further increasing her sense of isolation and sadness.

DIFFERENCES IN THE PREVALENCE OF DEPRESSION BETWEEN FEMALES AND MALES

About equal numbers of boys and girls exhibit symptoms of depression or have depressive disorders. Beginning in early to middle adolescence, there is a fairly dramatic increase in depression in females and either a small increase or no increase in depression in males (Angold & Rutter, 1992; Petersen, Sarigiani, & Kennedy, 1991). This trend continues until, by adulthood, women are about twice as likely as men to have depressive disorders (e.g., Nolen-Hoeksema, 1987). Research over the past two decades has explored several reasons for this dramatic change in rates of depression among females and males as they go through adolescence.

Biological Changes at Puberty

Since the change in the prevalence of depression between males and females begins about the time as the biological changes of puberty, it is reasonable to hypothesize that these biological changes influence depression. However, research has found almost no support for this hypothesis. For example, Angold and Rutter (1992) reasoned that, if the hormonal changes associated with puberty influenced depression, one would find different levels of depression, at any given chronological age, among children and adolescents who had completed the biological changes of puberty, those who were in the midst of the changes, and those who had not yet begun the changes. However, they detected no such pattern. Several researchers have explored the influence of hormones on depression in adolescence and adulthood, reasoning that the relatively dramatic differences in types of hormones found in females and males beginning at puberty may influence depression. However, none of these studies have found consistent correlations between hormone levels and depressive symptoms (Brooks-Gunn & Warren, 1989; Nolen-Hoeksema & Girgus, 1994).

The Psychological Consequences of Maturing as a Female or a Male

Attention has also been focused on the psychological consequences of sexual maturation. The gender intensification hypothesis suggests that, as boys and girls mature, they take on increased stereotyped gender roles and that feminine roles are associated with increased risk for depression (Hill & Lynch, 1983). The research in this area is mixed, however. There is conflicting evidence about whether gender-stereotyped roles increase at puberty (Peterson, et al., 1991). In addition, it appears that higher levels of stereotyped feminine roles are not associated with increased depression in adolescents or adults (Petersen, Sarigiani, & Kennedy, 1991), although high levels of stereotyped male roles are associated with lower levels of depression (Stoppard & Paisley, 1987). Thus, stereotypical feminine characteristics do not seem to account for increases in depression among female adolescents.

The psychological consequences of physical changes during puberty have also been hypothesized to increase depression in females. Girls, particularly those who mature early, tend to view their physical changes more negatively than boys view their physical changes (Nolen-Hoeksema & Girgus, 1994). In addition, body dissatisfaction has a stronger association with depression in girls than in boys (Allgood-Merten, Lewinsohn, & Hops, 1990). Females who are dissatisfied with their bodies may engage in problematic eating, which can also influence levels of depression (see chapter 9, on eating disorders). Thus, the research suggests that physical changes are associated with body dissatisfaction in girls and that this type of dissatisfaction is particularly influential on feelings of depression in girls.

Different Pathways for Expressing Despair

A 20-year longitudinal study found that males and females express despair in different ways throughout much of their lives (Block, Gjerde, & Block, 1991). Males are more likely to express despair through externalizing, acting-out behaviors, and females are more likely to express their despair through internalizing behaviors, including depression. A mix of biological issues and cultural expectations probably influence these differences. Observations of sad males at age 18 showed that their interactions with others often involve patterns of antagonism and a lack of behavioral restraint. Sad females, however, do not appear hostile and withhold behaviors that are aversive to others (Gjerde & Block, 1996). Although this longitudinal study is the only one to look at these issues separately for males and females, it does raise the possibility that distressed females are more likely to be depressed, while distressed males are more likely to be aggressive and hostile.

Stress and Coping in Females and Males

As described earlier, stress has been linked to depression. Could the differences in depression in females and males be explained by differences in the levels or types of stressors they experience? Research on differences in the amount of stress experienced by female and male adolescents is inconclusive. Some studies have found somewhat higher stressors for females, but others have found no differences between males and females (Compass, 1987; Garrison et al., 1987; Rubin et al., 1992; Schraedley, Gotlib, & Hayward, 1999). However, some research has shown that similar levels of stress may result in a higher incidence of depression in females. For example, Schraedley, Gotlib, and Hayward (1999) found that female children and adolescents have higher levels of depressive symptoms than males when experiencing moderate to high levels of stress.

Some differences in the types of stress associated with depression have been found for males and females. Stress associated with sexuality, a depressed mother, and body dissatisfaction is associated with depression for females but not for males (Fergusson, Horwood, & Lynskey, 1995; Rubin et al., 1992). The stress of having a family member or friend commit suicide is associated with higher rates of depression for males but not for females (Rubin et al., 1992). This research suggests that females experience more depression because the types of stressors associated with depression that females experience are far more common than the types of stressors associated with depression in males.

Differences in the frequency with which multiple stressors occur simultaneously may also influence the differences in rates of depression between males and females. For example, pubertal changes occurring at the same time as school change into junior high is correlated with increased depression for both boys and girls (Petersen, Sarigiani, & Kennedy, 1991). However, these simultaneous changes are more likely to happen to girls, because of their earlier physical maturation. Thus, many more girls experience the simultaneous stressors of puberty and school change that are associated with increased depression.

Differences in the ways that females and males cope with stress may also influence their levels of depression. Females are more likely to deal with stressful events by ruminating about them and thinking negatively of themselves, while males are more likely to use distracting behaviors and turn against others (Cramer, 1979; Nolen-Hoeksema, 1987). People who engage in protracted rumination experience more severe depressive symptoms of longer duration (Lyubomirsky & Nolen-Hoeksema, 1993), suggesting that the response to depression that is more common among females may intensify and lengthen their depression.

A Summary of Differences between Rates of Depression in Females and Males

Hypotheses about differences between female and male depression that focus on biological changes or on gender-role behaviors have received little research support. Several lines of research suggest that important differences exist in the relationship between stress and depression in males and females. The types of stress associated with depression in females are more common than the types associated with depression in males, and females experience more depression than males at moderate and high levels of stress. In addition, females appear to react to stress in ways that increase depression, while males react in ways that are not associated with depression but may be associated with other problematic behaviors, such as aggression. At this time, it appears that gender differences in coping with and expressing stress may provide the best explanations for higher rates of depression in females.

INTERVENTIONS FOR DEPRESSION

Interventions commonly used with depressed adolescents are antidepressant medications, cognitive therapy, and social-skills training. Usually, interventions are combined in the development of a treatment strategy, which reflects the previously noted views that most adolescents' depressions are influenced by

HELPING

YOURSELF AND OTHERS

Responding to Depression in Yourself or Others

MDD and dysthymia are serious disorders that often require the intervention of a professional. Indications that you or another person should seek professional help include (but are not limited to)

- Feelings of sadness or lethargy that are so severe that a person feels unable to go to class or a job or to meet other important obligations
- Frequent sleep disturbance (inability to fall to sleep, middle of the night waking with an inability to return to sleep, early morning waking)
- Significant weight loss or a loss of interest in eating
- A loss of interest in activities that the person once found pleasurable or a general lack of interest in doing anything or going anywhere
- Suicidal thoughts or actions (see chapter 7, on suicide, for a fuller discussion)
- Hallucinations or delusions

Colleges and universities typically have counseling services, junior high and high schools typically have a school psychologist, and many communities have counseling centers. Arrangements need to be made for a depressed person to see a mental health professional (e.g., psychologist, psychiatrist, clinical social worker) in one of these settings. Often, however, the depressed person will not have the interest or energy to seek help. In addition, the negative thoughts of many depressed people result in their thinking that they will not get better and that no one will be able to help them.

If you are concerned about a depressed friend, encourage your friend to seek help. Acknowledge that she may feel that it is hopeless, but tell her that you know that it is not. Perhaps you could help make the call for an initial appointment and/or go with her to the first appointment to provide support (although you will not be able to go into the interview, you can provide support on the way to the therapist's office and while in the waiting room).

If you are depressed, realize that your negative thoughts are an impediment to your seeking help, and work to seek help despite them. Ask a friend or family member to encourage you to seek help and maybe go with you to your first appointment. Tell this friend or family member that you are concerned that you will back out of the appointment at the last minute and ask her to cajole you into going, even if you want to back out.

several issues. Antidepressant medications alone, for example, are unlikely to influence enduring negative patterns of thinking. Cognitive therapy may influence these thinking patterns, but an ongoing lack of social skills may continue to reinforce the accuracy of a depressed adolescent's negative self-evaluation. Only minimal research on the effectiveness of interventions with depressed adolescents has been completed (Geller et al., 1999; Lewinsohn & Clarke, 1999).

Several antidepressant medications are effective with depressed adults. Monoamine oxidase inhibitors (MAOIs) and tricyclic antidepressants have been used for several decades, and selective serotonin re-uptake inhibitors (SSRIs), such as Prozac, have become popular in the past decade or so. These medications alter the neurotransmission process in the brain, which often results in a marked decrease in depressed mood.

The few studies of the use of tricyclic antidepressants with children and adolescents, however, have shown that adolescents on medication recover at the same rate as those on placebo (Geller et al., 1999; Sommers-Flanagan, 1996).

HELPING
YOURSELF AND OTHERS

Reducing Feelings of Sadness and Anger

You can apply the principles of cognitive therapy to yourself when you are feeling sad and angry. Monitor your thinking during these times. You are likely to find that it is dominated by negative thoughts that have some of the qualities described in this chapter. Monitor the times when you begin thinking them. When they arise, or when you notice yourself ruminating about them, tell yourself to stop: "OK, here they are again; now just stop thinking these things." Force yourself to think about something else. It sounds impossible, but you can do it. As you try to think about other things, the negative thoughts will try to creep back into your mind. Maybe you will begin to say, "I'll never be able to stop thinking these things" (which is simply another negative thought). Block these thoughts as well. Make yourself start a task, make lists of things you need to do, or think about a pleasant event in the past or something that you are looking forward to.

Stopping your negative thoughts may sound too simple to accomplish anything. However, for almost everyone, a reduction in negative thinking will result in decreased feelings of sadness and anger. You may not even notice that the sadness and anger are decreasing—but suddenly you will notice that you just feel better (such as when you suddenly notice that your sore throat does not hurt anymore).

People tend to withdraw from others when they are sad or angry, and this often deepens their feelings. Remember this when you are feeling sad or angry. Make yourself go out with friends when they ask, even if your initial reaction is to stay home. Keep involved in school, religious, community, or social activities, even if you feel like dropping them. By forcing yourself to maintain positive contact with others, you may find that your sadness or anger begins to diminish.

The following are some hypothesized reasons for the lack of effectiveness of tricyclic antidepressant medications with adolescents: (a) the causes of depression in adolescents may be more varied than the causes in adults, with medications influencing only a few of these causes; (b) the greater variations in the speed with which children and adolescents metabolize antidepressant medications lead to difficulty in determining an effective dose for them; and (c) developmental differences in brain receptor functioning among children, adolescents, and adults may result in the medications having minimal influence on the biology of children and adolescents (Remschmidt & Schulz, 1995).

Emslie et al. (1997) did find that Prozac (an SSRI) is more effective than placebo in reducing depression in children and adolescents with MDD (56 percent on Prozac improved, while 33 percent on placebo improved). However, the percentage of children and adolescents responding to Prozac was not as high as the percentage of adults responding to Prozac.

Cognitive therapy has been shown to be effective in the treatment of depression in children and adolescents (Lewinsohn & Clarke, 1999). The main focus of cognitive therapy is on identifying and changing thoughts associated with depression (Karasu, 1990). The therapist acts as a "collaborative empiricist," helping the adolescent (a) identify patterns of negative thinking, and when they arise, (b) analyze these patterns to see if, given all the available evidence, they are accurate, and (c) change the patterns to more accurately reflect reality, if warranted (Beck et al., 1979). Overall, the focus is on ending inappropriate, reflexive, negative thoughts and replacing them with realistic, intentional thoughts. Particular attention is paid to

- Automatic thoughts: thoughts that reflexively emerge during a particular type of situation (e.g., "Everyone hates me" in response to any negative interactions with a peer)
- Selective attention: attending only to the negative aspects of a situation (e.g., focusing on the 2 people who did not vote for you while ignoring the 25 who did)
- Overgeneralization: using a single event to make sweeping conclusions (e.g., concluding that admission to medical school is impossible based on a poor grade on one exam)
- Personalization: feeling responsible for events over which one has little control (e.g., "Everyone will blame me because our class didn't win the award") (Kovacs & Beck, 1978)

Social-skills training can be an important part of therapy for depression (Stark, Rouse, & Kurowski, 1994). As previously described, depressed adolescents are often evaluated more negatively by peers during social interactions, which can lead to the adolescents' withdrawal or rejection and reinforcement of their negative view of themselves and world (Birmaher & Brent, 1998). In addition, chronically depressed adolescents may have been withdrawn from social interactions for so long that they have failed to develop the social skills necessary for successful interactions with others. In this mode of therapy, the therapist acts as teacher and coach. Through the adolescent's descriptions of her social interactions, potential problem areas are identified. The therapist suggests alternate behaviors and may engage in role plays to allow the adolescent to practice these behaviors. The therapist encourages the adolescent to use these new skills in social interactions outside therapy, and they are discussed in subsequent therapy sessions. Not only does this help increase the adolescent's positive social interactions, but it also increases the adolescent's sense of self-determination and demonstrates that her life can improve.

CHAPTER SUMMARY

Depression, as both depressive disorders and depressive symptoms, is common in adolescence. About half of all adolescents are likely to experience significant depressive symptoms at some point before adulthood. Female adolescents are more likely to experience depression than males, and older adolescents are more likely to be depressed than younger adolescents. Left untreated, depression is likely to recur periodically during adolescence and adulthood. Depression is associated with high levels of school drop out, substance abuse, conduct problems, and suicide.

Several explanations for the development, intensification, and maintenance of depressive symptoms have been proposed. These include genetic heritability, biologically based abnormalities in neurotransmitters or hormones, stress, patterns of cognitions, and interpersonal relationships. It is likely that several of these influences occur in each case of depression and that the ways in which they combine and their relative strength are different for each depressed adolescent.

Common interventions for adolescent depression include antidepressant medication, cognitive therapy, and social-skills training. The multiple influences on adolescent depression indicate that multiple interventions may be needed in most cases. These interventions may take several months, or maybe even years, to end a longstanding depressed mood. Given the alternative of recurring and possibly intensifying depression, these efforts are likely to be well worthwhile.

Revisiting Elise

Elise experienced stress as an overweight child who was often teased. She had few friends for support, and her parents appear to have offered only minimal support. Elise's mother's behavior as a child suggests that she may also have been somewhat depressed. If she was depressed, Elise's mother may have passed genetic predisposition for depression to Elise, or her parenting may have been affected by depression. This may have resulted in Elise's reacting to the teasing by withdrawing from her peers, rather than by angrily lashing out at them.

Elise's depressive symptoms were heightened in high school, as is true for many females. As many depressed adolescents do, Elise claimed to others that she was not depressed. Finally, Elise was referred for an assessment of her depression, which resulted in a program of psychotherapy and medication. Even as her depression lifted, however, Elise had to cope with her reputation as a depressed, withdrawn person, although she may be able to flourish in her new environment at college.

- What might have hindered Elise's teachers from recognizing her depression and prompted than to simply see her as a child who was not living up to her potential?
- What issues might have discouraged Elise from telling her parents, teachers, or peers that she was depressed?
- What experiences in college might help or hurt Elise's chance of forming a new life?

Part of a Conversation During Cognitive Therapy for Depression

THERAPIST: So, can you tell me about what happened the last time you were feeling depressed?

CLIENT: It was in math, yesterday. The teacher asked for the answer to a problem, and I thought I knew it. You've been telling me that I should speak up more in class, so I raised my hand and she called on me. I gave the right answer, but then she asked a second question that I got wrong. I was so embarrassed! I just sat there the rest of the class and got more and more depressed.

THERAPIST: I think it's great that you took the chance to answer the question. Tell me what you were thinking when you decided to raise your hand.

CLIENT: Well, I thought, "I think I know the answer, but sometimes I'm wrong even then. I hate it when I'm wrong—I feel so stupid. But, I'm supposed to talk more in class, so I'll give it a shot."

THERAPIST: And then what were your thoughts when you couldn't answer the second question?

CLIENT: I thought about how it was a mistake to even raise my hand—that I always look stupid when I talk in class—that I HATE IT when I'm wrong and everyone sees how stupid I am.

THERAPIST: And then what happened when you had those thoughts? [Here the therapist makes the connection among the client's thoughts, feelings, and behaviors.]

CLIENT: I told you, I got more and more depressed and didn't say anything the rest of the class.

THERAPIST: So let's look at your thoughts, as we've done in the past. Did you look stupid when you talked in class? I thought you said that you gave the correct answer.

CLIENT: I did, but it was the next question I got wrong.

THERAPIST: So, you thought you knew the answer, and you were right about that. So it seems to me that you aren't always wrong. When you think you know the answer, how often are you right?

CLIENT: I guess most of the time—but not always.

THERAPIST: Are the other people in your class always right when they give an answer?

CLIENT: No, other people are wrong sometimes too.

THERAPIST: Just as you are wrong sometimes. You said that everyone would know that you are stupid. How do you know that they think that? Did they laugh?

CLIENT: Well, no. They were all busy writing down the right answer.

Therapist: And when other people give a wrong answer sometimes, do you think that they are stupid?

CLIENT: No.

THERAPIST: So, it seems to me as if your thinking wasn't all that accurate. You automatically thought that you'd give the wrong answer, but you didn't. You based your evaluation of your performance only on the part of the answer that you got wrong, and you assumed that everyone thought that you're stupid, even though they gave no indication of this.

[The therapist and client then go on to identify what thoughts would have been more accurate, how the client engages in automatic thinking and overgeneralization, and how the client could stop this type of thinking and engage in more accurate thinking.]

CHAPTER 7

Suicide

Lee's family arrived the day before his college graduation. They were looking forward to celebrating his accomplishments, including his degree with distinction in electrical engineering. However, he was not in his apartment when they arrived, and he could not be found with any of his friends. The police were called, and a search for him began. There was fear that he might have been kidnapped. Two days after graduation, his body was found in a ravine, where he had apparently jumped from a bridge. His friends and family were overwhelmed with sadness and surprise. Interviews with his friends after his body was found showed that Lee had strong feelings of failure, despite his accomplishments. He worried that his family was displeased with him, even though he acknowledged that they never expressed disappointment. Although he was going to graduate fifth in his class, his failure to win one of the two undergraduate engineering awards made him feel that he had not lived up to his obligations to his family—a family that had sacrificed to send him to college. His friends consistently pointed out all of his accomplishments but felt that he focused only on what he perceived were his deficits. The night before Lee's parents arrived, he and his friends had had a party. He was quiet and withdrawn, which was not unusual. He left the party early, after going to each of his friends, shaking their hands, and congratulating them for all that they had accomplished in school and thanking them for being his friends. No one saw him alive again.

Adolescents who attempt suicide often feel that their lives are nothing but pain and that their futures will be nothing but the same. They often feel overwhelmed by problems, although others may see these problems as relatively unimportant. They can feel completely alone with their problems and their intense unhappiness, even when they have friends and a supportive family. They come to see suicide as a solution to what they believe is an unendurable life (Shneidman, 1991, 1993).

About 2,500 adolescents in the United States commit suicide each year, and suicide is the third leading cause of death for adolescents (behind accidents and homicides) (Holinger et al., 1994). Estimates of the percentage of adolescents who have thought about suicide in the past year range from 15 to 25 percent, and 6 to 13 percent of adolescents attempt suicide during their adolescence (Holinger et al., 1994). About 45 percent of adolescents know someone who has attempted suicide, and 15 percent know someone who has completed suicide (Gallup, 1991).

In this chapter we will explore adolescent suicide by examining who thinks seriously about suicide, who attempts suicide, and who succeeds at suicide. We will try to understand the events that can lead to suicidal behavior, and we will explore how this understanding can be used to prevent suicide and provide effective interventions to suicidal adolescents.

The Plan: Following the pattern of most chapters, this chapter starts by defining several terms related to suicide—suicidal ideation, suicide attempt, suicide gesture, and completed suicide. The incidence of suicide and how current incidence rates compare with rates over the past few decades are then presented. In the main part of the chapter, we will explore the development of suicidal thoughts and behaviors. We will do this in four steps. Most researchers believe that serious thoughts about suicide can begin when an adolescent is under high stress, so the types of stressors associated with thoughts about suicide will be explored first. Next, we will explore some of the issues that can pull an adolescent toward suicide and death. We will then examine the ways in which suicidal adolescents' thoughts, feelings, and behaviors are changed by this pull, as well as how these changes increase the pull toward death. Finally, we will explore the issues that push some suicidal adolescents to the point at which they make a suicide attempt. In the final part of the chapter, we will apply our knowledge about the development of suicide to consider effective interventions to prevent suicide attempts and to help those who have attempted suicide.

DEFINITIONS OF SUICIDAL THOUGHTS AND BEHAVIORS

Suicidal Ideation

Suicidal ideation refers to serious thoughts about suicide (Lewinsohn, Rohde, & Seeley, 1996). The fleeting thoughts that many adolescents have about suicide are generally not considered suicidal ideation. Some adolescents who experience suicidal ideation attempt suicide; most decide not to make any attempt at all.

Suicide Attempt

A suicide attempt is a purposeful act that a person believes can or will result in his death but that does not cause death (Lewinsohn, Rohde, & Seeley,

1996). Life-threatening behavior that is accidental or simply ill-chosen is not considered a suicide attempt. For example, an adolescent who ingests so much alcohol during a party that he almost dies is not considered to have attempted suicide.

Determining whether an adolescent has attempted suicide can be difficult when his intent is unclear. For example, consider a case in which a very intoxicated adolescent is found asleep in his car, in the garage, with the motor running. Is he attempting suicide or did he simply pass out after getting the car into the garage and closing the garage door? It is possible to simply ask the adolescent if he intended to kill himself, but he might lie and deny a suicide attempt because of shame or fear of hospitalization.

Some clinicians and researchers have divided suicide acts into two categories: suicide gestures and suicide attempts. A suicide gesture is an act that could be lethal but is less likely to be lethal because it has a low likelihood of producing death or because there is a good likelihood that the person will be discovered and that others will take steps to save the person's life (Garrison et al., 1991). For example, consider an adolescent who fights with his parents; tells them, "You'll be sorry that you ever made me do this"; and then storms into his bathroom and takes a handful of aspirin. This could be considered a suicide gesture because of the relative uncertainty that the aspirin tablets will kill him, because of the possibility that his parents will investigate and take him to the hospital, or both. Suicide attempts are seen as events in which there is a high likelihood of death because the act is highly lethal and because there is only a small likelihood that the person will be discovered and saved.

Distinguishing between suicide gestures and suicide attempts may identify suicidal adolescents whose risk of death is higher than others. The distinction between a suicide gesture and a suicide attempt is often vague, however, and many suicidal acts could be classified as a gesture by some people but an attempt by others. In addition, both suicide gestures and suicide attempts can be lethal, and many adolescents die after making what would be classified as a suicide gesture. As a result, some would argue that making the distinction between gestures and attempts is not useful.

Completed Suicide

Completed suicides are those that result in death. In some cases, it is clear that an adolescent's death is a suicide. However, determining that a death is suicide can be difficult in other cases—even more so than after a suicide attempt because the adolescent cannot be asked about the act. For example, it may be unclear if an adolescent who is killed after driving into a highway overpass at high speed was intending to kill himself. A suicide note can resolve questions about an adolescent's death in some cases, but only a minority of adolescents who kill themselves leave a suicide note (Leenaars & Lester, 1995).

THE PREVALENCE AND INCIDENCE OF SUICIDE

Obtaining an accurate estimate of the number of adolescents who think about, attempt, or complete suicide is difficult (Holinger et al., 1994). Because suicide is often stigmatized, some adolescents may be reluctant to admit to thinking seriously about suicide or suicide attempts. Coroners and others who must determine the cause of an adolescent's death may avoid labeling it as a suicide for many reasons: insurance companies may deal with a suicide differently than an accidental death, some religions may not allow religious funerals or burials for those who commit suicide, and families may have to cope with much greater anguish if their child is determined to have committed suicide (Holinger et al., 1994). Thus, reported rates of suicide for adolescents probably underrepresent the actual number of suicides (Madge & Harvey, 1999). Overall, the data on suicidal behavior show that many adolescents think seriously about suicide at some time in their adolescence, that a small percentage of these adolescents attempt suicide, and that a minority of attempts result in completed suicide (Fergusson & Lynskey, 1995; Vannatta, 1996).

Completed Suicide

Contrary to popular belief, adolescents are not at a higher risk for completed suicide than adults. Adults are at higher risk for suicide than adolescents, and older adults are at the highest risk (Holinger et al., 1994). For example, in 1995 the rate of suicide per 100,000 population for 5- to 14-year-olds was 0.9; for 15- to 24-year-olds, 13.3; and for 25- to 44-year-olds, 15.3 (Anderson, Kochanek, & Murphy, 1997).

Adolescents are at much higher risk for suicide than are children, and the risk increases with age during adolescence (see table 7.1). Several reasons have been suggested for increased suicide risk in older adolescents: they may experience greater stress than younger adolescents, they may have moved further from the support of their families and may not have found similar levels of

TABLE 7.1. Rate of Suicide per 100,000 in 1992

	Males	Females
White		
10–14 years	2.6	1.1
15–19 years	18.4	3.7
Black		
10–14 years	2.0	0.4
15–19 years	14.8	1.9
Other		
10–14 years	1.1	0.2
15–19 years	17.5	5.0

Reprinted and adapted with permission. American School Health Association, Kent, Ohio. From "Suicide Among Children, Adolescents, and Young Adults—United States, 1980–1992." *Journal of School Health*. Vol. 65, No. 7, pp. 272–273, September 1995.

support in their peer network, they are under the direct supervision of adults less frequently, and they may have easier access to lethal weapons or other means for causing death (Holinger et al., 1994).

Male adolescents have higher rates of completed suicides than females. Native American adolescents have the highest rate of suicide (Berlin, 1987), and white adolescents have higher rates than African American adolescents or adolescents of most other racial or ethnic groups. The higher rate of completed suicides in males is probably due to their frequent use of more immediately lethal means, such as guns (Jurich & Collins, 1996). Few explanations for higher suicide rates among white adolescents have been suggested. This pattern is particularly puzzling, since poverty and lack of opportunity, characteristics that are more common in minority communities, are associated with increased risk for suicide (Fergusson & Lynskey, 1995).

The rate of completed adolescent suicides has risen over the past 40 years. The rate of suicide for 15- to 19-year-old females rose slightly but steadily from 1960 (when it was about 2 per 100,000) until the end of the 1980s, when it leveled off (compare to the more recent rates described in table 7.1). The rate for males has increased steadily and dramatically from 1960 (when it was about 5 per 100,000). The rate for white males leveled off in the late 1980s; however, the rate for nonwhite males had one of its more dramatic increases between 1985 and 1992 (Holinger et al., 1994).

Suicide Attempts

The incidence of suicide attempts is usually estimated from surveys of high school students or undergraduates. Many adolescents report that they have attempted suicide at some point in their lives, and two to three times as many females report attempts as males. What is generally unknown, however, is how potentially lethal these attempts are, since most researchers leave it to the adolescent who is responding to a survey to define an attempt. When studies rate the lethality of suicide attempts, they generally show that about 10 percent of attempts are highly likely to result in death, about one-third of attempts have a moderate chance of resulting in death, and about half of the attempts have a low chance of resulting in death (although even attempts with a low chance of death occasionally do result in death) (Centers for Disease Control and Prevention, 1999; Dubow et al., 1989; Lewinsohn, Rohde, & Seeley, 1996).

Suicide attempts at some point in their lives have been reported by 16 percent of the female and 8 percent of the male high school seniors in Minnesota (MDE, 1989); 15 percent of the females and 9 percent of the males in a large sample of junior and senior high school students (Dubow et al., 1989); 10 percent of the females and 4 percent of the males in a sample of 14- to 18-year-olds (Lewinsohn, Rohde, & Seeley, 1996); and 6 percent of the females and 3 percent of the males in a study of 18-year-olds in the United States (Reinherz et al., 1995). The reasons for the differences in the findings are unclear and may relate to the researchers' instructions about how to classify a suicide attempt.

A study of 16,000 high school students in the United States reported that 12 percent of the females and 5 percent of the males had attempted suicide in the past year (Centers for Disease Control and Prevention, 1999). Three percent of the adolescents had made an attempt that required medical attention. Contrary to most of the research on age and completed suicide, this study showed that more ninth-graders than twelfth-graders had made attempts (10 percent and 5 percent, respectively) and attempts that required medical attention (4 percent and 1 percent, respectively).

A few studies have reported on the method of suicide attempts (Fergusson & Lynskey, 1995; Lewinsohn, Rohde, & Seeley, 1996). The most common methods are intentional drug overdoses and wrist cutting. About 25 percent of males hang or shoot themselves, but these methods are less common among females.

Suicidal Ideation

Suicidal ideation is common among adolescents. Surveys of high school students have reported rates of serious suicide ideation during the past year of 25 percent (MDE, 1989) and 21 percent (Centers for Disease Control and Prevention, 1999). Thirty-six percent of a large sample of junior and senior high school students reported ideation in the past year, and 7 percent of the students reported "extremely troubling" ideation (Dubow et al., 1989). About twice as many females as males experience suicidal ideation (Centers for Disease Control and Prevention, 1999; Reinherz et al., 1995).

Reinherz et al. (1995) reported that 23 percent of a community sample of 15-year-olds reported current suicidal ideation. However, Lewinsohn, Rohde, and Seeley (1996) reported a much lower, 3 percent rate of current suicidal ideation. Differences in the measurement of suicidal ideation probably caused the discrepancy in these estimations (Reinherz et al. asked about ideation; Lewinsohn, Rohde, and Seeley relied on results from a structured interview).

THE DEVELOPMENT OF SUICIDAL
THINKING AND BEHAVIOR

For most of our lives, most of us feel a strong desire to live. As just described, however, many people feel ambivalent about life (Shneidman, 1991). Their desire to live is accompanied by a desire to die. This desire to die is only slight in

Death - - - - - - - - - - - - +- Life
                 Suicide attempt

most people who feel it; however, it can be quite strong in others, and irresistible in a few.

One way to think about the desire to live, or to die, is to consider a continuum with life on one side and death on the other. Imagine two forces being exerted on a person—a pull toward life and a pull toward death—with the person's tendency toward suicide being determined by the relative strength of these two forces. Most of us consistently feel pulled toward life, and we would be placed at the "life" end of the continuum. Many people experience an occasional pull toward death, and they can be imagined to move along the continuum toward the "death" side—with the distance that they move reflecting the strength of the pull they experience. Most of these people continue to experience a stronger pull toward life than toward death; although they may consider suicide, they do not attempt it. Some people, however, experience a pull toward death that is about as strong as their pull toward life. This can cause them to be very ambivalent about living. They struggle with the question of whether to live or take their lives, and they can struggle with this decision for years. For most of these people, the strength of the pull toward death diminishes over time, and their likelihood of suicide is reduced or eliminated. However, the pull toward death becomes strong enough for some people (or, alternately, their pull toward life becomes weak enough) that they decide to attempt suicide. This would be reflected on the continuum by the person's passing a point at which the pull toward death overcomes the pull toward life.

In the next sections, we will explore the development of this pull toward death. We will start by exploring the range and variety of stressors that may begin the process of adolescents' thinking seriously about suicide. Next, we will explore the influences on a steadily increasing pull toward death that some adolescents experience. We will then explore the emotions, cognitions, and behaviors of those who are thinking about suicide and the ways in which their decisions about whether to attempt suicide are influenced by their emotions, cognitions, and behaviors. Finally, we will discuss what it is that pushes some adolescents "over the edge" to making a suicide attempt.

Stressors and Resources

Most scholars in the area of suicide suggest that the first step toward understanding the development of suicidal ideation is to consider the stressors on a person and the resources that the person has to deal with these stressors (e.g., Henry et al., 1994; Jurich & Collins, 1996). As stressors outweigh an adolescent's resources to deal with them, he can begin to feel overwhelmed, and some of these overwhelmed adolescents may begin to think about suicide as a solution to the stress they are under. No specific stressors have consistently been associated with suicide, and it is the accumulation of stressors and the lack of resources to deal with them that are associated with the development of suicidal ideation (Huff, 1999; Lewinsohn, Rohde, & Seeley, 1993).

Individual Stressors

Experiencing depression or anxiety can stress adolescents, and the link between depression or anxiety and suicide is especially strong if depression or anxiety develops in childhood or early adolescence (Reinherz et al., 1995). Experiencing physical diseases, such as epilepsy or AIDS, or being the victim of traumatic experiences, such as physical or sexual assault, are also stressful and are associated with increased risk for suicide (Anderson, 1981; Brent, 1987; Laederach et al., 1999; Vannatta, 1996). Some suicidal adolescents show a history of early childhood behavior problems, which may have caused them stress throughout childhood. Childhood aggression and attention problems have been linked to suicide for females, and overdependency has been linked to suicide for males (Reinherz et al., 1995). Besides the stress of these circumstances, all of them may cause a child or an adolescent to withdraw from family and friends, thereby reducing the ability of the adolescent's family and friends to provide support and other resources.

Family Stressors

Many suicidal adolescents come from families that are chaotic, unsupportive, or overly intrusive (Jurich & Collins, 1996). Some suicidal adolescents report parental expectations that are more than they feel they can achieve, even when they are achieving at high levels (Dukes & Lorch, 1989). Problematic relationships within the family, particularly with the mother, have been associated with suicide. For example, risk for suicide is associated with insecure attachments to mothers (de Jong, 1992), mothers described as emotionally unresponsive (Fergusson & Lynskey, 1995), and lower levels of affection between mothers and adolescents (King et al., 1990).

Pulls Toward Life and Death

A clear illustration of the simultaneous pulls toward life and death felt by suicidal adolescents came from a 15-year-old whom I was treating in a psychiatric hospital. One day she asked urgently to see me and said that she was worried she would be overwhelmed by her strong suicidal urges and that she would kill herself. She asked that the hospital staff monitor her closely, so that she would not have the opportunity to kill herself. She clearly had a strong pull toward life, or she would not have asked for the assistance of the hospital staff, but she was also experiencing a strong pull toward death, which she was afraid would overwhelm her. She was placed on a one-to-one suicide watch, in which an additional staff person was brought in to keep her constantly in sight 24 hours a day. After two days, she reported that her suicidal urges had diminished, and the one-to-one watch was replaced by a visual check on her every 15 minutes for two additional days. She reported that her suicide ideation had ended during this time, and she never made a suicide attempt.

Higher incidences of parental criminality, substance abuse, and attempted and completed suicide have been found in the families of suicidal adolescents (Fergusson & Lynskey, 1995; Pfeffer, Normandin, & Kakuma, 1994). All these conditions may reflect ongoing family dysfunction, which can increase the stress on an adolescent and reduce his opportunity to receive support from his family. Living in a low-income family also has been associated with increased risk for suicide (Henry et al., 1994; Jurich & Collins, 1996). This may reflect the increased family stress that can be caused by few economic resources, or it may reflect a variety of parental problems that can both reduce family income and cause turmoil in the life of an adolescent.

Peer Stressors

Adolescents who receive little support from their families may come to depend even more on peers for support (Jurich & Collins, 1996). However, suicidal adolescents often report feeling isolated from and rejected by their peers (Garland & Zigler, 1993). Characteristics associated with alienation from peers and suicidal tendencies have included sexual identity problems, poor social skills, and academic giftedness (Delise, 1986; Garland & Zigler, 1993). Adolescents who have recently ended a serious romantic relationship or who are having ongoing problems with a boyfriend or girlfriend also are at greater risk for suicide (Allen, 1987).

Community Stressors

Research focused on the influence of community stressors on adolescent suicide has not been done; however, several authors have commented on the potential for community stressors to influence suicide. For example, living in a violent community may increase depression or anger because of being the victim of aggression or because of losing a friend or family member to community violence; living in a community where few social or economic opportunities exist can result in increased hopelessness; and living in a highly transient community can reduce the chance of an adolescent developing a support network of peers or adults (Jurich & Collins, 1996).

A Summary of Stressors

All adolescents experience stress, and most experience high levels of stress periodically. The types of stress that seem more common in adolescents who are suicidal appear to be chronic, such as ongoing psychopathology or physical disease, family dysfunction, isolation from peers, and day-to-day life in a dangerous community. Thus, these adolescents have little relief from their stress and are unlikely to believe that they will get relief in the future. This constant stress can result in feelings of depression or hopelessness and can sap an adolescent's energy. Some of these chronically stressed adolescents may begin to see suicide as the only way to escape their highly stressful lives.

The Pull Toward Death

An imbalance of stressors and resources is not sufficient for the development of suicidal ideation, since many stressed adolescents do not become suicidal. All adolescents know about suicide, and most have fleeting or mildly serious thoughts about it. Why are suicidal thoughts dismissed by most stressed adolescents but grow dramatically in others? There is little research directly related to this, but there is some information and theory that suggest that a growing intensity of personal pain and isolation, as well as a growing sense of hopelessness, can strengthen the pull toward death in overstressed adolescents.

The severity and constancy of the pain from the stressors in their lives can be an important force pulling adolescents toward death. The severity of the pain felt from stressors can depend on their number or on the importance that an adolescent attaches to them (Jurich & Collins, 1996). For example, breaking up with a girlfriend could be moderately upsetting to one adolescent yet devastating to another, either because the relationship was of central importance to the adolescent's life or because the breakup was another in a long string of painful stressors.

Adolescents who have experienced stress for most of their lives may easily develop the hopeless view that, since nothing has changed so far in their lives, there is little hope for the future. This sense of hopelessness may pull adolescents further toward death, because they can see no other way of ending the unendurable pain that they are experiencing.

Isolation from family and peers can strengthen the pull toward death in several ways (Gould et al., 1996). Isolation is painful to many adolescents and, thus, can increase their overall feeling of pain. As the adolescent comes to believe that others do not value him and his life, he may see little reason to continue living. Isolation also can eliminate people from the adolescent's life who could challenge the adolescent's growing belief that suicide is a reasonable solution to his pain and who could give an adolescent more time to focus on himself and on the problems that he is facing.

BROADENING Perspectives

Sink or Swim?

Consider this: you are on a cruise ship and suddenly fall overboard. You watch the ship sail away and are left alone in the middle of the ocean with little chance of being rescued. Would you struggle and struggle and struggle and struggle to stay alive, until you were physically incapable of continuing your struggle? Or would you decide to avoid what is likely to be a fruitless struggle and go underwater, expel the air from your lungs, and sink to your death? In some ways, this is the type of choice that many suicidal adolescents feel that they are faced with.

The Experience of Suicide

Many adolescents who feel a strong pull toward death have particular patterns of thinking, feeling, and behaving. Not all suicidal adolescents follow these patterns, but many do. Some of these patterns reflect the turmoil that suicidal adolescents feel. More important, many of them help maintain or deepen suicidal ideation and may drive an adolescent to making a suicide attempt.

There appear to be two types of experiences for suicidal adolescents. The first is characterized by depression, self-blame, withdrawal, and concern about being liked and accepted by others. The second is characterized by anger, aggression against people and property, and the blaming of others (Borst, Noam, & Bartok, 1991). Although these styles of behaving may seem like opposites, both can have profound pain and hopelessness at their foundation. For reasons that are not clearly understood, some adolescents respond to this pain and hopelessness by withdrawing from the world, others respond by lashing out at the world, and others alternate between both styles.

Emotions and Suicide

The common emotional experience of suicidal adolescents is psychological pain (Shneidman, 1991). The pain can come from many sources, including a fundamental sense of being a failure, ongoing sexual or physical assault, shame and guilt over acts or thoughts, and changes in lifestyle due to illness or disability. The pain often feels intolerable and is so strong and dominant for some adolescents that it seems to define their emotional experience.

Most, but not all, suicidal adolescents are depressed. For example, Fergusson and Lynskey (1995) found that 69 percent of adolescents who attempt suicide and 33 percent of those with suicidal ideation have depression or another mood disorder. Intense, ongoing anger is also found in some suicidal adolescents (Borst & Noam, 1993; Brown et al., 1991), and suicidal adolescents have scored higher on scales of anger than nonsuicidal adolescents (Lehnert, Overholser, & Spirito, 1994).

The relationship between suicide and depression can be complex. In some cases, the causes of the suicidal tendencies and the depression can be the same, with no direct link between them. For example, an adolescent recently diagnosed with AIDS might be very depressed and very suicidal, with the suicidal and depressed feelings being independent from each other and both caused by learning about the diagnosis. In other situations, strong feelings of depression can be so painful that they cause an adolescent to be suicidal. An adolescent with chronic and severe depression, for instance, may come to believe that suicide is the only way to escape his painful life. Alternately, being suicidal may increase depression. For example, the shame about considering suicide may increase an adolescent's feelings of depression.

The relationship between anger and suicide is also complex. It seems unlikely that high levels of anger would push a person to suicide. However, high levels of anger may be present and directed at events or people that have increased the adolescent's suicidal feelings. For example, an adolescent considering suicide because of school failure, the breakup of a relationship, or sexual abuse may feel high levels of anger toward a teacher, an ex-girlfriend, or an abusing parent. In addition, higher levels of aggression are associated with suicide in some adolescents (Brent et al., 1996), possibly reflecting their style of dealing with problems in an aggressive and angry way, even if the aggression and anger are aimed at themselves.

Cognitions and Suicide

The thoughts of many suicidal adolescents are characterized by "constriction" (Shneidman, 1991), a narrowing of a person's view of the world. One way that cognitions can be constricted is through biased perception. As discussed in chapter 6, depressed adolescents perceive their world in a biased way: they readily notice and remember negative events, classify many neutral events as negative, and fail to notice or remember most positive events. Angry/aggressive adolescents also have a biased perception, in that they see more aggression aimed at them than actually occurs, and they are likely to disregard the supportive nature of some events and relationships. As they perceive their world more negatively, these adolescents' depression or anger/aggression may grow. This can bias their perceptions further, which in turn can increase their depression or anger/aggression.

Cognitions can also be constricted through "tunneling," which occurs when a person's attention gradually becomes focused on one or two issues. Many suicidal adolescents' thinking becomes focused on their stressors and on the problems that are causing them pain, and they are unlikely to notice or think about other events or relationships (Leenaars & Lester, 1995). In addition, once an adolescent begins to consider suicide seriously, much of his attention may be focused on suicide. Consequently, thoughts of suicide and stress may begin to gradually dominate his attention and may eventually become the only important issue in his life.

The cognitions of a suicidal adolescent are also characterized by hopelessness (Kashani, Dandoy, & Reid, 1992). It is not clear whether suicidal adolescents have higher levels of hopelessness than adolescents with other psychiatric problems, although some studies show that they do (e.g., Kashden et al., 1993) and some show that they do not (e.g., Spirito, Overholser, & Hart, 1991). It is clear, however, that many suicidal adolescents do feel a strong sense of hopelessness, which is often associated with depression, and Beck's (1976) cognitive theory describes how this can occur. Beck describes a depressed person as someone who believes that he is inadequate—a "born loser." The depressed person sees negative events as resulting from enduring personal defects but sees positive events, when he notices them at all, as occurring because of temporary luck. This pessimistic style of thinking results in a pattern of behaviors, such as lack of effort on tasks, that make failure inevitable and thereby reinforces his pessimism. A person with this view sees no reason for the future to be an improvement over the dismal present, and the result is a sense of enduring hopelessness.

Hopelessness and constriction can reinforce each other. As a suicidal adolescent's thinking becomes more constricted and negative, his hopelessness may increase. After all, he sees no positive aspects of his life and, so, has little hope that his life will improve. Similarly, expectations of a bleak future can constrict the way that an adolescent views his current life by increasing his attention on his current and future unhappiness. Both hopelessness and constriction seem to work together to pull an adolescent toward suicide: they encourage a negative view of his current life—a life dominated by the issue of suicide—and provide little sense that his future will be any different.

Behaviors and Suicide

Two clusters of behaviors are associated with adolescent suicide, and they are related to the emotions of depression and anger. The first cluster is a set of withdrawn and passive behaviors common to depression (Rickgarn, 1994). Suicidal adolescents may withdraw from activities they once enjoyed, as well as from friends and family. They may be physically absent from school and other activities or psychologically absent if physically present. Their hopelessness results in few attempts to take initiatives, even in situations in which initiative is needed to defend themselves. Thus, suicidal adolescents are at greater risk for negative experiences, such as unwanted physical or sexual aggression.

The second cluster of behaviors consists of aggressive behaviors often associated with anger. Studies of community samples of adolescents and adolescents in a psychiatric hospital found significant correlations between violent behavior and suicidal ideation and attempts (Apter et al., 1995; Borst & Noam, 1993; Vannatta, 1996). Suicidal adolescents also have more contact with legal authorities than nonsuicidal adolescents and some engage in property damage and vandalism (Fergusson & Lynskey, 1995).

Heavy alcohol and other drug use is more frequent among suicidal adolescents than nonsuicidal adolescents (Levy & Deykin, 1989; Windle, Miller-Tutzauer, & Domenico, 1992). Drug use may be an attempt to blunt the adolescent's pain or to relieve his anguish as he struggles with the issue of whether to commit suicide.

Suicide Attempts

Many adolescents have little control over the stressors they face or the emotions that these stressors evoke. Consequently, they often have little control over the events and feelings that can lead to suicidal thoughts and urges. However, suicidal adolescents make decisions about whether or not to make a suicide attempt. These decisions are often influenced to a great degree by severe feelings of depression, anger, and hopelessness, but they are decisions nonetheless.

Adolescents who feel a strong pull toward death must wrestle with the decision about whether to attempt suicide. When the pull toward death is particularly strong, adolescents often must wrestle with this decision on a daily, or even hourly, basis. Most suicidal adolescents repeatedly decide not to attempt suicide. However, some decide, at some point, to make a suicide attempt. Two explanations have been suggested for understanding these decisions (Brown et al., 1991). One is that the slow build-up of stressors finally becomes too much for an adolescent to handle, and he decides to attempt suicide. The second involves a more impulsive decision by an adolescent who has just experienced a significant stressor. Some authors have suggested that these are competing explanations (e.g., Fergusson & Lynskey, 1995), but each has empirical support and provides useful information.

Those who are not impulsive in their decision to attempt suicide describe considerable thought about an attempt before it is made. Often, they have struggled with the decision about suicide for many months or years. Some adolescents attempt suicide soon after an event that is stressful but does not seem to be stressful enough to encourage an attempt by itself, such as the breakup of a romantic relationship or a poor test grade at school (Beautrais, Joyce, & Mulder, 1997; Fergusson & Lynskey, 1995b; Henry et al., 1994). These stressors may be the "straw that breaks the camel's back" for those who have been seriously contemplating suicide.

Those who make an apparently impulsive suicide attempt often describe little planning or thought about suicide (Brown et al., 1991), although these adolescents typically experience high levels of stress right before their attempt. Several findings may help explain impulsive attempts. Some adolescents who have completed suicide had unusually low levels of the neurotransmitter serotonin in their brains and blood; lower levels of serotonin have been associated with increased impulsivity in a variety of contexts (Horesh et al., 1999). Thus, a genetic or another influence that results in lower levels of serotonin may increase some adolescents' risk for an impulsive suicide attempt (Brent et al., 1996). Borderline personality disorder, that has as a symptom impulsivity in many contexts, is more common among those who attempt suicide than in the general population (Brent et al., 1993), again suggesting a role for impulsivity in some suicides. The disinhibiting effects of alcohol and other drugs can also encourage impulsive suicide attempts (Levy & Deykin, 1989; Windle, Miller-Tutzauer, & Domenico, 1992). For example, a suicidal adolescent who gets drunk after breaking off a relationship may be at an increased risk for making an impulsive suicide attempt while drunk. In addition, the easy availability of the means for a very quick and apparently painless death, such as firearms, may also facilitate impulsive suicides (GAP, 1996).

Whether awareness of a recently committed suicide encourages suicide attempts (known as suicide contagion) continues to be debated. Some case studies suggest that suicide contagion does occur. For example, increased rates of adolescent suicide attempts and completed suicides have been noted in areas where there is extensive media coverage of a suicide (Phillips & Carstensen, 1986). However, not enough empirical evidence exists to clearly support the existence of suicide contagion among adolescents. Brent et al. (1989) reported on 2 completed suicides, 7 suicide attempts, and 23 cases of strong suicidal ideation in a single high school, all of which occurred within 18 days of two earlier suicides at that school. Most of those who became suicidal after the earlier suicides had clear evidence of a psychiatric disorder before the earlier suicides. These findings suggest that awareness of a suicide may push disturbed adolescents toward an impulsive suicide attempt but that awareness of a suicide may not influence other adolescents.

Summary and Conclusions

Suicidal behavior appears to begin as an adolescent who is under stress starts to think about suicide as a solution to the problems he faces. As the stress and the number of problems increase to the point at which he feels overwhelmed, the pull toward death and away from life may increase. His attention may become focused on these problems until he can see little in his life except them, resulting in feelings of hopelessness. As his view of his life becomes more hopeless, he may struggle more and more with the decision about whether to commit suicide, further constricting his thinking and his view of the world. Suicide can become the primary issue in his life, as he struggles with a stronger and stronger pull toward death. Some adolescents in this situation appear to slip over the edge of suicide and decide to attempt suicide in the face of one additional stressor, problem, or disappointment. Other adolescents appear to make an impulsive suicide attempt—possibly without experiencing the high levels of stress, depression, or hopelessness that other suicidal adolescents come to feel.

SUICIDE PREVENTION

Strategies for reducing adolescent suicide come in many forms. Some are aimed at all adolescents, and others focus on adolescents with serious suicidal ideation. Knowledge about how suicide develops and who is at risk for becoming suicidal is used to guide both types of prevention efforts.

Prevention Aimed at All Adolescents

Education is a critical element of suicide prevention (GAP, 1996; Rickgarn, 1994). Some educational efforts aimed at all adolescents can be found in public service television or radio ads, in special presentations in school or the community, or in part of a school's curriculum. Some of these efforts are designed to help adolescents identify their own suicidal feelings, to inform them that these feelings are not uncommon but are potentially dangerous, to encourage them to seek help, and to inform them of the variety of places where they can receive help. Other efforts focus on helping adolescents notice behaviors associated with suicide in their friends and then react in a helpful way. The effectiveness of these programs for changing adolescents' attitudes about suicide and reducing suicide rates has not been well tested, however (Garland & Zigler, 1993). In one study of three school-based programs, although the adolescents reported that they found the programs informative, there was no change in the students' attitudes toward suicide or in their willingness to seek help when feeling suicidal (Vieland et al., 1991).

The education of adults who are in frequent contact with adolescents is an important prevention strategy (Spirito & Overholser, 1993). Teachers, physicians, ministers, juvenile detention facility staff members, coaches, and others need to learn to notice the indications that an adolescent might be suicidal, to ask the adolescent about suicide in an effective and supportive way, and to refer suicidal adolescents to appropriate services. Educating parents about suicide can give them the skills to intervene with their own children or the children of friends and neighbors (GAP, 1996; Rickgarn, 1994).

Communities can support a variety of services for suicidal adolescents (GAP, 1996; Spirito & Overholser, 1993). Some suicidal adolescents may want to talk with a school counselor or psychologist, others may prefer to talk with a therapist or minister, and still others may be willing to discuss their suicidal feelings only with an anonymous person on a suicide prevention hot line. Besides providing these resources, it is important for communities to make their existence known and to make them easily accessible to all adolescents (Shaffer et al., 1988).

HELPING
YOURSELF AND OTHERS

Signs of Possible Suicidal Intent

There are several indications that an adolescent may be suicidal (Leenaars & Lester, 1995). Their presence should raise significant concerns about suicide and should prompt a referral to a mental health professional or a physician for an assessment of whether the adolescent is suicidal. It is critical to note, however, that the absence of the following indications cannot be taken to mean that an adolescent is not suicidal:

- Talking of suicide. Even casual comments about suicide or death must be taken seriously.
- Indications of hopelessness, including doubt about having a future or about resolving current problems.
- Having a sudden sense of peacefulness and contentedness after a period of anxiety and confusion. The peacefulness may be the result of an end to the struggle about whether to commit suicide and a decision to do so.
- Giving away prized possessions
- Visiting favorite places or people one more time
- Having a sudden interest in death—visiting cemeteries, writing a will, or discussing the afterlife
- Buying or borrowing a gun; saving large quantities of medication

Prevention Aimed at Adolescents at Higher Risk for Suicide

Some prevention efforts are aimed primarily at adolescents experiencing circumstances that research has shown are associated with increased suicide risk. These interventions often involve individual discussions with adolescents in an attempt to identify any suicidal tendencies. For example, Brent et al. (1989) described prevention efforts in a high school after two students had committed suicide within four days. Mental health professionals met with each homeroom class to talk about the suicides and the students' reactions to them. One hundred ten of the 1,500 students in the school were then referred for an individual interview with a clinician. The students who were referred had either asked for additional help, had been referred by a friend as needing additional help, had been visibly upset during the homeroom meeting, had been a friend of one of the suicide victims or had attended one of the funerals, or had been known to have prior psychiatric problems. Of these 110 students, 16 were referred for clinical intervention because of significant suicidal ideation.

Adolescents in other circumstances associated with higher risk for suicide may also need more direct intervention to prevent suicide (Shaffer & Craft, 1999). For example, adolescents who have recently experienced a loss due to the death of a friend or family member (GAP, 1996) and adolescents with chronic or fatal diseases (Brent, 1987) are at higher risk for suicide and may require periodic assessment of their risk for suicide. Similarly, attention to the suicide risk of adolescents who have just been incarcerated or who appear at shelters for homeless adolescents may prevent suicide attempts.

CLINICAL INTERVENTIONS WITH SUICIDAL ADOLESCENTS

Clinical interventions with adolescents who have serious suicidal ideation or who have attempted suicide fall into two general categories: (1) acute interventions to ensure the adolescent's safety and (2) ongoing interventions to address the issues that influenced the suicidal ideation or behavior. Although the

---

BROADENING Perspectives

Suicide as Manipulation

Some people believe that many suicide threats are simply manipulative and designed to obtain sympathy from others. While this may be true occasionally, almost all threats of suicide come from people who are seriously thinking about it as a solution to their problems. Therefore, it is unsafe to assume that a suicide threat is not serious.

acute and ongoing interventions must be tailored to the needs of each adolescent, their overall focus is influenced by knowledge about the development of suicide in adolescents. All interventions should be conducted by mental health professionals who have received special training in work with suicidal adolescents.

Acute Interventions

The safety of a suicidal adolescent is of paramount importance (GAP, 1996; Kirk, 1993; Rickgarn, 1994). A clinician must assess the lethality of the adolescent, by exploring the specifics of any suicide attempts and by determining whether he has a specific plan for committing suicide and whether the plan has been put into effect (e.g., finding a gun, collecting pills). The clinician also must assess both the extent to which the adolescent has control over his suicidal urges and the extent to which the adolescent, and those in his life, are capable of ensuring his safety.

Hospitalization is an option if the adolescent's suicidal urges are strong or under little control, or if there is concern about the ability of others to monitor the adolescent closely. Although hospitalization is the most cautious approach (GAP, 1996), financial constraints or opposition from the adolescent or the adolescent's family may make hospitalization complicated. However, involuntary commitment to a hospital is possible, subject to judicial review, if an adolescent is in clear danger of harming himself. Suicidal adolescents with high levels of depression and low levels of family support are more likely to be hospitalized (Dicker et al., 1997).

If hospitalization is not necessary but the threat of suicide is still significant, the clinician may provide frequent clinical services and engage the adolescent and his family in a process of ensuring his safety between services. The adolescent must agree to cooperate by communicating with the family about any escalation in his suicidal tendencies. Family members commit to providing face-to-face supervision of the adolescent at all times, so that he is never out of the view of at least one family member. The family also agrees to consult immediately with the clinician if concerns about a suicide attempt arise. An agreement such as this not only helps ensure the adolescent's safety but also empowers a family that may be feeling helpless and can strengthen the bonds of the family (GAP, 1996).

The clinician may also make a suicide prevention contract or agreement with the adolescent (Kirk, 1993). The agreement states that the adolescent will contact the clinician if he is experiencing a suicidal urge or before he takes any actions toward suicide. Sometimes this contract is written to impress the adolescent with its seriousness.

Ongoing Interventions

Short-Term Interventions

Short-term interventions focus on helping reduce the constriction of the adolescent's thinking and expand his view of his life and future (GAP, 1996;

Reynolds & Mazza, 1994). These interventions can help identify reasons for living that the adolescent may not be considering and may reduce the strength of the reasons for dying by suggesting ways by which the adolescent's seemingly unsolvable problems may be addressed. Depressed suicidal adolescents may have an exclusively negative view of themselves, and the clinician can expand this view to include some positive personal characteristics. Thinking in time-frames that include more than the immediate is encouraged as a way to instill hope for more positive changes in the future.

Another focus is on identifying and addressing some of the issues that are causing the adolescent pain (Patros & Shamoo, 1989). This helps infuse a sense of self-efficacy and reduces helplessness. A common strategy for doing this is to identify techniques that the adolescent has used to cope with problems successfully in the past and explore ways that they could be used in the current situation or to brainstorm and then refine new strategies. With the clinician's help, these strategies can be put into action, and reports of the success and failure of the strategies can be used to modify them.

Long-Term Interventions

Long-term interventions focus on addressing the issues that influenced the suicidal ideation or attempts, repairing problems that may have resulted from the adolescent's suicidal feelings and providing skills to detect the onset of future suicidal ideation and to seek help for them:

- Depression and other mood disorders, conduct disorders, or anxiety disorders that either led to or resulted from the adolescent's suicidal tendencies are addressed.
- Efforts are made to reduce stressors, in some cases through a reevaluation of the adolescent's priorities (e.g., that he must be a star on the football team or achieve the best grade point average in his class) and in others through solving problems (e.g., helping him find a job to relieve financial concerns).
- Ongoing efforts are made to reduce problematic cognitions, such as cognitive constriction and negative and irrational thinking.
- Problems with interpersonal relationships are identified, and interpersonal skills are built. This may be of particular importance if depression or suicide has led to long-term withdrawal from others.
- Strategies for reducing anger, or for dealing with it in socially acceptable ways, are explored.
- Work with the adolescent and his family focuses on encouraging more effective family functioning and reintegrating the adolescent into his family if necessary.
- Once the adolescent is no longer actively suicidal, the development of his suicidal ideation is explored. This provides the opportunity for him to reflect on the issues that were important enough to drive him toward suicide. It also can alert him to early signs of suicidal thinking and provide the skills to notice and act on these early signs.

CHAPTER SUMMARY

Adolescent suicide is a significant public health problem. Suicide is the third leading cause of death among adolescents, and the rate of completed and attempted suicides has increased dramatically during the past 40 years. About one-quarter of all adolescents report contemplating suicide. About 6 to 16 percent of females and 3 to 8 percent of males report making a suicide attempt.

Most people experience a consistent strong pull toward living throughout their lives, but many adolescents feel a pull toward death. Although it is unknown how this pull starts, most researchers suggest that high levels of stress, with few resources for handling this stress, are associated with initial thoughts about suicide as a solution to the problems that an adolescent faces. Emotions such as depression or anger and styles of thinking that are characterized by negativity and hopelessness appear to deepen some adolescents' thoughts about suicide. Constriction of thinking may cause the issue of suicide, and the problems that the suicide is meant to solve, to consume the adolescent's life. Some adolescents gradually become ever more weighed down by their problems, until one additional problem or stressor results in a suicide attempt. Some suicidal adolescents appear to make more of an impulsive attempt in the presence of a new stressor.

Suicide prevention takes many forms, including efforts to inform all adolescents about suicide, the signs of suicidal ideation in themselves and their friends, and the ways to seek help. Communities concerned about suicide prevention can develop a number of ways to provide help to adolescents, including the training of school, religious, and medical personnel and the creation of anonymous suicide hot lines. Interventions with suicidal adolescents include immediate interventions to assure their safety. In some cases, hospitalization is required. Once a suicidal adolescent is safe, ongoing interventions focus on helping the adolescent feel less hopeless and on beginning the process of solving the problems that encouraged his suicidal thinking or behavior. Long-term interventions focus on providing the suicidal adolescent with new skills to cope with stressful situations, reintegrating the adolescent into his family and peer group, and helping him develop the skills to recognize any recurrence of his suicidal thinking and to seek help for it.

Revisiting Lee

It is difficult for most people to understand why Lee killed himself. He was very successful and about to celebrate many of his successes with his family. One might think that the end of college represents a relief from many stressors, not an increase in stress. Why wouldn't he kill himself before or during finals? Why would the stress become so unbearable after all the stress of college was over?

Feelings of success and failure, or feelings about what is stressful and what is not, are very individual. Being fifth in a graduating class might be a great success for some people but feel like a terrible failure to others. Similarly, taking exams might be very stressful to

HELPING
YOURSELF AND OTHERS

Asking Friends About Suicide and Applying Psychological First Aid

As seen in the section on prevention, there are several signs that may indicate that someone is suicidal. In particular, talking about suicide, ending pain, or making people regret their actions can be signs of suicide, as can giving away possessions or visiting friends or favorite places "one more time." A suicidal person may express feelings of hopelessness and helplessness. Some of these expressions may be indirect, such as "I don't see why I should even bother to finish my degree" or "There's no sense in ever trying to get anyone to like me."

Experts on suicide agree that, if you know someone you think might be suicidal, the best thing to do is to ask him about this directly (GAP, 1996; Kirk, 1993). Research has shown that adolescents are unlikely to initiate a discussion of their suicidal feelings, but they are often willing to disclose suicidal feelings if asked about them (Garrison et al., 1991). I suggest the following, asked in a sensitive way, when you and your friend are alone: "Lately I've been learning that many people who feel the way you feel think about killing themselves. Have you been thinking about killing yourself?" Some people find this a very difficult question to ask. It can feel awkward and intrusive, but it is direct and shows concern. Hinting or asking an indirect question (e.g., "Have you been thinking about doing something harmful/silly/wrong?") is usually ineffective.

Some people worry that their friend will be upset at the question. In some cases, this is true. But asking about suicidal thoughts indicates that you are concerned about your friend. Another worry is that, by asking about suicide, you may plant the idea in someone's mind and, thus, increase his chance of suicide. Experts agree that there have been no reports of this (GAP, 1996). Everyone knows about suicide already—your question will not make a friend think about suicide for the first time.

If a friend is actively considering suicide, then psychological first aid is needed. First aid, in medical terms, generally refers to actions taken to stabilize a person's condition, so that he can be taken for an intervention by an expert. The best way to provide psychological first aid for a suicidal friend is to stay with the friend and encourage him to seek the help of an expert. You may need to help your friend make an appointment at a counseling center and then accompany him to the appointment, to help him call a suicide prevention hot line, to help him contact his family, or to take him to a hospital. It may be important for you to stay with your friend until he receives some professional help. You do not have the expertise to intervene with your friend, but you can give him support and guidance until he receives expert help.

Be kind and supportive during your friend's crisis. You may need to enlist the aid of other friends or family members. At some point, you may even need to call a counseling center, hospital, or police department for assistance. The goal is to help maintain your friend's life through the crisis, then get him to an expert.

some but not others. It may be that Lee felt a terrible sense of failure, even though most of us would be very pleased to achieve what he achieved. Perhaps Lee considered facing his family to be even more stressful than facing final exams. When looking at the stresses experienced by anyone, it is important to see those stresses through their eyes, not through our own.

Lee's thinking and behaviors may have influenced his suicide. It is likely that he focused more and more on his "failure" as a student, to the point at which his sense of failure dominated his life. He may have interpreted every question that he got wrong on an exam as an indication of his failure, rather than seeing the few incorrect answers within the context of an entire exam on which he received an *A*. As he struggled to achieve more and more in his classes, he may have withdrawn from friends and social activities. His isolation may have increased his focus on his failures, by eliminating feedback from others about how well he was doing.

Lee's behavior during his last night alive gave hints about his decision to kill himself. He seemed at peace with his decision and said goodbye to people in the same way that people do when they plan never to meet again. Unfortunately, none of Lee's friends recognized the motivation for his behavior.

- If one of Lee's friends had become concerned that he was suicidal, what should the friend have said (say this out loud, for practice)? What should the friend have done if Lee had said that he was suicidal?
- The pull toward death overwhelmed Lee's pull toward life. If people had known about Lee's suicidal tendencies, what might they have done to strengthen his pull toward life? What changes in his emotions or cognitions might have increased his pull toward life and decreased his pull toward death?
- What programs might Lee's university have put into place to aid suicidal students? (Think more broadly than just having a suicide prevention phone line; consider programs to help students experiencing the stresses that might eventually lead to suicide.)

CHAPTER 8

Drug Use and Abuse

Maureen struggled with shyness for most of her life and felt that her shyness stopped her from being popular. She attracted the attention of many boys at her high school, but they would soon turn their attention to others when Maureen's social awkwardness made it difficult to be with her. At a party during her sophomore year, Maureen had several beers and became slightly drunk for the first time. The next day, her friends commented on how much fun she was at the party, and she was asked to two parties the next weekend. She had several beers at both parties and had a great time. She also enjoyed the attention that she received from several popular boys. Part way through her senior year, Maureen found that the pressures of grades, college entrance exams, and college applications were keeping her from falling to sleep at night. She began keeping some vodka in her room and having one or two drinks late at night to help her fall asleep.

Maureen's drinking increased when she entered college. She began drinking at social gatherings during the week as well as the weekends. Other students encouraged her to try marijuana and cocaine. She liked the feelings she had with these drugs and enjoyed the social aspects of taking them with her new friends. As the number of drugs she took increased, Maureen became concerned about the amount she was consuming. She also became concerned that her drinking and other drug use were interfering with her academic performance. She decided to stop taking all drugs for two weeks but found that she had difficulty falling asleep and that she did not enjoy her social interactions as much as before. She slipped twice during those two weeks: once she had two drinks to help her sleep when she felt exhausted, and once her friends got her to smoke marijuana during a party. Her inability to halt all drug use concerned her, but Maureen's friends told her not to worry and she felt that she could not discuss the issue with her parents or siblings. Maureen continued her drug use for the next year and took slightly increasing amounts of drugs each month. She came to believe that the drugs were no longer having a negative influence on her academic work, and in fact, felt that being relaxed at night helped her study. She was sure that she could stop all drug use if it clearly became problematic.

Adolescents use drugs[1] for many reasons, including experimenting, escaping from problems, reducing depression or anxiety, and getting along with friends (Novacek, Raskin, & Hogan, 1991). Experimental use of tobacco and alcohol is common among junior high school and high school students, and experimentation with illegal drugs such as marijuana is common among high school and college students (Stevens, Mott, & Youells, 1996). Most adolescents, including those who do not use drugs, are generally accepting of drug use by their peers and view drug use as an issue of personal choice rather than an issue that should be determined by social norms or expectations (Nucci, Guerra, & Lee, 1991).

Persistent or heavy use of drugs can harm internal organs, influence central nervous system functioning, and cause lasting changes in the brain (O'Brien, 1996; Segal & Stewart, 1996). However, the consequences of occasional drug use by adolescents are not well understood. Negative physical consequences often do not occur among adolescents who use drugs occasionally (O'Brien, 1996), and deaths by overdose or accidents related to drug use are rare. Consequently, the point at which adolescent drug use becomes problematic is often unclear.

In this chapter, we will focus on the issues that encourage and discourage drug use among adolescents—from occasional experimental use of legal drugs to chronic use of drugs that cause permanent changes in brain functioning. By understanding the range of drug use, we may be in a better position to prevent problematic drug use or intervene effectively with adolescents whose drug use is impairing their health or development.

The Plan: We will first explore ways to distinguish drug use from drug abuse. Is any use abuse? If not, how does one determine when someone crosses the line from using a drug to abusing it? Next we will examine the prevalence of adolescent drug use and abuse and the trends that the use of drugs have taken over the past few decades. In the main part of the chapter, we will focus on the development of drug use. Because there are many forms of drug use, from drinking alcohol occasionally to compulsive use of heroin, it is not helpful to describe the development of drug use as if it were one process. Rather, we will use the following strategy: we will first examine a model of the issues that create an urge for an adolescent to use a drug and that then influence her decision about whether or not to use the drug. We will then discuss a five-stage model of drug use, from experimental use to compulsive use. We will then combine the two models and explore the issues that are most likely to influence drug use at each of these stages. We will then use this knowledge to explore prevention and intervention efforts.

---

[1]The terms *drug* and *substance* are often used interchangeably. The *DSM-IV* states that "the term substance can refer to a drug of abuse, a medication, or a toxin" (APA, 1994, p. 175). This chapter focuses on drugs of abuse, and for ease of presentation the term *drug* will be used throughout the chapter, rather than substance.

DEFINITIONS OF DRUG USE, ABUSE, ADDICTION, AND DEPENDENCY

The terms *use, abuse, addiction,* and *dependency* are used to describe drug-taking behaviors. The term *drug use* is clearly defined for the most part, since it is generally clear when something labeled a drug is being used. However, the term *drug abuse* is more vague and may mean different things to different people. *Addiction* and *drug dependency* often refer to the compulsive use of a drug (APA, 1994); however, the line between compulsive and noncompulsive drug use can be vague (Kaminer, 1994).

Distinguishing Drug Use from Drug Abuse

Several guidelines have been used to distinguish drug use from abuse, and each of them has benefits and drawbacks. None of the guidelines is generally accepted as superior to the others, and two or more of them might be used together in some situations. As a result, some people might consider a certain form of drug use to be abuse, while others would simply consider it drug use. Most of these guidelines are the same as those used to designate which adolescent behaviors are problematic in general. Since these guidelines are described in chapter 2, they are only mentioned briefly here.

Any use is abuse. This guideline is very straightforward: any use of a specified drug is abuse. The primary advantage of this approach is that abuse is defined clearly and in the same way for all people. The primary disadvantage is that it creates a large and diverse group of abusers. For example, if everyone who ever used marijuana were considered to have abused marijuana, the "drug abuser" group would consist of those who tried it once, those who smoke it periodically, and those who get stoned every day. This group of "abusers" would be so mixed that drawing any conclusions about those in the group might be impossible.

Use by underage individuals is abuse. This guideline is used for drugs that are legal for adults to use, such as nicotine and alcohol. It also can be applied in a clear way and results in a large and diverse group of "abusers." An additional weakness is that it relies on age cutoffs that are arbitrary. There is no evidence, for example, that supports the law allowing smoking only after a person's 18th birthday, rather than after her 17th or 22nd birthday.

Use that harms the individual is abuse. Advantages to this guideline are that it considers individual differences in the ways that drugs influence people and that it may appear to be more reasoned to adolescents, because it is based on demonstrable harm, rather than "because it is illegal" or "because you are only 19." A disadvantage is that measurable physical harm is not apparent in most adolescents who use drugs, since it often takes many years of use before a drug produces this level of harm (O'Brien, 1996). This may result in a small "abuser" group consisting only of those who have taken huge amounts of several drugs.

Distinguishing Drug Abuse from Drug Dependency or Addiction

In common usage, *drug addiction* and *drug dependency* are used interchangeably (IM, 1997). The American Psychiatric Association began to distinguish between drug abuse and drug dependency in 1980 (APA, 1980). Both abuse and dependency require a maladaptive pattern of drug use that results in significant adverse consequences and impaired functioning (showing that the APA relies on the "harm to the individual" guideline). Dependency, but not abuse, requires a pattern of compulsive use. Compulsive use can be shown by the presence of tolerance or withdrawal (these terms are described later in this chapter), unsuccessful efforts to limit drug use, or a great deal of time being spent procuring and taking drugs. Therefore, dependency is generally seen as a more serious and chronic problem (O'Brien, 1996).

Defining the Terms Used in This Chapter

In much of this chapter, we do not need to distinguish among drug use, abuse, and dependency. Our primary goal is to understand how various levels and types of drug use develop. Determining whether a certain type of drug use should be labeled abuse or dependency does nothing to promote our understanding of how that type of drug use developed. Therefore, we will mostly use the general term *drug use,* but will use the term *drug abuse* occasionally—in situations where there is clear harm to an individual.

THE PREVALENCE OF DRUG USE

An important source of information about adolescent drug use comes from a yearly survey funded by the National Institute on Drug Abuse (NIDA) (Johnston, O'Malley, & Bachman, 1999). This survey started in 1975 as a survey of twelfth-graders and was expanded to include eighth- and tenth-graders in 1991. The survey involves about 15,000 students each year, from schools representing a broad range of ethnic and religious backgrounds and geographic locations.

There are two main concerns about the accuracy of drug use estimates from surveys of high school students. The first relates to the honesty of the students' responses. The surveys are anonymous to encourage honesty. However, some students may underreport drug use out of embarrassment or fears of having their drug use discovered; other students may overreport drug use to boost their social standing. Researchers generally agree that these surveys are good approximations of drug use, however. Those who overreport use may balance those who underreport.

A second concern is that students who are frequent or heavy drug users are likely to be underrepresented in the surveys because they are less likely to be at school when the surveys are conducted. Drug use by high school dropouts, for example, can be two to six times higher than use by high school students (Swaim et al., 1997). In addition, heavy drug users are more likely than other students to be absent on the days that the survey is taken, even if they have not dropped out of school. As a result, these surveys may underestimate heavy or frequent drug use.

Tables 8.1 and 8.2 show the percentage of students who responded that they had ever used a drug (lifetime use), that they had used the drug within the past 30 days, or that they had used the drug daily for each of the past 30 days (daily use). The survey asked about many types of drug use; some (e.g., inhalants, heroin, stimulants) are not presented here because of space limitations. As can be seen, there are different patterns of drug use over the 23-year period for the twelfth-grade students, partly reflecting differences in the popularity of drugs over time. A general pattern of drug use emerges: relatively high use in 1975 to 1980, a decrease in use from 1985 to 1991, and then an increase in use during the 1990s (Weinberg et al., 1998).

TABLE 8.1. Drug Use Among Twelfth-Grade Students

	1975	1980	1985	1991	1995	1997	1998
Cigarettes							
Lifetime use	73	71	69	63	64	65	65
30-day use	37	31	30	28	34	37	35
Daily use							
(½ pack +)	27	21	20	10	12	14	13
*Alcohol**							
Lifetime use	90	93	92	88	81	82	81
30-day use	68	72	66	54	51	53	52
Daily use	6	6	5	4	4	4	4
Marijuana/hashish							
Lifetime use	47	60	54	37	42	50	49
30-day use	27	34	26	14	21	24	24
Daily use	6	9	5	2	5	6	6
Cocaine							
Lifetime use	9	16	17	8	6	9	9
30-day use	2	5	7	1	2	2	2
Daily use	0.1	0.2	0.4	0.1	0.2	—	—
LSD							
Lifetime use	11	9	8	9	12	14	13
30-day use	2	2	2	2	4	4	3
Daily use	<.05	<.05	0.1	0.1	0.1	—	—

Numbers are percent of respondents; percents greater than 1 percent are rounded to nearest whole number.
*The survey beginning in 1993 required heavier alcohol use to elicit a positive response.
Source: Johnston et al., 1999.

TABLE 8.2. Drug Use Among Eighth- and Tenth-Graders

	Eighth-Graders				Tenth-Graders			
	1991	1995	1997	1998	1991	1995	1997	1998
Cigarettes								
Lifetime use	44	46	47	46	55	61	60	57
30-day use	14	19	19	19	21	30	30	28
Daily use								
(½ pack +)	3	3	4	4	7	9	9	8
*Alcohol**								
Lifetime use	70	55	54	53	84	71	72	70
30-day use	25	25	25	23	43	39	40	39
Daily use	0.5	0.7	0.8	0.9	1	2	2	2
Marijuana/hashish								
Lifetime use	10	20	23	22	23	34	42	40
30-day use	3	10	10	10	9	17	21	21
Daily use	0.2	0.8	1	1	0.8	3	4	4
Cocaine								
Lifetime use	2	4	4	5	4	5	7	7
30-day use	0.5	1	1	1	0.7	2	2	2
Daily use	0.1	0.1	—	—	0.1	0.1	—	—
LSD								
Lifetime use	3	4	5	4	6	8	10	9
30-day use	0.6	1	2	2	2	3	3	3
Daily use	<.05	0.1	—	—	<.05	<.05	—	—

Numbers are percent of respondents; percents greater than 1 percent are rounded to nearest whole number.
*The survey beginning in 1993 required heavier alcohol use to elicit a positive response.
Source: Johnston et al., 1999.

Each year, surveys are sent to some students who participated in an earlier study of high school seniors, one to four years after they have graduated. Based on responses from 1,000 to 1,400 people each year, estimates of drug use among college students have been developed (see table 8.3).

TABLE 8.3. Drug Use Within the Past Month Among College Students

	1980	1985	1990	1995	1997
Cigarettes	25	22	22	27	28
Alcohol*	82	80	75	68	66
Any illicit drug	38	26	15	19	19
Marijuana/hashish	34	24	14	19	18
Cocaine	7	7	1	0.7	2
LSD	1	0.7	1	3	1

Numbers are percent of respondents; percents greater than 1 percent are rounded to nearest whole number.
*The survey beginning in 1993 required heavier alcohol use to elicit a positive response.
Source: Johnston et al., 1999.

> ### *Notice the Prevalence of No Drug Use*
>
> Discussions of the prevalence of drug use can occasionally lead to an inflated perception of the percentage of adolescents who use drugs. Notice in tables 8.1 and 8.2, for example, that only a small percentage of adolescents smoke cigarettes daily and that a very small percentage have ever used cocaine. While the harmful use of drugs by even a small percentage of adolescents is worthy of concern, it is important to have a clear understanding of the percentage of adolescents who do and who do not use drugs.

THE DEVELOPMENT OF DRUG USE AND ABUSE

Several obstacles exist to developing a comprehensive theory to explain the development of drug use. In this section, we will examine some of these obstacles and then will discuss a strategy for understanding drug use that minimizes them.

The first obstacle is the large number of influences that researchers have found to be related to drug use. Each of these influences is related to drug use in some adolescents but unrelated to drug use in others. As a result, models of the influences on drug use are often very large and cumbersome and may be difficult to apply to individual cases.

The second obstacle is the many different types of drug use that need to be explained. For example, drug use includes the initial use of alcohol, occasional use of marijuana, and chronic use of heroin. It is not reasonable to expect that an explanation for the initial use of alcohol would also apply to chronic heroin use. Therefore, developing a single explanation for the entire range of drug use is probably impossible.

The third obstacle is that the influences on an individual's drug use can change from one use to another. For example, the influences on smoking right after waking in the morning (e.g., withdrawal) can be different from the influences on smoking a second cigarette after dinner (e.g., to prolong the dinner conversation). As a result, trying to develop one explanation for all drug use, even by an individual, may be impossible.

To minimize these obstacles, I will use the following strategy. First, I will focus on individual instances of drug use rather than on drug use overall and will argue that each time an adolescent uses a drug she has decided to do so. Next I will present a diagram of the variety of issues shown to influence these decisions to use a drug. Then I will present a model that groups drug use into five categories and describe the issues that are most likely to influence the decision to use a drug in each of these categories. This strategy will allow us, for example, to consider the issues that might influence smoking marijuana at a party separately from the issues that might influence the habitual use of marijuana. This should provide a more manageable way of exploring the many influences on the development of different types of drug use.

Many models exist for understanding drug use. The two presented in this chapter are useful, particularly when implemented together. Other models are also useful, and some people might find that other models are better than the ones presented here. As research continues to contribute to our understanding of drug use, new, more complete models will likely emerge.

Decisions to Use or Not Use Drugs

All adolescents decide whether or not to use a drug each time they are faced with the opportunity to do so. Some always decide not to use a drug, some decide to use a drug occasionally, and others frequently decide to use a drug when given the opportunity.

This is not to say that decisions to use or not use drugs are made completely freely. Significant pressures to use or not use a drug often exist. Pressures can come from parents, peers, and social institutions, and they may be felt acutely when drug use or abstinence is tied to an adolescent's independence, morality, or other desired characteristic. Even those who are physically addicted to a drug make decisions about using it. Their decisions may be greatly influenced by the pain associated with withdrawal, and they may be made with a mind that has been significantly altered by drug use, but they are decisions nonetheless.

Viewing drug use as a series of decisions is helpful, because it allows us to focus on the influences on those decisions. It might be impossible to answer the question "Why is this person a daily user of marijuana?" However, it might be possible (although hardly easy) to answer the question "Why did this person decide to smoke marijuana in this situation?" By understanding the reasons for these decisions, we can come to a clearer understanding of the complexity of an adolescent's abstinence, or her occasional or chronic use of a drug.

A Model of the Process of Deciding to Use or Not Use a Drug

Jaffe (1992) presents an informative and complex model of the influences on drug use (see figure 8.1). The model describes biological and social influences on drug use, as well as the ways in which earlier decisions about drug use influence subsequent decisions. Jaffe suggests that an urge to use a drug begins a cognitive assessment of the benefits and risks of using the drug and that this assessment results in a decision to use or not use a drug. An initial urge may be influenced by factors such as angry or depressed feelings, the easy availability of a drug, and physical symptoms of withdrawal. Alternately, feelings of contentment or hope may reduce an urge to use a drug. Many factors can influence the assessment of the risks and benefits of using a drug. For example, perceived social benefits, previous positive experiences using a drug, and the ability of the drug to reduce withdrawal symptoms can encourage a positive assessment of drug use. Alternately, fear of the consequences of drug use, previous negative experiences with drugs, and previous positive experiences from deciding not to use a drug can encourage a negative assessment of drug use.

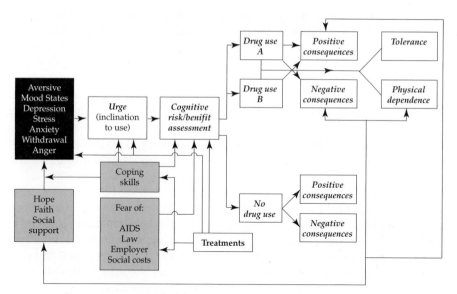

FIGURE 8.1. Current concepts of addiction.
From O'Brien, C.P., Childress, A.R., McLellan, A.T. & Ehrman, R. (1992), A Learning Model of Addiction. In C. O'Brien & J. Jaffe (Eds.), Addictive States (pp. 157–177). New York: Raven Press. Reprinted with permission.

Applying knowledge about adolescent development to this model can help explain the high use of drugs by adolescents. Many influences that increase the urge to use drugs, such as depression, stress, anxiety, and anger, occur frequently among adolescents (Birmaher et al., 1996; Goodyer, 1995) (also see chapters 6 and 10). Similarly, factors that can decrease the urge to use drugs, such as hope, faith, and social support, may be at relatively low levels during adolescence because of the relative uncertainty of adolescents' futures and a reduction in their use of family support (Gardner, 1993). In addition, as described in chapter 4, the risk-benefit assessments made by adolescents are more likely to be influenced by the immediate and potentially positive aspects of an outcome and less likely to be influenced by the long-term or potentially negative aspects of an outcome (Furby & Beyth-Marom, 1992). Consequently, negative experiences with drugs and the long-term physical or psychological consequences of drug use may have relatively little influence on an adolescent's assessment, while potential positive physical sensations, peer-group acceptance, and relief from aversive moods may have a relatively strong influence.

The Stages of Drug Use

Nowinski (1990) suggests that there are five stages of drug use: experimental, social, instrumental, habitual, and compulsive. Although each stage tends to involve increased frequency of drug use, they are distinguished by the primary motivation to use drugs in each stage.

The model is not used to describe people, but to describe drug use. Consequently, the model is not used to label someone as an experimental or a habitual user of drugs, but to describe each drug use. On any one day, some drug use by an adolescent may fall into one stage, and other drug use may fall into another. In addition, the stages in the model are not mutually exclusive, and some drug use may be described best by a mixture of stages—for example, experimenting with a new drug in a social setting may best be described as experimental and social use. The lack of discrete stages does not reduce the value of the model, however, because its goal is not to classify every drug use into one category. Rather, it is designed to describe the variety of motivations for drug use, as well as the different influences on each of these motivations.

The primary motivations for drug use in the experimental stage are curiosity and risk taking. While an adolescent may experience the mood-altering effects of a drug, it is the excitement of experimentation that is primarily important during this stage. Drug use in this stage is occasional, and experimentation may occur with other adolescents or alone. Adolescents using drugs in this stage return to their normal mood state after the drug wears off, except for the possibility of a hangover or other short-term consequence.

Social acceptance is the primary motivation for drug use in the social stage. The mood-altering effects of drug use may be a positive consequence, but the primary motivation is to influence an adolescent's social standing. Drug use may be heavy at times, and even life-threatening, but it always takes place in a social context. As with the experimental stage, mood state returns to normal after the effects of the drug wear off.

Drug use in the instrumental stage is primarily motivated by the mood-altering effects of a drug. Nowinski suggests two types of instrumental use: hedonistic and compensatory. Hedonistic use is aimed at increasing positive emotions. A typical motivation is to feel happy or to disinhibit behavior. Compensatory use is aimed at coping with stress and negative feelings by suppressing emotions. A goal might be to stop feeling depressed or anxious or to reduce feelings of emptiness or failure. In the instrumental stage, the adolescent returns to a normal mood state as the drug wears off. Consequently, there is typically just a positive mood-altering effect of using drugs and no subsequent negative effect. This is one factor that distinguishes instrumental use from habitual or compulsive use.

Nowinski refers to the habitual stage as the boundary between purposeful drug use and compulsive use. Coping with the physiological consequences of earlier drug use becomes an important motivation at this stage. The adolescent's emotional state does not return to normal after using drugs but, instead, becomes more negative than before drug use. For example, a depressed adolescent will feel less depressed while under the influence of a drug but will feel more depressed than usual for a time after the drug wears off. These feelings provide a strong urge for subsequent drug use and can influence the decision to use drugs again. The battle for control is the hallmark of the habitual stage. Adolescents may be frightened by their increasingly strong urges to use drugs and may fear that they are losing control over their drug use. They may develop rules to limit use, such as how much of a drug to use or on which days to use it. Some adolescents can regain a solid sense of control over their drug use at this point; however, others find themselves breaking their own rules because of their growing physical and psychological need for the drug. Adolescents who lose the battle for control find themselves using drugs compulsively.

The adolescent who is preoccupied with drug use is in the compulsive stage. She has lost the battle for control, and the need to use drugs begins to dominate her life. Anhedonia (the inability to experience pleasure) is the adolescent's prevailing mood, and it is only through drugs that it can be lifted. Maintaining a steady supply of drugs becomes an important issue for her, and she may become a dealer or the girlfriend of a dealer. A compulsive user may make occasional efforts to limit drug use, but these typically fail quickly.

Influences at Each Stage of Drug Use

Combining Jaffe's and Nowinski's models helps us explore the development of different types of adolescent drug use. Jaffe's model helps us understand the influences on both the urge to use a drug and the subsequent cognitive assessment about drug use, and Nowinski's model suggests that these influences may differ from stage to stage.

Drug use tends to develop by progressing through the stages of Nowinski's model. Initial experiences with drugs tend to fall into the experimental or social stages, and most adolescents engage in this type of drug use. Many of these adolescents will eventually engage in at least some instrumental drug use. Some instrumental users will engage in habitual drug use, and some of these adolescents will use drugs compulsively. While it is true that all adolescents who use drugs compulsively once used drugs on an experimental or social basis, it is not true that those who use drugs experimentally or socially are likely to become habitual or compulsive users (Golub & Johnson, 1998). Some adolescents at each stage of drug use will continue to the next stage, but others will not. In some ways, a description of the development of drug use is a description of the issues that influence some adolescents to progress through the stages of drug use and others to stop their use at one stage—perhaps staying there for the rest of their lives.

The Experimental Stage

The urge to use drugs in the experimental stage comes primarily from curiosity and interest in risk taking—two characteristics that many adolescents have in abundance (Segal & Stewart, 1996). The effects of the drug itself have little influence on urge in this stage, although interest in experimenting with these effects can motivate experimental use. Adolescents who are leery of experimenting with new experiences may have little urge for experimental use (Shelder & Block, 1990).

Cognitive assessments that may encourage drug use at this stage include beliefs about the benefits of trying something new or risky. On the other hand, beliefs about the impropriety of drug use may discourage use. For example, stronger religious affiliation has been associated with decreased likelihood of drug use, and many religious institutions discourage drug use among adolescents (Adlaaf & Smart, 1985). Fear about the consequences of the experimental use of drugs (e.g., death, eventual addiction) or about what it would mean to be a person who experiments with drugs (e.g., the inability to resist peer culture influences) could also discourage drug use. For example, Shelder and Block (1990) found that 18-year-olds who had never experimented with marijuana were highly self-controlled and leery of new experiences.

It is noteworthy that experimental drug use is not focused on overcoming a negative mood or life circumstance. The motivations for experimental drug use are primarily positive (e.g., trying new things, learning about the world), although many people would view drug use itself as negative. This may be one reason that experimental drug use is so widespread among adolescents, including those who are successful and content with life.

The Social Stage

The urge to use drugs in the social stage comes from a desire to improve or maintain one's social standing. Drug use or drug abstinence may be a source of mutuality and cohesion within some peer social groups, and drug use may be a way of solidifying one's place within the adolescent culture (Segal & Stewart, 1996).

A primary focus of the cognitive assessment at this stage is an evaluation of drug use and social standing. Adolescents whose friends use drugs may see more benefit to drug use, whereas those whose friends actively avoid drugs may see more liability in drug use. This may be why adolescents whose friends use drugs are much more likely to use drugs themselves (Kandel, 1982; Stevens, Mott, & Youells, 1996). Another influence on the cognitive assessment is the positive and negative consequences of earlier drug use. For example, a bad hangover from the experimental use of alcohol may discourage social use. Previous social responses to drug use, such as condemnation from a friend for drug use, are likely to be even more powerful.

Adolescents may also be conscious of their standing in their nuclear and extended families. Therefore, the actual or anticipated consequences of drug use on their standing within their families can influence social drug use by some adolescents. Adolescents who are living in families in which drug use is condoned are more likely to use drugs (Barnes & Welte, 1986; Dishion, Patterson, & Reid, 1988), and their drug use may be influenced by the enhancement of social standing within both their family and peer group. Adolescents whose families do not condone drug use may need to balance the effects of drug use on their social standing among peers with the effects on their standing within their family.

The Instrumental Stage

The urge to use drugs during the instrumental stage comes primarily from the drugs' ability to enhance positive moods and decrease negative moods. Many adolescents cite drugs' mood-altering qualities as the primary reason for using them—for example, to relieve tension, boredom, and distress (Khantzian, 1985;

Segal & Stewart, 1996). In addition, adolescents experiencing negative moods for a variety of reasons are more likely to use drugs. For example, adolescents who experience mood disorders, anxiety disorders, and conduct disorders are more likely to use drugs. Regular drug use usually follows the onset of these disorders, rather than preceeding the disorders, suggesting that drugs are being used to cope with the negative feelings associated with them (Brook et al., 1995; Wilens et al., 1997). Being the victim of childhood physical or sexual abuse is related to depression and anxiety, as well as to increased risk for drug use (Fendrich et al., 1997; Mezzich et al., 1997). As previously mentioned, adolescents who come from families in which there is ongoing drug use are more likely to use drugs themselves. While this may be partly due to easier drug availability, genetic vulnerability, or modeling of drug using behavior, it may also be due to higher levels of chaos in these families, which an adolescent could find emotionally troubling (Brook et al., 1992; Dishion et al., 1988). As suggested by Jaffe's model, adolescents who have the skills to cope with their negative moods and experiences, or who have the support from others to cope with these situations, may experience less of an urge to use drugs.

The cognitive assessment of drug use in the instrumental stage is influenced primarily by the mood-altering effects of previous drug use. Adolescents who experience few positive moods; who are seldom able to achieve positive moods through success in school, sports, or social activities; or who experience many negative moods may be particularly vulnerable to the mood enhancing qualities of drugs (Stevens, Mott, & Youells, 1996; Wilens et al., 1997). Mood enhancement by earlier drug use can encourage ongoing use, and previous decisions to avoid drug use that were followed by a continuation of a negative mood state may increase the likelihood of future decisions to use a drug.

On the other hand, drug use may be accompanied by several aversive emotions—for example, fear of being discovered, guilt over drug use, and anxiety about potential punishment. Adolescents who are more likely to feel and respond to these emotions may assess the overall value of drug use as negative, despite the mood-enhancing qualities of the drugs.

Instrumental Use

One of my therapy cases in an adolescent inpatient psychiatric hospital was a 14-year-old boy who had been raised in a highly chaotic family and neighborhood. He had smoked marijuana almost daily since age 8. He explained this by saying, "The only times that I ever stopped feeling depressed was when I was smoking." It was easy to see how the urge to smoke marijuana and the assessment of the benefits of smoking marijuana would be strongly influenced by the drug's ability to produce the only relief from depression that he had ever experienced.

The Habitual Stage

The urge to use drugs in the habitual stage comes primarily from the molecular, cellular, and functional changes that occur in a person's brain after sustained use (Leshner, 1997). The body's attempts to counter the effects of repeated drug exposure result in a chronic physical state resembling withdrawal when the drug is not active in the body (Koob & Le Moal, 1997) (see the box on the development of withdrawal). It is the presence of this chronic physical state that distinguishes drug use in the instrumental stage from drug use in the habitual stage, and it is this persistent negative state that produces a powerful urge for drug use.

Adolescents whose drug use is habitual are likely to have experienced important changes in their lives, such as declines in their academic or athletic performance (Brown et al., 1994; Hops, Davis, & Lewin, 1999; Johnson & Kaplan, 1990). These changes can increase their stress, anxiety, or depression, either because of declines in their self-satisfaction or because of criticism from parents, teachers, peers, and others. Increases in these negative states can add to the urge to use a drug.

The drugs' ability to improve mood, even if only temporarily, is a powerful component of the adolescent's cognitive assessment about drug use in this stage. Further, a decreasing ability to achieve positive mood states through other activities reduces the mood-enhancing options available to the adolescent. Adolescents whose drug use is habitual may have drifted away from old friends and into a new group of friends where drug use is common (Stevens, Mott, & Youells, 1996). They may both give and receive social reinforcement for drug use within their new group of friends, and this may further encourage the assessments that drug use is appropriate.

Some adolescents can pull back from habitual use into instrumental use, but others experience an increasing lack of control over their drug use and slip into a pattern of compulsive use. The influences on this are not well understood. Genes play an important role in the development of the compulsive use

---

Development of Tolerance

Tolerance occurs when a person must take increasing amounts of a drug to achieve a desired effect. Tolerance develops because of the body's physiological responses to drug use.

An organism attempts to maintain its physical systems within appropriate limits. When the organism is challenged through the introduction of a drug, it attempts to maintain equilibrium through actions that counter the effects of the drug (Koob & Le Moal, 1997; Nutt, 1997). Thus, when a drug is introduced, the body initiates physiological responses that counter those produced by the drug. As the body's responses become efficient, more of the drug must be taken to achieve the same effect. As more of the drug is taken, the body initiates even stronger countermeasures, requiring that even more of the drug be taken.

HELPING
YOURSELF AND OTHERS

Your Drug Use and Control

Control is what primarily distinguishes instrumental from habitual drug use. If you use drugs, how much control do you have over your use? Probably the only way to find out is to decide to stop using a drug for a couple of weeks and monitor how easy or difficult it is for you to be free of that drug. Self-monitoring in this type of situation can be difficult, however, since people are often good at fooling themselves into thinking that they have more control than they do. For example, deciding after one week that "This is silly—I don't need to prove anything to myself," or "Why should I let some guy who wrote a textbook tell me how to live my life?" may be a sign that you have less control than you believe you have. If you find it difficult to maintain abstinence for two weeks, you may be closer to habitual use than you believe. Consultation with a physician, counselor, or therapist might be useful.

of alcohol, but the role of genes in the development of the compulsive use of other drugs is not known (IM, 1997; Weinberg et al., 1998). Interventions by family, friends, or others may help reduce negative feelings such as anxiety, loneliness, or depression, and this may result in a decreased urge toward drug use. One or two influential adults or peers may help an adolescent assess drug use in new ways or may help her see ways of meeting goals other than by taking drugs. At a fundamental level, what is needed in this stage is a reduction in the amount of drugs taken, since continued use raises the risk of further changes in the brain that lead to compulsive use.

The Compulsive Stage

Leshner (1997) suggested that, at some point in drug use, a switch in the brain seems to be thrown, resulting in changes in brain functioning that result in chronic urges for drug use. The areas of the brain most affected are those controlling emotion and motivation, thus affecting the compulsive drug user's insight and control over drug use (IM, 1997). Nestler and Aghajanian (1997) provided a good example of how these brain changes produce ongoing urges for drug use. Acute opiate use inhibits the adenosine 3',5'-monophosphate (cAMP) pathways in the brain. The body adapts to repeated opiate use by up-regulating the cAMP pathways in the brain, resulting in a chronic up-regulation of these pathways. The hyperactivity of the cAMP pathways is associated with many of the withdrawal symptoms of opiate use. Thus, the chronic up-regulation of this pathway results in a chronic state of opiate withdrawal, providing a strong urge to use opiates. As more opiates are used, the pathways become increasingly active, requiring more opiates to reduce withdrawal symptoms.

As described in the box on conditioned withdrawal, environmental clues that drug use is likely to occur result in drug-opposite responses even before they are taken, and this results in a worsening of withdrawal symptoms and an increased urge for drug use. For example, if an adolescent uses opiates during lunch and right after school, the environmental clues associated with the closeness of lunchtime or the end of school (e.g., the beginning of the class period just before lunch or at the end of the school day) will result in the body's initiating drug-opposite responses, which will result in heightened withdrawal symptoms during these times. These heightened withdrawal symptoms will further increase the urge to use opiates. As the adolescent uses the opiates at lunch and after school, the negative reinforcement (cessation of withdrawal symptoms) and positive reinforcement (elevation of mood) encourage subsequent drug use. The physiologically driven urge to use drugs will have an increasing influence on the adolescent's life. For example, if the adolescent's withdrawal symptoms become intolerable during the periods before lunch and at the end of school, she may skip these periods to take the drugs earlier. This leads to new environmental clues for drug use—in this case, the beginning of the classes before those that she is now skipping. This can eventually lead her to skip these periods as well.

Alleviating the chronic symptoms of withdrawal dominate the adolescent's cognitive assessment of drug use at this stage. Factors that could influence drug abstinence in the compulsive stage are very weak in comparison with the influences to use drugs. The adolescent may receive little social reinforcement for reduction in drug use. Peer or family influences may have little effect because of the adolescent's withdrawal from family members and peers who do not use drugs. School, social, and athletic performance may have become so

---

Development of Withdrawal and Conditioned Withdrawal

Cessation of drug use after chronic use can produce physical withdrawal symptoms. These symptoms are severe for some drugs (e.g., heroin, alcohol) but moderate for others (e.g., crack cocaine, methamphetamines) (Leshner, 1997). Symptoms of withdrawal can also appear after each use. The body's efforts to counter the effect of the drug persist after the drug has become metabolized, resulting in a "rebound effect" of physical and emotional consequences that are opposite of those produced by the drug (O'Brien, 1997).

Just as with tolerance, after repeated use of a drug the body learns (through classical conditioning) to begin drug-opposite responses when in an environment that has repeatedly preceded drug use in the past. This can produce withdrawal symptoms prior to drug use (conditioned withdrawal), which can be a strong motivator for subsequent drug use. Conditioned withdrawal symptoms can last years after a person has stopped using a drug, which may contribute to a relapse even in people who have been drug free for years (O'Brien et al., 1992).

compromised that improvement in these areas with a halt in drug use may seem remote or impossible (Brown et al., 1994; Johnson & Kaplan, 1990).

A Summary of the Development of Drug Use and Abuse

Drug use, whether infrequent or chronic, can be thought of as a series of decisions to use or not use a drug. There is a wide range of influences on these decisions, from physiological changes in the brain to an adolescent's social environment. Rather than trying to develop an overall model of drug use, it is best to consider drug use as falling into stages and to develop models of the influences on drug use and abstinence at each stage. Drug use in the experimental and social stages is primarily encouraged by normal adolescent curiosity and interest in social acceptance. Interest in experimentation and the extent to which an adolescent's peer group and family condone or encourage drug use are likely to have the primary influence on drug use in these stages. Beginning in the instrumental stage, a drug's ability to influence mood becomes increasingly important. The drug's ability to alleviate negative moods or to bring on positive moods will encourage use. The negative moods, such as guilt or fear, that accompany actual or anticipated drug use will discourage use. Chronic use of drugs results in changes to the brain that can have powerful influences on the urge to take drugs and on the decision to take drugs when this urge is present. These brain changes, and the chronic drug use that they encourage, often results in significant changes in the adolescent's academic and social lives, and these changes can encourage compulsive drug use—leading to further changes in brain functioning and the adolescent's social environment.

THE PREVENTION OF DRUG USE

Prevention is a complex issue because of the many reasons for adolescent drug use. For prevention efforts to be successful, they must have targeted goals (e.g., the nonuse of drugs, the nonuse of illegal drugs, a delay in initial use of drugs), since strategies that can prevent one type of use may not be effective with others. In addition, these strategies must address the complexity of the issues that encourage or discourage drug use among adolescents. Unfortunately, many prevention programs do not specify what they are trying to prevent and focus on only one or two influences on drug use.

Public Policy Prevention Efforts

Laws have been used for many years to attempt to reduce or eliminate drug consumption. The most obvious efforts are those imposing criminal penalties on the use or sale of certain drugs. Other efforts are designed to reduce the use of legal drugs such as tobacco and alcohol, such as by prohibiting their use until a certain age and prohibiting their use in certain settings (e.g., public buildings).

Warning labels on alcoholic beverages and cigarettes have also been used to reduce consumption, but there is little research on their effectiveness. One study of the influence of alcohol warning labels on pregnant women showed that women who drank very little decreased their alcohol consumption after the labels were required, but women who drank at least one drink a day did not change their drinking patterns (IM, 1997). This suggests that warning labels may be least effective with those who should heed them the most.

Another strategy to reduce smoking and drinking has been for the government to increase the tax on tobacco and alcohol (IM, 1997). The results of these efforts have been mixed, however. One study found that increasing the price of beer and hard liquor resulted in decreased consumption by adolescents who consumed three to five drinks per day (Grossman, Coate, & Arluck, 1987). A 25 cents per pack increase in the cost of cigarettes in California in 1988 reduced the number of adult smokers, but not adolescent smokers. However, a cigarette price increase in Canada did result in a decrease in adolescent smoking (IM, 1997).

Media Presentations

Public service announcements on television and radio provide health information about drug use, portray drug use in a negative light, provide support for refusing drugs when they are offered, and encourage adolescents to remain drug free. These announcements by themselves do not appear to reduce initial or ongoing drug use, although they can reinforce and strengthen information received during school-based prevention programs (IM, 1997).

School-Based and Community-Based Programs

Many school-based programs to prevent drug use have been implemented over the past three decades. Some are nationally known, such as the D.A.R.E. program, and many others are used in individual schools or school districts (Stoil & Hill, 1996). Some programs are designed to improve family strength or enhance self-esteem and, consequently, reduce stress, which might lead to anxiety, depression, and drug use (e.g., Callison, Colocino, & Vasquez, 1995; LoSciuto et al., 1999; Spoth, Redmond, & Lepper, 1999). Others focus on providing knowledge about the consequences of drug use, based on the belief that this will help adolescents decide not to use drugs. An increasingly popular part of many programs is designed to prevent experimental and social drug use by giving children and adolescents the skills to resist peer pressure to use drugs. Research on the effectiveness of these prevention programs is mixed and sometimes contradictory. However, some general trends can be described (for reviews, see Herrmann & McWhirter, 1997; Stoil & Hill, 1996).

Based on the number of adolescents who have tried legal and illegal drugs, programs to prevent experimental and social use of drugs must be seen as failures. Even intensive programs to prevent experimental and social drinking and drug use among adolescents have been unsuccessful (e.g., Brown, D'Emidio, &

Caston, 1995; Stevens et al., 1996). Programs designed to increase knowledge about the consequences of drug use do increase adolescents' knowledge, however, but have almost no influence on their drug use. Programs that give students strategies to resist peer pressure result in increased knowledge about refusal skills and have a moderate influence on drug use. However, this influence fades within a year unless "booster programs" are offered in subsequent years. For example, programs delivered in elementary school (such as D.A.R.E.) have no influence on drug use in junior high school and high school (Dukes, Ullman, & Stein, 1996; Ennett et al., 1994). Finally, programs that include the active practice of skills (such as role playing) produce better results than those that simply tell students how to behave.

CLINICAL INTERVENTIONS FOR DRUG USE AND ABUSE

As with prevention programs, clinical interventions can be aimed at a wide range of drug use—from intervening with adolescents who are experimenting with drugs to intervening with those who have been using drugs compulsively for years. Successful interventions for one type of drug use are likely to differ from successful interventions for other types.

An issue often ignored in the clinical literature is how to determine when an intervention is called for. In cases where an adolescent has little control over her drug use, it is easy to argue that intervention is needed. However, it is less clear whether interventions are needed for other adolescents—for example, for someone who drinks for the first time at a high school party and is found drunk later that evening or for someone who smokes marijuana on the weekends with her friends but never during the week. Early use of drugs, particularly early heavy use, is associated with later habitual or compulsive use, so it could be argued that early intervention for any drug use could reduce the chance of later problematic drug use (Ellickson, Hays, & Bell, 1992). However, it is not clear which early users will go on to become heavy users (Waldron, 1997), and it is not currently possible to identify the early users that need intervention.

Interventions for Experimental or Social Use

Interventions for drug use in the experimental and social stages can focus either on reducing or eliminating use or on encouraging safe use. One strategy for eliminating or reducing use is to influence adolescents' decision-making process. Information about the potential harm of starting drug use or of the possibility of death occurring with even one use can discourage use by some adolescents, but not by most. Strengthening ethical, moral, or religious prohibitions against drug use may also discourage use, as may encouraging adolescents to be friends only with those who do not use drugs. Currently, however, the effectiveness of these strategies is unknown.

Other interventions acknowledge the possibility of drug use and focus on discouraging dangerous behaviors associated with drug use. An example of this strategy is a parent who discourages drinking, but whose primary prohibition is against drinking and driving and who offers to pick up the adolescent anywhere, anytime—with no questions asked—to prevent the adolescent from having to ride with someone who has been drinking.

Interventions for Instrumental Use

Interventions for drug use in the instrumental stage typically focus on resolving the issues that are encouraging an adolescent to use drugs. Adolescents who are using drugs in a compensatory way are helped to find other solutions to the problems they face. For example, interventions might be aimed at reducing the depression or anxiety that is fueling the adolescent's drug use. Adolescents who are using drugs in a hedonistic way are helped to find other ways of producing positive feelings—for example, an adolescent may be helped to enhance or develop academic, athletic, social, or recreational skills.

Several studies have shown that family therapy is an important component of successful interventions for adolescent drug use, and that it can be superior to individual therapy for an adolescent (e.g., Azrin et al., 1994; Liddle & Dakof, 1995; Weinberg et al., 1998). This may be due either to a decrease in the family-related stressors that are influencing drug use or to an increase in family support or monitoring for the adolescent as she attempts to decrease or eliminate drug use.

HELPING

YOURSELF AND OTHERS

Reducing Habitual or Compulsive Drug Use

Adolescents whose drug use is in the habitual or compulsive stage may find it very difficult to reduce or end their drug use. Most often, the help of a mental health professional or of a well-established self-help program (such as Alcoholics Anonymous) is needed. The location of these professionals or self-help groups can be found through campus organizations or in the telephone book. If a friend has a serious drug problem, she may need your support and encouragement to seek help. You may be able to be with her while she makes a call to set up an appointment or to find a meeting place for a self-help group. It might be helpful for you to drive her to the first appointment or meeting—to provide encouragement. If you have a serious drug problem, you need to find a way to get the courage that you will need to make an appointment or attend a meeting, so that you can begin to recover. Perhaps by confiding your concerns to a close friend, you could receive the encouragement that you need to start on the road to better health.

Interventions for Habitual or Compulsive Use

Successful interventions for drug use in the habitual and compulsive stages must be extensive and complex because of the physical, psychological, and social problems associated with chronic drug use (O'Brien, 1997). Interventions typically involve three stages—detoxification (eliminating the drugs from the system), rehabilitation (returning the person to effective levels of functioning and ending drug use), and follow-up (maintaining or improving a person's functioning and preventing relapse of drug use). Biologically based and psychologically based interventions are used at each stage (IM, 1997). Inpatient treatment during the detoxification stage and the early part of the rehabilitation stage may be necessary (IM, 1997).

Medications can be useful during the detoxification process for drugs such as nicotine, alcohol, and opiates. For example, detoxification from nicotine is helped by using nicotine patches or gum. Alcohol withdrawal, which can be life-threatening if not handled properly, is aided by benzodiazepines. Opiate withdrawal, which is painful but not life-threatening, can be eased through opiate-based drugs such as methadone (O'Brien, 1997). However, medications are not currently available during detoxification for cocaine or other stimulants, hallucinogens, inhalants, or cannabinoids (O'Brien, 1997).

Medications can also be effective during the rehabilitation stage for addressing the long-lasting changes in the brain that result from chronic drug use (O'Brien, 1997). For example, methadone can reduce craving for opiates, and naltrexone can block the effect of opiates, eliminating the benefits of taking them (IM, 1997). The antidepressant bupropion has been shown to reduce craving for nicotine, and naltrexone reduces craving for alcohol (O'Brien, 1997).

Conditioned withdrawal can lead to relapse of drug use during the rehabilitation or follow-up stages, and interventions based on classical conditioning can reduce the influence of conditioned withdrawal. This is done by repeatedly pairing aspects of the environment where drugs were previously taken with a therapeutic environment where no drugs are taken (e.g., a therapist taking an adolescent to the street setting where she once took drugs and sitting there for periods of time without taking drugs). With many pairings, the ability of the previous environment to produce the anticipatory physical responses that create feelings of withdrawal is gradually reduced (Higgins, 1997). Operant conditioning principles can also be used to encourage ongoing abstinence. For example, rewarding treatment participants with gift certificates when they have a clear drug screen through urinalysis can encourage abstinence (Higgins et al., 1993).

Many of the interventions described for instrumental drug use are necessary during the rehabilitation and follow-up stages of treatment. The issues that originally prompted drug use need to be addressed. In addition, extensive work may be needed to reestablish constructive relationships with friends and family members whom the adolescent is likely to have angered and alienated. Moreover, long-term drug use will have interfered with academic and social development, and strategies to overcome these deficits will be needed. Ongoing support groups may help the adolescent's reentry into a nondrug-using peer culture and may facilitate the development of prosocial skills. Twelve-step groups such as Alcoholics Anonymous and Narcotics Anonymous can provide support to some adolescents, although the efficacy of these programs for maintaining abstinence for adolescent drug users has not been tested (IM, 1997).

CHAPTER SUMMARY

Drug use by adolescents is widespread, although the amount of drug use among current adolescents is lower than it was in the 1970s and 1980s. Current surveys show that about half of all eighth-graders have tried tobacco and alcohol, nearly half of all twelfth-graders have tried marijuana, and that about one-fifth of all college students have used an illicit drug within the previous month.

Nowinski suggested that there are five stages of drug use: experimental, social, instrumental, habitual, and compulsive. One stage is distinguished from another by the primary motivation for using drugs at each stage. Although these stages can overlap, they are helpful because they allow us to consider different types of influences on drug use at each stage. For example, peer pressure is an important influence during the social stage but has little influence during the compulsive stage, where the primary influence is the change in brain functioning caused by long-term drug use. Understanding the variety of influences on drug use at each stage provides direction to programs for preventing drug use and helping adolescents whose drug use has become problematic.

Programs to prevent initial drug use and to prevent drug use from developing into drug abuse take place on several levels. Public policy can affect drug use—for example, by changing ages at which drugs can be consumed and raising the taxes on legal drugs such as alcohol and tobacco. Prevention programs taught during one year at school appear to have some short-term benefits, but, without ongoing follow-up prevention efforts, these one-time programs appear to have little influence on drug use and abuse in subsequent years. Many interventions have been used with adolescents who use drugs, and they differ with the type of use for which they are designed. Interventions range from efforts to reduce the negative consequences associated with drug use (avoid driving if you have been drinking) to inpatient programs to detoxify chronic drug users.

Revisiting Maureen

The progression of Maureen's drinking and other drug use seems to have followed a clear path that is similar to the one suggested by Nowinski. Her initial drinking seemed to be in the experimental and social stages, with the party providing an opportunity to experiment with drinking and gain some approval from her friends by drinking with them. During her experimental and social drinking, it is likely that Maureen was learning that alcohol could be helpful in other ways—it reduced her feelings of shyness in social situations and allowed her to enjoy them more. To the extent that she drank to reduce her shyness, Maureen's drinking could be classified as being in the instrumental stage, and her drinking was clearly in the instrumental stage when she drank to help herself fall asleep at night. Since, during this time, Maureen limited her drinking to weekend parties and times when she had difficulty falling asleep, it suggests that her drinking had not entered the habitual stage.

On entering college, Maureen's drinking appeared to be in the social and instrumental stages. She took new drugs when encouraged by her friends and enjoyed the camaraderie of taking these drugs with them; she also liked the physical and psychological effects of the drugs. As Maureen took several different drugs on a fairly frequent basis, her body began to accommodate to the effects of the drugs. The chronic physical changes brought on by this accommodation made it difficult for Maureen to stop using drugs when she became concerned about the frequency of her drug use. Her brief struggle to limit her drug use was also influenced by her friends who encouraged her not to worry about it—encouragement that might have been based partly on her friends' concerns about their own drug use. Maureen's continued drug use resulted in ongoing physical changes (e.g., tolerance, withdrawal), which provided strong motivation for even more drug use. Maureen appears to have resolved the negative emotions caused by her earlier concerns about her drug use by dismissing these concerns and deciding that her drug use was completely under her control. Maureens' increasing focus on her drug use raises concerns that her use may be slipping from the habitual stage into the compulsive stage.

- Are there specific indications that Maureen's drug use is excessive? What other information might be useful in determining whether her drug use is excessive?
- What types of interventions are needed if Maureen's drug use is to be reduced? Are there people who might be in the best position to help Maureen reduce her drug use? Would encouragement from certain people make Maureen *less* likely to reduce her drug use?
- Are there actions that could have been taken in high school to change the path of Maureen's drug use? (Try to avoid limiting yourself to answers such as "She should have been warned of the dangers of drug use.")

CHAPTER 9

Anorexia Nervosa and Bulimia Nervosa

Leslie was very excited about entering college. She had only a few friends in high school and was looking forward to a new environment where she could create a new, popular image. During orientation, she talked with members of the college varsity crew team, and they encouraged her to join the crew as a boatswain, because of her short, slight build. She threw herself into her classes when they began and was determined to become the varsity boatswain during her first or second year. Although there was a minimum weight for boatswains, she was about 5 pounds heavier than the minimum, and, at the encouragement of her coach and the other members of the crew, she began a diet. She lost 5 pounds fairly easily but found that keeping her weight down was more difficult. Her weight would often bounce up or down by 2 or 3 pounds during a week. She redoubled her efforts to reduce her eating, so that she could maintain the minimum weight. Although she was often very hungry, she ate only a small amount of food, in part because of the encouragement from her friends and in part because of her determination to make her body do what she wanted it to do. About halfway through her first year, she replaced the woman who was the boatswain because of her developing skills as a boatswain and her ability to keep her weight at the minimum (a goal that the other boatswain was unable to meet). Rather than feeling excited about becoming the varsity boatswain, however, Leslie felt increased anxiety about her weight and about the possibility that she might be replaced. She began to focus more and more on her weight, and she weighed herself several times a day. If she were even a half pound over the minimum weight at any time, she felt anxious and depressed. She began to find that even small amounts of food resulted in a temporary weight gain, and so she further restricted her eating. As she focused more and more on her weight, she found that she could not concentrate on her academic work. Her grades began to slip. Because of her inability to focus on her schoolwork, she began to devote more and more of her energy on her skills as a boatswain and on her weight.

Eventually, Leslie found that her hunger seemed to have disappeared. This made it easier for her to eat very little each day. She also discovered, however, that her weight had slipped below the minimum allowed for a boatswain. As this would make her ineligible to be the boatswain, she tried to eat a little more each day. However, she found that eating anything made her anxious, as she was concerned that she would begin to eat too much and would lose control of her eating. Although she tried to eat, she often found that she just could not. She struggled to eat as she had once struggled not to eat. Despite her efforts to eat more, her weight continued to decline, until she was very underweight and about 7 pounds below the minimum for a boatswain. Finally, two of her friends on the crew convinced her to let them take her to a nearby clinic for people with eating disorders. Her physical examination revealed that her body had begun to consume her muscle tissue to survive, including her heart muscle. She was admitted immediately to an inpatient clinic, where a slow process of refeeding began, and where she began psychotherapy.

Many children, adolescents, and adults struggle with anorexia nervosa or bulimia nervosa every year. In addition, many others who do not meet the specific diagnostic criteria for these disorders struggle relentlessly to control their eating or weight. Many more females than males struggle with eating disorders, and intelligent, high-achieving females are particularly likely to have an eating disorder (Attie & Brooks-Gunn, 1995). Odds are that almost everyone reading this text has either had significant problems with eating or has a friend who has had these problems. Many readers will be experiencing an eating disorder now or will be concerned about helping a close friend or roommate who has one.

The consequences of eating disorders can be severe and permanent (Steiner & Lock, 1998). Permanent damage to the heart and digestive system can occur. Preadolescent girls with anorexia nervosa may permanently lose their ability to ovulate. Death is the result for some people with eating disorders, either by suicide or because one or more of their body's systems simply stops functioning and cannot be restarted.

Early research and clinical work with adolescents who had eating disorders resulted in simple theories about their development. Some theories suggested that eating disorders were caused by society's expectation that females be thin, adolescents' desire to remain prepubescent or to have control over their lives, or the functioning of the adolescents' families (e.g., Bruch, 1973; Furnham & Manning, 1997; Minuchin, Rosman, & Baker, 1978). What is clear now, however, is that these theories provide only partial explanations for the development of eating disorders. Current theories suggest that eating disorders develop through a complex combination of biological, cognitive, emotional, family, and cultural issues, each of which can have a different influence at different times.

The Plan: After defining eating disorders, we will examine the prevalence and course of eating disorders. We will then look at the many consequences of eating disorders—some of which can be irreversible or life-threatening. In the main part of the chapter, we will explore the development of eating disorders. We will do this by using a four-stage, sequential model. This model will help us see the variety of influences on the development of eating disorders and the ways in which some of these influences are primarily important in one stage but may have little importance in other stages. Finally, we will examine efforts to prevent eating disorders and to intervene with adolescents who have them.

THE DEFINITION OF EATING DISORDERS

The *DSM-IV* specifies the diagnostic criteria for anorexia nervosa and bulimia nervosa (APA, 1994).

Anorexia nervosa is characterized by (a) purposeful starvation resulting in weight that remains at least 15 percent below the minimum normal weight for a person of a given age and height; (b) intense fear of becoming fat; (c) a distorted body image, a reliance on body size for self-evaluation, or denial of the seriousness of current low weight; and (d) in females, a failure to initiate menstruation or a loss of menstruation for at least three consecutive periods (APA, 1994).

Several changes in the diagnostic criteria for anorexia nervosa have occurred over the past two decades. The weight criteria changed in 1987 from 25 percent to 15 percent, representing the belief that such severe weight loss was not necessary for the diagnosis (APA, 1987). Early criteria required a distorted body image, such that the person perceived at least parts of her body to be larger than they were. However, subsequent research showed that many people who met the other criteria for anorexia nervosa did not have a distorted body image (e.g., Horne, Van Vactor, & Emerson, 1991). Some adolescents with anorexia nervosa even see their bodies as thinner than they are (Probst et al., 1998). Consequently, the characteristic about body image was broadened to include an excessive reliance on body image for self-evaluation or a denial of the seriousness of being underweight (Ponton, 1996). The diagnostic criteria for anorexia nervosa included two subtypes beginning in 1994: the binge-eating/purging subtype, in which occasional cycles of bingeing and purging occurs, and the restricting subtype, in which these cycles do not occur (APA, 1994).

Bulimia nervosa is characterized by cycles of bingeing followed by attempts to avoid weight gain by purging (e.g., vomiting or use of laxatives), excessive exercise, or fasting (APA, 1994). Binges are defined as discrete periods of time in which an amount of food is eaten that is "definitely larger than most people would eat" and during which the person feels a lack of control over her eating (APA, 1994, p. 549). The binges must occur, on average, at least twice a week for two months. In addition, the person's self-evaluation must be unduly influenced by body size and shape. The *DSM-IV* also includes a provisional category (a category that may be adopted in future editions of the *DSM*) of atypical binge eating. This is binge eating that occurs at least twice a week for at least six months and that is not accompanied by purging, excessive exercise, fasting, or other compensatory behaviors to avoid gaining weight.

Many adolescents have unhealthy patterns of eating that do not meet the diagnostic criteria for an eating disorder (Ponton, 1996). Polivy and Herman (1987) even suggested that, given the periodic or continuing dieting that characterizes the eating of most adolescent females, the normal eating patterns of female adolescents should be considered disordered eating. The development of these problematic eating patterns may be similar to the development of anorexia nervosa and bulimia nervosa, and they may respond to interventions useful in cases of anorexia nervosa and bulimia nervosa.

THE PREVALENCE AND COURSE OF EATING DISORDERS

Determining the prevalence of eating disorders is difficult, because many who have eating disorders try to keep them secret (Attie & Brooks-Gunn, 1995). Some adolescents with eating disorders are too embarrassed to seek help and, so, are not identified as having an eating disorder. Others are unwilling to participate in research, so community surveys may underestimate the prevalence of eating disorders (Beglin & Fairburn, 1992).

Prevalence

The prevalence of bulimia nervosa has been estimated to be 1 to 2.5 percent for adolescent and young-adult females, and the prevalence of anorexia nervosa is about 0.2 percent (Fairburn & Beglin, 1990; Whitaker et al., 1990). Interestingly, a higher percentage of children and young adolescents have anorexia nervosa than have bulimia nervosa (Robin, Gilroy, & Dennis, 1998).

Many adolescents engage in bingeing, purging, and restricting behaviors that may have health consequences but do not meet the severity or frequency requirements for a diagnosis of an eating disorder (Herzog et al., 1993; Steiner & Lock, 1998). For example, French, Story, and colleagues (1995) studied 36,000 seventh- to twelfth-graders and found that 12 percent of the females and 2 percent of the males had dieted at least 10 times in the previous year and that 15 percent of the females and 7 percent of the males had engaged in purging behavior in the past year. In a study of 5,500 high school students, Whitaker (1992) found that 63 percent of the females had dieted, that 17 percent of them had used diet pills, and that the average weight loss on a diet was 11 pounds.

The prevalence of eating disorders has increased significantly among adolescents and young adults over the past few decades. Lucas and his colleagues (Lucas, 1992) studied the prevalence of anorexia nervosa in Rochester, Minnesota, for 45 years. They found no overall increase in the prevalence of anorexia nervosa from the 1930s to the 1980s for the entire community. However, they did find a significant linear increase from the 1930s to the 1980s among females ages 15 to 24. Among 10- to 14-year-old girls, there was a decrease in prevalence from the 1930s to the 1950s, then a sharp increase since the 1960s.

Many more females than males have eating disorders. The ratio of females to males with anorexia nervosa is about 10:1; and with bulimia nervosa, about 5:1 (Attie & Brooks-Gunn, 1995; Steiner & Lock, 1998). However, some researchers argue that there may be more underreporting of eating disorders among males, because of their greater unwillingness to acknowledge that they have an eating disorder or their rationalization of eating-disordered behavior (e.g., "I eat this way only during wrestling season") (Carlat & Camargo, 1991). There is some suggestion that gay male adolescents may be at higher risk for developing an eating disorder (Andersen & Holman, 1997; Carlat, Camargo, & Herzog, 1997).

Eating disorders appear more common in those from families with higher incomes than in those from low-income families. However, this pattern appears to hold mostly for those above the age of 15—there appears to be little pattern based on family income in children under the age of 15 (Attie & Brooks-Gunn, 1995).

College students have higher rates of eating disorders than their peers who do not attend college. Surveys of college women have found rates of anorexia nervosa between 1 and 2 percent and rates of bulimia nervosa between 3 and 19 percent (Alexander, 1998). In one study, 61 percent of the college women reported problematic eating patterns that did not rise to the level of an eating disorder (Mintz & Betz, 1988). Some studies have reported higher rates of disordered eating among college women in sororities (e.g., Meilman, von Hippel, & Gaylor, 1991), but another study found no difference in disordered eating between college women in sororities and those not in sororities (Alexander, 1998).

Course

Eating disorders often first appear in adolescence. Attie and Brooks-Gunn (1989) found that many eating disorders first emerge soon after puberty in females. Halmi and colleagues (1979) found two peaks of age of onset of anorexia nervosa: 14.5 years and 18 years. However, it appears that there has been a trend over the past two decades for eating disorders to develop in many school-age children (Field et al., 1999). The courses of both anorexia nervosa and bulimia nervosa are variable. Some adolescents experience one relatively short occurrence of an eating disorder, but others struggle for years with one episode of an eating disorder or fluctuate between periods of healthy eating and periods of disordered eating (Steiner & Lock, 1998).

Patterns of disordered eating are often very resistant to change, with anorexia nervosa being even more resistant to change than bulimia nervosa. Over a period of one year, Herzog and colleagues (1993) found that only 10 percent of the patients with anorexia nervosa they studied had made a full recovery and that 56 percent of those with bulimia nervosa had made a full recovery. North, Gowers, and Byram (1997) interviewed 35 adolescents two years after their diagnosis of anorexia nervosa and found that 55 percent had made a good recovery, 39 percent continued to experience some eating problems, and 7 percent continued to have significantly disordered eating. Smith and colleagues (1993) interviewed 23 women six years after they had been hospitalized for anorexia nervosa and found that 43 percent met the criteria for an eating disorder at the time of the interview. Herzog and colleagues (1999) examined the recovery of females with anorexia nervosa and bulimia nervosa 7.5 years after diagnosis and found that only 33 percent of those with anorexia nervosa had made a full recovery; 74 percent of those with bulimia nervosa had made a full recovery.

THE PHYSICAL CONSEQUENCES OF ANOREXIA NERVOSA AND BULIMIA NERVOSA

Anorexia nervosa and bulimia nervosa have many physical consequences. Some consequences are irreversible, even if a person resumes healthy eating. The consequences to those who develop anorexia nervosa and bulimia nervosa in childhood or early adolescence are particularly severe (Attie & Brooks-Gunn, 1995). For example, some girls with anorexia nervosa may never menstruate.

The consequences of anorexia nervosa range from dermatological problems to changes in heart functioning. Skin is often dry, fingernails become brittle, scalp hair is thin and dull, and a downy type of hair—lanugo hair—may develop on the face and neck. The hands and feet may take on a bluish tint because of a lack of oxygen in the blood, or the skin may take on a yellow tint because of liver dysfunction (Kaplan & Woodside, 1987). The digestive system slows, resulting in constipation and a prolonged sense of fullness after eating. In severe cases, the digestive system may cease to work altogether (Kaplan & Woodside, 1987). Density and mineral content of the bones can become significantly reduced, particularly in adolescents with longstanding anorexia nervosa (Bachrach et al., 1990). This can lead to osteoporosis, and even young women's bones may become brittle and break easily. Heart rate and blood pressure are often significantly reduced (Kreipe & Harris, 1992). Growth retardation, delay in the onset of puberty, and structural abnormalities in the brain are common (Steiner & Lock, 1998).

The physical consequences of bulimia nervosa are also far-ranging. Skin damage and irritation from gastric juices can occur around the mouth. Tooth decay is caused by repeated exposure to stomach acid, and salivary ducts can become blocked (Kaplan & Woodside, 1987). Extensive damage to the mouth, throat, and esophagus from stomach acid occurs, and in severe cases the esophagus can rupture, causing death. Dehydration and electrolyte imbalances, caused by repeated vomiting, can harm many internal organs (Steiner & Lock, 1998). Stomach damage and hiatal hernias are common. The overuse of laxatives can impair the functioning of the bowel to the point where some adolescents with bulimia are unable to have a bowel movement without laxatives (Kaplan & Woodside, 1987).

Death occurs in some cases of anorexia nervosa and bulimia nervosa. Studies of adolescents with anorexia nervosa have reported mortality rates of 3 percent and 6 percent after follow-up periods of 5 and 12 years, respectively (Neumarker, 1997). About half of those who died had committed suicide; the other deaths were due to the physical consequences of anorexia nervosa, such as metabolic collapse, circulatory failure, and shock. Patton (1988) found a mortality rate of 3 percent among a group of adolescents and adults with bulimia nervosa.

THE DEVELOPMENT OF ANOREXIA NERVOSA AND BULIMIA NERVOSA

Of all the problematic behaviors discussed in this text, the literature on the development of eating disorders is perhaps the most complex and most difficult to summarize. Theories about the causes of eating disorders abound. Dozens of physiological, psychological, family, and cultural variables are related to eating disorders. In addition, most adolescents are concerned about their weight and most diet at one time or another, yet only a small percentage develop an eating disorder. Many characteristics of adolescents who develop eating disorders are found in adolescents who do not develop eating disorders. It is all very confusing.

To facilitate our understanding of the development of eating disorders, we will use a sequential model that involves four somewhat separate stages. Each stage has features that distinguish it from the others; however, the stages often blend into each other, so they are not completely distinct. The early stages of the model involve restrained eating and do not constitute an eating disorder. However, the biological and behavioral changes that occur during these early stages can lead to the development of an eating disorder. This model is similar in many ways to the model used to describe the development of compulsive drug use (see chapter 8). Many adolescents are involved in the early stages of the model (dieting, experimental or social use of drugs); the early stages are often condoned or encouraged by society or by an adolescent's peers; and a steadily decreasing number of adolescents continue to the next stage as the model progresses.

As with the other problematic behaviors discussed in this text, the model is based on the belief that adolescents make decisions about engaging in the behaviors at each stage. Adolescents decide to diet, decide to end or intensify their dieting, and decide to vomit after bingeing. Pressures to make decisions in certain ways can be very strong at each stage, however, so one cannot consider that an adolescent has complete free will when making any of them. Pressures that influence an adolescent's decisions at one stage may have little influence in others, and dividing the model into stages allows us to examine these influences more carefully. As with decisions made to take drugs, influences on decisions made during the early stages of the model come largely from the environment (e.g., reinforcement from friends to be thinner or to take drugs), and the influences on decisions made during later stages are increasingly influenced by a person's biology. A biologically based craving for food can encourage an adolescent with an eating disorder to binge, just as a biologically based craving for a drug encourages ongoing drug use.

As shown in figure 9.1, the four stages are

1. An adolescent decides to begin dieting, develops a strategy to lose weight, and puts it into action.
2. The dieting strategy leads to success (meaningful weight loss) or failure, and the adolescent decides to end the diet, continue it, or intensify it.
3. For some adolescents who decide to continue or intensify their dieting, the physical and psychological changes caused by extended dieting, in combination with the adolescents' personal characteristics, lead to prolonged food restriction and a preoccupation with food and weight.
4. The physical and psychological changes associated with prolonged food restriction and preoccupation with food and weight result in severely disordered eating patterns that constitute an eating disorder. The level of control that the adolescent has over her eating determines whether the eating disorder involves bingeing and purging.

Throughout the discussion of these stages, it will be important to keep in mind that each stage is affected by a combination of personal characteristics, family influences, and cultural influences (Ruderman & Besbeas, 1992). No one or two issues result in an eating disorder—it is not simply cultural pressures to be thin, dysfunctional families, or individual problems.

This model remains incomplete. In many ways, we do not know enough about eating problems to create a clear model describing their development. This model is a step forward, but many steps remain to be taken.

The Decision to Diet

The first stage of this sequential model involves an adolescent's decision to diet. Many factors can influence this decision. Some adolescents engage in healthy dieting (eating well-balanced meals and avoiding high-calorie snacks) to attain reasonable goals (e.g., they are currently overweight and want to attain a healthier weight). Little concern might be raised about these adolescents. Others, however, might diet even though they are currently underweight or might diet in an unhealthy way (e.g., eating only salads).

Cultural Influences

Cultural values about the importance of physical attractiveness and the role of thinness in physical attractiveness for females are clear to adolescents (Striegel-Moore, 1993). Magazines, movies, and television programs consistently reinforce the value of thinness by showing thin people as desirable and

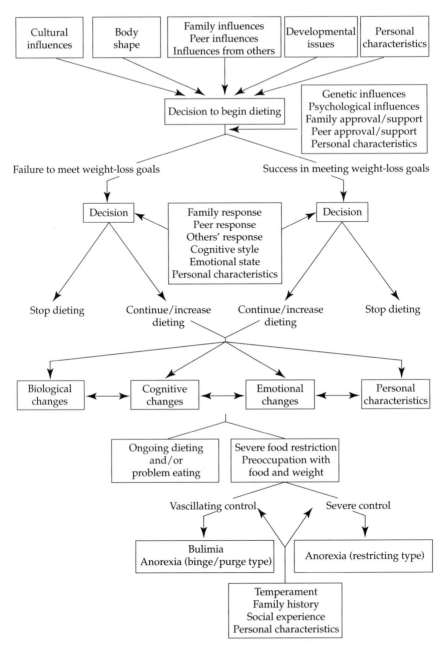

FIGURE 9.1. A model for the development of eating disorders.

happy and often by using people who are not thin in negative roles (Strong & Huon, 1998). In addition, many adolescents feel pressure to be thin, so that they can attract a boyfriend or girlfriend (Striegel-Moore, 1993).

Family and Peer Influences

Pressure to diet can come from family members and peers. Young adolescents who are dating are more likely to diet than those who are not dating (Cauffman & Steinberg, 1996). Adolescents in social groups that are more concerned about their attractiveness may experience considerable pressure to diet, particularly if they are concerned that they will be excluded from their social group if they are considered unattractive (Attie & Brooks-Gunn, 1995).

Parental encouragement to diet is even more potent on young adolescents' dieting than is peer encouragement to diet (Strong & Huon, 1998). Parents who want to have physically attractive children, who believe that their children would be happier if more physically attractive, or who are consistently concerned about their own weight are more likely to have children who diet (Attie & Brooks-Gunn, 1995; Pike & Rodin, 1991). Also, parents who are intrusive and overprotective, or who are disengaged and emotionally unavailable, have daughters who are more likely to diet (Attie & Brooks-Gunn, 1998). The underlying issue in these families appears to be the girls' lack of autonomy (Strong & Huon, 1998).

Body Shape

Adolescents with rounder shapes (primarily females) are more likely to diet than are those with thinner shapes (Davis et al., 1993; Graber et al., 1994). However, some adolescents (again, primarily females) with thin shapes diet to make themselves thinner overall or to reduce the size of specific body areas. Females who are dissatisfied with their body shape are at higher risk for the development of serious dieting and eventual eating disorders than are those who are satisfied with their shape (Attie & Brooks-Gunn, 1995; Strong & Huon, 1998), and adolescents who were teased as children about their body shape are more likely to diet than those who were not teased (Thompson & Heinberg, 1993).

Developmental Issues

Physical development at puberty can encourage many females to diet. The physical changes, which include breast development and increases in subcutaneous fat, can be very alarming for females who feel the need to be thin (Gross, 1984). The timing of physical changes is also important. They often occur as girls are making the first significant transition in their social lives—the move from elementary school to junior high school—where dating, relationships, and physical attractiveness are suddenly more important (Attie & Brooks-Gunn, 1995). Many girls report feeling adrift during this social transition and embrace the goal of physical attractiveness as one over which they have control and which will launch them successfully into their new social environment.

Personal Characteristics

Adolescents who feel insecure or who have low self-esteem may believe that being thin will help them achieve acceptance by others, and this may encourage them to begin dieting (Smolak & Levine, 1996; Striegel-Moore, 1993). This issue may be particularly important for females, as females tend to base their self-esteem on the success of their interpersonal relationships. Adolescents who are higher in perfectionism also are more likely to diet (Hewitt, Flett, & Ediger, 1995).

Dieting Success or Failure and the Decision to Stop or Continue Dieting

Some adolescents who begin to diet will meet their goals for weight loss, but others will not. Those who do not meet their weight-loss goals must decide whether to continue or intensify their efforts or to stop dieting. Similarly, adolescents who meet their weight-loss goals must decide whether to stop dieting or to maintain or intensify their dieting to lose even more weight. In this section, we will explore the influences on the success of meeting weight-loss goals and the influences on the decisions to stop or continue dieting.

As with the previous stage, adolescents in this stage are not considered to have an eating disorder; some engage in dieting that is healthy, while others engage in unhealthy dieting. The biological and behavioral changes experienced by those who decide to engage in long-term or rigorous dieting in this stage may begin to set the stage for the development of serious problematic eating during the next stage.

Failure or Success in Meeting Weight-Loss Goals

Dieting is difficult, as anyone who has been on a diet knows. Many dieters feel consistently hungry and spend much of their time thinking about the food that they are denying themselves. It is no wonder that most of us regularly fail to meet our weight-loss goals when we diet. However, the difficulty of dieting is not the same for everyone. Several biological, psychological, and social factors influence the extent to which an adolescent's attempts to lose weight will be successful. Adolescents have control over some of these factors, but not all of them.

Genetic Influences. Genes influence body size and shape. Adolescents whose dieting goals involve weight levels that are difficult to reach because of their genetically influenced body size may find it difficult to meet their weight-loss goals. This difficulty may decrease the likelihood of their meeting their goals (Attie & Brooks-Gunn, 1995).

Hunger and Self-Control. The sense of hunger occurs very quickly following the onset of a diet. The body and mind have evolved strong mechanisms to encourage eating when a person is hungry. Considerable self-control is required to overcome these mechanisms. Adolescents who are less able to deprive themselves in the face of hunger pains are more likely to fail to reach a weight goal.

Self-Reinforcement. As anyone who has dieted knows, losing a pound or even a fraction of a pound can be very reinforcing, particularly at the beginning of a diet. The pleasing response of initial weight loss can reinforce ongoing dieting. The dieting adolescent may initially feel an increase in self-esteem and pride because she has set a goal and is working successfully toward achieving it. This increase in self-esteem and pride may reinforce ongoing dieting and increase the chance of meeting weight-loss goals. On the other hand, adolescents who are unable to lose some weight quickly may become discouraged. Adolescents who are depressed or who seldom feel that they can control their lives may be particularly vulnerable to this discouragement. Discouragement and a lowering of self-esteem will likely reduce an adolescent's ability to meet her weight-loss goals.

Peer and Family Approval/Support. Reinforcement and support from friends and family can encourage dieting success (Strong & Huon, 1998). Comments about noticeable weight loss can encourage continued efforts to meet weight-loss goals. Compliments about an adolescent's control when she avoids eating lunch or snacks at social events can reinforce her dieting. Because many adolescents diet, each dieting adolescent may receive support from others and give support in return, and this can improve the chances of meeting weight-loss goals. Parents may focus attention on a dieting adolescent by monitoring her weight or providing low-calorie meals, and this attention can also encourage ongoing weight loss. Conversely, a lack of peer or family support for dieting, or the failure of anyone to notice and comment on initial weight loss, may discourage dieting and thus the ability to meet weight-loss goals. In some situations, however, parental discouragement can promote ongoing dieting efforts if the adolescent gains something by acting contrary to her parents' wishes.

The Decision to Stop Dieting or Continue Dieting

Adolescents who have started dieting are faced with the decision of when to stop. The decision may come at specific points, such as when a goal of losing 10 pounds is reached, or it may be an ongoing process occurring each day or perhaps at every meal. Those who meet their weight-loss goals may decide to continue dieting toward a lower weight, increase their food intake somewhat with the plan of maintaining their weight loss, or consider themselves successful and stop dieting. Those who do not meet their goals may increase their dieting efforts, or they may consider themselves as dieting failures and stop dieting. As with the other stages in this model, several factors may influence these decisions.

The Responses of Family, Peers, and Others. The responses of many people in an adolescent's life can influence her decision to stop or to continue dieting. Adults and peers who discourage ongoing dieting may dissuade an adolescent from continuing a diet; however, peers and parents who express ongoing dissatisfaction with the adolescent's body size may influence continued dieting (Strong & Huon, 1998). Positive responses to the adolescent's ability to restrict food intake may influence ongoing dieting, because these responses would stop if she were to resume normal eating. These positive responses may be particularly powerful for adolescents who receive few other positive comments from others. Adolescents who have failed to attain their weight-loss goals may be encouraged to redouble their efforts ("I know that you can do it if you'd just try harder"), which can encourage continued dieting. Adolescents in families and social groups in which perfection or high levels of success are expected may be particularly vulnerable to this argument (Hewitt, Flett, & Ediger, 1995). Adolescents may hear from others about a "rebound effect" in which they will regain some weight if they begin eating normally, and this may encourage them to lose weight beyond their weight-loss goal so that the rebound will not take them above their goal.

Positive responses from coaches, teachers, and others engaged in certain sports or activities (e.g., gymnastics, ballet) may encourage continued dieting. Comments about how thinner figures are always better, with no specifics about whether a point could be reached at which someone is too thin, may be particularly influential. Female and male college athletes report slightly higher rates of eating-disorder symptoms than do nonathletes (Hausenblas & Carron, 1999). Females in judged sports (e.g., gymnastics) are at a higher risk than those in refereed sports (e.g., soccer) for ongoing dieting (Zucker et al., 1999).

Cognitive Style. Certain styles of thinking may influence some adolescents to continue dieting. Dichotomous thinking, in which things are viewed as one or another extreme rather than throughout their range, may encourage ongoing dieting (Kales, 1989; Polivy & Herman, 1993). Adolescents with a dichotomous thinking style believe that they are either thin or fat. If they weigh even 1 pound over their weight goal, they believe that they are fat. This style encourages ongoing dieting because the adolescent must constantly be at or below her weight goal to avoid believing that she is fat (rather than believing that she is still thin but 1 pound heavier than she would like to be).

Egocentric thinking, in which an adolescent views herself as the center of attention, can encourage ongoing dieting. Adolescents with egocentric thinking may believe that any small, temporary weight gain will be observed by others and thus that they will be seen by others as failing. As a result, they are under strong pressure to remain at or below their weight goals.

Self-Worth. Adolescents with a greater sense of self-worth are less likely to continue dieting (Strong & Huon, 1998). It may be that they feel an increased sense of self-worth if they have reached a reasonable weight goal, and they may focus on other, more successful aspects of their lives if they are unable to reach their weight goal. Adolescents who are perfectionistic are more likely to continue dieting, and this may be related to a lower sense of self-worth when they compare their own views of perfection with what they see in themselves (Hewitt, Flett, & Ediger, 1995).

The Development of Prolonged Food Restriction and a Preoccupation with Food and Weight

In several controlled studies of restricted eating, researchers have taken healthy young adults, restricted their diets for several days to several months, and found many changes in the participants' biological, cognitive, and emotional functioning (e.g., Fichter & Pirke, 1986; Keys et al., 1950; Schweiger et al., 1986). Because these changes occurred in healthy individuals after a period of food restriction, a strong argument can be made that it was the food restriction that caused them. Many of these changes have also been noted in adolescents on extended diets. Ongoing dieting appears to make adolescents more unstable biologically and psychologically, and this lack of stability contributes to the development of prolonged food restriction and a preoccupation with food and weight, which can subsequently lead to the development of an eating disorder (Lowe, 1993; Polivy & Herman, 1993). In this section, we will explore these changes and the ways in which they can lead to prolonged food restriction and a preoccupation with food and weight.

Biological Changes

Studies of complete food abstinence for three weeks (Fichter, 1992) and food restriction to 1,000 calories per day (Schweiger et al., 1986) showed several neuroendocrine and neurotransmitter changes during food restriction, with a reversal of these changes after a subsequent period of normal eating. Many changes resulted in a lowering of the body's energy output and an improvement in the efficiency with which calories were absorbed and used by the body. Other changes increased the desire to eat and the willingness to obtain and consume food. For example, food deprivation may lead to increased physical activity—a response that may have benefited our distant ancestors who were starving and needed to seek food.

Levels of a luteinizing hormone, follicle-stimulating hormone, and growth hormone are all changed during food restriction. Levels of the neurotransmitters serotonin and norepinephrine are both reduced significantly, and shortened rapid eye movement (REM) latencies are observed during sleep. The daily cycle with which the hormone cortisol is released is changed. What is noteworthy about these changes is that they are all considered biological markers of depression (Fichter, 1992). This suggests that the depressed mood that many people feel when dieting may be the direct result of the biological changes initiated by reduced food intake.

Emotional Changes

Many emotional changes have been observed during food restriction (e.g., Keyes et al., 1950; Schweiger et al., 1986). The most notable emotional change is the increase in depression (Smoller, Wadden, & Stunkard, 1987). As noted in chapter 6, one of the symptoms of depression is heightened irritability, which is also commonly found during food restriction. Adolescents with bulimia nervosa overestimate their body size when they are feeling depressed (Kulbartz-Klatt, Florin, & Pook, 1999) and, as a result, may feel an even stronger need to restrict their eating.

An increase in emotional lability has also been associated with ongoing dieting. Moods can change quickly, and levels of depression and elation are heightened (Polivy & Herman, 1993). Small failures in dieting often evoke higher levels of emotion than would have been experienced earlier in a diet. Many of these changes in emotional functioning do not reverse soon after the resumption of normal eating; rather, they often remain for several weeks or months after normal eating resumes. This is noteworthy because the lack of a more satisfying mood soon after resuming normal eating may encourage the return to dieting.

Cognitive Changes

Personal styles of thinking that may encourage initial dieting can be heightened by ongoing dieting. Dichotomous thinking may be exacerbated, with the adolescent monitoring her weight closely and seeing any small increase as an indication that her diet is a failure. In addition, dichotomous thinking can result in any deviation from a strict diet being seen as a complete failure. Dieters who eat small amounts of high-calorie or other "forbidden" foods are likely to binge (Polivy & Herman, 1985). This may be partly the result of dichotomous thinking: "I have ruined my diet [after eating a small amount], so I might as well just eat all that I want."

Long-standing food restriction may also result in a dieter's thinking becoming more constricted, in part because of the depression she is experiencing (see chapter 6). As a dieter's thinking becomes more constricted, she focuses more and more on her diet, her weight, and the food she is trying to resist. Other aspects of her life can fade into the background as her self-image becomes increasingly based on her weight and her restricted eating.

Dieting also can alter a person's perception of the attractiveness of food overall or of certain types of food (Polivy & Herman, 1993). Whereas food might have been difficult to resist before, it now becomes so attractive that it is almost irresistible (Keyes et al., 1950). The enjoyment of the taste of food may be heightened, which further increases the desirability of food. At the same time, the dieter's cognitions can become completely focused on food. This can dull her inhibitions against eating and consequently can increase the likelihood that she will eat or binge on these foods that are highly attractive (Polivy & Herman, 1993).

Severe Food Restriction and the Development of an Eating Disorder

At this point in the four-stage model, we have an adolescent whose ongoing dieting has resulted in a series of interacting biological, cognitive, and emotional changes. The adolescent's personal characteristics interact with these changes to produce a person who is preoccupied with food restriction and weight. This preoccupation produces a strong psychological desire to continue severe food restriction, since it is only through this restriction that the adolescent can maintain a positive self-image. Opposing this psychological desire to continue food restriction, however, is a strong biologically based urge to eat based on millions of years of evolution. Consequently, the adolescent is caught between two very strong forces: a psychologically based urge to continue restricting food and a biologically based urge to consume food. These forces result in behaviors, biological functioning, and psychological functioning that constitute an eating disorder.

Most of those with eating disorders develop a cycle of bingeing and purging (Heatherton, Herman, & Polivy, 1991). Some are diagnosed with bulimia nervosa and others with anorexia nervosa (binge/purge type), depending on their other symptoms. Most research shows that dieting leads to the development of the binge/purge cycle (Lowe, 1993). After a period of food restriction, biological urges, operating through both biological and psychological mechanisms, create an irresistible urge to consume large amounts of food. The adolescent succumbs to this biologically based pressure and eats a large amount of food. In addition, bingeing relieves the depression and anxiety that extended dieters often experience (Elmore & DeCastro, 1990), so bingeing is negatively reinforced by the reduction in distressing emotions and hunger. However, the positive consequences of eating or bingeing are short-lived. Soon after eating, most dieters feel strong increases in distressing emotions (e.g., depression, anxiety) and distressing cognitions (e.g., "I'll become hugely fat") (Elmore & DeCastro, 1990). To reduce these emotions and cognitions, they purge. This relief is also short-lived, however, as distressing emotions and cognitions focused on the purging or on the overall binge/purge cycle return. As the adolescent continues her determined dieting, she repeats the pattern of eating to dispel hunger and purging to dispel the food she just consumed.

A minority of those with eating disorders do not binge and purge but restrict their food intake consistently. There is some indication that some adolescents who have severely restricted their eating for a considerable time are less sensitive to feelings of hunger (Lowe, 1993). These adolescents may feel less of an urge to eat or to binge, which may reduce their likelihood of developing a binge/purge cycle. However, this relative lack of hunger does not develop

BROADENING Perspectives

Why Purge, Knowing the Emotional Consequences?

One might ask why an adolescent would purge after eating, since she knows from past experience that she will experience distressing emotions after doing so. A reasonable answer is to consider her state before and after purging. They both involve uncomfortable emotions and cognitions. Her state before purging, however, also includes knowledge that she will be gaining weight—that all her previous efforts at dieting will be for naught (whether this knowledge is an accurate reflection of reality is debatable, but she still believes it). Therefore, it can be seen that her state after purging, no matter how negative it might be, is usually less negative than her state before purging. Why, one might ask, does she start the cycle once again by bingeing? It is because she succumbs to the irresistible biological urge to eat.

BROADENING Perspectives

An Alternate Route to Bingeing and Purging

Although binge eating and purging are most often preceded by extended dieting, they also occur in some people who do not diet. Some people who binge eat or are overly involved with food in other ways appear to have genetically influenced differences in neurotransmitter functioning that influence their eating (Drewnowski, 1995). Some binge eaters, as well as some who overeat regularly but do not binge, may develop the strategy of purging to maintain their weight at reasonable levels (Mitchell & Mussell, 1995).

quickly, and these adolescents may have had to endure many months of feeling the same biologically driven urge to eat that is felt by those who develop a binge/purge cycle.

The issues that influence whether an adolescent develops a binge/purge cycle or restricts food intake consistently have not been investigated extensively. Some differences have been found between the personal characteristics of those who binge and purge and those who restrict consistently, and some differences have been found in their families and their relationships with their parents (Attie & Brooks-Gunn, 1995; Connors, 1996; Laliberte, Boland, & Leichner, 1999). However, it is not clear how these differences affect eating styles. One interesting avenue of inquiry focuses on the consistency of the adolescent's control over her eating. The strong biological urges to eat erode most adolescents' control. Their control vacillates, and they find themselves in a binge/purge cycle. The length of time between binges may be an indication of the consistency of their control. A relatively small percentage of adolescents can maintain control over their eating consistently, despite their strong urges to eat, and they develop a consistent restricting pattern of eating. Since most adolescents who have severely restricted their food intake are unable to maintain control over their eating in the face of biological urges to eat, more adolescents develop binge/purge cycles than develop consistent restricting eating patterns. The specific personal, family, or social characteristics that influence whether an adolescent has vacillating or consistent controls over her eating remain unknown.

A Summary of the Stages in the Sequential Model

This section focused on a four-stage model for understanding the development of an eating disorder. None of the stages are clearly distinct from each other, but they provide a model for considering how different cultural, social, family, and individual characteristics can eventually result in the development of an eating disorder. The first stage involves an adolescent's decision to begin a diet—a decision often based on cultural, peer, and family pressures. Some adolescents have an easier time meeting their weight-loss goals, and the second stage focuses on whether the adolescent continues dieting after either meeting her weight-loss goals or failing to meet them. The biological, emotional, and cognitive changes associated with ongoing dieting, and the ways in which these changes focus the adolescent's attention on her weight and her diet constitute the third stage. The strength of the eating patterns that develop as the adolescent focuses on her weight and her diet results in an eating disorder, the fourth stage of the model.

THE PREVENTION OF EATING DISORDERS

Efforts to prevent anorexia nervosa and bulimia nervosa, as well as less severe forms of eating disturbances, have taken many forms. Primary prevention programs (those designed to prevent a problem from ever developing) have usually been aimed at early adolescents, while secondary prevention programs (those designed to prevent the exacerbation or continuation of a problem) are usually aimed at middle and late adolescents.

Most prevention programs are designed to counteract risk factors identified as increasing an adolescent's likelihood of developing problematic eating. For example, themes common among prevention programs include learning about the composition of healthy and unhealthy diets, understanding the role of the media in establishing body shape standards that are impossible for many females to attain, learning about the variety of body shapes and the genetic influence on body shape, feeling more comfortable with one's body shape, and resisting urges to diet in unhealthy ways (Piran, 1998).

Some prevention programs are presented as part of a junior high or high school's health curriculum. Programs for college students are presented through campus health centers, sororities, and other groups. Unfortunately, there is little evidence that prevention programs are effective. Several programs aimed at junior high school girls have shown some increase in knowledge about eating and eating disorders but little or no difference in eating or dieting behaviors (e.g., Killen et al., 1993; Moreno & Thelan, 1993). It may be that the many themes presented by the programs, and the limited time for the presentation of each theme, result in a relatively ineffective program for most of the participants (Ponton, 1996).

Concern has been raised that some prevention efforts may be counterproductive. For example, Carter and colleagues (1997) found that a group of 13- to 14-year-old girls reduced dieting behavior immediately after a prevention program but that six months later they had increased their dieting over the levels present before the prevention program. A program for undergraduates in which several students who had recovered from an eating disorder described their experiences to those who had never had an eating disorder resulted in increases in dieting among those who had participated in the program. The authors suggested that efforts to destigmatize disordered eating, so that the participants would be more willing to seek help for their disordered eating, may have inadvertently normalized the behavior (Mann et al., 1997)

Other types of efforts have been organized to identify adolescents with disordered eating and refer them for therapy. Ponton (1996) noted, for example, that primary physicians often miss the presence of disordered eating in their female adolescent patients and that efforts to encourage physicians to ask about eating and dieting behaviors might identify many adolescents whose disordered eating may develop into an eating disorder. As another example, student attendants in the gyms at Cornell University are instructed in ways to identify students whose exercise patterns suggest that they have an eating disorder (e.g., exercising for very long periods or when injured), and these students are approached by counseling staff.

THE TREATMENT OF EATING DISORDERS

Because of the biological, psychological, and social issues that adolescents with anorexia nervosa or bulimia nervosa face, treatment for these problems must be multifaceted (Steiner & Lock, 1998). Efforts to increase weight and stabilize metabolic functioning, change eating patterns, reduce troubling emotions, change destructive patterns of thinking, and improve family and social relationships are often needed. Several interventions may occur concurrently, with each focused on an important aspect of helping the adolescent return to healthy biological, psychological, and social functioning. For example, an adolescent with anorexia nervosa may see a nutritionist to monitor her physical functioning and weight and to help her create healthy daily menus. A psychologist might work with the adolescent to change dysfunctional cognitions and to help her struggle with

---

HELPING
YOURSELF AND OTHERS

Do All Dieting Adolescents Need Psychotherapy?

Because dieting behaviors, as well as weight, lie along a continuum, it is often difficult to determine whether psychotherapy, nutritional counseling, or another intervention is needed for a dieting adolescent. Woodside (1995) suggested several characteristics of a dieting adolescent that indicate the need for an intervention:

- Dieting that is accompanied by steadily increasing weight-loss goals (as opposed to the adolescent feeling satisfied when reaching a weight-loss goal)
- Dieting accompanied by increasing criticism of one's body (as opposed to feeling pleased with a body shape that many would consider improved)
- Dieting accompanied by social isolation
- Dieting accompanied by amenorrhea
- Dieting accompanied by purging

various emotions and changes in social relationships as she gains weight and eats healthier foods. The same psychologist or another therapist might work with the adolescent and her family to change problematic patterns of family functioning or to help the family support and monitor the adolescent's eating. A psychiatrist might consult about antidepressant medication.

Determining the effectiveness of treatment for anorexia nervosa and bulimia nervosa may be difficult. Success is often determined by changes in weight and eating patterns. However, often an assessment of the extent to which adolescents are content after treatment is not made, and many adolescents have felt coerced to gain weight or change their eating patterns (Jarman & Walsh, 1999).

Hospitalization

Hospitalization is an important intervention for some adolescents with anorexia nervosa and a small number of adolescents with bulimia nervosa. Hospitalization may be needed in cases of severe malnutrition and weight loss, when medical complications are present, when suicide or other psychiatric emergencies are present, or when the adolescent is severely depressed (Robin et al., 1998). A few years ago, hospitalization could last for several months, during which a "refeeding" process gradually helped the patient gain weight and reestablish healthy eating patterns. Currently, however, changes due to managed care programs often mean that hospitalization lasts only through an acute medical crisis—often a week or so (Robin, Gilroy, & Dennis, 1998; Steiner & Lock, 1998).

The primary goals of hospitalization are: (a) to save the adolescent's life if her biological functioning has become precarious and (b) to begin the process of recovery that will be continued in therapy after the adolescent leaves the hospital. Hospital interventions usually focus on helping the adolescent eat reasonable amounts of nutritious foods to begin the process of weight gain. Behavioral interventions are often used in this process. For example, patients can earn visiting or television privileges by eating appropriately, and may need to stay in bed, without visitors, when refusing to eat (Robin, Gilroy, & Dennis, 1998).

Partial hospitalization programs provide services to adolescents 8 to 12 hours a day, with their returning home to sleep. They are used when there are fewer immediate, severe concerns about the adolescent's physical health but when consistent monitoring of the adolescent's eating is needed. The goals of partial hospitalization are often similar to the goals of full hospitalization. Many partial hospitalization programs have been successful in helping patients achieve appropriate weight gain, and they are much less expensive than full hospitalization (Danziger et al.,1988).

Nutritional Counseling

Interventions by a nutritionist are usually focused on helping the adolescent create and follow a healthy eating plan. The nutritionist also monitors the adolescent's physical functioning, such as her weight and metabolic rate. The goals of these interventions are to continue the process of returning the adolescent to physical health and to facilitate improvement in the biologically based emotional and cognitive consequences of prolonged dieting, bingeing/purging, and starvation (Steiner & Lock, 1998).

Family Therapy

Family therapy is commonly used with adolescents who have anorexia nervosa or bulimia nervosa. The goals of various family therapy approaches differ, but most have the primary focus of helping the family function in a way that will promote the adolescent's ongoing recovery. Some family therapy approaches consider the eating disorder as resulting from problematic family functioning, and they work to change the family functioning in order to eliminate the need for the eating disorder within the family (e.g., Minuchin et al., 1975). Others focus on establishing the family as a force to help the adolescent regain her health, with the issue of why the adolescent has an eating disorder receiving little or no attention (e.g., Dare & Szmukler, 1991). Family therapy has generally been an effective treatment in cases of anorexia nervosa (Robin, Gilroy, & Dennis, 1998). Russell and colleagues (1987) found that family therapy was more effective than individual therapy in cases in which the onset of anorexia nervosa was below the age of 18 and was of short duration and that individual therapy was superior in cases with older clients.

Individual Therapy

Several styles of individual therapy have been used with adolescents with anorexia nervosa or bulimia nervosa. These strategies usually focus on exploring and changing cognitions or emotions that can impede healthy eating, on repairing social and family relationships, and on supporting the adolescent through the many difficult transitions she must make as she recovers from an eating disorder. Some therapists focus on a particular strategy, and some combine strategies when appropriate.

Cognitive-behavioral therapy has been widely used with adolescents who have anorexia nervosa and bulimia nervosa (Peterson & Mitchell, 1999). It focuses on enhancing self-esteem and exploring and changing the cognitions (e.g., "I must be thin to be liked") and thought patterns (e.g., dichotomous thinking) that can lead to food restriction. Adolescents may be asked to keep detailed records of their food intake and to monitor and record their thoughts about themselves, their eating, and their social relationships. Cognitive-behavioral therapy is often directive, with the therapist taking an active role in encouraging the adolescent to maintain healthy eating patterns and to change problematic patterns of thinking (Fairburn, Marcus, & Wilson, 1993). Cognitive-behavioral therapy has received considerable research attention and has been shown to be useful in many cases of bulimia nervosa and anorexia nervosa. About 75 percent of clients improve their eating patterns, and about 40 percent develop healthy

---

HELPING

YOURSELF AND OTHERS

If You or a Friend Has Problematic Eating

The earlier that problematic eating patterns can be stopped, the less likely it is they will develop into unyielding eating styles. Those struggling with eating problems that are not severe enough to be an eating disorder may benefit from consultations with a nutritionist or psychotherapist, and the consultations may provide increased control over healthy eating patterns. Those with severe eating problems often need the intervention of professionals to regain control over their eating.

If you have an eating problem or are concerned that you might be developing one, gather your courage and make an appointment with a therapist or nutritionist who can give you needed information about your diet and your eating. You may find that her help is very valuable. If you have a friend with problematic eating patterns, encourage her to see a professional. You may want to help her make the call for an appointment or accompany her to the first appointment, to show your support and concern. Raising your concerns with your friend can be difficult, but doing so is an indication of your friendship and a sign that you care. Many adolescents with eating disorders are worried about their eating and are relieved when someone shows concern and helps them make changes in their behaviors.

The health centers at most colleges have professionals who are expert in the area of eating disorders. Many community mental health centers also have experts on these disorders, particularly those focused on adolescent health or women's health. Call and find someone who can help.

---

eating patterns that continue for months or years after therapy (Peterson & Mitchell, 1999).

Psychodynamic individual therapy is less directive than cognitive-behavioral therapy. It focuses on helping the adolescent explore concerns about her identity, her interpersonal issues with family members and peers, her ability to cope with challenges, and the role of weight and size in these issues (Robin, Gilroy, & Dennis, 1998). Therapists focus less on promoting changes in eating patterns and more on helping the adolescent understand the role that food plays in her life and her ability to modify that role. A few assessments of psychodynamic individual therapy have shown it to be effective in many cases of anorexia nervosa; it has not been evaluated in the treatment of bulimia nervosa (Robin, Gilroy, & Dennis, 1998).

Psychopharmacological Interventions

Some drugs have been used in the treatment of adolescent eating disorders, but their effectiveness has not been evaluated systematically (Steiner & Lock, 1998). In some cases, medication works effectively in conjunction with other forms of therapy. Antidepressant medication has been used to reduce depression, particularly during long-term recovery to prevent a relapse of problematic eating. Low doses of antipsychotic drugs have been used in a small percentage of cases to reduce obsessional thinking about food.

CHAPTER SUMMARY

Anorexia nervosa is an eating disorder characterized by purposeful starvation, intense fear of becoming fat, problems with body image, and loss of menstruation in females. About 0.2 percent of all adolescent and young adult females have anorexia nervosa. Bulimia nervosa is characterized by cycles of bingeing and purging that occur at least twice a week for at least two months. Estimates of the prevalence of bulimia nervosa among adolescent and young-adult females range from 1 to 2.5 percent. There is a higher prevalence of anorexia nervosa and bulimia nervosa among females than males and a higher prevalence among females in college than among the same-age females not in college.

The physical consequences of anorexia nervosa and bulimia nervosa can be severe and permanent. The consequences of anorexia nervosa include changes in heart rate and blood pressure, decreased bone density, growth retardation, changes in skin color and texture, and growth of facial hair. The consequences of bulimia nervosa include damage to the mouth, throat, and esophagus from vomiting; damage to the digestive system from the use of laxatives; and damage to vital organs from electrolyte imbalances. Death is a consequence for 3 to 6 percent of those with anorexia nervosa or bulimia nervosa.

This chapter presented a four-stage model for the development of anorexia nervosa or bulimia nervosa. Individual, family, social, and cultural issues influence each of these stages, with some issues having primary influence at one stage but little influence at others. As with the development of other problems discussed in this text, each of these stages involves decisions made by the adolescent. The first stage is the decision to diet, a decision often made because of cultural, peer, or family pressures. In the second stage, several issues influence the extent to which the adolescent can successfully meet her weight-loss goals. Those who successfully meet their weight-loss goals must decide whether to stop dieting, increase their food intake slightly so that they do not regain weight, or set a lower weight-loss goal and continue dieting. Those who do not meet their weight-loss goals must decide whether to stop dieting or redouble their efforts. In the third stage, adolescents who continue dieting for an extended period begin to experience changes in their biological functioning, their emotions, and their thinking. These changes often focus their attention on their weight and on their food restriction. In the fourth stage, as they struggle to maintain their restricted eating, some adolescents succumb to their biological urges to eat, often in large amounts. Many of these adolescents then purge the food to avoid gaining weight. This often develops into the binge-purge cycle that is bulimia nervosa or anorexia nervosa (binge/purge type). Some adolescents can maintain their food restriction, and this develops into anorexia nervosa (restricting type).

Given the many influences on the development of anorexia nervosa and bulimia nervosa, treatment for these disorders is multifaceted and often extends over a long period of time. Hospitalization is required when an adolescent's life is in peril or when she is unable to change her eating patterns in outpatient treatment. Several forms of individual and family therapy have been found effective.

Revisiting Leslie

Leslie's development of anorexia nervosa followed a pattern similar to that of many adolescents. She began dieting for a purpose related to her social interactions and self-esteem. Being on the crew was important to her, and she was willing to diet to attain her goal. Although she attained her initial weight-loss goals, she struggled to maintain her weight loss. As she continued to struggle with eating, she found that much of her energy was focused on her weight and on her food restriction. She became less focused on other issues, increasing the importance of weight in her life. Feelings of depression and anxiety increased, probably due in part to her decreased food consumption. Her mood further exacerbated her struggles with eating. At some point, Leslie experienced what many with anorexia nervosa experience—a shift from the struggle to avoid eating to the struggle to eat. Eating even small amounts of food had such strong meaning to her, and evoked such strong emotions, that she found herself unable to eat as much as she wanted. Luckily for Leslie, two of her friends intervened on her behalf and were able to take her to a hospital before the development of life-threatening health problems.

- What forms of positive and negative reinforcement did Leslie experience for restricting her eating?
- What biological or psychological changes resulted in Leslie's inability to eat, even when she wanted to?
- Were there signs that Leslie's friends might have noticed earlier that would have encouraged them to help Leslie seek help for her problematic eating?

CHAPTER 10

Physical Aggression

Within days of entering a preschool program, it was clear that Mary was a very aggressive child. She lashed out at other children, and they became afraid of her and avoided her when she tried to play with them. This often led to additional angry and aggressive outbursts. One day Mary went to school with welts on her legs, and the school administrator informed the state's child protective services. A subsequent investigation showed that Mary had been repeatedly beaten by both her mother and father. She was removed to a foster home, where she lived for one year. She was then returned to her parents but was removed again two years later, when a teacher took her to the hospital because of a head injury.

Throughout elementary and junior high school, Mary was in periodic trouble for threatening others, and she had an explosive temper. She was often in trouble for fighting in physical education courses. She always claimed that the other student had initiated the fighting and that she was just defending herself, but her teachers reported that the other student was usually just playing the game according to the rules. Mary often fought with other foster children in her foster home and occasionally threatened her foster parents. As a result, Mary was moved from one foster home to another, and she never lived in any foster home for more than two years.

Mary had no friends until she was a freshman in high school, when she started hanging out with three other aggressive students—two of whom were juniors. It was assumed that she and her friends were responsible for vandalism around their high school, but they were never caught. It was also well known among the students that Mary was extorting money from several freshmen by threatening them with physical harm. When she was a sophomore, Mary and two of her friends stole money from several people and left town. Mary's foster parents and classmates never heard from her again. Most people were relieved that Mary had left, and many felt that, if she had been put in jail or had met some type of violent end to her life, she had gotten what she deserved.

Negative images often come to mind when people think about aggression. However, there is also a positive side to aggression, and many of our social institutions encourage and nurture aggression, particularly in adolescents. Coaches pressure high school and college athletes to be aggressive, and even members of the chess and math clubs are encouraged to be aggressive in their tournaments. The army expects aggression in its soldiers, the youngest of whom are adolescents or young adults. Fans cheer for the most aggressive players on the field or ice and call for the removal of those who are not being aggressive enough. Even home-team players who give another player a "cheap shot" often receive cheers of approval.

In our society, aggression is usually viewed positively in situations in which everyone agrees to be aggressive: the boxing ring, lacrosse field, and battlefield. It is often viewed negatively where not everyone agrees to be aggressive: the golf course, a party, or a tavern. Interestingly, our society has come to expect adolescents to turn their aggression on and off almost instantly as they move from one situation to another. The soldier, football player, and field hockey player are expected to abstain from aggression as soon as they leave the battlefield or playing field. The basketball player with an "in-your-face" style of play is expected to stop being aggressive when she leaves the basketball court. It is not clear whether this is a reasonable expectation.

The focus of this chapter is on the development of physical aggression. As just noted, not all aggression is problematic, and, as discussed in chapter 2, a value judgment is needed to decide whether an act of aggression is problematic. Societies and cultures can differ in their judgment of whether some forms of aggression are problematic, and groups and individuals within societies and cultures may have widely different views about certain types of aggression (Feshbach, 1997). These views may be influenced by tradition or the necessities of current living situations. Consequently, as we discuss the development of aggression, we must be mindful that some of the aggression we discuss will be designated as problematic by some in our society, but not by all.

Two general strategies have been used to study aggression—official arrest reports and self-report surveys. Official arrest reports underestimate aggression. Only 15 to 30 percent of violent and aggressive offenses result in an arrest, and first arrests typically take place after a person has been offending for months or years (Coie & Dodge, 1998; Huizinga & Elliott, 1987). Self-report surveys reveal a more accurate picture of aggression than do arrest reports. However, even self-report surveys underestimate aggression, especially severe forms of aggression and aggression that adolescents want to remain hidden. Adolescents may be hesitant to describe their own aggression honestly, even if promised that their reports will be confidential. Finally, the two strategies often result in different views of aggression. For example, arrest records show a much larger difference between the frequency of aggression committed by African American adolescents and that committed by European American adolescents than do self-report surveys, because minority adolescents are more likely to be arrested (Coie & Dodge, 1998).

The Plan: As with all other chapters, we will first explore the definition of aggression. We will next examine the characteristics of problematic adolescent aggression and the influence of gender and age on its prevalence. The main part of the chapter focuses on the development of aggression. As with other problems explored in this book, however, the development of aggression is too complex to explore as if it were one large issue. Consequently, we will consider the development of aggression in the following way. First, we will focus on four patterns of aggression: aggression that remains consistent throughout childhood and adolescence, aggression that increases through childhood and adolescence, aggression that decreases through childhood and adolescence, and aggression that becomes a problem for the first time in adolescence. Next, the many influences on aggression are described. Then, we will explore which of these influences are most likely to affect each of the four pathways. Exploring the development of aggression in this way should give us a clearer view of the complexity of adolescent aggression. Finally, we will examine interventions to prevent or reduce adolescent aggression.

THE DEFINITION OF AGGRESSION

In the research literature, aggression is generally considered behavior designed to harm or injure another person (e.g., Bushman, 1993; Loeber & Stouthammer-Loeber, 1998). Intent to harm is required in many definitions of aggression to distinguish it from accidents (Coie & Dodge, 1998). In its broadest sense, aggression does not have to be physical. For example, Crick (1995) studied relational aggression in girls, consisting of the exclusion of peers from social groups, gossip, and other forms of character defamation. Some researchers consider aggression to include threats to inflict harm (e.g., Loeber & Hay, 1997), although others do not (e.g., Johnson, 1996; Vitielo & Stoff, 1997). Harm to self (e.g., suicide) or to the property of others is also considered aggression by some researchers (e.g., Young et al., 1994), but not by others.

Some authors distinguish between aggression and violence. For example, Loeber and Stouthammer-Loeber (1998) define violence as aggression that causes serious harm, such as aggravated assault or murder. Other authors use the terms interchangeably or simply refer to aggression without mentioning violence (e.g., Lore & Schultz, 1993; Shaw & Campo-Bowen, 1995).

In this chapter, we will focus on physical aggression toward others, so will not consider suicide, property damage, character defamation, and nonphysical forms of aggression. We will focus on overt forms of aggression rather than threats of aggression. When it is used, *violence* will refer to more severe forms of aggression.

THE SUBTYPES OF AGGRESSION

Much of the research on aggression has been conducted with animals other than humans. Several subtypes of aggression have been identified in these animals,

Instrumental and Affective Aggression

Although instrumental and affective aggression are controlled by different parts of the brain in many animals, they are clearly related and people can move from one to the other quickly. Consider one of the goals of "talking trash" in many athletic events: moving another player from instrumental to affective aggression. To the extent that a basketball player can be made angry or frustrated, she may begin to engage in affective rather than instrumental aggression on the court. Not only may she hit another player and be ejected from the game, but her focus will be shifted from the controlled, purposeful instrumental aggression needed for her to perform well to anger-driven, affective aggression.

including predatory, intermale, territorial, maternal, irritable, fear-induced, and instrumental. Each subtype involves distinct behavioral patterns, and each can be activated or suppressed by stimulating specific parts of the brain (Vitielo & Stoff, 1997). Animal aggression has also been divided into two larger categories: predatory and affective. Predatory aggression is proactive and offensive, and it involves little arousal, such as a cat stalking and pouncing on a mouse. Affective aggression is reactive and defensive, and it involves high levels of arousal, such as the furied attack by the same cat when a dog backs it into a corner.

Human aggression has commonly been classified into these same two categories, although different labels for them have been used. Predatory aggression is often called instrumental aggression, although it has also been called covert, proactive, offensive, or controlled aggression. The label of affective aggression is commonly used for both humans and other animals, although this type of aggression has also been called hostile, overt, reactive, defensive, or impulsive aggression (Shaw & Campo-Bowen, 1995). Instrumental aggression is characterized by low levels of arousal and is generally focused on achieving a goal other than physical harm to the victim, such as winning a game or stealing a purse. Affective aggression is typically accompanied by fear or anger and high levels of arousal. It is often unplanned and impulsive and can escalate quickly to levels never intended by the aggressor (Vitielo & Stoff, 1997).

While a few adolescents engage primarily in one type of aggression, most engage in both types (Dodge & Coie, 1987). In addition, many acts of apparently instrumental aggression have a hostile component. This suggests that, although many acts can be primarily instrumental or affective aggression, both types are present to some degree in most aggressive situations (Vitielo & Stoff, 1997).

THE CHARACTERISTICS OF HUMAN AGGRESSION

Stability of Aggression

When the term *stability* is used in social science research, it does not refer to the extent to which a behavior stays the same across a person's lifetime.

Rather, *stability* refers to the extent to which the ranking of individuals within a group on the behavior stays the same over time. For example, a researcher might gather a teacher's ratings on the aggressiveness of a class of kindergarten children and rank the children from the most to least aggressive. If the researcher then were to gather teachers' ratings of aggressiveness for the same children in the third, fifth, and seventh grades, a measure of the stability of their aggression would be obtained by analyzing how similar the rankings were over time. Even if the aggression of the entire group were to drop from kindergarten to the seventh grade (as typically happens), there would still be high stability of aggression if the rankings remained similar over time.

Aggression is highly stable for both males and females, and it is often as stable as characteristics such as intelligence (Coie & Dodge, 1998). Young children ranked high on aggression are ranked high on aggression as adolescents and then as adults. For example, Huesmann and colleagues (1984) found high levels of stability when comparing peer ratings of aggression in 8-year-old boys, peer ratings of the boys' aggression at age 18, and their wives' ratings of their aggression when they were 30.

Age Patterns of Aggression

Patterns of aggression often begin early in life. For example, Loeber and Hay (1997) studied aggressive children and found that regular patterns of aggression had emerged by age 2 years for 55 percent of the boys and 41 percent of the girls, with an additional 25 percent of the boys and 34 percent of the girls showing patterns of aggression by age 5.

Minor aggression, such as pushing or hitting, decreases for many children when they enter school at age 4 or 5, and continues to decline gradually during the school-age years. There is a sharp increase in physical fighting during early adolescence, particularly for boys, with a subsequent reduction in fighting during middle and late adolescence. Rates of aggression for boys peak around age 16 and decline quickly after that. Rates for girls peak around age 13 and decline slowly and steadily throughout adolescence (Cairns, et al., 1989; Elliott, Huizinga, & Morse, 1987; Loeber & Hay, 1997).

However, while minor forms of aggression often decline during adolescence, serious and violent forms of aggression increase dramatically for some adolescents. Self-reported rates of criminal violence peak between ages 16 and 18 for males and 13 and 15 for females, and the highest rates of aggravated assault and other forms of criminal violence occur during adolescence and young adulthood (Campbell, 1994). In addition, increased strength and the use of weapons result in higher rates of injury or death after physical confrontations between adolescents (Loeber & Hay, 1997). Consequently, adolescence is when the clearest distinctions in aggression emerge: most adolescents engage in less aggression than they had as children, but a few adolescents engage in more aggression and more serious aggression (Loeber & Stouthammer-Loeber, 1998).

Gender and Aggression

Few differences exist between the amounts and types of aggression initiated by boys and that initiated by girls before age 3 years. Beginning at about age 3, boys engage in more aggression than girls, and this difference holds across socioeconomic groups and cultures (Coie & Dodge, 1998).

Boys continue to be more physically aggressive than girls during the school-age years. Two lines of research are worth noting, however. As already mentioned, Crick (1995) found that school-age girls engage in more verbal aggression, gossip, and character defamation than boys. Thus, it may be that girls can be as hostile to their peers as boys, just hostile in different ways. Also, Pepler and Craig (1995) studied bullying by boys and girls on school playgrounds: (a) girls reported that they engaged in less bullying than boys, (b) playground observers reported less bullying by girls than boys, but (c) observations of bullying made surreptitiously with wireless microphones found no differences between the amounts of bullying done by boys and girls. This research suggests that girls may be better than boys at hiding their physical aggression.

Differences between the amounts of male and female aggression grow during adolescence. Arrest records and self-reports show that three to nine times as many males as females engage in aggression (Campbell, 1994). Conflicts between females tend to become less violent during adolescence, whereas the level of violence and confrontation among males does not decline (Cairns & Cairns, 1994). In addition, cross-gender aggression increases dramatically during adolescence—with far more cross-gender aggression initiated by males than females (Loeber & Hay, 1997).

Characteristics and experiences during childhood that predict higher levels of aggression in adolescence may be different for boys and girls. One study found that early academic problems was the strongest predictor of later aggression for girls; peer rejection was the best predictor for boys (Lewin, Davis, & Hops, 1999). This suggests that similar experiences may have different influences on the development of aggression in boys and girls.

THE DEVELOPMENT OF PHYSICAL AGGRESSION

There are many influences on the development of problematic physical aggression. Some influences are primarily biological, others are based on cultural or social expectations, and others are based on individuals' experiences within their cultural, social, or family contexts. Consequently, exploring the development of aggression in adolescents is a complex process.

We will use the following strategy to cope with this complexity. First, we will examine four pathways to aggression across childhood and adolescence. We will then discuss the variety of influences on the development of aggression. Finally, we will look at the influences that are most likely to be important in the development of each pattern of aggression. This should help us explore the complexity of the development of aggression in a more structured way.

Pathways to Adolescent Aggression

In their ongoing longitudinal study of aggression in children and adolecents, Loeber, Stouthammer-Loeber, and their colleagues described four pathways to aggression (e.g., Loeber & Hay, 1997; Loeber & Stouthammer-Loeber, 1998):

1. An onset of aggression in early childhood with an ongoing decline of aggression during childhood and adolescence
2. A generally consistent pattern of aggression beginning in early childhood and continuing through adolescence
3. Aggression that begins in early childhood and increases in intensity and frequency during adolescence
4. A pattern of aggression that emerges for the first time in middle to late adolescence (although incidents of aggression occur in childhood)

Most people in the United States follow the first pathway, and the fourth pathway seems to occur relatively rarely. The percentages that follow each pathway are unknown, however. These patterns suggest that our exploration of the development of aggression needs to address several questions: (a) what influences result in unusually high aggression in some children, (b) what influences encourage the onset of aggression in adolescence among those who have largely been nonaggressive as children, (c) what influences result in increases in aggression during adolescence, and (d) what influences result in a decrease of aggression in adolescence.

Influences on the Development of Aggression

The influences on aggression are often divided into those that are biologically based and those learned through the environment. However, biological and environmental influences cannot be thought of as completely separate, since they often interact (Pepler & Slaby, 1994). For example, genetic influences can make a person more reactive to environmental learning that encourages aggression (Goldsmith & Gottesman, 1996). Alternately, environmental stimuli, such as being in a dominant relationship to others, can increase levels of testosterone in males (Archer, 1994). Therefore, it is important to consider the ways in which biological and environmental influences work together to encourage aggression.

As with the other problematic behaviors discussed in this text, no single factor causes aggression in an individual—aside from rare situations in which a brain injury has a fundamental influence on aggression. Instead, each influence is best thought of as a risk factor—an influence that increases the likelihood that an individual will be aggressive. Research has consistently shown that individuals with more of these risk factors are more likely to be aggressive than are those with fewer risk factors (Loeber & Hay, 1997).

Biological Influences on Aggression

Several biologically based characteristics influence aggression. Genes influence some of these biologically based characteristics, while other characteristics are influenced by environmental factors and injuries.

Genetic influences. The influence of genes on adolescent aggression remains unclear (Coie & Dodge, 1998; Loeber & Stouthammer-Loeber, 1998). Twin and adoption studies have shown genetic influences on aggression in adulthood and on delinquent behavior in childhood and adolescence. However, a clear influence of genes on childhood or adolescent aggression has not been found (Young et al., 1994).

Even in adults, no evidence of an aggression gene exists (Goldsmith & Gottesman, 1996). Rather, a combination of genes appears to influence characteristics such as impulsivity and emotional reactivity, which can increase the likelihood of aggression. A person's environment and experience act in combination with these genetic predispositions to create patterns of behavior. As a result, a genetic predisposition may influence different patterns of behavior, depending on a person's learning. Goldsmith and Gottesman (1996), for example, suggest that the same genes that influence a mugger to impulsively grab a woman's purse and disappear down a dark alley can influence a police officer to immediately dash down the dark alley in pursuit without much thought to her safety.

Temperament influences. *Temperament* refers to basic styles of relating to the environment and other people. Temperament styles are often apparent from very early in life and, so, are believed to be primarily genetically based. Children with a fearless, uninhibited temperament or an uncontrolled, impulsive temperament are more aggressive than children with other temperaments (Henry et al., 1996; Pepler & Slaby, 1994). These children are often more difficult to socialize, and they respond less to reinforcement and punishment from parents and other adults. They often seek out novel, risk-taking activities, and aggression often becomes part of the excitement and daring that they seek. In addition, the parents of young children with difficult temperaments often become permissive in the face of their children's behavior, and this can lead to steadily increasing aggression (Olweus, 1980).

Hormonal influences. The influence of testosterone on aggression has been investigated extensively, because of heightened aggression in males and an increase in aggression around the time of puberty. Testosterone can influence aggression in several ways. At the biological level, testosterone appears to diminish neurotransmitters that inhibit behavior, thus increasing the chance of impulsive behavior (Loeber & Stouthammer-Loeber, 1998). At a social level, children with higher levels of testosterone may engage in more active, rough-and-tumble play. These early peer group preferences may be maintained through childhood and adolescence, resulting in higher levels of activity and aggression (Maccoby, 1988).

However, several lines of research suggest that testosterone may have only an indirect influence on aggression in boys and young adolescents. Schall and colleagues (cited in Coie & Dodge, 1998) found that boys who were social leaders had higher levels of testosterone, even if they were not physically aggressive, and that boys who were aggressive but not leaders had testosterone levels no higher than those who were neither leaders nor aggressive. They suggested that testosterone may be primarily associated with social leadership or dominance but only indirectly related to aggression because some socially dominant boys were aggressive toward lower-status boys. Similar conclusions were reached by Tremblay and colleagues (1998), who found that testosterone was related to social dominance in boys and that physical size was related to higher levels of aggression, regardless of testosterone levels.

Research with adult prisoners and military veterans has shown a positive correlation between higher levels of testosterone and aggression. However, similar studies with adolescents have presented mixed results, and it appears that the influences of testosterone and aggression may be bidirectional (Coie & Dodge, 1998). For example, artificially increasing testosterone has resulted in heightened aggression in some studies, suggesting that testosterone influences aggression (Archer, 1994). However, males who win games, even when the results are artificially manipulated or due to chance, often have higher levels of testosterone after the competition but not before the competition. This suggests that being dominant in a social situation can increase testosterone (McCaul, Gladue, & Joppa, 1992).

The influences of brain injuries or abnormalities.   Animal studies have shown that lesions to certain brain structures can increase or inhibit aggression (Vitielo & Stoff, 1997). In addition, autopsies on unusually violent humans and brain scans and neuropsychological testing on aggressive adolescents and adults have shown injuries or abnormalities in several areas of the brain (Young et al., 1994). For example, damage to the hypothalamus can produce uncharacteristic feelings of rage, which can result in violence that a person regrets afterward. Damage to the amygdala has resulted in intense anger following minor problems or confrontations, with aggression occurring occasionally. Injury to several areas of the prefrontal cortex can result in impulsive behavior, including aggression (Lueger & Gill, 1990; Young et al., 1994).

The influences of alcohol.   In low doses, central nervous system depressants such as alcohol appear to promote aggression. The ways in which this occurs remain unclear, however. When reviewing the laboratory studies of alcohol and aggression, Bushman (1993) found that the strongest effect of alcohol occurred when a person was given alcohol and knew that he or she was drinking alcohol. Thus, it appears that both the physiological and psychological effects of drinking alcohol are needed to promote aggression. The effect of alcohol consumption on aggression might result from reduced inhibitions, decreased self-awareness, or decreased ability to make an accurate assessment of the risks and benefits of various behaviors.

The biological influences of child abuse.   Perry and colleagues (e.g., Perry et al., 1995) have argued that severe child abuse and other traumatic experiences can result in abnormal brain development in infants and young children, as well as changes in brain functioning in older children. One outcome of the repeated fear and anger experienced by abused children is that many neural connections for experiencing these emotions are created in the brain. As a result, the brain becomes more sensitive to these emotions, and they are more easily evoked in a wide range of situations. Perry has shown that, when abused boys are asked to describe their abuse experiences, they have a general increase in autonomic nervous system functioning similar to that experienced during affective aggression. Maltreated girls, interestingly, often have the opposite reaction when describing their experiences, with a decrease in CNS functioning. Thus, maltreatment may make children, especially boys, experience increased emotional arousal to stressful situations and act more aggressively when they occur.

Delville, Melloni, and Ferris (1998) provided an interesting animal model of the influence of physical abuse on adolescent aggression. They found that adolescent hamsters that were physically attacked daily by an adult later developed a submissive style when around other adults but an aggressive style toward younger hamsters. They found density increases in the parts of the hypothalamus associated with aggression in these adolescent hamsters, which may have resulted from the abuse they experienced and which subsequently influenced their style of behavior.

Cultural Influences on Aggression

The culture in which a child is raised can influence the likelihood of her being aggressive in many ways. Cultures in which aggression is prized, allowed, or necessary may provide a background against which aggression is more easily learned or practiced, and cultures in which aggression is discouraged or unnecessary may provide a background against which little aggression is learned or used. For example, children growing up in high-crime areas may observe the value of aggression for obtaining money and prestige, and children growing up in schools with high levels of violence may learn that they must be aggressive to avoid being victimized constantly. As another example, cultures that prize artistic freedom for moviemakers and television executives may allow high levels of violence in the media rather than institute censorship, and this violence may increase the aggression of some children. However, it is important to note that not all children growing up in high-crime areas, attending violent schools, or watching violence in the media become aggressive. Other cultural influences—such as the culture of a particular religion, neighborhood, or family—may influence some children to avoid aggression.

Environmental Learning Influences on Aggression

Children and adolescents can learn to be aggressive by being reinforced for aggression or by observing others obtaining what they want through aggression. This learning can take place within the family, peer groups, or the community and can be influenced by observing violence on television and through other forms of communication.

Coercive family processes.   Patterson and colleagues (e.g., Patterson, 1996; Patterson, Littman, & Bricker, 1967) have constructed a model for the development of aggression that starts with the interactions between a young child and her parents. The first part of the model involves a parent making a demand on a child (e.g., get ready for bed, pick up your toys) and the child responding with verbal or physical aggression (e.g., yelling "No", throwing a toy at the parent). How the child learned this behavior is not important to the model; the child may have observed this behavior or it may simply be random. If the parent withdraws in the face of the child's aggression (e.g., drops the demand that the child go to bed, leaves the child's room), the parent's withdrawal of the demand negatively reinforces the child's aggression. This increases the likelihood that the child will respond aggressively when the parent makes a demand in the future. If this pattern is repeated, the child can develop a repertoire of aggressive behaviors in response to demands from others. When the child enters school, she is likely to use this repertoire of aggressive behaviors when confronted with demands by teachers and peers. This is likely to result in her being rejected by her peers (Coie & Dodge, 1998) and treated as a discipline problem by her teachers. Because of this rejection by others, she is likely to associate with other aggressive children who have also been rejected. Within this group, her aggression will often be positively reinforced by others, and she will reinforce their aggression. By the time that she is an adolescent, aggression will have become a consistent part of her behavior.

Physical punishment and physical abuse.   Children in families in which moderate forms of physical punishment are consistently used for discipline and in which there is little parental warmth are more likely to be aggressive than are children in families in which physical punishment is seldom used (Coie & Dodge, 1998). Children whose parents use harsh physical punishment or physically abuse their children have high rates of aggression (Dodge, Bates, & Pettit, 1990; Farrington, 1991). Because of their experiences, abused children expect that others will be aggressive toward them. Consequently, they are hypervigilant for aggression from others, often misinterpret others' behavior as aggressive, and act aggressively in response to this misperceived aggression (Dodge, Bates, & Pettit, 1990).

Television violence.   Coie and Dodge (1998) argue that there is no greater cultural influence on violence among children and adolescents than television. They note that television viewing accounts for about 10 percent of the variability in childhood aggression and that this is similar to the influence that cigarette smoking has on lung cancer. The effects of television violence are long-lasting. In one study, the amount of television violence observed at age 8 predicted aggression at age 18, even after the level of aggression at age 8 and the amount of television violence observed at age 18 were taken into account (Eron et al., 1972).

Besides having aggression modeled on television, repeatedly observing violence can desensitize children and adolescents to its occurrence, so that it comes to be commonplace and expected. Donnerstein, Slaby, and Eron (1994) provide an interesting reciprocal model of the influences of television violence (see figure 10.1). It suggests that observing television violence gives children and adolescents examples of violent ways to interact with others, and they practice these ways in fantasy or actual interactions. As the child or adolescent interacts violently with others, she becomes increasingly unpopular. As a result, she watches more television by herself, and this increases her identification with violent television characters. Because of this increased identification, she acts violently in more and more social interactions.

Influences of violence in schools, neighborhoods, and communities. The violence and aggression that are frequent in some schools, neighborhoods, and communities can encourage aggression in children and adolescents, even those who come from nonviolent and nonaggressive families (Garbarino, 1999). Children and adolescents can observe the value of violence for obtaining goods and compliance from others. Further, they may observe the inability of the schools, police, and other community agencies to protect anyone from aggression and, thus, may learn that they must be aggressive to protect themselves.

FIGURE 10.1. The mass media and youth aggression.
Copyright © 1994 by the American Psychological Association. Reprinted with permission.

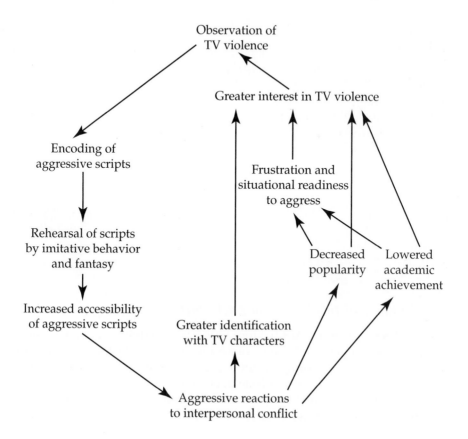

Emotional and Cognitive Influences on Aggression

Several theories have focused on the links among thoughts, emotions, and aggression. Many theories suggest that an adolescent's thoughts have an influence on her emotions and, consequently, on her aggressive behavior.

One of the earliest theories of aggression focused on the influences of frustration (Dollard et al., 1939). The theory suggested that, when a person becomes frustrated, a natural drive toward aggression is activated. The more the frustration, the stronger the drive to be aggressive. Berkowitz (1989) expanded on the frustration/aggression theory by suggesting that frustration activates the strong emotional response of anger and that anger increases the likelihood of an attack on the person or situation perceived to be causing the frustration. Thus, Berkowitz connected the cognitive experience of frustration to the emotional experience of anger and the subsequent behavior of aggression. Subsequent research has shown that frustration causes aggression in some instances but also that frustration is not always accompanied by aggression and aggression can arise in nonfrustrating situations (Pepler & Slaby, 1994).

Beck's (1999) cognitive theories focus on the ways in which patterns of thinking can activate emotions such as anger and, consequently, aggression. Aggressive children and adolescents often believe that others are being hostile toward them, even when no hostility is intended (Fondacaro & Heller, 1990; Graham, Hudley, & Williams, 1992). For example, an aggressive adolescent who is accidentally bumped from behind is likely to consider the bump an intentional push. Believing that others are acting in a hostile way often evokes fear or anger, and these thoughts and emotions can result in the conclusion that retaliatory aggression is warranted.

Aggressive adolescents' thinking often involves overgeneralization. This may cause them to believe that all people with certain characteristics are hostile toward them (e.g., "All jocks are out to hurt me"), because they were once hurt by someone with that characteristic (Beck, 1999). This can result in anger and aggression in many situations.

Although it is often assumed that aggressive children and adolescents have low self-esteem, research shows that many have inflated self-esteem (Baumeister, Smart, & Boden, 1996). Their inflated self-esteem promotes their belief that they are often being slighted or shown disrespect, even when others are acting normally. Believing that others being disrespectful can activate anger, which can encourage an aggressive response.

Developmental Influences on Each Pathway to Aggression

Now that we have examined the four pathways to adolescent aggression and the influences on the development of aggression, we will explore several ways in which the influences can play out in each pathway. As with the other problematic behaviors explored in this text, however, many different sets of influences can affect each pathway, so the following are only examples of how aggression can develop along each pathway.

BROADENING Perspectives

Settings, Thoughts, Emotions, and Aggression

Beck (1999) provides the following thought-provoking example for considering the way in which a person's thoughts can influence emotions and aggression:

Suppose you see a flying object in the distance. As it comes closer, you decide that it is probably a bird. If you are not particularly interested in birds, your attention wanders to other things....Now imagine that your country is at war....Your attention is riveted to the distant flying object. If you think it may be an enemy aircraft, your psychological and physiological systems are totally mobilized....Also, as you move about off duty, you will be poised to recognize enemy agents who might be mingling in the crowd....You will focus on small details such as a man's slight foreign accent, his ignorance of certain sports figures in your country, or his secret, suspicious-looking meetings with other strangers. (pp. 71–72)

Because of their experiences, some adolescents believe that they are living in a hostile environment. They are quick to conclude that others are dangerous or hostile; they often view others' behaviors with suspicion; and they are quick to act aggressively in response to the hostility they believe surrounds them.

An Onset of Aggression in Early Childhood with an Ongoing Decline of Aggression During Childhood and Adolescence

As noted earlier, this is the pathway taken by most children and adolescents. Several scientists have considered human aggression to be an instinct (e.g., Freud, 1950; Lorenz, 1966), which may help explain the relatively high levels of aggression among toddlers and young children, even those who live in generally nonaggressive environments. Aggression in very young children may have had some evolutionary value, as children who aggressively sought out and kept food and belongings may have been more likely to survive.

Socialization by family members, older children, other adults, and social institutions such as schools appears to be the primary way in which aggression diminishes for many children. It is unknown whether any instinctual influence on aggression diminishes during childhood and adolescence. Children and adolescents who are reinforced for nonaggressive behavior and punished for aggressive behavior are likely to decrease aggression.

A Generally Consistent Pattern of Aggression Beginning in Early Childhood and Continuing Through Adolescence

This pathway may begin similarly as the previous pathway—with a general tendency in early childhood to be aggressive. The socialization away from aggression experienced by many children and adolescents may be absent for some who follow this pathway. In other cases, a child's temperament or other biological predisposition may make attempts to socialize her less effective.

Ineffective or problematic parenting may encourage the continuation of aggression in some cases. Patterson's model is a good example of the way in which parenting practices can result in ongoing aggression in children, even if this is

---

Controversy
Extreme Aggression

Troubling examples of extreme forms of adolescent aggression can be shocking and incomprehensible—for example, when adolescents beat other adolescents to death because they are gay, African American, or Jewish or when adolescents take assault weapons to school and kill many students and teachers. Because these incidents are so rare, we have little systematically collected data with which to understand them. Consequently, we do not know whether the development of these forms of aggression—often characterized by extreme levels of hatred—develop in ways similar to less lethal forms of aggression.

It is important to note, however, that lethal aggression is part of many adolescents' lives—for example, children and adolescents living in high-crime urban areas. Unfortunately, the aggression with which they must live often becomes so commonplace that it seldom receives the media attention that the same level of violence occurring in less violent neighborhoods receives. It is also noteworthy that an average of five children are beaten or starved to death by their parents every day in the United States—another form of extreme aggression about which we seldom hear (U.S. Department of Health and Human Services, 1998).

---

not the parents' intention. Some parents may believe that aggressiveness in their children is a desirable characteristic and purposefully reinforce aggression. This may be due to the parents' own aggressiveness or to their belief that the environment in which their child is being raised requires that the child be aggressive.

Once children reach school age, their prior learning or biologically based predispositions may make it difficult for teachers and other adults to change the children's aggressive behaviors. Aggressive children often associate with each other, and they may reinforce each other's aggression. In addition, aggressive children are likely to believe that the world is an aggressive place (which may be an accurate assessment of their immediate environment), and this may encourage them to act aggressively.

During this time, however, social institutions such as schools may be exerting an influence on these children to become less aggressive, either by punishing their aggression or by teaching them nonaggressive ways of handling social situations. These influences will compete with a child's biological tendencies and previous learning. It is possible that a child's tendencies toward aggression would be somewhat balanced by influences from others to avoid aggression, resulting in a stable level of aggression. This pattern may continue into adolescence.

Aggression That Begins in Early Childhood and Increases in Intensity and Frequency During Adolescence

Adolescents on this pathway are likely to have experienced the same influences on aggression just discussed. At issue here are the factors that result in an intensification of aggression during adolescence.

Physical changes during adolescence may cause an intensification of aggression. Rising levels of testosterone in adolescent boys can intensify preexisting patterns of aggression, and hormonal changes may be particularly strong in adolescents whose aggression is influenced by differences in neurotransmitter or brain functioning (Archer, 1994). Even something as simple as change in height and weight may influence aggression. For example, boys and girls who have been repeatedly abused by parents or others may find themselves big enough in adolescence to be aggressive toward those who had abused them.

Normal developmental processes during adolescence also can result in increased aggression. For example, children who have been rejected by many of their peers because of their aggression may become adolescents who decide to make increasing levels of aggression a central part of their emerging sense of identity. Some of these adolescents may become part of groups that encourage heightened levels of violence and aggression, such as gangs. In addition, alcohol and other drugs may increase the tendency toward aggression in some adolescents. Drug use may decrease inhibitions against aggression, particularly in adolescents with high levels of anger and those whose cognitions result in errors about the amount of aggression aimed at them.

Aggression That Emerges for the First Time in Middle to Late Adolescence

A small minority of aggressive adolescents develop patterns of aggression beginning in middle to late adolescence. Loeber and Stouthammer-Loeber (1998) suggest that adolescents with late-onset aggression are likely to have used high levels of self-control to inhibit strong urges toward aggression during their childhood and early adolescence. In addition, significant people in their lives may have helped them develop self-control over their aggressive tendencies. For some, the tight control they have maintained over their aggressive tendencies loosens during adolescence. In some cases, this is because of decreased influence from parents or other adults and, in other cases, because of high levels of stress that cause their control to finally "crack."

A Summary of the Development of Aggression

Early experiences can set a child on a developmental track toward high levels of aggression that is reinforced and expanded during childhood and adolescence. Some of these early experiences may be influenced by the child's temperamental and biological tendencies. Biological tendencies and learning experiences can often interact. For example, a child whose impulsive or difficult temperament encourages aggression may have a parent with the same temperament and aggressive tendencies, resulting in an aggressive home environment, in which the child is reinforced for aggression.

Aggressive children are often rejected by peers and labeled as problems by adults. This can result in social and academic failure and a tendency to associate with other aggressive children. These groups of aggressive children can reinforce each other's aggression. Furthermore, living in an environment that is often characterized by aggression is likely to result in children's developing beliefs or cognitions about the aggressiveness of their world. These beliefs can make them misinterpret many acts as aggressive and results in their acting aggressively in response to the aggression they perceive is aimed at them.

Aggression can be an integral part of the identity of some adolescents. Some of these adolescents may find that their lack of academic and social success precludes them from many mainstream avenues for success. They may experience frustration and may turn to heightened aggression to give themselves some successes. Some of these adolescents can control their aggression sufficiently in late adolescence to find a job and friends that do not require aggression; however, others will expand their aggression throughout their adulthood.

INTERVENTIONS FOR AGGRESSION

Interventions for problematic physical aggression take many forms—legal interventions designed to deter aggression or punish adolescents who are aggressive, interventions with families and young children designed to interrupt the development of aggression at an early age, and interventions with aggressive adolescents designed to help them control the emotions and cognitions that may be encouraging their aggression.

Legal Interventions

Until recently, violent adolescents who had been arrested were dealt with by the juvenile court, with the primary goals of rehabilitation and treatment. However, in recent years, increasing numbers of violent juveniles have been dealt with by the adult criminal courts, reflecting a change in emphasis from treatment to community protection, punishment, and retribution (Tate, Reppucci, & Mulvey, 1995). This change has partly been in response to public outrage over apparent increases in the amount, viciousness, and senselessness of the most violent forms of juvenile crime. This change also has been in response to the apparent lack of effectiveness of many interventions for aggressive adolescents. Thus, many people in law enforcement and the general public have determined that locking violent adolescents away from society for many years is the best solution to juvenile violence.

Family-Based Interventions

Several interventions have been designed for families with aggressive young children. Since most aggressive adolescents were aggressive children, these interventions can be considered ways of preventing adolescent aggression. Most of the interventions are based on the belief that, by teaching parents more effective styles of parenting, their children will become less aggressive. For example, Patterson (1996) and colleagues have developed several programs to improve the assertiveness of parents and reduce the frequency with which they reinforce their children's aggression. Counselors go to the homes of children who are identified in preschool as overly aggressive and work with the parents to identify and modify the ways that they are reinforcing their children's aggression. Several assessments of these interventions show that children in these families become less aggressive and that this reduction in aggression lasts for many years.

Henggeler and colleagues (e.g., Henggeler & Borduin, 1995) have developed a multisystemic treatment program for serious juvenile offenders. Counselors meet in the family home with the adolescent and as many members of her family as possible. The counselor encourages the family to see how the adolescent's behavior is influenced by the family, her peers, her school, and other parts of the community. With guidance from the counselor, family members develop a plan to reduce the adolescent's aggression and other problems, such as substance abuse. This might include increased monitoring of the adolescent, helping her join a vocational education program or improve her classroom performance, and helping her find a job. Interventions typically last about four months and often end with greater family cohesion, better family functioning, and less aggression and other forms of offending by the adolescent (Henggeler, Melton, & Smith, 1992).

Individual and Group Interventions

Based on research showing the connection between aggression and emotions, cognitions, and social skills, several programs have been designed to address problems or deficits that aggressive adolescents may have in these areas. Some of these programs are delivered in group settings—such as schools, juvenile detention facilities, and residential treatment programs—and others are delivered during individual counseling sessions.

Anger-control treatment is based on the belief that aggressive adolescents are often overwhelmed by angry emotions and that they act on these feelings with little thought (e.g., Barfield & Hutchinson, 1990; Dangel, Deschner, & Rasp, 1989). Anger-control programs are designed to help adolescents recognize the early signs of increasing anger, tell themselves to stop this escalation, relax their upper torso muscles, and leave the anger-provoking situation if possible. The intervention is not designed to make adolescents passive or to eliminate their aggression; rather, it is designed to give them more cognitive control over their aggression and to reduce the effect that their angry emotions have on their behavior. Several anger-control programs have shown good short-term results, but their long-term influence has not been evaluated.

Cognitively based programs are designed to decrease the cognitive distortions of aggressive adolescents and to increase their repertoire of nonaggressive ways for handling difficult social situations. For example, Pepler, King, & Byrd (1991) designed an intervention that focuses on aggressive adolescents' cognitions and social problem-solving skills. First, the adolescent learns to pay better attention to others to reduce her distortion of their behavior (e.g., looking at others while they talk and thinking about what they are saying). Second, she is encouraged to reflect on her thinking patterns during social situations in which aggression can occur. This helps her understand the thoughts that might automatically occur (e.g., "This person is out to get me") and the ways in which they can evoke anger and other feelings. The therapist then helps the adolescent think about alternative interpretations of these social situations. Third, the adolescent learns a full range of responses to these social situations, so that she will not have to rely solely on aggressive responses. Fourth, she learns to stop before acting and to consider the range of responses available to her and the possible consequences of these responses. Finally, nonaggressive behaviors are practiced through role playing, and the adolescent is given homework assignments to practice her new skills outside therapy.

CHAPTER SUMMARY

Problematic aggression declines steadily throughout most individuals' childhood and adolescence. However, a small percentage of adolescents become increasingly aggressive and violent. Self-reported criminal violence, for example, peaks around ages 16–18 for males and 13–15 for females. Levels of aggression are very stable across individuals: aggressive adolescents are likely to have been aggressive children, and they are likely to become aggressive adults. Males are more aggressive than females beginning around age 3, and the difference between male and female rates of aggression increases during adolescence.

Some theorists have suggested that aggression is a human instinct and may be present from birth. Even if aggression is an instinct, individual levels of aggression are clearly influenced by many factors. Genes may play a role through their influences on temperament, impulsivity, and other characteristics. Hormones appear to be related to aggression in humans, although the strength of this influence is not clear. Brain injuries, including injuries resulting from child abuse, also can influence aggression.

Aggression can be learned from the environment. Children may learn to be aggressive by watching aggression among family members, on television, or in their neighborhoods. They may be reinforced for aggression by parents, teachers, or peers—in some cases, this reinforcement is purposeful; in others, accidental. Children who are the victims of child abuse may become physically abusive toward others. Aggressive children and adolescents often misperceive others' actions as aggressive, which can increase their aggressive responses. In addition, aggressive adolescents often have limited repertoires of response to social problems, often resulting in their using aggression in problem situations.

Some interventions for aggression in adolescents include helping them change their perceptions of the extent to which others are aggressive toward them and giving them a broader range of responses to problematic social situations. Anger-control interventions focus on helping an aggressive adolescent control her anger in social situations, so that her response is not based on high levels of anger. Other interventions focus on the aggressive adolescent's family—helping the family and adolescent work together to reduce aggression. Programs to improve the parenting of young children can also reduce adolescent aggression by helping parents reduce aggression in their developing child. Legal interventions also focus on reducing adolescent aggression, primarily by trying violent adolescents in adult court, where they can receive longer sentences if found guilty.

Revisiting Mary

Mary is one of the millions of children in the United States who are physically or sexually abused each year. In fact, an average of five children are beaten or starved to death each day in the United States (U.S. Department of Health and Human Services, 1998). Mary has experienced many of the risk factors for childhood and adolescent aggression. She has seen aggression modeled by her parents and possibly other members of her family. She probably has high levels of anxiety and anger because of her abuse, and the neural connections in her brain for experiencing and expressing anxiety and anger may be especially strong. Her history of abuse is likely to have resulted in beliefs about the world being an aggressive place, and she is likely hypervigilant for the aggression of which she has repeatedly been the target. She may have sustained brain injury during her abuse that increases her likelihood of acting aggressively, and she may have inherited tendencies toward aggression or impulsivity from her parents.

Mary's experience in school is typical of the experiences of aggressive children: they are often rejected by the other children and labeled as problems by the teachers. Aggressive children often react to rejection by being aggressive—forcing their way into a tetherball game or hitting another child during a basketball game. Teachers and peers often find it difficult to understand why aggressive children continue to act aggressively despite all the negative consequences of doing so. In part, they continue to act aggressively because it is all that they know.

It appears that Mary began emphasizing her aggressive nature in adolescence, as she began to form an identity. She did what many adolescents do—she found others who were forming identities in ways similar to hers. This gave her some support and a sense that she was not alone in the world. Unfortunately, as with many highly aggressive adolescents, her choices to continue and expand her aggressiveness may have led her to a lifetime of violence and aggression—a lifetime that is likely to be shortened or spent partly in prison.

- Are there actions that could have been taken by Mary's foster parents or social workers when she was a young child that might have resulted in a different outcome for Mary? Would some form of therapy have been useful?
- What strategies might have been taken by teachers, counselors, or others in Mary's life when she was in high school that could have reduced her aggression? Consider the reasons for, and goals of, her aggression. Are there ways that these goals could have been accomplished without aggression? How could she have been encouraged to meet these goals in ways other than through aggression?
- How much responsibility do Mary and the other people in her life have for her apparent problematic outcome?

CHAPTER 11

Sexual Assault and Sexual Coercion

Julie called her friend early Sunday morning and was very upset. She had been out with her boyfriend the night before, and they ended up having intercourse in his car, even though she did not want to. She said that they had been partly undressed and were kissing and fondling each other, when he began to talk about "finally doing it," took off his underwear, and began to take off hers. She had said "I don't want to do this" several times, but he seemed not to notice and just continued as if she had not spoken. She believes that she was clear about not wanting to have intercourse, but is not sure if she was clear enough. She did not physically resist his efforts, so he did not use physical force, and she worries that her failure to physically resist his efforts was wrong. She worries about pregnancy and disease (he did not wear a condom) and has no idea what she will do Monday, when she will probably see him in a course that they take together.

Julie's friend rushes over to her apartment. She agrees with Julie that it was a terrible experience and that she must have been very frightened and confused at the time, and must still be. She says that many women at their university have had to endure some form of sexual aggression and that she knows of a group at the student health center where women who have had these experiences can get help and give each other mutual support. She confides to Julie that she knows about this group because she was raped by someone she had met at a party the year before. Julie and her friend decide that Julie will not attend her class Monday and that Julie and her friend will go to the student health center together.

Every year, tens of thousands of adolescents are forced or pressured to engage in sexual behavior against their will. Some estimates suggest that as many as 60 percent of all adolescent females have had such an experience (Abbey et al., 1996). In 1997, almost 4,000 males in the United States, age 17 or younger, were arrested for forcible rape, and another 13,000 were arrested for other types of sexual offenses (Federal Bureau of Investigation, 1999).

Sexual assault can be a difficult topic to discuss because even the most fundamental issues are often contentious, such as how it is defined (Johnson & Sigler, 1997). For example, some authors have stated that "narrower definitions of rape have served the interests of men. In contrast, broader definitions would be more inclusive of the interests of women" (Muehlenhard et al., 1992, p. 25). Arguments about sexual assault often take place along gender lines, with women citing examples of ineffective legal interventions for women who have been raped and men citing examples of men convicted of rape after having sex that they believed was consensual. There is much room for anger and defensiveness in discussions about sexual assault.

Although females are more often the victims of sexual assault and males perpetrate sexual assault more often, it would be incorrect to assume that all victims of sexual assault are females and that all perpetrators are male.[1] Many males are sexually assaulted—some by females, some by other males—and females sexually assault both males and females (Moore & Waterman, 1999). Considering women as sexual aggressors and men as victims of sexual aggression can reduce the appropriate focus on women as frequent victims of sexual aggression (Muehlenhard, 1998; Struckman-Johnson & Anderson, 1998). Ignoring females as aggressors, however, constrains our view of sexual coercion and thus limits our ability to understand it. In addition, dismissing male victims ignores many men who have had a painful and degrading sexual experience (Muehlenhard, 1998). Keeping with this text's strategy of developing as broad a view of problematic behaviors as possible, I will strive to avoid the stereotyped view of all victims of sexual coercion being females and all perpetrators being male.[2] I will also work to avoid the assumption that all sexual coercion occurs in relationships between men and women. Unfortunately, little research exists on sexual aggression involving females as perpetrators or males as victims, or on sexual aggression in gay and lesbian relationships, so our discussion of these topics is limited.

A discussion of rape or sexual assault among adolescents is complicated by the different degrees of relationship between those involved. Some adolescents

---

[1]The terms *victim* and *perpetrator* were chosen after considerable thought. Some would object to the use of victim because it suggests helplessness and because it may suggest that those who have been sexually assaulted are powerless to recover from their experience. I use the term *victim* in this chapter because those who have experienced sexual assault have been victimized—that is, they have been injured or harmed by some event or person. I use the term *victim* to describe the person in the context of the sexual assault, not as a general description of the person's character, just as I could refer to the victim of a tornado or a flood. From my perspective, being a victim does not indicate whether a person can recover from her experience. Some victims of tornados, floods, and sexual assault are able to reclaim a feeling of control over their lives and move forward, while others remain frozen by their experiences. To perpetrate an act simply means to do it. It suggests a purposefulness to the act, so perpetrator is an appropriate label for someone who forces or coerces another into sexual activity.

[2]I do use the female pronoun for the victim of sexual coercion and the male pronoun for the perpetrator. Those concerned about this choice may take some comfort in my use of the female pronoun for the perpetrator in the chapter on physical aggression.

rape strangers, and some adolescents are raped by strangers. Others may be confronted by an unknown exhibitionist or expose themselves to a group of unknown children. However, the vast majority of sexual coercion involving adolescents occurs between adolescents who know each other (Craig, 1990). Consequently, this chapter will focus on this type of sexual coercion.

The Plan: We will first explore the definitions of the terms used for sexually assaultive behavior and will then explore the prevalence of rape and other forms of sexual assault. In the central part of the chapter, we will focus on how incidents of sexual coercion occur. We will use the strategy of considering the influences on sexual coercion as falling into two main categories: those that affect the development of an individual so that he is more likely to engage in sexual coercion and those that affect a specific situation so that sexual coercion is more likely to occur in that situation. After examining the developmental and situational influences on sexual coercion, we will explore the variety of ways in which they can combine to create an incident of sexual coercion. Efforts to prevent or reduce the frequency of sexual coercion are described at the end of the chapter.

DEFINITIONS OF RAPE, SEXUAL ASSAULT, AND RELATED TERMS

Many terms have been used to describe situations in which one person forces or coerces another into engaging in sexual behavior. Clear definitions of these terms are important in many contexts. Many refer to illegal acts, and the law requires that illegal acts be defined clearly, so that the public knows which behaviors to avoid (Romney, 1991). Research on sexual assault is conducted most effectively when similar definitions are used by several researchers. In addition, people discussing sexual assault need to have a clear understanding of the terms used in their discussion if they are to avoid confusion. However, the term applied to a particular incident is unimportant in other circumstances. For example, victims of all forms of sexual coercion need support from friends, family, and others, and the amount of support they receive should not depend on the term used to describe their experience.

Legal and Research Definitions

Rape is a legal term that is usually narrowly defined. For example, the federal Uniform Crime Reporting Program defines forcible rape as vaginal intercourse with a female forcibly and against her will or attempts to commit rape by force or threat of force (Federal Bureau of Investigation, 1999). The term *rape* has also been used in the clinical and research literature, although the definitions of rape vary in these contexts and often include a wide range of sexual acts (Muehlenhard et al., 1992).

Using the term *rape* in research can be problematic because it often results in significant under reporting. Many women who have experienced forcible sex against their will answer "no" to the question "Have you ever been raped?" (Russell, 1984). These women may assume that rape must occur with a stranger or involve physical restraint. Thus, although they know that they have been forced to have sex, they believe that they have not been raped.

Other terms, such as *sexual assault, sexual aggression,* and *sexual coercion,* have been used in research to describe a wide range of coercive sexual behaviors, from sexualized kissing to intercourse, and attempts to do any of these (Johnson & Sigler, 1997). The definitions of each of these terms can vary from one report to the next. Date rape has been used to label a wide range of sexually coercive behaviors occurring between two people who have a social or romantic interest in each other. Acquaintance rape has been used to label the same behaviors when they take place between two people with any level of acquaintanceship or friendship (Cowling, 1998).

The Determination of Whether a Sexual Act Is Consensual

An important issue in determining whether an act is or is not rape or sexual assault is whether those involved consented to the sexual activity (Muehlenhard et al., 1992). Many criteria have been used to determine whether a sexual encounter is consensual.

In some cases, the characteristics of the sexual encounter are used to determine consent. Situations in which one person has been coerced into having sex are usually viewed as nonconsensual. For example, the use or threatened use of force is always considered an indication of lack of consent. Situations in which consent cannot be given, such as when a victim is intoxicated, unconscious, or asleep, are usually viewed as nonconsensual (Muehlenhard et al., 1992). However, disagreement exists about whether pleading, pledges of love, and other statements that are not overtly threatening are considered inappropriately coercive (Craig, 1990).

The victim's actions and thoughts have also been used to establish consent. Some researchers have focused on the victim's observable behavior to determine nonconsent—for example, if the victim fights or cries out (Alder, 1985) or "makes it clear to the male either verbally or nonverbally" that she does not want to engage in sex (Muehlenhard & Linton, 1987, p. 188). Other researchers have used the victim's state of mind to determine nonconsent—for example, considering any sexual activity "when you didn't want to" as nonconsensual (Koss, Gidycz, & Wisniewski, 1987, p. 167). It should be noted that researchers who establish lack of consent solely on whether a person wanted it to occur may include some people who engaged in sexual behavior without complaint, and perhaps with active consent, but who did not want the sexual activity to occur (Cowling, 1998; Gilbert, 1992; Muehlenhard et al., 1992). Both males and females sometimes agree to engage in sex when they do not want to do so; when this occurs, it is often in an attempt to make a boyfriend or girlfriend happy, to improve a dating relationship, or because there seemed to be no good reason not to engage in sex (Johnson & Sigler, 1997).

An important issue in determining consent is whether it must be active. For example, if a man initiates gradually intensifying sexual activity, can he assume that his partner consents unless she says to stop (passive consent), or must he get her verbal approval for the initiation of any new sexual activity (active consent)?

Passive consent standards present several difficulties. First, they allow the initiator to engage in at least some sexual activity with anyone until told to stop. Similarly, when initial active consent has been given and a person instigates increasingly intrusive sexual activity until told to stop, the other person has to endure at least some unwanted sexual activity. In addition, distinguishing between passive consent and lack of consent can require the interpretation of ambiguous verbal or nonverbal behavior. Males and females often have different interpretations of these behaviors, and adolescents who are inexperienced in sexual relationships may be particularly poor at making accurate judgments about another person's consent (Craig, 1990).

Active consent standards eliminate many potential problems with passive consent. However, obtaining active consent can be awkward for many adolescents. Interrupting previously agreed-upon sexual activity to ask if a new type of activity can be initiated is difficult under many circumstances, and partners who have not been together long may find it awkward to agree beforehand about sexual activity.

The Terms Used in This Chapter

Because of its limited use in many contexts, the term *rape* will be used only when describing the results of studies in which the term is used. The term *sexual assault* will be used to describe a variety of sexual behaviors, from kissing to intercourse, obtained through force, through threats of force, or when a person cannot consent. The terms *sexual coercion* and *sexually coercive behavior* will be used to describe a broad range of sexual behaviors, including all those characterized as sexual assault, obtained through a broad range of verbal coercion or trickery. In short, sexual assault is sexual coercion that involves force, a threat of force, or a person who cannot consent to sexual activity.

THE PREVALENCE OF SEXUAL ASSAULT AND SEXUAL COERCION

Most females and many males are the targets of at least one incident of sexual coercion during their adolescence. As might be imagined, wide variations in the prevalence of sexually coercive behaviors have been reported—primarily because of differences in definitions. However, even with these differing definitions, the research clearly shows that sexual coercion is a frequent occurrence among adolescents.

Early studies of sexual coercion among undergraduates were completed by Kanin and colleagues (Kanin, 1957; Kirkpatrick & Kanin, 1957). In their sample, 13 percent of the freshmen and 21 percent of the sophomores, juniors, and seniors reported forceful attempts at intercourse during the previous year, and 5 percent of the freshmen and 6 percent of the others reported completed intercourse accompanied by physical force or threats of physical force during the previous year. Similar results were found by Kanin and Parcell (1977) 20 years later.

The research by Koss and colleagues is the most frequently cited more recent research on sexual coercion among undergraduates. Koss and Oros (1982) found that 54 percent of a large sample of female undergraduates had experienced some form of sexual coercion since the age of 14. Eighteen percent had experienced undesired sexual intercourse after verbal coercion, repeated arguing, or false promises; 24 percent had experienced some form of sexual contact through force or threat of force; and 12 percent had experienced intercourse through force or threat of force. Koss, Gidycz, and Wisniewski (1987) asked about these experiences over the previous academic year and found rates of 12 percent, 12 percent, and 15 percent, respectively.

Other research has also reported high rates of sexual coercion. For example, Abbey and colleagues (1996) found that 59 percent of a large sample of female undergraduates had experienced sexual coercion since age 14 and that 23 percent had experienced rape as it is defined legally. Fergusson, Horwood, and Lynskey (1997) found that 4 percent of a large sample of females in New Zealand had experienced rape or attempted rape between the ages of 16 and 18. Walsh and Foshee (1998) found that 9 percent of a sample of eighth and ninth grade girls had been the target of forced sexual activity during the previous six months.

Some researchers have asked males about sexual coercion that they initiated against women. In one study, Kanin (1967) found that 26 percent of the college males had used some degree of physical force to engage in sexual intercourse with a woman. Koss and colleagues (1985) found that 22 percent of the college men in their study had used extreme verbal coercion to engage in sexual intercourse with a woman and that an additional 4 percent had engaged in forcible rape. Muehlenhard and Linton (1987) found that 7 percent of the college men had engaged in sexual intercourse that they knew a woman did not want, and Abbey, McAuslan, and Ross (1998) found that 9 percent of the college males had committed an act meeting the legal standard for rape.

As previously noted, only a few studies have examined the experiences of men as victims of sexual coercion and of women as sexual aggressors. Muehlenhard and Cook (1988) asked undergraduates whether they had ever engaged in intercourse when they did not want to (the gender of the other person was not questioned, although 98 percent of the participants described themselves as heterosexual). Six percent of the women and 7 percent of the men said that they had been physically coerced into intercourse, and 12 percent of the women and 13 percent of the men said that they had been verbally coerced into intercourse. Surprisingly, more males than females said that they had engaged in unwanted intercourse because of intoxication (31 percent vs. 21 percent) or enticement (57 percent vs. 39 percent). Shea (1998) asked female undergraduates about times when they had had intercourse with a man "when she knew that he did not want to, by saying things she did not mean, making false promises, or just going ahead even though he said not to" (p. 95). Nineteen percent of the females had been involved in such an experience, with an additional 1 percent involved in an experience in which they used physical force to have sex with a male.

THE DEVELOPMENT OF SEXUALLY COERCIVE BEHAVIORS

In this section, we will explore the issues that can influence the occurrence of sexual coercion. As with other topics in this text, we will work to think expansively about the motivations for and influences on sexual coercion. To make our exploration more methodical, sexually coercive behaviors are divided into two broad categories—malicious and nonmalicious. (These two categories are described later in this chapter. In general, malicious sexual coercion occurs when a person engages in behaviors that he intends to be coercive; nonmalicious sexual coercion occurs when a person acts in ways that he does not intend to be coercive but that are experienced as coercive by another person.)

We will explore two sets of factors that influence the development of sexual coercion. One set influences the characteristics of an individual that make him more or less likely to engage in sexual coercion. These are called developmental factors, since they influence the development of the individual and his behavior. The second set of factors relates to the characteristics of a situation that increase or decrease the likelihood of sexual coercion occurring in that situation, called situational factors. Considering these two sets of factors separately facilitates our understanding of how some people are more likely to be sexually coercive but not in all situations, as well as how sexual coercion is more likely to occur in some situations but not by all the people there. It is important to note that developmental and situational factors can be related. Someone who enjoys sexually coercive encounters is likely to create situations in which they can occur (Craig, 1990). As a result, the situational factors found in many sexually coercive environments do not happen by chance—they are often created purposefully.

This strategy for understanding sexual coercion focuses on risk factors. No developmental or situational factor is necessary or sufficient for sexual coercion to occur. Rather, each of these factors increases the risk that sexual coercion will occur. Some risk factors may be particularly influential in the development of sexual coercion in some people or situations, while having little influence in others.

Malicious Sexual Coercion

The sexually coercive behaviors in this category are those that a person engages in purposefully, knowing that they are coercive, and intending that they will result in sexual activity, even if the other person resists. It is the intentional use of coercion that distinguishes malicious from nonmalicious sexual coercion. Two competing theories exist regarding the motivation for male sexual coercion (Ellis, 1991; Malamuth et al., 1991), and a third theory combines the two primary motivations (e.g., Marshall & Eccles, 1993). Empirical support exists for all three theories, suggesting that they each help explain the behavior of some men who engage in sexual coercion (similar theories for females do not exist).

- One theory argues that sexual assault and sexual coercion are "pseudo-sexual" acts that are primarily motivated by males' interest in enforcing their domination over females. The goal is domination—with sex used as the method through which domination occurs (e.g., Brownmiller, 1975; Groth, 1979; Herman, 1990).
- A second theory focuses on the sexual aspect of sexual coercion. Men have a strong genetically based sex drive and possibly a strong drive to have sex with multiple partners. Some men have difficulty obtaining the level of sexual activity they desire, and some of these men will use coercion to have sex. Sexual intercourse is the goal—with coercion used as one method of achieving the goal (Ellis, 1991).
- A third theory was developed by researchers working with rapists (Abel et al., 1977; Marshall & Eccles, 1993). They argue that some men are motivated to have sex accompanied by aggression. These men's arousal is increased when they force sex on a woman, so this is the type of sex they pursue.

In some cases, a person's sexually coercive behavior may be influenced completely by one motivation. However, a mixture of motivations is often present. For example, men who are high in sexual promiscuity and hostility toward women are more likely to engage in sexual assault than are men high in sexual promiscuity but low in hostility (Malamuth et al., 1991).

Developmental Factors

Many personal, social, and cultural characteristics are associated with increased risk for males initiating sexual coercion. Unfortunately, it is not known whether these characteristics influence sexual coercion by females. Some developmental factors are primarily related to sexual coercion that is sexually based, others are related to sexual coercion that is aggressively based, and others may influence more than one type of sexual coercion.

Biological influences. Ellis (1991) argued that a biologically based sex drive is stronger in men than in women and that its strength varies among men. Sex drive is influenced primarily by testosterone, and higher levels of testosterone have been associated with increased sexual intercourse, masturbation, and sexual fantasies (Dabbs & Morris, 1990; Gooren, 1987; Udry et al., 1985). Artificially decreasing testosterone in men reduces sexual behaviors (including sex crimes), and artificially increasing testosterone increases sexual desire, nocturnal erections, and masturbation (Davidson, Kwan, & Greenleaf, 1982; Thiessen,

Controversy
Do Certain Characteristics Distinguish Women Who Are More Likely to Be the Targets of Sexual Coercion?

Whether certain characteristics distinguish women who are more likely to be targets of sexual coercion is a controversial topic. Some argue that searching for or discussing these characteristics shifts responsibility for sexual coercion onto victims. Others argue that knowledge about any characteristics could be used to alert women with them about the need for increased vigilance and might help identify women who would gain the most from programs to prevent being the victim of sexual aggression (e.g., Himeline, 1999; Synovitz & Byrne, 1998). Most studies that have examined the characteristics that may increase a woman's risk of being a victim of sexual coercion report characteristics such as increased and earlier sexual activity, passivity in the face of initial attempts at coercion, and increased use of alcohol in dating situations (see Craig, 1990, for review). Increased frequency of sexual activity places a woman in more situations in which sexual coercion may occur, even if it occurs by chance, and alcohol use and passive response may decrease her ability to discourage coercive situations, particularly at their early stage of development.

1990). Ellis argued that men with higher sex drives are at increased risk for engaging in sexually coercive behaviors if they cannot find someone to engage in noncoercive sex. In addition, a stronger sex drive may interact with other factors to raise further the risk for sexual coercion. For example, men with strong sex drives may be particularly susceptible to the arousing influences of pornography.

Attitudinal influences. Several attitudes are found more frequently among men who engage in sexual coercion than among men who do not (these attitudes are often referred to as rape myths (e.g., Brownmiller, 1975). These attitudes tend to reinforce certain beliefs: (a) a man should be able to act as he wants when he is with a woman; (b) women are eager to engage in sex, although they may need pressure to do so; and (c) the consequences to those who are the targets of coercive sex are minor. Unfortunately, little information is available on how these attitudes develop, although they can develop early. In a study of 1,700 middle school children, 65 percent of the boys and 57 percent of the girls stated that it is appropriate for a man to force sex on a woman if they had been dating for at least six months (Teens Express Themselves, cited in Craig, 1990).

Many sexually coercive men have attitudes about relationships that focus on male dominance (Kanin, 1985). They accept the appropriateness of aggression in many types of interpersonal interactions, not just sexual interactions (Malamuth, 1986). Sexually coercive men are more likely than other men to think that certain women—such as those met in bar—are fair targets for sexual coercion (Kanin, 1985). In addition, they often believe that women are responsible for preventing unwanted sexual encounters and that social expectations require women to resist sexual advances, even when they would like to have sex (Koss et al., 1985). These attitudes can encourage men to press for sex in the face of a woman's refusal, because they believe that the woman does want to be sexual and that, after a period of obligatory refusal, she will agree.

Men who have engaged in coercive sex are more likely to believe that relationships between men and women are adversarial and that game playing and deception are common in male/female relationships (Craig, 1990). These beliefs may promote the belief that "when a woman says 'no,' she really means 'yes,'" which may increase the likelihood of steadily increasing coercion when a woman refuses to engage in sexual activity.

Peer influences.   Men whose peers place a high value on sexual prowess are more likely to engage in sexual coercion than are those whose peers do not (Koss et al., 1985). This peer influence can result in the basing of some men's self-esteem on the frequency with which they have sex, and this can increase the likelihood of coercive sex if they cannot have enough noncoercive sex. Similarly, men who believe that their peers engage in frequent sex are more likely to engage in coercive sex—possibly because they must coerce some women to be sexual to "keep up" with their peers (Abbey, McAuslan, & Ross, 1998).

Previous learning.   Sexually coercive males are more likely than noncoercive males to come from families in which they experienced or observed sexual or physical abuse (Foshee, Bauman, & Linder, 1999; Malamuth et al., 1991). From these experiences, they may have learned that a male can get what he wants through physical coercion. In addition, males who come from cultures or social environments that revere dominance, aggressiveness, and competitiveness may use sexual relationships to express these characteristics (Malamuth et al., 1991).

In some cases, males may be positively reinforced for engaging in sexual coercion. The sexual release after forcing sex on a woman may strongly reinforce the use of force in the future. When a woman succumbs to pressure to engage in sex, she provides positive reinforcement for the male's use of pressure, which can increase the likelihood of his using pressure in the future (in these situations, the woman does not intend to reinforce the man's behavior, but the reinforcement occurs in spite of her intent). This reinforcement may be particularly powerful for men with high sex drives (Ellis, 1991).

The effects of pornography.   Repeated viewing of sexually aggressive pornography increases the risk for engaging in sexual coercion (Donnerstein & Berkowitz, 1981). Sexually coercive pornography may create or reinforce beliefs that can encourage sexual coercion. For example, it may mislead a male into thinking that women are always eager to have sexual intercourse or that they are likely to yield to sexual aggression (Ellis, 1991). In addition, since this type of pornography often shows women resisting sexual intercourse but then enjoying it when it is forced on them, it may promote the belief that, if sex is forced on a woman, she will eventually enjoy it (Mulvey & Haugaard, 1986).

Cultural Influences on Sexual Coercion

The culture in which an adolescent is raised may influence his likelihood of engaging in sexual coercion. Adolescent males raised in a culture where women are denigrated or seen as inferior to men may develop attitudes that promote taking advantage of women in many ways. This denigration of women may occur throughout large cultural groups in many ways, such as through music, movies, or television shows. It may also occur in smaller groups, such as when mothers and sisters are mistreated in families or when girls are denigrated in schools or neighborhoods. Adolescents living in environments where they observe repeated coercion may see males being reinforced for sexual coercion (e.g., obtaining sex, being congratulated by other males), and this can increase the chance that they will be sexually coercive to obtain the same rewards. In addition, females in cultures where they are denigrated may come to see sexual coercion as normal and expected and, therefore, may not resist it or take steps to have a perpetrator arrested.

Patterns of sexual arousal.   Convicted rapists and college students who report being more likely to engage in coercive sex often experience heightened sexual arousal to audiotaped or videotaped depictions of a woman being physically assaulted (Malamuth & Check, 1993; Quinsey, Chaplin, & Upfold, 1984). Quinsey and colleagues (1984) also found that rapists' sexual arousal is higher when listening to audiotaped rape scenarios than to scenarios involving consensual sex. These arousal patterns appear to increase the risk for men engaging in sex that purposefully combines sex and aggression.

Situational Influences

Drinking alcohol, particularly the heavy use of alcohol, is associated with increased likelihood of sexual coercion in social situations (Abbey, McAuslan, & Ross, 1998). Alcohol and other drugs may increase the likelihood of a man's misinterpreting a partner's interest in sex, may decrease his ability to perceive her desire to stop sexual activity, or may numb his internal inhibitions against sexual coercion. In addition, it may reduce the woman's ability to notice initial attempts at coercion and to deflect them or effectively fend off an assault. However, sexual coercion does not occur only when one or both partners are intoxicated. Abbey and colleagues (1998) found that 53 percent of the cases of sexual coercion reported by their sample occurred when neither the man nor the woman had been drinking, and Abbey and colleagues (1996) found that neither the man nor the woman was drinking during 41 percent of the occurrences of attempted or completed rape.

Sexual coercion is more likely to occur when a couple is physically separated from others (Amick & Calhoun, 1987). This does not mean that the couple must be isolated, however, as most incidents of sexual coercion occur when a couple is alone in either the perpetrator's or the victim's home (Abbey et al.,

1996). Sexual coercion is also more likely to occur on a date when the man drives the couple somewhere (Muehlenhard & Linton, 1987). This may provide the man the opportunity to separate from others, and the woman may feel obliged to engage in unwanted sex because of her inability to get home without the man's cooperation.

Dates during which some sexual activity has occurred are more likely than other dates to result in sexual coercion (Craig, 1990). The male's arousal may make it more difficult for him to perceive the woman's reluctance to expand their sexual activity, or he may believe that the woman's refusal to expand their activity is insincere, given her willingness to engage in some sexual activity (Kanin, 1985).

Pathways to Malicious Sexual Coercion

The picture that begins to emerge for the sexually coercive male who is primarily motivated by sex is one of strong desire to have frequent sex, barriers to having sex as frequently as he would like, and attitudes or experiences that allow him to justify coercing women to be sexual with him. The desire to have frequent sex might be based on a heightened sex drive that is biologically based, on a sense of self-esteem influenced by the frequency with which he can have sex, or both. When the frequency of sex is not what he wants, certain beliefs (e.g., women enjoy coercive sex) or experiences (e.g., observing aggression in his family, being reinforced for earlier attempts at coercive sex) encourage him to coerce an available woman to be sexual with him. He may have identified situations that facilitate his ability to engage in sexual coercion, and he may create these situations so that he can force sex on his partner if she is unwilling to engage in consensual sex.

A different picture emerges for a sexually coercive male who is primarily motived by domination, anger, or aggression. He may have a history of being abused or of observing abuse in his home or neighborhood. He tends to be angry, particularly angry and hostile toward women. He often views women as inferior to men and deserving of harsh treatment. He engages in coercive sex because it allows him to express his aggression and hostility. This type of man may create situations facilitating sexual coercion. However, he is likely to create these situations to ensure that he can engage in sexual coercion, rather than to permit sexual coercion if consensual sex is not possible. This is because his primary motivation is to be aggressive and hostile, not to have sex.

Marshall and Eccles (1993) described one pathway for the development of men who want to have aggressive sex. They suggested that these men often experience a childhood characterized by poor parenting and poor socialization. As they enter adolescence, they do not have the skills for engaging others in social and physical relationships. Consequently, they fantasize about relationships in which they have total control, such as relationships in which they force sex on a woman. If they masturbate during these fantasies, the fantasies become paired with sexual arousal, and through classical conditioning the fantasies begin to create arousal on their own. In some cases, a lack of focus on nonaggressive sex may result in a loss of arousal to nonaggressive sex. These men are likely to seek out situations in which they can use aggression to obtain sex, such as situations in which women are intoxicated or are isolated from others, because they want to have aggressive sex—they tend to find consensual sex unsatisfying.

Nonmalicious Sexual Coercion

This category consists of behaviors that the initiator does not intend to be coercive but that are considered to be coercive by the person who is the target of the behaviors. Hypothetically, if these behaviors were observed by a panel of objective, uninvolved people from a variety of backgrounds, many panel members would label them as coercive, but there might be honest disagreement about their nature.

I created this category after struggling to form a model for the development of sexually coercive behaviors in which all behaviors were purposefully coercive. This was a problem because the literature on sexual coercion contains many descriptions of the ways in which men in general (not just sexually coercive men) incorrectly perceive many women's behaviors as indicating that they are interested in sex (Craig, 1990). In fact, it appears that almost every behavior in which a female adolescent engages during social situations is interpreted by some males as indicating an interest in sex. Further, miscommunication often occurs between males and females during sexual situations, and this miscommunication often precedes coercive behavior. From the perspective of trying to understand the development of sexually coercive behavior, behavior based on misinterpretations or misperceptions would best be understood in ways that are different from behaviors in which a man purposefully coerces a woman into having sex.

There are several potential problems with a category such as this, so several points should be made clear from the outset:

- Many convicted rapists argue that their victims "encouraged" their assaultive behaviors, "were asking" to be treated in an assaultive way, or "really wanted" to be raped. Their behaviors would not be included in this category. This category does not provide a haven for those who want to excuse their purposeful, assaultive behavior by claiming that it was justified. Purposeful coercion is not nonmalicious coercion, regardless of the circumstances under which it occurs.
- Some men believe that, if they have been "led on" or sexually aroused by a woman, forcing sex on her is acceptable (Abbey et al., 1996). These men would not be included in this category, even if their forced sex was brought on by their misperception of a woman's intention, because they willingly engaged in forced sex. Just because their willingness was prompted by a misperception does not make their forced sex nonmalicious.
- The coercive behaviors falling into this category are problematic and are not justified. They may be just as troubling as malicious coercive behaviors to the victim, and they can result in significant harm. It is

important to note that these behaviors are still labeled sexual coercion, even if they are considered nonmalicious.

- I am concerned that my use of this category is simply a way for me to excuse the behavior of many in "my" gender. I have struggled with this issue and have discussed it with several colleagues and students. To the extent that I can understand my own motivations, I do not believe that I am simply excusing the behavior of many males. Rather, I believe that understanding the development of these types of sexually coercive behaviors occurs best when they are separated from those that are malicious.

Developmental Factors

Little is known about the development of nonmalicious sexual coercion or the people who engage in it, because nonmalicious sexual coercion has seldom been examined separately from the broad range of sexually coercive behaviors. Some information is available from the general study of male/female sexual relationships, suggesting that attitudes and beliefs common among males in our society may set the stage for sexually coercive behaviors by men who do not intend to be coercive.

Males in general (not just sexually coercive males) tend to perceive many behaviors of a female as indicating that she would like to engage in sex—for example, if she dresses in a way that the male perceives as provocative, if she initiates the social interaction, or even if she is friendly (Abbey & Melby, 1986; Craig, 1990). Although these behaviors may sometimes show an interest in sex, many males misperceive females' interest in sex by assuming that the behaviors always indicate that the females are interested in sex. Misperception about a female's interest in sex, combined with our commonly accepted cultural script of the male instigating sexual activity, may lead to incidents of unwanted advances or unwanted sexual activity. This may be particularly true if the male also is using a sexual script common in our culture that expects the female to provide token resistance to sexual activity, even if she wants it to occur (Muehlenhard & Hollabaugh, 1988).

Situational Influences

The timing of a woman's refusal to continue or increase the intensity of sexual activity can influence sexual coercion that results in intercourse. Women who refuse to continue sex early in a sexual encounter are more likely to be heeded than are those who refuse after the sexual encounter has continued for a while (Shotland & Goodstein, 1983). In malicious sexual coercion, a male may perceive the woman's refusal correctly yet ignore it because of his own desire to continue. It is possible, however, that some males may misperceive a woman's refusal, either because their own arousal has reduced their ability to perceive accurately, because the woman's refusal is ambiguous, or both.

Pathways to Nonmalicious Sexual Coercion

Beliefs and practices common in our culture appear to increase the likelihood that males will overestimate females' interest in sex. If some of these males believe that it is their role to initiate or intensify sexual behavior, they may engage in unwelcome sexual behaviors. Sometimes they stop unwelcome sexual activity when the female's wishes become clear. However, there may be situations in which the male's arousal or misinterpretation of the woman's verbal or nonverbal behavior interferes with his ability to accurately perceive her wishes. In these cases, the male may engage in behavior that is unwanted and coercive, even though he does not intend to be coercive or to engage in behavior that was not mutually acceptable.

THE PREVENTION AND TREATMENT OF SEXUAL ASSAULT AND SEXUAL COERCION

Efforts to prevent sexual assault and sexual coercion have taken several forms. Some have focused on the potential victims—providing them with strategies and self-confidence for repelling sexually coercive behaviors or avoiding situations in which sexual coercion may occur. Preventive efforts have also focused on those initiating sexual coercion. However, few programs to prevent males from initiating sexual coercion have been developed. The reasons for this remain unclear. It may be that people in the field believe that such efforts would be useless (possibly because those in most need of the program would not attend).

Prevention also can take place through laws and public policy. For example, harsh penalties for sexual coercion and vigorous efforts to arrest and prosecute those accused of sexual coercion may provide an external constraint that will reduce sexual coercion in some people. Similarly, consequences for sexual coercion enforced by other organizations (e.g., expulsion from school or from a fraternity) may motivate some people to avoid initiating sexual coercion or to cease ongoing sexual coercion.

Prevention and Treatment Programs for Victims or Potential Victims

These prevention programs typically involve one or more sessions of lecture and discussion about sexual assault, including topics such as the prevalence of sexual assault on campus, cultural beliefs that may promote sexual assault, the identification of situational characteristics associated with a higher risk of sexual assault, the identification of signs that may alert a woman to the likelihood that a man is planning to engage in sexual coercion, strategies to clearly state expectations about sex and to deflect initial attempts at coercion, and strategies for dealing with assaultive behavior. These programs usually have been evaluated by assessing the knowledge of participants about these issues before and after the program or by comparing the knowledge of participants with that of groups of students who had not participated in the program. On the whole, many of these programs do appear to increase participants' knowledge about sexual assault and sexual coercion (Lonsway, 1996). However, evaluations that assess whether prevention program participants are less likely to experience sexual coercion have been discouraging. Two programs, each involving one session of information about sexual assault and taking place early in the academic year, did not result in a decrease in participants' rate of experiencing sexual coercion during that academic year, and they had little effect on participants' dating behaviors and communication about sex (Breitenbecher & Gidycz, 1998; Breitenbecher & Scarce, 1999). This research calls into question the value of some prevention efforts, despite their ability to increase participants'

HELPING
YOURSELF AND OTHERS

What To Do If You, Your Friend, or Your Partner Has Been Sexually Assaulted

Most people who have been sexually assaulted face many medical, emotional, social, and legal issues. They may have been physically injured, requiring an intervention by a physician who may need to conduct physical exams that can be painful and intrusive under the best of circumstances. Many victims of sexual assault experience depression and anxiety, and some become suicidal. They must decide whom to tell about the assault—including whether to tell family members, friends, and the police. They may have to face seeing the person who assaulted them in class or in social situations.

The number and intensity of these issues make it important for victims of sexual assault to seek help from professionals who have been trained to work with them. Many high schools and colleges have counselors or psychologists specially trained to work with sexual assault victims. Many communities have rape crisis centers, with professionals trained to work with victims of rape and of other types of sexual assault.

If you have been assaulted and do not know how to respond or to whom to turn, you should talk with someone who is knowledgeable about sexual assault and those who experience it. Many community or campus centers allow you to call without giving your name, and you can explore with the person on the phone how it would be best for you to respond. This leaves you with the power to decide what to do but gives you information and support as you decide.

If a friend or partner has been assaulted, you should help her seek professional help. You could call a rape crisis center and ask about available services. You could work to gently encourage your friend to call or visit a center and can ask whether going with her would be helpful. Try not to force yourself or your help on your friend, but be gently and sensitively persistent.

knowledge about sexual assault. It may be that the complexity of changing dating and sexual behaviors and attitudes requires that prevention programs be more intense and occur over a longer period than those currently described in the literature.

Therapeutic interventions for sexual assault victims are often extensive, since these victims can experience a wide range of physical, psychological, and interpersonal consequences (Wiehe & Richards, 1995). Consultation with a physician is essential either to identify any physical injury or disease or to inform the victim that she was not injured and did not contract a disease. This can be a distressing process for any victim, however, and emotional support from family and friends is essential. Treatment from mental health professionals may include individual therapy and group therapy with other victims. Group therapy allows victims to see that others have had experiences similar to theirs, and it gives all participants a supportive environment for exploring their responses to the assault and to others' reactions to it. Therapy and guidance for victims' families and friends may also be important. Family and friends may need the opportunity to explore their reactions to the assault, so that their interactions with the victim can be as helpful as possible. The recovery process for victims of sexual assault can be long and arduous, with ongoing support needed.

Victims of less violent or less physically intrusive forms of sexual coercion may also experience a wide range of consequences, with the consequences being intense and numerous for some victims and mild for others. Support is important for all victims, regardless of the intensity or number of consequences that are apparent. Helping victims express feelings about their experience, even if those feelings are more or less severe than one might expect, is an important way of showing support. Victims experiencing severe consequences, consequences that worsen over time, or consequences that persist after several months may need to consult with a mental health professional. Victims experiencing physical pain, or who are concerned about disease or injury, should consult a physician.

Prevention and Treatment Programs for Perpetrators or Potential Perpetrators

Programs to prevent men or women from initiating sexual coercion are rare. Many programs have been designed to prevent additional assaults by convicted rapists, but it is not clear if these programs would be appropriate for those who engage in sexual coercion other than rape. A cautionary note was raised by Winkel and de Kleuver (1997), who showed a videotape designed to change attitudes about sexual aggressiveness to a group of Dutch adolescents. The videotape showed vignettes of males acting in sexually aggressive ways, and each ended with significant consequences to the male (e.g., being sent to jail). However, they found that sexually aggressive attitudes were increased in the participants after viewing the videotape, possibly because of the modeling of these attitudes.

One prevention strategy aimed at a wide range of adolescents came from studies of the effects of pornography on sexual coercion. Researchers in the pornography studies were concerned that they might increase the incidence of sexual assault by showing aggressive pornography to male undergraduates, so they created an extensive debriefing process that described the ways that viewing pornography can change men's attitudes toward coercive sex. Later, they found that the undergraduates who had watched the pornography and had been told about its potential consequences had fewer attitudes supporting sexual assault than they did before watching the pornography (Mulvey & Haugaard, 1986). This suggests that helping people understand the ways in which their attitudes can be manipulated, and the ways in which these manipulated attitudes may increase their chance of initiating sexual coercion, may help them avoid being sexually coercive.

Treatment of rapists is often aimed at those who are primarily aroused by aggressive sex. Through a variety of behavioral methods, attempts are made to change their arousal patterns in response to aggression and aggressive sex. For example, rapists are encouraged to fantasize about engaging in aggressive sex and then receive self-administered shocks or other aversive consequences (e.g., a whiff of smelling salts). Theoretically, the pairing of the aversive act with the fantasy will reduce or eliminate the arousing qualities of the fantasized coercive activity (Abel et al., 1977). These efforts remain controversial, and their effectiveness continues to be debated.

CHAPTER SUMMARY

Rape, sexual assault, sexual coercion, and other terms have been used to describe many situations in which one person is forced or coerced into unwanted sexual activity. Unfortunately, none of these terms are defined consistently in the research, clinical, or advocacy literature. Therefore, it is important that the definitions of these terms are specified each time that they are used.

Most undergraduate women report at least one instance of being coerced into sex, and about 15 percent report being raped. Surveys of high school students show that many females experience some form of sexual coercion in high school or junior high school. About 25 percent of college men report coercing a woman into sexual activity at least once, and 5 to 10 percent acknowledge raping a woman. The minimal research on men as victims and women as perpetrators of sexual coercion suggests that many men are coerced or forced into being sexual, some by women and others by men, and that about 20 percent of college women report engaging in sexual intercourse with a man even though he said that he did not want to have sex.

Many influences are associated with an increased likelihood of sexual coercion. Some influences, called developmental factors, increase the likelihood that an individual will engage in sexually coercive behaviors, while other influences, called situational factors, increase the likelihood that sexual coercion will occur in a particular setting. Developmental factors include cultural beliefs about male/female relationships, individual attitudes and beliefs, inaccurate or incomplete perceptions of others' interest in engaging in sex, biologically based levels of sexual drive, pressure within peer groups to be sexual, physical or sexual abuse in childhood or the observation of family members being abused or assaulted, and deviant patterns of sexual arousal. Situational factors include drinking during social situations (particularly heavy drinking), being alone and away from other people, and being in a situation in which some types of consensual sexual activity have occurred.

Several programs have been instituted to prevent sexual coercion. Most efforts have been aimed at women—giving them the confidence and skills to recognize and diffuse potentially coercive encounters or to escape coercive encounters in which they find themselves. A few efforts aimed at males have focused on impressing them with the potential consequences of their actions, both for themselves and for potential victims. Unfortunately, most prevention efforts have had little or no influence on the likelihood that the participants will be the perpetrators or victims of sexual coercion.

Revisiting Julie

Julie's reaction to being sexually assaulted is similar to the initial reaction of many. She is emotionally upset and is confused about the incident and whether her actions might have played a role in it. Most victims of sexual assault experience a wide range of emotions and thoughts—and many of these conflict with each other. Telling sexual assault victims how they should feel or what they should think only heightens their distress, as these comments can be perceived as unsupportive and condemning.

Julie was sexually assaulted in circumstances that are similar to those experienced by many victims. She and her boyfriend were alone and away from others who might intervene on her behalf, and they were engaging in mutually consenting sexual activity. Although heavy drinking increases the likelihood of sexual coercion, many sexual assaults occur when a couple have not been drinking—as in Julie's case.

Julie's friend reacts in a supportive and helpful way. She goes to Julie so that Julie is not alone and allows her to express her confusing feelings. She encourages Julie to get help from a mental health professional and tells Julie that she will accompany her to the clinic in the morning. She confides that she was also sexually assaulted, letting Julie know that she is not alone in her experience. Julie's friend helps her make specific plans about how they will handle potentially troublesome situations (e.g., seeing Julie's boyfriend in class) and lets her know that she will be available to give Julie caring support.

- What would be the benefits and problems associated with Julie's telling other friends about being sexually assaulted?
- Are there ways in which Julie's friend can continue to be helpful to Julie?
- What struggles is Julie likely to face if she develops a physical relationship with another man?

CHAPTER 12

Gangs

Gabe and some of his friends, all of whom are about 25 years old, are sitting around in a park where their gang has hung out for many years, talking with a group of 9- and 10-year-old boys. "I was just like you guys when I was your age," he says. "I had to go to school, but it was a waste of time—who needs all that stuff here where we live? I started hanging out in this park when I was about 8 years old. My mother would hit me when she found out, and she cried and told me that I would be killed if I hung out with the gang. But if her boyfriend was there he'd hit her and tell her to shut up and tell her that men have to learn to keep what's theirs and the best way to do that is to hang out in the park and learn." Gabe then describes some of the fights that he has been in—some against other gangs and some against the police. He shows the boys two bullet scars on his arms and a scar from a knife wound on his side. "Sure, you can be like your mama and work for some rich man if you want," he continues, "or you can be like us and *take* what you want." He leans forward and grabs at the boys. Most flinch back, but one does not. He grabs this boy by the collar and pulls him forward. "You have to be like this," he continues, shaking the boy roughly. "Sure, it hurts sometimes," he says, hitting the boy on the side of the head, "but what if you don't stand up and take what you have to take—then you have no honor. With no honor—then you're just shit." He looks more closely at the boy he is holding. "You stay tough, kid—let these others be like their mamas." He lets go of the boy and says, "Now, you babies get out of here." The group runs off, clearly letting the boy who had been the center of attention run in front.

Adolescents have been forming into gangs for hundreds of years. There are reports from the Middle Ages of groups of French adolescents fighting with rival groups and committing crimes, as well as of English adolescents who formed gangs such as the Mims, Hectors, and Dead Boys (Fagan, 1996; Shelden, Tracy, & Brown, 1997). In the late 1700s, adolescent gangs began to develop in New York City, and the first organized gang, the Forty Thieves, was founded in the early 1800s. By the late 1800s, many gangs had formed in New

York City and Chicago, including the Bowery Boys, Roach Guards, and Plug-Uglies.

Although there has been long-standing concern about adolescent gangs, this concern grew dramatically in the 1980s and 1990s. For example, the number of gang-related articles in major newspapers and magazines grew from 36 in 1983 to 1,313 in 1994 (Shelden, Tracy, & Brown, 1997). Concern has been fueled by the increase in the number of gangs and by increases in their violence and drug trafficking. In a study of gangs in 1995, research found that although gang members made up only one-third of a sample of 1,000 adolescents living in high-crime areas in Rochester, New York, they committed 65 percent of the delinquent acts and 86 percent of the serious delinquent acts (Thornberry & Burch, 1997). Gang-related murders doubled in Los Angeles from the late 1980s to the middle 1990s, and in Chicago they increased by five times in that same period (Howell, 1999).

Gang members run a higher than average risk of violent death, injury, or incarceration (Flannery, Huff, & Manos, 1998). They are often targets of rival gang members and law enforcement agencies. Depending on the type of leadership of a gang, many members have little to say about gang activities or their roles in them. Potential members must endure a violent initiation, and members wanting to leave a gang may have to endure an even more violent "ranking out." Despite this, the number of gangs and gang members continues to increase. For example, in a national survey of more than 21,000 junior high and high school students, 15 percent reported the presence of gangs in their schools in 1989, with this percentage nearly doubling to 28 percent in 1995 (Chander et al., 1998). In this chapter, we will explore the rise in gang membership over the past few decades and the reasons for adolescents, joining gangs, despite the potentially severe consequences of doing so.

Our knowledge of gangs and their activities is limited because gangs are difficult to study. They often exclude outsiders and keep their illegal activities secret. To learn about gangs, some researchers have interviewed current and past gang members (e.g., Campbell, 1990), and others have associated with gangs and observed their activities (e.g., Jankowski, 1990). Although these research strategies provide useful information, gang members may hide their most violent or disturbing activities from researchers. Thus, direct information about some of most notorious gang activities probably remains unavailable.

The Plan: Before discussing gangs, we must first define what a gang is. As we will see, a generally accepted definition of what constitutes a gang does not exist, although researchers agree on several characteristics that gangs have in common. To gain some background on gangs, we will examine the demographics of gang membership and the various structures of gangs. We will then explore a variety of reasons for the existence of gangs. Understanding these reasons will provide insight into the decisions of some adolescents to join gangs. We will then explore two developmental issues: how gangs develop and how individuals develop into gang members. This will provide additional insight into the role of gangs in many communities and the ways in which children and adolescents become involved in them. Finally, we will explore several interventions used to discourage or limit gang activity.

DEFINITIONS OF A GANG

A generally accepted definition of a gang does not exist, and the characteristics used to define gangs have evolved over the past 80 years (e.g., Spergel et al., 1989). Local agencies are free to determine their own definition of a gang when gathering and reporting information. This allows groups such as the police and the media to use a definition that minimizes or maximizes the apparent prevalence of gangs if they choose to do so (Klein, 1995). The lack of a uniform definition of gangs or gang activity makes it difficult to gather consistent information on them.

Several characteristics appear consistently in definitions of a gang (Goldstein & Soriano, 1994; Parks, 1995; Shelden, Tracy, & Brown, 1997). These include self-identification as a distinct group; a distinctive name; some type of leadership; ongoing, purposeful involvement in illegal activities; and the claiming and defending of territory. Characteristics used in some definitions include being seen by others in the community as forming a distinct group, comprising those from a specific ethnic or economic group, meeting together frequently, having a specific initiation to join the gang, and using distinctive clothes, jewelry, markings, or hand signs.

While some adolescent groups are easily classified as gangs, it may be more difficult to determine whether other groups are gangs. For example, it is unclear whether six adolescents are considered a gang if they wear distinctive clothes, consider themselves a gang, and engage in only occasional minor vandalism. Similarly, the definition of gang activity is often unclear. A fight between a gang member and someone not in a gang, unrelated to any gang issue, might be considered gang violence in one city but not in another (Goldstein & Soriano, 1994). For example, Maxson and Klein (1990) found that applying the definition of gang membership used by the Chicago police to Los Angeles crime reports resulted in a 50 percent reduction in the number of homicides that would be considered gang-related in Los Angeles.

GANG DEMOGRAPHICS

The most recent national study of the prevalence of gangs was conducted in 1995 by mailing questionnaires to 4,120 police and sheriff departments (Moore, 1997). Fifty-eight percent of the respondents reported a gang problem in their city or area, and 23,388 gangs and 664,906 members were identified. Ninety percent of the respondents said that their problems with gangs were the same or getting worse. A study of 11 large and medium-sized cities found that 10.6 percent of eighth graders considered themselves to be members of a gang

(Esbensen, Deschenes, & Winfree, 1999). Lahey and colleagues (1999) estimated that about 24 percent of all boys enrolled in the Pittsburgh City Schools join a gang and that about 16 percent join a serious gang (one involved in gang fights, drug sales, stealing, or homicide).

Gang membership in large urban areas has increased over the past 30 years, and many gangs have formed in medium and small cities, as well as in rural areas (Moore, 1997). Although there has been concern that gangs from urban areas are purposefully creating satellite gangs in smaller cities, most gangs in smaller cities are started by local adolescents (Maxson, Woods, & Klein, 1996).

Most gangs are ethnically homogeneous, and most gang members come from lower-income families (Parks, 1995). Gangs in the early part of this century were comprised primarily of adolescents of European descent; however, beginning after World War II, the number of gangs of Hispanic or African American adolescents began to rise, and the number of gangs of adolescents of European descent began to fall (Fagan, 1996). Currently, most gang members are African American or Hispanic adolescents, with a smaller percentage of gangs comprising Asian American or European American adolescents (Flannery et al., 1998; Goldstein & Soriano, 1994; Klein, 1995).

Males outnumber females as gang members (Taylor, 1993), and most of a gangs' illegal activities are committed by males (Goldstein, 1994). For many years, females were primarily auxiliary members of male gangs or formed gangs closely allied to male gangs. However, increasing numbers of independent female gangs began to be established in the 1980s (Campbell, 1990). This has led to an increase in the percentage of gang members who are female. Recent studies have found that females comprise 20 percent (Cohen et al., 1995) and 38 percent (Esbensen, Deschenes, & Winfree, 1999) of the adolescents who consider themselves to be gang members.

Until the mid-1970s, most gang members were between the ages of 12 and 21, with the most active members being between the ages of 13 and 16 (Goldstein, 1991; Harris, 1994). However, the age range of members has widened over the past 20 years to include 9- to 30-year-olds, primarily because of the expansion of drug trafficking (Goldstein & Soriano, 1994). Younger members are needed as lookouts and carriers of drugs, and some members remain in the gangs longer because of the ongoing availability of a lucrative income from drug selling. Most members of well-established gangs are adults, while about 90 percent of those in emerging gangs are adolescents (Flannery et al., 1999). There is some indication that females enter and leave gangs at younger ages than males (Esbensen, Deschenes, & Winfree, 1999).

Gang members engage in more illegal activities than their peers who are not members of gangs (Flannery et al., 1999; Lahey et al., 1999). Males are most commonly arrested for assaults on other gang members, and males are more likely than females to be involved in violent offenses. Females are more likely than males to be involved in stealing and other property offenses. Contrary to public perception, selling drugs is not a primary activity for most gangs, although some gangs focus on drug sales. Even the well-publicized shootings by gang members tend to result from turf battles, rather than drug selling (Huff, 1996).

THE STRUCTURE OF GANGS

The structure of gangs can be described in several ways: by their leadership structure, by the roles of members of various ages, and by the degree of the involvement of members.

Leadership Structure

Based on his observation of many gangs, Jankowski (1990) described three types of leadership structures. The first is a vertical/hierarchical structure, with a clear hierarchy of leadership and one or two members at the top of the hierarchy (also see Patton, 1998). Members are often divided into levels of importance, with those at higher levels having considerable influence over the activities of the others. This structure helps the gang maintain discipline, implement strategies to defend themselves and their territory, and conduct money-making activities efficiently. Jankowski found that many gangs in New York City had this structure, and he suggested that it was influenced by the hierarchical structure of adult organized crime families.

The second style of leadership structure is horizontal/commission. It is a confederation of many small gangs, with the leaders of these gangs having approximately the same level of power within the confederation. Jankowski found this type of structure in emerging gangs, as several smaller gangs began to create a larger gang, or in hierarchical gangs that were becoming less organized. He also found this structure in many ongoing gangs in Los Angeles. He suggested that this is due to two factors: (a) a cultural emphasis on loyalty to family and a subsequent difficulty of gangs to accept leadership from other families and (b) a greater emphasis on defending local neighborhoods as gang territory.

The third type of leadership is labeled influential. There is no enforced hierarchy in these gangs, and a few members hold most of the power because of their influence over others and the willingness of others to see them as leaders.

Age-Based Structure

Whatever their leadership structure, most gangs have different roles for members based on their age. For example, Huff (1992) described three age groups in gangs. Children 9 to 12 years old are potential gang members and may be peripherally involved in some gang activities. These children often hang out in their own age-based groups and view older gang members as role models. Twelve- to 14-year-olds may be considered junior members of gangs. They may gradually participate in more gang activities as they develop the skills necessary to become central members of the gang. Full members of the gang are typically between 14 and 20 years of age. As already noted, however, the age range of these members is expanding to include those up to age 30 or 40. Veterans are older members who are only periodically involved in gang activities and who can be looked to for guidance by current members (Goldstein & Soriano, 1994).

The Degree of Member Involvement

Observers of gangs have noted differing levels of involvement in gang activity by members (Reiner, 1992; Thornberry et al., 1993; Vigil, 1988). At the center of the gang are regular, or hard-core, members. They are strongly attached to the gang, are consistently involved in gang activities, and are the most influential members. They typically make up 10 to 15 percent of a gang's membership. Gang activities are less central to the lives of associate or peripheral members, but, when they participate in gang activities, they have a strong attachment and dedication to the gang. Temporary members tend to join the gang at a later age and remain in the gang a short time. They participate in gang activities, but the strength of their commitment to the gang is not as strong as that of regular and associate members. Situational members join the gang for certain activities, such as a fight against another gang, but mostly remain disconnected from active involvement. Wannabes are children and early adolescents who are too young for membership and who aspire to membership and emulate gang members' behaviors. Wannabes can also be adolescents who would like to be gang members but who have not been admitted to the gang because they are not considered worthy. Finally, veterans, or veteranos, are those who were once regular or associate members but who have limited their involvement in the gang as they have gotten older and taken on other responsibilities.

WHY GANGS EXIST

Gang members face many risks, often on a daily basis. Although some gang members "age out" of the gang, many members cease active involvement because of being killed, permanently disabled, incarcerated, or chronically addicted to drugs (Jankowski, 1990). Although some adolescents are coerced into joining gangs, many others join freely; still others would like to join but are not admitted (Shelden, Tracy, & Brown, 1997). Understanding why gangs exist and what they offer to members helps us understand why they flourish in some environments.

A Source of Opportunity

Gangs often flourish in communities that provide adults and adolescents few opportunities for success (Goldstein, 1994). Gang membership can provide opportunities for success in several ways.

A Sense of Belonging

Many gang members are estranged from their families, schools, and communities (Belitz & Valdez, 1994). The gang is often the only place where members feel that they belong and are important. Members often have strong, positive feelings toward their gang and fellow members. They are committed to

BROADENING Perspectives

A Brief Exercise

On a piece of paper, list five reasons for your joining the students at your college or university, in your fraternity or sorority, or in any other social group. Then list five reasons why adolescents join gangs.

If your responses are like many others, your reasons for joining your college or social group will be mainly positive or focused on building a positive future, and your reasons for an adolescent's joining a gang will be largely negative or focused on overcoming an existing deficit.

Gangs are different from universities or fraternities, and gang members engage in many behaviors that are violent and unacceptable to most of society. However, why do we tend to assume that their reasons for joining a gang are much more negative than the reasons that others have for joining a college, sorority, or social club?

---

the gang and its members and know that the other members are willing to stand up for them (Harris, 1994; Molidor, 1996; Patton, 1998).

Monetary Success

Although there is little research on the money-making activities of gangs, drug selling and other illegal activities can provide significant income to some gangs (Fagan, 1996). The ways in which this income is distributed among members are not clear; however, many members achieve higher levels of material wealth through gang activities than they could through legal employment (Jankowski, 1990; Klein, 1995). Gang membership seems to provide a benefit even among those engaged in illegal activities: Huff (1996) found that gang members selling drugs on a daily basis make more money on each drug sale than do daily drug sellers who are not in a gang.

Self-esteem

Not every adolescent who wants to join a gang is admitted. Thus, being admitted can be a source of both self-esteem and esteem within a community or peer group (Calabrese & Noboa, 1995). Being able to survive, defend one's territory and honor, and perpetrate violence can be sources of pride. Gang membership can also be seen as a statement that the adolescent is resisting joining a legal employment market that shows little respect or appreciation for the jobs typically held by his parents or other members of his community (Campbell, 1990; Shelden, Tracy, & Brown, 1997).

Aggression and Violence

Gang activities often provide an opportunity to be aggressive and violent. Gang membership may be attractive to adolescents who want to act violently toward people in general or toward specific people.

Understanding Gang Members

A criticism that I often receive when I lecture on gangs is that I do not emphasize their negative nature enough and that I make gang members appear too "normal." Gangs are very violent, and their violence often affects innocent children, adolescents, and adults. Gang members often engage in criminal activity, including drug sales to children and adolescents. However, to understand gang members requires that we understand their motivations for joining gangs and participating in gang activities. Recognizing that these motivations may be the same as those that influence choices that all of us make can help our understanding of gangs and can help those interested in developing interventions to reduce gang membership or to reduce gang violence. It does not help to think of gang members as inhuman—even though many of their actions are not humane.

Protection

In an apparent paradox, gang membership can provide protection from violence (Esbensen, Deschenes, & Winfree, 1999; Patton, 1998). Vigil (1988) quotes a gang member as saying, "It was either get your ass kicked every day or join a gang and get your ass kicked occasionally by rival gangs" (p. 154). Adolescents who are not in a gang may be potential targets of many gangs or of adolescents not associated with a gang. Becoming a gang member provides protection because others know that they will face consequences if they attack someone in a gang. Some females join gangs for protection from physically and sexually abusive family members or peers (Chesney-Lind, Shelden, & Joe, 1996), and one reason that many females have formed their own gangs is for protection from the sexual assault and victimization that many of them face if they are involved in male gangs (Esbensen, Deschenes, & Winfree, 1999; Joe & Chesney-Lind, 1995).

A Commitment to Community

Gangs have existed in some communities for generations, and many gang members have parents or other relatives who are or have been members. Some members see their participation as helping to perpetuate a gang that is an important part of their community (Shelden, Tracy, & Brown, 1997; Vigil, 1988).

Recreation

The primary activity of gang members is hanging out together (Flannery et al., 1999). They drink or take other drugs together, party, meet members of the opposite sex, and enjoy each other's company. They may come from communities with few opportunities for group activities, or they may have become estranged from community organizations that provide these activities. Thus, gang membership can provide a place for recreation and comradeship (Fagan, 1996; Joe & Chesney-Lind, 1995; Shelden, Tracy, & Brown, 1997).

THE DEVELOPMENT OF GANGS

Exploring the social and community issues that have led to the development of gangs is another way of understanding why some adolescents join gangs and how gangs become important in the lives of individual adolescents and the communities in which they live.

Historically, gangs developed in areas of little economic or social opportunity. Because few jobs and activities were available to them, and because they were often estranged from school and other community organizations, adolescents hung around with each other and had little to do. They seldom had adult supervision, because their parents and other adults either had little interest in them or had to work at several low-paying jobs to survive financially. The nucleus of many gangs formed from these informal groups of adolescents spending time together (Shelden, Tracy & Brown, 1997).

Several influences resulted in some of these informal groups developing into cohesive gangs. In some cases, members of these fledgling gangs began to engage in illegal activities, and the structure of the gang developed as they planned and carried them out. The structures of adult organized-crime groups may have been copied by some gangs (Jankowski, 1990). As these gangs accumulated money, others may have tried to take it away from them or to take over their illegal activities. This would have encouraged the gangs to become even more cohesive, in order to safeguard their activities and the territories in which they took place. In addition, actions by the police or others to stop this illegal activity or to arrest gang members would have encouraged cohesiveness for self-protection.

In other cases, these fledgling gangs may have been confronted by groups from other neighborhoods, local business owners, or the police, even before they began any illegal activities. This confrontation would have resulted in some groups disbanding, others joining other gangs for protection, and others developing a stronger sense of cohesion so that they could defend themselves (Huff, 1992; Moore, 1991). As some of these groups became more cohesive, they may have used their cohesiveness to develop illegal activities or challenge other gangs.

As these gangs coalesced, they began to achieve status because of their ability to accumulate money, and because of their ability to maintain honor by effectively defending themselves and their territory (Horowitz, 1987). Children and adolescents envied this status—a commodity that was relatively rare in their economically and socially depressed neighborhoods—and sought to become part of the gang. As the gang grew and became more widely known, it was likely to come under increased pressure from rival gangs or from the police. This pressure encouraged the gang to grow further, so that it could better defend itself, its activities, and its territory. It also encouraged members to make the gang an important focus of their lives. As the gang became more powerful in a neighborhood, it had more influence on the socialization and aspirations of children and adolescents in the neighborhood, resulting in a steady flow of new gang members to replace those who voluntarily stopped gang activity or those who were killed, injured, or incarcerated (Jankowski, 1990; Shelden, Tracy, & Brown, 1997).

This general description helps us see some of the environmental influences on gang development: a lack of economic and social opportunity and an increasing need to defend oneself, one's honor, and one's neighborhood. It also helps us see how the developing gang's ability to generate money through illegal activities and to defend its neighborhood and its members' honor would be powerful incentives for others to strive to join the gang. As a successful gang continued to develop, it attracted adolescents in increasing numbers and began to create its own social world where behaviors that promote the goals of the gang were rewarded.

THE DECISION TO JOIN OR LEAVE A GANG

Many researchers have studied neighborhoods in which gang members live, as well as the experiences of gang members before and after entering gangs. These observations have provided information about the ways in which some children and adolescents become gang members. Unfortunately, only a few researchers have compared the experiences of gang members with those of peers who have not become gang members. As a result, there is only preliminary information about the characteristics of adolescents and their environments that increase the likelihood that some will join a gang.

An interest in becoming a gang member often begins during a child's early school-age years. Some children look up to gang members because of their power, prestige, or economic prominence or because relatives are associated with a gang. Many of these children have few supports at home and have already begun to do poorly in school. They decide to avoid family and school and begin to hang out together on the streets—often by the age of 7 to 9 (Vigil, 1988). These children emulate gang members, wear clothes with gang colors, and hang out where gang members congregate. Their interest in the gang—and the gang's attitudes toward school, community, and family—may result in their withdrawing more and more from school and family, increasing the gang's influence on their socialization. The gang may encourage these children and slowly allow them to participate in gang activities to further socialize them into the gang culture (Sheley et al., 1995). In addition, rival gang members, police, and others may label these children as members of the gang, encouraging them to turn to the gang for support and protection (Parks, 1995).

Boys who display increasing rates of antisocial behavior during their adolescence, particularly violence against other people, are more likely than their peers to join gangs (Lahey et al., 1999). Also, young adolescents who have delinquent or violent friends are more likely to join gangs (Lahey et al., 1999;

Thornberry, 1998), as are young adolescents who receive lower levels of parental supervision. Interestingly, adolescents who join gangs at an older age often experience higher levels of parental supervision than their peers who do not join gangs. Lahey et al. (1999) hypothesized that this high parental supervision may have kept these adolescents out of a gang for several years but that other forces finally overwhelmed the parental supervision and the adolescent joined the gang when he was older.

Initiation into a gang often takes place around age 13 (Huff, 1996; Vigil, 1996). Not all adolescents who want to join a gang are admitted, because of perceived weakness, excessive drug use, or some other undesirable characteristic. Some adolescents enter a gang in the same way that many college students enter college—it has always been assumed that they would do so, perhaps because relatives or friends are gang members (Shelden, Tracy, & Brown 1997). Other adolescents make a more deliberate decision to join a gang at a certain point. Still others enter a gang because they are coerced into joining by threats from the gang (Jankowski, 1990). Initiation for males typically involves a physical fight between selected current members and the new member (Patton, 1998; Vigil, 1996). The new member is not expected to win the fight but is expected to display courage during it. Females can be admitted into male-dominated gangs in two ways: by demonstrating courage in fights or by being "sexed in" (Miller, 1998). Being "sexed in" often involves having sex with multiple members of the gang. Females admitted in this way are often viewed by the males in the gang as continually available for sex. These females may have a much lower status than females admitted because of their fighting ability or courage, and they may experience considerable sexual victimization in the gang. Little information about initiation into female gangs is available.

Once an adolescent has joined a gang, the characteristics of the gang and his experiences in the community can encourage his increased devotion to the gang. Gangs often discourage members from having close friends outside the gang, and this can make the gang the only source of a member's social activities, support, and protection (Spergel et al., 1989). Romantic and sexual relationships may be difficult to find except among gang members or members of affiliated gangs. Gang membership may seriously limit an adolescent's chance for employment, causing him to rely on the gang for income (Thornberry et al., 1993). The police, schools, other community agencies, and members of rival gangs may target gang members—increasing their need to turn to the gang for protection. The process of planning and participating in risky criminal activities may also bring members of a gang closer together.

Many gang members are actively involved in gang activities for only a year or two. Most members who remain longer than a year or two either leave the gang or dramatically reduce their participation as they reach the end of adolescence (Thornberry et al., 1993). Decisions to leave a gang are often motivated by a combination of increased maturity, aging, and concern about violence (Decker & Lauritsen, 1996). Members with growing ties outside the gang are more likely than others to leave. For example, those who develop stable romantic relationships, become parents, find legal jobs, or develop supportive relationships outside the gang often find that the disadvantages of remaining an active member begin to outweigh the benefits. (As described in chapter 13, the same pattern often influences cult members to leave a cult.) After deciding to leave a gang, many members simply reduce their participation in gang activities over time, to the point where they are no longer actively involved (Decker & Lauritsen, 1996). Others endure a "ranking out" of the gang, generally consisting of the type of physical beating similar to the initiation into the gang (Jankowski, 1990). Other members move to a new area, and still others are incarcerated, permanently disabled, or killed (Jankowski, 1990).

INTERVENTIONS

Prevention Programs for School-Age Children

Programs to prevent children and young adolescents from pursuing gang membership have been presented in many schools and community groups. Many have been modeled after the D.A.R.E. drug abuse prevention program, such as Gang Resistance Education and Training (GREAT). These programs often target elementary school children and try to discourage their emulation of gang members and encourage their involvement in more socially acceptable activities. An initial evaluation of the GREAT program was discouraging and showed little influence on children and young adolescents' behaviors (Palumbo & Ferguson, 1995). A more recent, multisite evaluation involving more than 5,000 eighth-grade students showed some modest differences in attitudes about gangs and in the tendency to join a gang between students receiving the GREAT program in the seventh grade and those not (Esbensen & Osgood, 1999). Thus, the program may show some promise, but it is not having a major influence on gang membership.

Interventions with Gangs and Gang Members

During the 1950s and 1960s, interventions with gangs were done primarily by social workers who left their offices and interacted with gang members in their neighborhoods (these workers were known as *detached workers*). The primary goal of the detached workers was to transform the values of gang members rather than discourage gang membership (Goldstein, 1994). They held dances and organized trips, car washes, and athletic teams. Unfortunately, no formal evaluations of these programs were undertaken, so it is impossible to know if they were successful. Klein (1995) argued that these programs may very well have contributed to an increase in gang membership. He argued that it is the cohesiveness of gangs that promotes their continuation and that anything that promotes cohesiveness promotes the size and strength of gang membership. By promoting prosocial gang activities, the detached workers may have promoted gang cohesiveness and, consequently, their strength.

Many interventions during the 1970s and 1980s focused on improving the social and economic climates in neighborhoods where gangs were present. The theory was that, since gangs flourished in economically and politically power-less neighborhoods, enhancing the economic and political power of the neigh-borhoods would reduce gang membership (Klein, 1995). Further, it was believed that reducing poverty would give potential gang members greater op-portunities to follow legal pathways to economic success and thus reduce their interest in gangs (Spergel et al., 1989). Although projects in several large cities were begun, no evaluation of their effectiveness was undertaken, so their value remains unknown (Goldstein, 1994).

Based largely on frustrations with the lack of success of earlier efforts and concerns about escalating gang violence and drug trafficking, efforts in the 1980s changed to the suppression of gang activities (Klein, 1995). Suppression took several forms, including large-scale police sweeps and arrests through gang neighborhoods, new laws that held any identified gang member responsi-ble for the actions of other gang members, the restriction of gang members from parks and other community areas, the imposition of maximum jail sentences on gang members for any legal violation, and the public posting of fliers with the pictures of gang members who had been convicted of crimes. In addition, schools were allowed to prohibit students from wearing gang colors and using hand signs or other indications of gang affiliation. Klein (1995) argued that many of these efforts, while pleasing to the public, increased cohesiveness among gang members. As the police, school, and other agencies challenged the gangs, the gangs responded by becoming more cohesive in their fight against these "enemies."

Some current interventions include local efforts to promote the psychologi-cal growth of gang members and reduce gang violence, rather than to dis-courage gang membership. For example, Belitz and Valdez (1994) provided individual and group psychotherapy programs to gang members. The therapy focused on helping the adolescents overcome their anger and frustration about their family and neighborhood life, take responsibility for their behaviors, and interact with members of rival gangs in a prosocial way. As another example, Tabish and Orell (1996) organized mediation programs at middle schools, in or-der to defuse gang-related tensions and reduce the violence and pervasive sense of fear that exist in schools where gang tensions are high.

CHAPTER SUMMARY

Much of society deplores gangs and their violent and illegal activities. However, the number of gangs and gang members continues to increase despite efforts by the police, social work, and other community agencies to suppress gang mem-bership or direct gang activity in more prosocial directions. Adolescents join gangs for many reasons. Gang membership can enhance members' self-esteem, increase their income, and give them a close-knit support network similar to that provided by a family. Gang membership may reduce the likelihood of being the target of violence, although gangs periodically act very violently. Females who have formed their own independent gangs describe them as protection against sexual and physical aggression from family members, other adults, and male peers.

Although gangs are now present in rural communities to large metropolitan areas throughout the country, they began in areas in large cities with little social or economic opportunity. Many gangs evolved from informal groups of adolescents, as they became more focused and cohesive in order to carry out illegal activities or to protect themselves from the actions of police, businesses, or other groups of adolescents. As the gangs coalesced, adolescents with few other opportunities strived to become members, resulting in increased gang membership. As gangs became better organized, they drew more attention from police and rival gangs—attention that they met by continuing to expand and becoming more cohesive.

Some children growing up in neighborhoods with gang activity use gang members as role models. The children begin to hang out together and strive to take on characteristics of the gang. In early adolescence, some of these children will be admitted to a gang. Some of them will make the gang the center of their lives, although many others will be more peripherally involved in gang activity while remaining involved in other social, educational, and job pursuits. Although some gang members remain active into their thirties, most begin to reduce gang activity in their early twenties. The development of relationships, other employment possibilities, and concerns about being the victim of violence appear to encourage many gang members to slowly reduce their involvement, although many will continue to have some involvement as gang veterans, or veteranos.

Revisiting Gabe

The 9- and 10-year-old boys that Gabe is talking with may take the same path of gradually increasing involvement in a gang that many gang members follow. Gabe is probably aware of this and is engaging is some subtle recruitment for the gang. He appears to have spotted one boy who may be particularly brave, confident, and tough. He has tested the boy a little and has raised the boy's esteem in the eyes of his peers. He has also spent some time teaching the boys some of the principles on which the gang is based. He may pass along information about this boy to other members of the gang, and they may work to gradually bring the boy into gang activities, if he proves as competent as he appears to Gabe. Although interventions from nongang adults may dissuade the young boy from ever joining a gang, it is clear that he is impressed and influenced by Gabe and the attention that Gabe has given him.

- What strategies might Gabe and other gang members use to increase the boys' interest in the gang? Does knowing these possible strategies suggest interventions that could be used by those attempting to reduce the number of children and adolescents who join gangs?

- Does knowing the reasons that gangs exist provide guidance about the types of community programs that might decrease gang membership or gang activity?
- Is joining a gang the same as joining a fraternity or sorority? Does the eagerness with which some undergraduates pursue membership in a fraternity or sorority shed any light on the eagerness with which some adolescents pursue gang membership?

CHAPTER 13

Cults

Allison's first contact with members of the New Age of the Kingdom cult was at a street fair near her college. She was attracted to the cult members' friendliness and to their immediate acceptance of her and her quest for greater meaning in her life—something she had not experienced from her family and peers. She was also attracted to the straightforwardness and clarity of the beliefs professed by the cult members and by their message of personal fulfillment through bringing a higher standard of morality to society. At the suggestion of several cult members, she attended a weekend workshop sponsored by the cult. After the workshop, she decided to skip a week's worth of classes to attend a retreat that included lectures, discussions, and communal living with members of the cult. She maintained contact with the cult during that academic year, and at the end of the year she took a leave of absence from college and joined the cult. She withdrew about half her savings and donated it to the cult. Her parents were amazed to hear that she had joined the cult and were concerned that they would never hear from her again. However, they did receive a letter from her each month that contained mostly long descriptions of her deepening understanding of the cult's beliefs. They did not know if she ever received the letters they mailed her.

The teachings of the cult emphasized hard work, obedience to the cult leaders, communication of the message of the cult to potential new members, and abstinence from drugs and sex. Allison found aspects of the cult's communal living difficult and the social control exerted by the leaders occasionally oppressive. However, she felt closer to the other members than she had felt to people for years and found that the support of the other members helped her through difficult times. Further, she felt that the sacrifices she was making by remaining in the cult were justified by the potential that the cult's message had for improving life throughout society.

After two years, she became close friends with Tom, who had been in the cult for one year. Although they had never had a physical relationship, they gradually became very close emotionally. About six months after their friendship began, two leaders of the cult told Allison and Tom that they would have to end their relationship and stop spending so much time together. When pressed for a reason, the leaders said that Allison and Tom would need to obey the directive and that they did not feel the need to justify their decision. Although they stopped meeting,

Allison and Tom were very angry with the leaders' decision and passed messages to each other furtively. About one month later, they decided to leave the cult, so that they could resume their relationship. They told no one of their decision and one night walked 10 miles from the cult's living quarters to a nearby town. They then hitchhiked to Allison's parents' home.

When most people think about cults, they recall incidents such as the mass suicide/murder at the People's Temple in Jonestown in 1978, the siege of the Branch Davidian compound in Waco in 1993, and the 1995 poison gas attack in the Tokyo subway by Aum Shinrikyo (Hexham & Poewe, 1997). They might also recall hearing about the mass weddings performed by the Reverend Sun Myung Moon, founder of the Unification Church, for hundreds of church members and the partners that the church leaders had chosen for them (Galanter, 1989). Encounters with an orange-clad member of the International Society for Krishna Consciousness (better known as the Hare Krishnas) at an airport or on the street might also come to mind. However, most cults are neither murderous nor well recognized by the public, and they often exist in relative obscurity.

Most members join a cult during their late adolescence or early adulthood (GAP, 1992). Most who join a cult stay for only a year or two, while others make a long-term commitment (Galanter, 1980). Some are willing to die or to commit murder when instructed to do so by a cult leader.

In this chapter, we will focus on cults and the adolescents and young adults who join them. Understanding of cults and cult members is significantly limited, however, by the difficulty of getting information about them. By their nature, cults are isolated from the rest of society. They may be leery to interact with a researcher because of fears that the researcher is bent on exposing or destroying them. As a result, much of the information about cults comes from previous members, some of whom have gone through extensive psychotherapy, or "deprogramming," and may have particularly negative views of cults. Some researchers have been allowed to interview current cult members and observe cult activities (e.g., Galanter, 1989; Wright, 1987). However, whether cult leaders prohibited them from observing activities that would reflect negatively on the cult remains unknown, and it is not clear whether they were allowed to interview only cult members who the leaders knew would represent the cult in the most positive way.

The literature on cults is more divided than the literature on any other topic in this text. One side refers to cults as "destructive cults"; focuses on descriptions of physical, psychological, and sexual abuse; cites examples such as Jonestown and Waco to illustrate how cults operate; and accuses the other side of being duped by the cults through interviews with carefully selected members. Many on the other side refer to cults as "new religious movements," attribute the negative descriptions of cults by some previous members to manipulation by deprogrammers or others who have counseled them after leaving the cult, see Jonestown and Waco as aberrations, and believe that the other side is too emotionally involved to have an objective view of cults. The stark differences in their perspectives make it difficult to interpret the literature. In this chapter, however, we do not need to determine whether cults and their activities are primarily positive or negative. We are more interested in understanding why adolescents join cults, remain with cults, and leave cults. For example, judging whether a particular strategy for recruiting members is coercive or unethical will not be a goal of this chapter; however, we will try to understand why that strategy is effective with some adolescents.

The Plan: We will first explore what a cult is. The term *cult* has been applied to a wide range of religious groups. Although there is general agreement about some characteristics of cults, there is disagreement about whether all cults have other characteristics. We will then review some basic information about cults, such as how many exist and who the members are. The main part of the chapter focuses on the cult members themselves. We will explore why adolescents and young adults decide to join cults, why they remain members despite the hardships they face, and why some of them decide to leave their cult. We will then examine some interventions for cult members and previous members, including a brief look at the controversial practice of deprogramming.

DEFINITIONS OF A CULT

The term *cult* has had religious significance for thousands of years. The traditional meaning of *cult* is a group that engages in a specific form of worship or ritual within an established religion (Saliba, 1996). Some religious writers have distinguished cults from sects: a sect deviates from currently accepted religious practice by returning to earlier or more traditional beliefs and practices, while a cult deviates from current religious practice by promoting novel beliefs and practices (Stark & Bainbridge, 1987). Some religious groups that are generally accepted today could once have been labeled cults or sects, such as the Mormons, Seventh Day Adventists, and Jehovah's Witnesses (Hexham, & Poewe, 1997; Saliba, 1996).

For many people, the term *cult* has taken on a pejorative meaning, suggesting that the group is suspect, the leaders are unscrupulous, and the members possess irrational beliefs (GAP, 1992). The definitions of a cult suggested by some authors, for example, include characteristics such as using methods of mind control, using deception to recruit new members, and exploiting members (Cushman, 1984).

Other researchers, however, have used a less pejorative definition of cults. For example, Galanter (1982) use the following definition of cults and other charismatic groups:

> Members of charismatic groups typically (a) adhere to a consensual belief system, (b) sustain a high level of social cohesiveness, (c) are strongly influenced by group behavioral norms, and (d) impute charismatic (or divine) power to

the group or its leadership. The concept of *cult* adds the issue of religious deviancy and rejection of participation in majority culture. (p. 1539)

Galanter's definition allows for the inclusion of a diverse group of cults because it does not require that a group engage in deception or manipulation. Thus, his definition will be used as a general guideline in this chapter.

This chapter will not focus on satanic cults. Although there has been recent concern about satanic cults (Belitz & Schacht, 1994; Clark, 1994), many of them appear to be small, short-lived, and focused on abuse and violence. Thus, they are often quite different from other cults. In addition, very little research exists on satanic cults and most of the information about them comes from anecdotal reports by those in therapy or police custody (e.g., Miller et al., 1999).

CULT DEMOGRAPHICS

Accurately estimating the number of cults and cult members is impossible because of their physical and social isolation. Consequently, estimates of the number of people involved with cults vary dramatically. For example, Robinson, Frye, and Bradley (1997) suggested that between 2 and 5 million adolescents and young adults were involved in cults in the United States in 1997. A Gallup poll in 1981 suggested that 13 million adolescents (about half the adolescents in the United States) were involved with cults to some degree, but that estimate seems inflated (GAP, 1992). Other estimates of cult membership have been as low as 150,000 to 200,000 people in the United States (Hexham & Poewe, 1997).

Most cult members come from middle-income or upper-middle-income backgrounds, and most cult members and their parents have attended college (Galanter, 1996; GAP, 1992). About twice as many males as females join cults, and most cult members are white and single (GAP, 1992; Wright, 1987).

Little information about the families of cult members is available, and most of it comes from clinical reports. Some clinicians have described these families as tightly enmeshed; others, as troubled, and still others, as intact, close-knit, and achievement-oriented (Galanter, 1996; GAP, 1992). Since these descriptions fit many families in the United States, it is impossible to say that a certain type of family may predispose an adolescent to become a cult member.

Psychological disturbance among many adolescents and young adults who join cults has been found in some studies (e.g., Galanter et al., 1979) but not in others (e.g., Barker, 1984; GAP, 1992). Thus, it remains unclear whether psychological or emotional disturbance may encourage cult membership. It does appear, however, that many cult members were lonely and without many social ties before joining a cult (Galanter, 1996).

CHARACTERISTICS OF CULTS

Although there is considerable variability in the beliefs and practices of cults, most of them share several characteristics, some of which play an important role in recruiting and retaining members.

Strong Religious Beliefs

At the foundation of most cults are deeply held beliefs about God and the special relationship between members of the cult and God. These beliefs can help members feel special or superior to others and can create a sense of cohesion within the cult and separateness from those outside the cult. Many core members of cults have had unusual religious experiences, such as visions or speaking in tongues, that have reinforced their religious beliefs (Hexham & Poewe, 1997). Some cults reinterpret religious documents such as the Bible or develop new religious documents. A central belief of some cults is that an apocalyptic event will occur in the near future and that members of their cult will be among the few who survive (Hexham & Poewe, 1997; Saliba, 1996).

A Charismatic Leader

Cults often develop around one leader who evokes awe and obedience from others. Many cult leaders emerge after years of leading quiet and obscure lives, and often after a period of personal hardship and revelation. They often emerge during times of social unrest and proclaim a rebellious message in ways that capture the attention of others (GAP, 1992). Many leaders believe they have a special relationship with God or are God's representative on Earth (Saliba, 1996). The specific qualities that make some people charismatic leaders remain unknown.

Isolation

Many cults physically remove themselves from the rest of society by creating a communal living environment on an isolated piece of property (Galanter, 1996). Cult members in urban environments may live communally in one building and avoid interactions with those outside the cult to create psychological distance between themselves and others. Members often call themselves family and see this family as different from the rest of society.

A communal and isolated existence has many benefits for the cult. It can reduce or eliminate the flow of outside information to cult members, putting the leaders in a better position to provide only the information that they want to provide. Cult members are likely to become more dependent on the cult when no one outside the cult is available for support or guidance. In addition, the enforcement of behavioral expectations and beliefs is easier in an isolated environment.

Leadership Hierarchies and Codes of Conduct

Most cults have a strict hierarchy of leadership (Galanter, 1989). The charismatic leader in larger cults may be surrounded by several tiers of leaders, who often have strong or even complete control of those under them. Even smaller cults may be organized so that some members are required to obey the instructions of others. The ways in which cult leadership hierarchies emerge are unclear, and members typically have little or no say in choosing those who are in a position of power over them.

Cults often have specific behavioral expectations about sex, interpersonal relationships, and drugs. The heavy use of drugs is prohibited in most cults, and some discourage any drug use (Galanter, 1996; Saliba, 1996). Sex between members is often prohibited, especially in communal living situations, although there have been reports of cult leaders encouraging or even demanding sex between themselves and others (Saliba, 1996). Deep friendships can be discouraged because they interfere with members' relationship to the cult as a whole, and in some cases parents in cults have been prohibited from having close relationships with their children (Wright, 1987). Romantic relationships and marriages may be dictated by cult leaders (Galanter, 1989; Wright, 1987).

Enthusiasm and a Sense of Mission

The enthusiasm of cult members for their beliefs and for taking those beliefs to others is one of the most visible qualities of many cults. People without strong religious beliefs often find this enthusiasm difficult to understand and may misinterpret it as phoney (Saliba, 1996). Typically, however, members' outward enthusiasm matches their feelings. Members' enthusiasm is often fueled by their commitment to the cult's values and by their belief that they are playing an important part in the cult's efforts to transform society.

Some cults engage in active proselytizing of their beliefs (Saliba, 1996). Trying to convince others of the legitimacy of their beliefs can reinforce members' commitment to these beliefs and to the cult. In addition, these activities can identify potential new members of the cult—a high priority of many cults. New members can contribute money to a cult and help extend its message to others. Moreover, the addition of new members shows current members that their cult is a vibrant, growing group and that their cause is just and supported by God.

THE DEVELOPMENT OF CULT MEMBERSHIP

In this section, we will explore the processes by which adolescents and young adults join cults, deepen their commitment to cults, and leave cults. Although there are examples of people being tricked into joining cults and forced to remain members, it appears that most members make relatively free decisions to join and leave cults.

Joining a Cult

Several authors describe adolescents and young adults who join a cult as "seekers" (e.g., Galanter, 1996; Saliba, 1996; Wright, 1987). For some, this seeking is primarily positive: it is part of their identity development or an attempt to develop a meaningful religious foundation for their life. For others, the seeking is based on a perceived deficit: they are trying to reduce feelings of emptiness or depression or to find a supportive social or peer group.

Late adolescence is a time when cult membership may be particularly desirable (Hunter, 1998). Some late adolescents see themselves as ending one part of their lives, they may see little direction to their future, and they may be seeking solutions to personal and social problems. Cult membership provides clear directions for life and easily understood answers to many, if not all, of life's problems. A cult can provide structure and clear sets of rules and expectations that are not forced on the adolescent by parents or teachers but, rather, are embraced by the adolescent. In addition, late adolescence is a time of minimal commitments to people and institutions, and this lack of commitment can make it easy for an adolescent to change life direction and join a cult.

Some adolescents and young adults may actively seek out a cult, with the thought of learning more about it and possibly joining for a trial period. Others come across cult literature or meet cult members more by accident and are intrigued by the possibility of cult membership. Why a person joins a particular cult is not clear, and it may be a matter of coming across cult members who have the right message at the right time in the person's life.

Those who show interest in a cult may be encouraged to join activities with current members or to attend an orientation meeting. During these activities, they are often showered with affection and acceptance by current members (Galanter, 1996). While they learn about the cult's beliefs, they may feel a level of acceptance that they have not experienced before. This can be a strong inducement to join the cult, particularly for adolescents who are lonely.

The ways in which cult membership can enhance their lives may be described repeatedly to potential members. Being surrounded by current members who are obviously happy and fulfilled may provide powerful examples of the contentment that would follow a decision to join the cult. In addition, the mission of many cults is to achieve a better society by spreading their beliefs. Helping achieve a better society can provide strong motivation for some adolescents to join a cult.

Deepening Commitment

Although many adolescents who join cults stay for only a few weeks or months, some maintain a commitment of several years (Galanter, 1980; Wright, 1987). A match between the needs of the person and what she gets out of cult membership often encourages an ongoing commitment. In addition, several ways in which cults function can deepen commitment to the cult.

Many new members of cults report a "relief effect" of joining (Galanter, 1989, 1996). A sense of purpose and a sense of belonging increase, and depression and anxiety decrease. Those who had struggled to find meaning in their life may be relieved by the structured beliefs of cult members. As one cult member said, "Being told what to accept was a relief. You could give up the constant struggle" (GAP, 1992, p. 30). Some members report giving up the use of alcohol and other drugs, and if they live with the cult they may have a healthier diet and their physical activity probably increases (Saliba, 1996). As a result, their physical health and sense of physical well-being may improve. All these results can be powerful reinforcement for joining the cult, and they can encourage an ongoing and deepening commitment.

Stress on new cult members can be significant, however. They may need to adjust to communal living, spending many hours a day at physically demanding work, attending hours of religious lectures and discussions, and having their personal and social habits tightly controlled. Interestingly, this added stress may deepen commitment in two ways. The first is through the process of cognitive dissonance (Galanter, 1996). The theory of cognitive dissonance states that two incompatible thoughts cannot be held in the mind at the same time and that, if two incompatible thoughts exist, the mind works to change one of them so that they are no longer incompatible (Festinger, 1957). For example, most people would find the following two thoughts of cult members to be incompatible: (a) "The group to which I belong is only mildly important" and (b) "The sacrifices I am making to be in this group are justified." The two thoughts are incompatible because no sensible person could justify making great sacrifices to be in a mildly important group. Because of their dissonance, one of these two thoughts is likely to change. Some people will decide that the group is only mildly important and change their belief that their sacrifices are worth making. They are likely to leave the cult. Others will continue to believe that their sacrifices are justified and, consequently, will believe that the cult is very important. As they come to see the cult as very important, their commitment to it is likely to increase.

The second way in which this stress can increase commitment is described by Galanter (1989) as a psychological pincer. The cult creates stress on the member, but it is through the support and fellowship of the other cult members that the stress is relieved. As a result, the cult creates a situation in which stress relief occurs because of a member's ongoing affiliation with the cult and cult members. This process can tie members closer to each other and, consequently, closer to the cult to which they all belong. In addition, physical or psychological isolation from those outside the cult means that cult members receive support and reinforcement only from other cult members. Support, love, and proper guidance come only from within the cult; anxiety, depression, lack of direction, and lack of support lie outside the cult.

The physical and psychological isolation of cults also restricts information to cult members (GAP, 1992; Saliba, 1996). Leaders of a cult may spend considerable time describing those outside the cult as weak or immoral, or as enemies of the cult and the cult's beliefs. With little outside contact, cult members have no evidence that the leaders' message is wrong and may gradually come to believe the message wholeheartedly. "Brainwashing," or coercion, is not required for this. A lack of other perspectives and a constant association with other members who believe the cult's perspective are often sufficient to produce a wholehearted acceptance of the cult leaders' beliefs. In addition, members may be expected to express their acceptance of the cult's beliefs in front of other members and to defend the strength of their acceptance when challenged by leaders

BROADENING Perspectives

Brainwashing

Are cult members brainwashed into joining cults? *Brainwashing* originally referred to the treatment of prisoners of war who were held in complete isolation, subjected to starvation and physical and psychological torture, and later appeared to take on the beliefs of their captors. Although cult members do live in isolation, there is no evidence that they experience the extreme physical deprivation and torture associated with brainwashing (Barker, 1984). In addition, Saliba (1996) notes that most people who contact cults decide not to join, so their recruiting methods must not be irresistible.

Some cults are adept at using strategies that encourage joining and remaining with a cult, such as isolation of the cult, control of social contacts, and reinforcement for accepting cult teachings. It does not appear that this is brainwashing, although it may be very effective indoctrination into a certain style of thinking, believing, and acting.

or other members. This process of publicly defending their allegiance to the cult can reinforce their commitment to it.

Finally, contemplating leaving the cult may result in considerable anxiety for members. They may have severed ties with those outside the cult and, thus, believe that no one will be available to them if they leave. They may recall their negative emotional state before joining the cult and fear its return if they leave. If the cult is physically isolated, they may face the daunting task of having to walk to a nearby community, possibly with other members trying to find them and return them to the cult. If a member who is considering leaving the cult decides not to leave, her anxiety will be relieved; thus, she will be negatively reinforced for maintaining her affiliation with the cult.

Leaving a Cult

Some members are physically trapped in a cult, either because of their remote location (e.g., members of the People's Temple living in the jungle of Guyana) or because of the cult's vigilance in keeping them on the cult's property. However, many cult members have the option of leaving, even though that option may be difficult to take.

For some, the physical and psychological demands of cult life encourage them to leave. Some members find the communal living and physical labor distasteful or the long hours of religious teaching and discussion boring. Others may experience physical illnesses because of the communal living or change in diet, and others experience increased depression or guilt (GAP, 1992). These members may leave after only a few weeks or months.

Those who stay with a cult past their first few months may be tempted to leave if their expectations when joining the cult are not met. For example, some may leave if they do not experience ongoing social or emotional support. Others may leave if an initial reduction in depression or anxiety is not maintained. Members may leave because of the cult's lack of progress in transforming society or attracting a large membership (Wright, 1987). Lack of progress may call into question the leaders' closeness to God or the cult's special place in the world. Some who leave cults express disappointment in the leader's inability to live an exemplary life.

Events that decrease cult members' isolation appear to increase the likelihood of their leaving the cult. For example, members are more likely to leave a cult after visiting family and friends away from the cult (Wright, 1987), and an ongoing attachment to family and friends outside the cult is also associated with a higher likelihood of leaving (GAP, 1992). In addition, developing a close emotional bond with a fellow cult member may lead to leaving if the new bond

BROADENING Perspectives

Deadly Cult Activities

Although suicide and murder are rare cult activities, they are disturbing and often incomprehensible. How can people kill themselves, their children, or their friends on the instructions of a cult leader? Although this question cannot be answered conclusively, it may be instructive to consider other situations in which people kill others or are willing to die themselves.

Throughout history, people have been willing to kill others or to die for their religious beliefs, including the belief that their actions will increase their stature in the eyes of their god. Many religions glorify martyrs from history, and some people today are willing to kill for their religious beliefs.

Soldiers and police officers are trained to kill to protect themselves, others, and national ideals. Soldiers, police officers, firefighters, and many others have sacrificed their own lives to protect others and beliefs that they hold dear. Although we might view the goals of deadly activity by soldiers, police officers, and cult members quite differently, they all may be motivated by similar influences.

The isolation of cults, their tight behavioral controls, and their practice of requiring that members publicly acknowledge their allegiance to the cult, its beliefs, and its leaders contribute to the ability of some cult leaders to induce members to engage in deadly activities. Cult members may come to believe that those outside the cult are evil and dedicated to destroying the cult and its ideals, just as citizens of one country may come to believe this about the citizens of another country. Cult members may become convinced that their most hallowed beliefs and their way of life are being threatened by others. Without other sources of information, longtime cult members may come to believe wholeheartedly the warnings voiced by cult leaders and may be willing to act in deadly ways to protect themselves and their beliefs.

provides needed support and acceptance or if the cult leadership prohibits the continuation of the relationship (Wright, 1987).

Galanter (1983, 1996) found that leaving a cult increases many members' anxiety, depression, and guilt. The loss of social support from fellow members may be troublesome to those leaving a cult, and they may be reentering a world where they experienced little support in the past. Substituting the regimentation of cult life for a life that is largely unstructured may be difficult. They may feel guilt about leaving the other cult members and may fear that others will be punished by their leaving. However, several years after leaving a cult, most of these emotional problems are reduced significantly, perhaps as the result of the person's becoming established in society outside the cult.

A Summary of the Development of Cult Membership

Adolescents and young adults join cults for many reasons, although most of them appear related to filling a void in the person's life. Many who join cults are disillusioned with the cult or are unable to adjust to the demands of life in the cult, and they leave soon after joining. However, some members develop a deep commitment to a cult. Many members report strong feelings of belonging and friendship after joining the cult. Communal living and working, changes in diet, a focus on the mission of the cult, and prohibitions against heavy alcohol and other drug use may improve physical health and reduce feelings of anxiety or depression. The physical or psychological isolation of the cult often means that members hear only what the leaders want them to hear, and this can deepen commitment to the cult. Many members eventually decide to leave their cult. Some leave after becoming disillusioned with the cult's leaders or beliefs, finding that the sacrifices of cult membership are not being matched by the progress toward social reform that they expected, or discovering that the benefits of cult membership can be obtained in other ways with fewer sacrifices.

INTERVENTIONS

Not much information is available regarding interventions with cult members. Some groups advocate prevention programs to warn adolescents and young adults about the dangers of cults and to dissuade them from joining (see Langone, 1993). Warnings are often given in public service announcements and through churches and religious schools. Warning students about cults in public schools is problematic, however, because such warnings could be interpreted as discouraging specific religious beliefs, thus interfering with the separation of church and state.

Counseling adolescents who are considering joining a cult could be beneficial. The number of members who leave cults soon after joining suggests that their decision to join was a mistake (Saliba, 1996). Giving potential members a realistic picture of cult membership and encouraging them to consider carefully their reasons for joining a cult may result in fewer people joining and then leaving a cult soon afterwards.

HELPING
YOURSELF AND OTHERS

What to Do If You or a Friend Are Considering Joining a Cult

Although some writers caution strongly against anyone joining a cult, it would be inappropriate for me to give advice about whether joining a cult is wise or unwise. It does seem appropriate, however, to suggest that a decision to join or not join a cult should be based on a great deal of information and should be considered carefully.

Any decision to join a cult should be made only after becoming as familiar as possible with all its activities and expectations. Talking with a wide range of people already in the cult may be necessary to gain a full understanding of the members' experiences. Observing all their activities may not be possible, since many religions restrict certain activities to certain people. Caution is appropriate if only a select group of cult members is available for conversations or questions or if you are prohibited from talking with a certain member. Determining the ease with which a person can leave the cult is important, especially if the cult expects new members to live in physically isolated areas.

Remember that the cult will put its best face forward when encouraging new members to join—as is true for any organization. Positive and enjoyable activities will probably be emphasized, and stressful or strenuous activities will be downplayed. Current members who talk with you are likely to be those who are most enthusiastic about the cult. Evaluate what you learn about the cult in this light.

Ask for advice from those you trust, and listen carefully to all the points they make. As with any transaction, resist attempts to make a quick decision to join any cult or cult activity.

Parents may initiate contact with a therapist, counselor, or support group when they discover that their son or daughter has joined a cult. Parents can be quite distraught and may fear that they will lose contact with their child forever. The Group for the Advancement of Psychiatry (GAP, 1992) recommends that it is often important to reduce the parents' distress so that they can get a more realistic view of the situation. They can be told that many cult members leave the cult within a short period. By encouraging them to neither overwhelm their child with demands to leave the cult nor abandon their child to the cult, they can be in the best position to maintain ongoing contact and to give their child support if she decides to leave the cult. GAP also recommends a face-to-face interview with a cult member to assess whether she is freely maintaining cult membership. If there are signs of a break with reality or if the person's cognitive ability seems markedly impaired, then it is possible for her to be placed in a psychiatric hospital for observation and assessment, even against her will. If, on the other hand, she is alert and competent, then it is unlikely that there is any reason for an intervention for which she does not ask.

Some parents of cult members have hired a "deprogrammer" for their child. Deprogramming is controversial and typically involves forcibly removing the person from the cult and isolating her with the deprogrammer for several days of lengthy conversations about the "true nature" of the cult and how the person had been coerced into joining (Langone, 1993). Those who approve of deprogramming see it as an essential strategy against the physical and psychological coercion they perceive to be inherent in cults. Those who disapprove of deprogramming see it as nothing more than the physical and psychological coercion that the deprogrammers claim the cults use.

Those who leave cults voluntarily may also need counseling or therapy (Saliba, 1996). They may need help reintegrating themselves into their families or old social networks, or they may need help establishing new social networks outside the cult. In addition, they may need assistance overcoming the issues that encouraged them to join a cult and in integrating their cult experiences, and their decision to join the cult, into their new lives outside the cult (Galanter, 1996).

CHAPTER SUMMARY

Highly publicized and deadly activities have raised concerns about cults over the past few decades. However, little is known about most cults because of their isolation. Although cult practices can vary considerably, most of them share several characteristics, such as strong religious beliefs and sense of mission, physical or psychological isolation, a charismatic leader, a hierarchy of leadership, and strict codes of behavior.

Some adolescents who join cults hope that their involvement will help the cult promote a better world. Others join because of the friendliness and acceptance that they experience from other cult members. Still others hope that by joining they will achieve a sense of meaning in their lives or that problems, such as depression or anxiety, will be reduced.

Most people who join cults leave within a short time, often because of the restrictions of cult life or disillusionment with the cult. Those who stay longer can develop a commitment to the cult and its activities that can last for years. Several factors can influence a deep commitment to a cult, including relief from problems experienced before joining the cult, a "pincer effect" of stress caused by cult membership being relieved by association with cult members, the ability of many cult leaders to restrict information available to cult members, and anxiety about resuming life outside the cult.

Counseling for potential cult members may help them make an informed decision about joining a cult. Counseling the parents of those who join cults often involves helping them develop a realistic picture of cult life and maintain constructive contact with their child. The controversial practice of deprogramming involves forcibly removing someone from a cult and convincing her of the ways that she was deceived into joining and remaining with the cult. Members who leave cults voluntarily may benefit from some therapy or counseling, because of the significant changes that they may face in their new life outside the cult.

Revisiting Allison

Allison's experience with a cult is similar to the experiences of many older adolescents and young adults. She was originally attracted to the cult because it appeared to meet some of her needs at the time—a need for closeness to people, a need for acceptance by others, and a need to find a guiding purpose for her life. She was immediately attracted to the friendliness and acceptance she felt from members of the cult—friendliness and acceptance that may have been motivated in part by true feelings and in part because they are valuable for recruiting new members. Allison joined the cult with little warning to others; her parents and friends were probably quite surprised. However, Allison's decision was not an impulsive one. It is just that she did not discuss the decision-making process with others as she was going through it.

Allison seems to have enjoyed her experiences in the cult, although it is clear that she found it difficult to adjust to the communal living. As her fellow members supported her through her struggle to integrate into the cult, she grew closer to them and thus to the cult. Allison's closeness with Tom may have worried some of the cult leaders, as close personal relationships can reduce the intensity of the relationship that some members have with their cult. When the leaders prohibited the relationship, Allison and Tom decided to end their involvement with the cult. Perhaps the support and closeness that they felt when around each other gave them the strength to leave the support and closeness that they had felt within the cult. Leaving the cult in the middle of the night suggests that they may have been concerned about the leaders' reactions if their plans to leave were discovered. They were able to leave safely, although the physical isolation of the cult made leaving more difficult.

- What strategies might the current cult members have used when they first encountered Allison, to increase the likelihood that she would decide to join the cult?
- What characteristics of the cult or of life within the cult helped to increase Allison's commitment to it once she joined?
- What difficulties might Allison face in her life outside the cult?

CHAPTER 14

Conclusion and Final Thoughts

As we finish our exploration of problematic behaviors during adolescence, it seems appropriate to revisit and highlight a few points made throughout the text and to leave you with a few additional ideas.

RECOGNIZING THE COMPLEXITY OF INFLUENCES ON BEHAVIOR

Each of us enters and progresses through adolescence with a unique set of genes and a unique set of experiences. It is no wonder, then, that our behaviors in adolescence are motivated by a complex web of influences and that this web is different for each of us. Even experiences that many of us share, such as being bombarded with advertising images of thin people and having friends encourage us to experiment with drugs, interact with our unique biology and psychology to influence our behaviors in different ways.

The complexity of influences on our behavior require that we recognize that complexity and discard all simple explanations for the development of problematic behaviors during adolescence (e.g., advertizing with thin models causes eating disorders; peer influences cause drug use). Each of the problems described in this text is influenced by many issues, and the relative strength of these influences varies for each individual. In addition, influences that may be particularly strong at one point in the development of a problematic behavior may be unimportant at other points. Those trying to understand problematic behaviors during adolescence must be willing to embrace this complex range of influences rather than struggle to simplify them.

As discussed throughout this text, efforts to prevent problematic behaviors during adolescence or to help those with problematic behaviors must be based on an understanding of the ways in which the behaviors develop. Those working with individual adolescents (e.g., therapists, teachers, parents) must know about the range of influences on one or more problems, be willing to investigate which of the influences appear to be particularly strong with an adolescent, and then tailor their interventions to those influences. Extensive knowledge about a problem and an ability to apply that knowledge in distinctive ways when interacting with individuals are the hallmarks of those who are best able to intervene successfully with adolescents.

FOCUSING ON PEOPLE

As I wrote this text I was often struck by the suffering caused by problematic behaviors—in particular, when describing the experiences of the adolescents that began and ended each chapter. I am often moved by the depths of sadness felt by those who are depressed or who are narcissistic, the trauma experienced by those who are sexually or physically assaulted, and the confusion felt by those with an eating disorder or who are thinking about joining or leaving a cult. I am also moved as I think about the friends and families of adolescents who are experiencing these problems: how difficult it is to see a painfully shy child struggle to have a social life, how frightening it can be to see a close friend act in reckless ways.

Part of my motivation for writing this text was to help others understand problematic behaviors more clearly, so that they can intervene with troubled adolescents now or in the future. The effective prevention of problematic behaviors can save many from unnecessary suffering, and effective interventions with those experiencing problems can improve their lives and the lives of many around them. Effective prevention or intervention can be done by those in many professions. Some professionals, such as teachers, psychologists, and physicians, may work directly with adolescents. Others may work on their behalf, such as lawyers advocating for increased medical and behavioral research or business executives encouraging their corporations to sponsor agencies such as suicide prevention phone lines. And, of course, every parent and every neighbor can play significant roles in helping adolescents avoid or overcome problematic behaviors.

HELPING OTHERS OR YOURSELF

Every year, I talk with several students who ask how they can help a roommate, friend, or sibling who is struggling with one or more problematic behaviors. A few students ask about help for themselves. In addition, many students want to pursue careers helping children, adolescents, and families, and some of them volunteer in programs to improve the lives of individuals, families, and the community. It seems appropriate to conclude this text with some thoughts on the importance of helping people with problems and some suggestions for ways that you might be able to help.

Helping People You May Never Meet

There are many ways to have an influence on the lives of adolescents you may never meet. Activities on your own, with a group of friends, or through a social, preprofessional, or collegewide club can influence the lives of adolescents. Some examples of ways you can prevent problematic behaviors among adolescents or help those experiencing problems are

- Volunteer for a suicide prevention phone line, where you may be able to provide guidance and support to a suicidal adolescent.
- Work for Habitat for Humanity or a similar organization. Helping a family settle in a neighborhood and create a pleasant home environment will strengthen it and, thus, may prevent problems in their children and adolescents.
- Be a Big Brother or Big Sister. The guidance and support you give to a child or young adolescent may provide the motivation for them to struggle against making decisions in their adolescence that will have negative consequences.
- Participate in a rape-awareness rally, in which you can show support for victims and encourage the strict enforcement of laws against sexual assault.
- Work with the administrators at your college to develop programs to help the youth in your community.
- Stop people from telling jokes or making disparaging comments about people who are depressed, are shy, are too thin, or have other problems. Such comments promote an environment that inhibits adolescents from seeking help or getting better.

Helping Friends

Seeing a friend struggle with a problem can be very difficult. It is even more difficult when friends are acting in unhealthy ways or contemplating a decision that may have an important influence on their lives. Many people wrestle with whether to talk with their friend about the problem, intervene in some other way, or avoid intruding in their friend's life. Many people worry that expressing concern about a problem will be seen as an unwelcome intrusion and may hurt their friendship, but they also worry that, by standing idly by, they may not provide the support or guidance that their friend would welcome. It can be a huge dilemma.

When a student asks me about approaching a friend who is struggling with a problem, I usually suggest the following:

- Expressing concern to your friend and offering your help are acts of friendship. Most friends appreciate it when their friends express concern or would like to help them. Troubled adolescents often feel alone, and knowing that a friend is concerned can be very helpful.
- Do not be judgmental. Avoid phrases such as "What you're doing is harmful/wrong/hurting others." This is likely to make your friend defensive. If your friend is depressed, judgmental statements may increase the depression.

- Be honest, and mention two things: (a) that you are concerned about your friend and (b) that you feel somewhat awkward about raising the issues. Then state that your concern is strong enough that you want to talk, even though it feels somewhat awkward. This is often a good way to get the conversation started.
- Describe your concerns clearly. Do not beat around the bush—that usually just results in garbled communication. For example, clear statements such as "I'm concerned about the amount of drugs that you've been taking lately" or "I'm concerned about how sad you've been lately" can be helpful. If you are worried about your friend being suicidal, see the discussion of how to intervene in chapter 7.
- Be sensitive. Listen to what your friend has to say.
- Remember that this is not an attempt to convince your friend that your perspective is right. There are no winners and losers in this type of a conversation. You are simply stating your concern and offering to help. That is all. Do not feel that you have to strong-arm your friend into agreeing with you or into taking some action. Your friend might decide to act, but, if not, you should not see the conversation as a failure.

It is unlikely that anyone reading this text has the expertise to intervene effectively with friends who are experiencing meaningful levels of problematic behavior. Trying to intervene with a friend who has depression or an eating disorder, for example, is about the same as trying to set a friend's broken leg. The safest and best intervention is to provide support and to encourage your friend to seek the help of a professional who has been trained to handle the type of problem your friend has. Think of yourself as applying psychological first aid. It is like carefully carrying your friend with a broken leg to the physician to be set—it is not setting it yourself.

It may be helpful for you to investigate the appropriate professionals for your friend to see. This is often another indication of your concern and willingness to help your friend. You may, for example, get the telephone number of a rape crisis center, a clinic focused on eating disorders, or the counseling center at your college. You might even call ahead and see they have drop-in hours or whether an appointment needs to be made.

It is often difficult for someone to seek help for themselves, but they might be willing to seek help with a friend's assistance. You might give your friend the phone number of a clinic that you have learned about and encourage your friend to call for an appointment while you are there. You can offer to drive your friend to the appointment or ride on the bus with your friend. You might even go with your friend into the clinic. Do not be intrusive and tell your friend what you will do. Rather, ask your friend what would be the most helpful.

Showing concern and asking if you can help are clear indications of your concern and your friendship. Even if it is difficult to raise your concerns with friends, doing so can have a marked influence on their lives (and maybe even your own).

Helping Yourself

Seeking help for a problematic behavior is difficult for most of us. Although we would not hesitate to call for an appointment with a physician because of a bad rash or strep throat, most people are hesitant to call a counselor or therapist because they are painfully shy, are afraid to leave their apartment after being assaulted, or are too depressed to study. Many of us might hide our problems from friends or make excuses when asked about them, so our friends may not know about the difficulties we are experiencing.

Many people hesitate to seek help because they have the sense that they are at fault for their problems. Although most people would not feel at fault for having asthma or the flu, they do feel at fault for being shy or depressed. When we believe that a problem is our fault, we often believe that we must suffer with it or that we must solve it completely on our own. This is not an effective way of thinking. Solving a problem is the goal—if it can be solved with the assistance of others, then that assistance is appropriate.

Some people are able to find a therapist or counselor and get to an appointment on their own. For others, talking with a friend and asking the friend to help them get to an appointment is best. Either strategy for getting some help is fine. The issue is to get started in the process of addressing a problem.

AN INVITATION

Many opportunities exist for those interested in preventing problematic behaviors during adolescence or in helping troubled adolescents and their families. Professionals in medicine, teaching, clinical psychology, social work, law, and public policy can all influence the lives of adolescents in positive ways. Those conducting research, those providing direct services, and those influencing public policy all play important roles within the effort to reduce problematic behaviors during adolescence. Come join the effort.

Glossary

adjustment disorder   A *DSM-IV* classification in which symptoms occur that are related to a stressful event but are not severe enough to warrant another classification.

adolescence   The developmental period between childhood and adulthood, usually defined by age (e.g., 12 to 21) or educational standing (e.g., the time from junior high school through college).

affective aggression   Aggression characterized by autonomic nervous system arousal and high levels of emotional arousal.

aggression   Behavior designed to harm or injure another person or to overcome another person through physical force.

amygdala   An almond-shaped mass of gray matter at the base of the temporal lobe; part of the limbic system.

anaclitic depression   Depressed and withdrawn symptoms observed in many institutionalized infants who are raised with minimal human contact.

anhedonia   An inability to experience positive emotions.

anorexia nervosa   An eating disorder characterized by purposeful starvation, intense fear of becoming fat, problems with body image, and loss of menstruation in females.

attachment theory   Personality theory, initially described by John Bowlby, that focuses on the short- and long-term consequences of an infant's initial attachment to a primary caregiver.

attributional style   A person's way of understanding the causes of positive and negative events.

bipolar disorder   A *DSM-IV* classification for a mood disorder characterized by alternating periods of depression and mania (an exaggerated feeling of positive well-being).

bulimia nervosa   An eating disorder, characterized by cycles of bingeing and purging that occur at least twice a week for at least two months.

cognitive behavioral therapy   Psychotherapy focused on helping a person change irrational styles of thinking that are contributing to emotional and behavioral problems.

consensual   Based on mutual agreement.

continuum   A linear representation of a characteristic that occurs on a continuous basis (e.g., age), as opposed to one that occurs in groups (e.g., gender).

cortex   The outer layers of the brain surrounding the cerebrum and the cerebellum.

cult   A religious group that deviates from current religious practice by promoting novel beliefs and practices.

cultural influence   An influence on a person's development that emanates primarily from the beliefs and practices of the culture in which the person develops.

D.A.R.E.   Drug Awareness and Resistance Education: a program, usually delivered during the fifth grade, designed to prevent drug use.

dependence   State of relying on someone or something or being heavily influenced by someone or something.

depression   A psychological disturbance; can be used to describe transient or prevailing moods; and is a label for several mood disorders (e.g., major depressive disorder).

detached workers   Social workers who went into the community to interact with gangs and gang members, to reduce their antisocial behaviors and increase their prosocial behaviors.

detoxification   In drug abuse treatment, the process of removing the biological effects of a drug while minimizing withdrawal symptoms.

deviant   Someone whose behavior deviates from the accepted norm.

drug abuse   Wrongful or harmful use of drugs.

dysfunction   Impaired functioning.

dysthymia   A *DSM-IV* classification characterized by a long-term depressed mood that is not as severe as that found in major depressive disorder.

egocentrism   Focus on oneself.

fallacious   False, deceptive, or misleading.

fearful shyness   Shyness or withdrawal that usually begins during the first year of life and that occurs when an infant or a young child encounters an unfamiliar adult.

gang   An adolescent peer group whose primary activities are antisocial or delinquent.

genetic   Relating to a person's genes.

G.R.E.A.T.   Gang Resistance Education and Training: a program, delivered to elementary school children, designed to reduce gang involvement.

heroin   A narcotic, derived from morphine, with strong physical and psychological addictive properties.

hormone   Chemical substance secreted by one or more endocrine glands.

hypothalamus   A part of the brain that controls visceral functions, such as sleep cycles and body temperature, and the functioning of the pituitary gland.

inhibition   Something that restrains actions or thoughts.

instrumental aggression   Aggression characterized by low autonomic system arousal and low emotional arousal.

intervention   An attempt to influence someone or something.

intoxicate   To temporarily diminish physical or mental control through alcohol or other drugs.

introverted   Describes those who prefer to be alone, are comfortable being alone, and have little difficulty interacting with others when necessary or desired.

juvenile delinquency   Adolescent or childhood behavior that is not in accordance with the law.

longitudinal study   A study following the same group of individuals over time.

major depressive disorder (MDD)   A depressed mood that is severe but typically of shorter duration than that of dysthymia.

marijuana   The leaves and flowers of the cannabis plant.

masturbation   Manual erotic stimulation of the genital organs.

melancholia   A *DSM-IV* classification characterized by extreme depression and lack of interest in people and activities that a person once found pleasurable.

metacognitive   The process of thinking about one's thinking.

narcissism   Self-love or adoration (comes from the Greek myth of Narcissus); often involves self-centeredness, grandiosity, a sense of entitlement, exploitiveness, sensitivity to criticism, and hostility.

National Institute on Drug Abuse   Founded in 1974, NIDA is part of the United States National Institutes of Health and supports over 85 percent of the world's research on the causes and consequences of drug abuse and addiction.

neurotransmitters   Chemical substances that transmit signals across the synapse between two neurons.

pathological   Altered/abnormal; affected by disease.

peer groups   Groups of individuals belonging to the same societal group (based on age, grade or status).

predisposition   A susceptibility to something.

problematic behaviors   Behaviors that are perplexing and troublesome, and that call out for some type of solution.

psychiatry   Branch of medicine that deals with mental, emotional, or behavioral disorders.

psychoanalytic theory   Personality theory, originally described by Sigmund Freud, that focuses on the influences of unconscious conflicts and processes on behavior.

psychology   Science of mental processes and behavior.

psychotherapy   Treatment of mental, emotional, or behavioral disorders or of related physical disorders, by psychological means.

rape   Used in some circumstances to describe a wide range of nonconsensual sexual activities; in law, commonly refers to nonconsensual sexual intercourse.

reckless behavior   Risk-taking behaviors that have substantial potential personal costs and over which an individual has little control over the outcome of the behavior.

retrospective study   Research in which the participant is asked to describe events that occurred in the past (e.g., an adolescent completing a questionnaire about childhood experiences).

risk-taking behavior   Sensation-seeking behaviors that have a clear potential for injury or other negative outcomes.

self-consciousness   The degree to which one is aware of one's thoughts or emotions; often used to describe uncomfortable feelings related to one's thoughts or emotions (e.g., being concerned about feelings of guilt, anger, or shyness).

self-esteem   One's estimation of the positive or negative nature of one's self-image.

self-image   Concept of oneself.

sensation seeking   Engaging in behaviors that result in physiological arousal and psychological excitement.

sexual assault   A wide range of sexual behaviors obtained through force, through threats of force, or when a person cannot consent (e.g., when he or she is very intoxicated).

sexual coercion   A wide range of sexual behaviors obtained through force, through threats of force, when a person cannot consent, or through a broad range of verbal coercion or trickery.

shyness   Anxiety that occurs in social or interpersonal situations and that is characterized by physiological changes and emotions indicating anxiety, negative thoughts about one's social self, and awkward social behaviors.

social anxiety   Persistent, high anxiety related to social situations that might expose a person to scrutiny from others (e.g., attending a party, speaking in public).

suicide   Voluntarily and intentionally taking one's own life.

suicide ideation   Serious thoughts about whether to attempt suicide.

superego   Structure that is part of Freudian personality theory (id, ego, and superego) and that refers to one's "conscience" or the extent to which one has integrated societal expectations into one's own standards of behavior.

References

Abbey, A., & Melby, C. (1986). The effects of nonverbal cues on gender differences in perceptions of sexual intent. *Sex Roles, 15*, 283–298.

Abbey, A., McAuslan, P., & Ross, L. T. (1998). Sexual assault perpetration by college men: The role of alcohol, misperception of sexual intent, and sexual beliefs and experiences. *Journal of Social and Clinical Psychology, 17*, 167–195.

Abbey, A., Ross, L. T., McDuffie, D., & McAuslan, P. (1996). Alcohol and dating risk factors for sexual assault among college women. *Psychology of Women Quarterly, 20*, 147–169.

Abel, G. G., Barlow, D. H., Blanchard, E. G., & Guild, D. (1977). The components of rapists' sexual arousal. *Archives of General Psychiatry, 34*, 895–903.

Abramson, L. Y., Metalsky, G. I., & Alloy, L. B. (1989). Hopelessness depression: A theory-based subtype of depression. *Psychological Review, 96*, 358–372.

Adlaaf, E. M., & Smart, R. G. (1985). Drug use and religious affiliation, feelings, and behavior. *British Journal of Addiction, 80*, 163–171.

Alden, L., & Cappe, R. (1986). Interpersonal process training for shy clients. In W. Jones, J. Cheek, & S. Briggs (Eds.), *Shyness: Perspectives on research and treatment* (pp. 39–46). New York: Plenum Press.

Alder, C. (1985). An exploration of self-reported sexually aggressive behavior. *Crime and Delinquency, 31*, 306–331.

Alexander, L. A. (1998). The prevalence of eating disorders and eating disordered behaviors in sororities. *College Student Journal, 32*, 66–75.

Allen, B. P. (1987). Youth suicide. *Adolescence, 22*, 271–290.

Allgood-Merten, B., Lewinsohn, P. M., & Hops, H. (1990). Sex differences and adolescent depression. *Journal of Abnormal Psychology, 99*, 55–63.

Alm, C., & Lindberg, E. (1999). Attributions of shyness-resembling behaviors by shy and non-shy individuals. *Personality and Individual Differences, 27*, 575–585.

American Psychiatric Association (APA). (1980). *Diagnostic and statistical manual of mental disorders* (3rd ed.). Washington, DC: Author.

American Psychiatric Association (APA). (1994). *Diagnostic and statistical manual of mental disorders* (4th ed.). Washington, DC: Author.

Amick, A. E., & Calhoun, K. S. (1987). Resistance to sexual aggression: Personality, attitudinal, and situational factors. *Archives of Sexual Behavior, 16*, 153–163.

Andersen, A. E., & Holman, J. E. (1997). Males with eating disorders: Challenges for treatment and research. *Psychopharmacology Bulletin, 33*, 391–397.

Anderson, L. S. (1981). Notes on the linkage between the sexually abused child and the suicidal adolescent. *Journal of Adolescence, 4*, 157–162.

Anderson, R. N., Kochanek, K. D., & Murphy, S. L. (1997). *Report of final mortality statistics, 1995. Monthly vital statistics report* (Vol. 45, No. 11, Supp. 2). Hyattsville, MD: National Center for Health Statistics.

Angold, A., & Rutter, N. (1992). Effects of age and pubertal status on depression in a large clinical sample. *Development and Psychopathology, 4*, 5–28.

Angold. A., & Costello, E. J. (1995). The epidemiology of depression in children and adolescents. In I. Goodyer (Ed.), *The depressed child and adolescent: Developmental and clinical perspectives* (pp. 127–148). Cambridge, England: Cambridge University Press.

Apter, A., Gothelf, D., Orbach, I., Weizman, R., Ratzoni, G., Har-Even, D., & Tyano, S. (1995). Correlation of suicidal and violent behavior in different diagnostic categories in hospitalized adolescent patients. *Journal of the American Academy of Child and Adolescent Psychiatry, 34*, 912–918.

Apter, M. J. (1992). *The dangerous edge: The psychology of excitement*. New York: Free Press.

Archer, J. (1994). Testosterone and aggression: A theoretical review. *Journal of Offender Rehabilitation, 21*, 3–39.

Arnett, J. (1992). Reckless behavior in adolescence: A developmental perspective. *Developmental Review, 12*, 339–373.

Arnett, J. (1995). The young and the reckless: Adolescent reckless behavior. *Current Directions in Psychological Science, 4*, 67–71.

Asarnow, J. R., & Bates, S. (1988). Depression in child psychiatric inpatients: Cognitive and attributional patterns. *Journal of Abnormal Child Psychology, 16*, 601–615.

Asendorpf, J. B. (1993). Abnormal shyness in children. *Journal of Child Psychology and Psychiatry, 34*, 1069–1081.

Attie, I., & Brooks-Gunn, J. (1989). Development of eating problems in adolescent girls: A longitudinal study. *Developmental Psychology, 25*, 70–79.

Azrin, N. H., Donohue, B., Besalel, B. A., Kogan, E. S., & Acierno, R. (1994). Youth drug abuse treatment: A controlled outcome study. *Journal of Child and Adolescent Substance Abuse, 3*, 1–16.

Backteman, G., & Magnusson, D. (1981). Longitudinal stability of personality characteristics. *Journal of Personality, 49*, 148–160.

Bandura, A. (1977). *Social learning theory*. Englewood Cliffs, NJ: Prentice Hall.

Barker, E. (1984). *The making of a Moonie*. London: Blackwell.

Barnes, G. M., & Welte, J. W. (1986). Patterns and predictors of alcohol use among 7–12th grade students in New York State. *Journal of Studies on Alcohol, 71*, 59–69.

Bauman, K. E. (1980). *Predicting adolescent drug use*. NY: Praeger.

Baumrind, D. (1987). A developmental perspective on adolescent risk taking in contemporary America. In C. Irwin (Ed.), *Adolescent social behavior and health* (pp. 93–125). San Francisco: Jossey-Bass.

Beautrais, A. L., Joyce, P. R., & Mulder, R. T. (1997). Precipitating factors and life events in serious suicide attempts among youths aged 13 through 24 years. *Journal of the American Academy of Child and Adolescent Psychiatry, 36*, 1543–1551.

Beck, A. (1999). *Prisoners of hate*. New York: HarperCollins.

Beck, A. T. (1976). *Cognitive therapy and the emotional disorders*. New York: International Universities Press.

Beck, A. T., Rush, A. H., Shaw, B. F., & Emery, G. (1979). *Cognitive therapy of depression*. New York: Guilford Press.

Beck, K. H. (1990). Monitoring parent concerns about teenage drinking and driving: A random digit dial telephone survey. *American Journal of Drug and Alcohol Abuse, 16*, 109–124.

Beglin, S. J., & Fairburn, C. G. (1992). Women who choose not to participate in surveys on eating disorders. *International Journal of Eating Disorders, 12*, 113–116.

Belitz, J., & Schacht, A. (1994). Satanism as a response to abuse: The dynamics and treatment of satanic involvement in male youths. *Family Therapy, 21*, 81–98.

Belitz, J., & Valdez, D. M. (1994). Chicano gang youth: A need for mental health intervention and advocacy. *The Quarterly, 17*, 10–12.

Berkowitz, L. (1989). Frustration-aggression hypothesis: Examination and reformulation. *Psychological Bulletin, 106*, 59–73.

Berlin, I. N. (1987). Suicide among American Indian adolescents: An overview. *Suicide and Life Threatening Behavior, 17*, 218–232.

Birmaher, B., & Brent, D. (1998). Practice parameters for the assessment and treatment of children and adolescents with depressive disorders. *Journal of the American Academy of Child and Adolescent Psychiatry, 37*, 63S–83S.

Birmaher, B., Ryan, N., Williamson, D. E., Brent, D., Kaufman, J., Dahl, R., Perel, J., & Nelson, B. (1996). Childhood and adolescent depression: A review of the past 10 years. Part 1. *Journal of the American Academy of Child and Adolescent Psychiatry, 35*, 1427–1439.

Bleiberg, E. (1994). Normal and pathological narcissism in adolescence. *American Journal of Psychotherapy, 48*, 30–51.

Block, J. H., Gjerde, P. F., & Block, J. H. (1991). Personality antecedents of depressive tendencies in 18-year-olds: A prospective study. *Journal of Personality and Social Psychology, 60*, 726–738.

Borst, S. R., & Noam, G. G. (1993). Developmental psychopathology in suicidal and nonsuicidal adolescent girls. *Journal of the American Academy of Child and Adolescent Psychiatry, 32*, 501–508.

Borst, S. R., Noam, G. G., & Bartok, J. A. (1991). Adolescent suicidality: A clinical-developmental approach. *Journal of the American Academy of Child and Adolescent Psychiatry, 30*, 796–803.

Bradshaw, S. D. (1998). I'll go if you will: Do shy persons utilize social surrogates? *Journal of Social and Personal Relationships, 15*, 651–669.

Breitenbecher, K. H., & Scarce, M. (1999). A longitudinal evaluation of the effectiveness of a sexual assault education program. *Journal of Interpersonal Violence, 14*, 459–478.

Brent, D. A. (1987). Correlates of the medical lethality of suicide attempts in children and adolescents. *Journal of the American Academy of Child and Adolescent Psychiatry, 26*, 87–89.

Brent, D. A., Bridge, J., Johnson, B. A., & Connolly, J. (1996). Suicidal behavior runs in families: A controlled family study of adolescent suicide victims. *Archives of General Psychiatry, 53*, 1145–1152.

Brent, D. A., Johnson, B., Bartle, S., Bridge, J., Rather, C., Matta, J., Connolly, J., & Constantine, D. (1993). Personality disorder, tendency to impulsive violence, and suicidal behavior in adolescents. *Journal of the American Academy of Child and Adolescent Psychiatry, 32*, 69–75.

Brent, D. A., Kerr, M. M., Goldstein, C., Bozigar, J., Wartella, M., & Allan, M. J. (1989). An outbreak of suicide and suicidal behavior in a high school. *Journal of the American Academy of Child and Adolescent Psychiatry, 28*, 918–924.

Brent, D. A. et al. (1993). Adolescent psychiatric inpatients' risk of suicide attempt upon six-month follow-up. *Journal of the American Academy of Child and Adolescent Psychiatry, 32*, 95–105.

Briggs, S. R. (1985). A trait account of social shyness. In P. Shaver (Ed.), *Review of personality and social psychology* (Vol. 6, pp. 35–64). Beverly Hills, CA: Sage.

Brook, J. S., Whiteman, M., Cohen, P., Shapiro, J., & Balka, E. (1995). Longitudinally predicting late adolescent and young adult drug use: Childhood and adolescent precursors. *Journal of the American Academy of Child and Adolescent Psychiatry, 34*, 1230–1238.

Brook, J. S., Whiteman, M., Cohen, P., Tanaka, J. S. (1992). Childhood precursors of adolescent drug use: A longitudinal analysis. *Genetic, Social, and General Psychology Monographs, 118*, 197–213.

Brooks-Gunn, J., & Warren, M. (1989). Biological contributions to affective expression in young adolescent girls. *Child Development, 60*, 372–385.

Brooks-Gunn, J., Petersen, A. C., & Compas, B. (1995). Physiological processes and the development of childhood and adolescent depression. In I. Goodyer (Ed.), *The depressed child and adolescent: Developmental and clinical perspectives* (pp. 81–110). Cambridge, England: Cambridge University Press.

Brown, L. K., Overholser, J., Spirito, A., & Fritz, G. K. (1991). The correlates of planning in adolescent suicide attempts. *Journal of the American Academy of Child and Adolescent Psychiatry, 30*, 95–99.

Brown, S. A., et al. (1994). Correlates of success following treatment for adolescent substance abuse. *Applied and Preventive Psychology, 3*, 60–73.

Brownmiller, S. (1975). *Against our will: Men, women, and rape*. New York: Simon & Schuster.

Bruch, H. (1973). *Eating disorders*. New York: Basic Books.

Bruch, M. A., & Cheek, J. M. (1995). Developmental factors in childhood and adolescent shyness. In R. Heimberg, M. Liebowitz, D. Hope, & F. Schneier (Eds.), *Social phobia: Diagnosis, assessment, and treatment* (pp. 163–182). New York: Guilford Press.

Bruch, M. A., & Heimberg, R. G. (1994). Differences in perceptions of parental and personal characteristics between generalized and nongeneralized social phobics. *Journal of Anxiety Disorders, 8*, 155–168.

Bruch, M. A., Heimberg, R. G., Berger, P., & Collins, T. M. (1989). Social phobia and perceptions of early parental and personal characteristics. *Anxiety Research, 2*, 57–63.

Bushman, B. J. (1993). Human aggression while under the influence of alcohol and other drugs: An integrative research review. *Current Directions in Psychological Science, 2*, 148–152.

Buss, A. H. (1980). *Self-consciousness and social anxiety*. San Francisco: Freeman.

Buss, A. H. (1986). A theory of shyness. In W. Jones, J. Cheek, & S. Briggs (Eds.), *Shyness: Perspectives on research and treatment* (pp. 39–46). New York: Plenum Press.

Byrnes, J. P., Miller, D. C., & Schafer, W. D. (1999). Gender differences in risk taking: A meta-analysis. *Psychological Bulletin, 125*, 367–383.

Cairns, R. B., & Cairns, B. D. (1994). *Lifelines and risks: Pathways of youth in our time*. Cambridge, England: Cambridge University Press.

Cairns, R. B., Cairns, B. D., Neckerman, H. J., Ferguson, L. L., & Gariepy, J. L. (1989). Growth and aggression: Childhood to early adolescence. *Developmental Psychology, 25*, 320–330.

Callison, W. L., Colocino, N. R., & Vasquez, D. A. (1995). *Substance abuse prevention handbook*. Lancaster, PA: Technomic.

Campbell, A. (1990). Female participation in gangs. In C. Huff (Ed.), *Gangs in America* (pp. 163–182). London: Sage.

Cantwell, D. P., & Baker, L. (1991). Manifestations of depressive affect in adolescence. *Journal of Youth and Adolescence, 20*, 121–133.

Carlat, D. J., & Camargo, C. A. (1991). Review of bulimia nervosa in males. *American Journal of Psychiatry, 148*, 831–843.

Carlat, D. J., Camargo, C. A., & Herzog, D. B. (1997). Eating disorders in males: A report on 135 patients. *American Journal of Psychiatry, 154*, 1127–1132.

Carlson, N. R. (1986). *Physiology of behavior* (3rd ed.). New York: Allyn & Bacon.

Carroll, B. J. (1982). The dexamethasone suppression test for melancholia. *British Journal of Psychiatry, 140*, 292–304.

Carroll, L., Hoenigmann-Stovall, N., & Whitehead, G. I. (1996). The interpersonal impact of narcissism. *Journal of Social Behavior and Personality, 11*, 601–613.

Carter, J. C., Stewart, D. A., Dunn, V. J., & Fairburn, C. G. (1997). Primary prevention of eating disorders: Might it do more harm than good? *International Journal of Eating Disorders, 22*, 167–172.

Castle, C. M., Skinner, T. C., & Hampson, S. E. (1999). Young women and suntanning: An evaluation of a health education leaflet. *Psychology and Health, 14*, 517–527.

Centers for Disease Control and Prevention. (1999). *1997 youth risk behavior surveillance system*. Washington, DC: Department of Health and Human Services.

Chandler, K. A., Chapman, C. D., Rand, M., & Taylor, B. (1998). *Students' reports of school crime: 1989–1995*. Washington, DC: U.S. Department of Education.

Cheek, J. M., Carpentieri, A. M., Smith, T. G., Rierdan, J., & Koff, E. (1986). Adolescent shyness. In W. Jones, J. Cheek, & S. Briggs (Eds.), *Shyness: Perspectives on research and treatment* (pp. 105–115). New York: Plenum Press.

Cheek, J. M., & Watson, A. K. (1989). The definition of shyness: Psychological imperialism or construct validity? *Journal of Social Behavior and Personality, 4,* 85–95.

Cheek, J. M., & Busch, C. M. (1981). The influence of shyness on loneliness in a new situation. *Personality and Social Psychology Bulletin, 7,* 572–577.

Chesney-Lind, M., Shelden, R. G., & Joe, K. A. (1996). Girls, delinquency, and gang membership. In C. Huff (Ed.), *Gangs in America* (pp. 185–217). London: Sage.

Cicchetti, D., & Toth, S. L. (1998). The development of depression in children and adolescents. *American Psychologist, 53,* 221–241.

Clark, C. M. (1994). Clinical assessment of adolescents involved in satanism. *Adolescence, 29,* 461–468.

Cohen, M. I., Williams, K., Bekelman, A., & Crosse, S. (1995). Evaluation of the national youth gang prevention program. In M. Klein, C. Maxson, & J. Miller (Eds.), *The modern gang reader* (pp. 266–275). Los Angeles: Roxbury.

Cohen, O. (1997). On the origins of a sense of coherence: Sociodemographic characteristics, or narcissism as a personality trait. *Social Behavior and Personality, 25,* 49–58.

Cohn, L., Macfarlane, S., Yanez, C., & Imai, W. (1995). Risk perception: Differences between adolescents and adults. *Health Psychology, 14,* 217–222.

Coie, J. D., & Dodge, K. A. (1983). Continuities and changes in children's social status: A 5-year longitudinal study. *Merrill-Palmer Quarterly, 29,* 261–282.

Compass, B. E. (1987). Stress and life events during childhood and adolescence. *Clinical Psychology Review, 7,* 275–302.

Connors, M. E. (1996). Developmental vulnerabilities for eating disorders. In L. Smolak, M. Levine, & R. Striegel-Moore (Eds.), *The developmental psychopathology of eating disorders: Implications for research, prevention, and treatment* (pp. 285–310). Mahwah, NJ: Lawrence Erlbaum Associates.

Cooper, A. M. (1986). Narcissism. In A. P. Morrison (Ed.), *Essential papers on narcissism* (pp. 112–143). New York: New York University Press.

Cooper, P. J., & Goodyer, I. (1993). A community study of depression in adolescent girls: I. Estimates of symptom and syndrome prevalence. *British Journal of Psychiatry, 163,* 369–374.

Cowling, M. (1998). *Date rape and consent.* Adlershot, England: Ashgate.

Coyne, J. C. (1976). Toward an interactional description of depression. *Psychiatry, 39,* 28–40.

Craig, M. E. (1990). Coercive sexuality in dating relationships: A situational model. *Clinical Psychology Review, 10,* 395–423.

Cramer, P. (1979). Defense mechanisms in adolescence. *Journal of Youth and Adolescence, 7,* 1–11.

Crick, N. R. (1995). Relational aggression: The role of intent attributions, feelings of distress, and provocation types. *Development and Psychopathology, 7,* 313–322.

Cushman, P. (1984). The politics of vulnerability. *Psychohistory Review, 12,* 5–17.

Dabbs, J. M., & Morris, R. (1990). Testosterone, social class, and antisocial behavior in a sample of 4,462 men. *Psychological Science, 1,* 1–3.

Dahl, R., et al. (1992b). Regulation of sleep and growth hormone in adolescent depression. *Journal of the American Academy of Child and Adolescent Psychiatry, 31,* 615–621.

Dahl, R., & Ryan, N. D. (1996). The psychobiology of adolescent depression. In D. Cicchetti & S. L. Toth (Eds.), *Adolescence: Opportunities and challenges* (pp. 197–232). Rochester, NY: University of Rochester Press.

Dangel, R. F., Deschner, J. P., & Rasp, R. R. (1989). Anger control training for adolescents in residential treatment. *Behavioral Modification, 13,* 447–458.

Dare, C., & Szmukler, G. (1991). The family therapy of short-history, early-onset anorexia nervosa. In D. B. Woodside & L. Shekter-Wolfson (Eds.), *Family approaches to eating disorders* (pp. 25–47). Washington, DC: American Psychiatric Press.

Davidson, J., Kwan, M., & Greenleaf, W. (1982). Hormonal replacement and sexuality in men. *Clinics in Endocrinology and Metabolism, 11*, 599–623.

Davidson, S. (1990). Management. In G. MacLean (Ed.), *Suicide in children and adolescents* (pp. 98–127). Toronto: Hogrefer & Huber.

Davis, C., Claridge, G., & Cerullo, D. (1997). Reflections on narcissism: Conflicts about body image perceptions in women. *Personality and Individual Differences, 22*, 309–316.

Davis, J., Gurevich, M., LeMaire, A., & Dionne, M. (1993). Body composition correlates of weight dissatisfaction and dietary restraint in young women. *Appetite, 20*, 197–207.

de Jong, M. L. (1992). Attachment, individuation, and risk of suicide in late adolescence. *Journal of Youth and Adolescence, 21*, 357–373.

Decker, S. H., & Lauritsen, J. L. (1996). Breaking the bonds of membership. In C. Huff (Ed.), *Gangs in America* (pp. 103–122). London: Sage.

Delise, J. R. (1986). Death with honors: Suicide among gifted adolescents. *Journal of Counseling and Development, 64*, 558–560.

Delville, Y., Milloni, R. H., & Ferris, C. F. (1998). Behavioral and neurobiological consequences of social subjugation during puberty in golden hamsters. *Journal of Neuroscience, 18*, 2667–2672.

DeWilde, E. J., Kienhorst, E. C., Diekstra, R. F., & Wolters, W. H. (1993). The specificity of psychological characteristics of adolescent suicide attempters. *Journal of the American Academy of Child and Adolescent Psychiatry, 32*, 51–59.

Dicker, R., Morrissey, R. F., Abikoff, H., Alvir, J. M. J., Weissman, K., Grover, J., & Koplewicz, H. S. (1997). Hospitalizing the suicidal adolescent: Decision-making criteria of psychiatric residents. *Journal of the American Academy of Child and Adolescent Psychiatry, 36*, 769–776.

Dishion, T. J., Patterson, G. R., & Reid, J. R. (1988). Parent and peer factors associated with drug sampling in early adolescence: Implications for treatment. In E. R. Rahdert & J. Grabowski (Eds.), *Adolescent drug abuse: Analyses of treatment research* (pp. 69–93). Rockville, MD: Department of Health and Human Services.

Dodge, K. A., Bates, J. E., & Pettit, G. S. (1990). Mechanisms in the cycle of violence. *Science, 250*, 1678–1683.

Dodge, K. A., & Coie, J. D. (1987). Social information processing factors in reactive and proactive aggression in children's peer groups. *Journal of Personality and Social Psychology, 53*, 1146–1158.

Dollard, J., Doob, L. W., Miller, N. W., Mowrer, O. H., & Sear, R. (1939). *Frustration and aggression.* New Haven, CT: Yale University Press.

Donnerstein, E., & Berkowitz, L. (1981). Victim reactions in aggressive erotic films as a factor in violence against women. *Journal of Personality and Social Psychology, 41*, 710–724.

Donnerstein, E., Slaby, R. G., & Eron, L. D. (1994). The mass media and youth aggression. In L. Eron & J. Gentry (Eds.), *Reason to hope: A psychosocial perspective on violence and youth* (pp. 219–250). Washington, DC: American Psychological Association.

Drewnowski, A. (1995). Metabolic determinants of binge eating. *Addictive Behaviors, 20*, 733–745.

DuBois, D. L., Felner, R. D., Bartels, C. L., & Silverman, M. M. (1995). Stability of self-reported depressive symptoms in a community sample of children and adolescents. *Journal of Clinical Child Psychology, 24*, 386–396.

Dubow, E. F., Kausch, D. F., Blum, M. C., Reed, J., & Bush, E. (1989). Correlates of suicidal ideation and attempts in a community sample of junior high and high school students. *Journal of Clinical Child Psychology, 18*, 158–166.

Dukes, R. L., & Lorch, B. (1989). The effects of school, family, self-concept, and deviant behavior on adolescent suicide ideation. *Journal of Adolescence, 12*, 239–251.

Dukes, R. L., Ullman, J., & Stein, J. A. (1996). Three-year follow-up of drug abuse resistance education (D.A.R.E.). *Evaluation Review, 20*, 49–66.

DuRant, R. H., Getts, A., Cadenhead, C., Emans, S., & Woods, E. R. (1995). Exposure to violence and victimization and depression, hopelessness, and purpose in life among adolescents living in and around public housing. *Developmental and Behavioral Pediatrics, 16*, 233–237.

Elkind, D. (1967). Egocentrism in adolescence. *Child Development, 38*, 1025–1034.

Ellickson, P. L., Hays, R. D., & Bell, R.M. (1992). Stepping through the drug use sequence: Longitudinal scalogram analysis of initiation and regular use. *Journal of Abnormal Psychology, 101*, 441–451.

Ellis, L. (1991). A synthesized (biosocial) theory of rape. *Journal of Consulting and Clinical Psychology, 59*, 631–642.

Elmore, D. K., & DeCastro, J. (1990). Self-rated moods and hunger in relation to spontaneous eating behavior in bulimics, recovered bulimics, and normals. *International Journal of Eating Disorders, 9*, 179–190.

Emslie, G. J., Weinberg, W. A., Kennard, B. D., & Kowatch, R. A. (1994). Neurobiological aspects of depression in children and adolescents. In W. Reynolds & H. Johnston (Eds.), *Handbook of depression in children and adolescents* (pp. 143–165). New York: Plenum Press.

Emslie, G. J., et al. (1997). Double-blind placebo-controlled trial of fluoxetine in depressed children and adolescents. *Archives of General Psychiatry, 54*, 1031–1037.

Ennett, S. T., Rosenbaum, D. P., Flewelling, R. L., Bieler, G. S., Ringwalt, C. L., & Bailey, S. L. (1994). Long-term evaluation of drug abuse resistance education. *Addictive Behaviors, 19*, 113–125.

Eron, L. D., Huesmann, L. R., Lefkowitz, M. M., & Walder, L. O. (1972). Does television violence cause aggression? *American Psychologist, 27*, 253–263.

Esbensen, F., Deschenes, E. P., & Winfree, L. T. (1999). Differences between gang girls and gang boys: Results from a multisite survey. *Youth & Society, 31*, 27–53.

Esbensen, F. A., & Osgood, D. W. (1999). Gang Resistance Education and Training (GREAT): Results from the national evaluation. *Journal of Research in Crime and Delinquency, 36*, 194–225.

Eysenck, S. B., & Eysenck, H. J. (1975). *Manual of the Eysenck Personality Questionnaire*. London: Hodder & Stoughton.

Fagan, J. (1996). Gangs, drugs, and neighborhood change. In C. Huff (Ed.), *Gangs in America* (pp. 39–73). London: Sage.

Fairburn, C. G., & Belgin, S. J. (1990). Studies of the epidemiology of bulimia nervosa. *American Journal of Psychiatry, 147*, 401–408.

Fairburn, C. G., Marcus, M., & Wilson, G. T. (1993). Cognitive-behavioral therapy for binge eating and bulimia: A comprehensive treatment manual. In C. G. Fairburn & G. T. Wilson (Eds.), *Binge eating: Nature, assessment and treatment* (pp. 361–404). New York: Guilford Press.

Farrington, D. P. (1991). Childhood aggression and adult violence: Early precursors and life outcomes. In D. Pepler & K. Rubin (Eds.), *The development and treatment of childhood aggression* (pp. 5–29). Hillsdale, NJ: Lawrence Erlbaum Associates.

Fendrich, M., Mackesy-Amiti, M. E., Wislar, J. S., & Goldstein, P. J. (1997). Childhood abuse and the use of inhalants: Differences by degree of use. *American Journal of Public Health, 87*, 765–769.

Fergusson, D. M., Horwood, L. J., Lynskey, M. T. (1995). Maternal depressive symptoms and depressive symptoms in adolescents. *Journal of Child Psychology and Psychiatry, 36,* 1161–1178.

Fergusson, D. M., & Lynskey, M. T. (1995). Childhood circumstances, adolescent adjustment, and suicide attempts in a New Zealand birth cohort. *Journal of the American Academy of Child and Adolescent Psychiatry, 34,* 612–622.

Feshbach, N. D. (1997). Empathy: The formative years—Implications for clinical practice. In A. Bohart & L. Greenberg (Eds.), *Empathy reconsidered: New directions in psychotherapy* (pp. 33–59). Washington, DC: American Psychological Association.

Festinger, L. (1957). *A theory of cognitive dissonance.* New York: Row & Peterson.

Fichter, M. M. (1992). Starvation-related endocrine changes. In K. Halmi (Ed.), *Psychobiology and treatment of anorexia nervosa and bulimia nervosa* (pp. 193–219). Washington, DC: American Psychiatric Press.

Fichter, M. M., & Pirke, K. M. (1986). Effect of experimental and pathologcial weight loss upon the hypothalamo-pituitary-adrenal axis. *Psychoneuroendocrinology, 11,* 295–305.

Field, A. E., Camargo, C. A., Taylor, C. B., Berkey, C. S., Frazier, L., Gillman, M. W., & Colditz, G. A. (1999). Overweight, weight concerns, and bulimic behaviors among girls and boys. *Journal of the American Academy of Child and Adolescent Psychiatry, 38,* 754–760.

Field, T. (1992). Infants of depressed mothers. *Development and Psychopathology, 4,* 49–66.

Fiscalini, J. (1993). Interpersonal relations and the problem of narcissism. In J. Fiscalini & A. Grey (Eds.), *Narcissism and the interpersonal self* (pp. 53–90). New York: Columbia University Press.

Flannery, D. J., Huff, C. R., & Manos, M. (1998). Youth gangs: A developmental perspective. In T. Gullotta, G. Adams, & R. Montemayor (Eds.), *Delinquent violent youth: Theory and interventions* (pp. 175–204). London: Sage.

Fondacaro, M. R., & Heller, K. (1990). Attributional style in aggressive adolescent boys. *Journal of Abnormal Child Psychology, 18,* 75–89.

Fordham, K., & Stevenson-Hinde, J. (1999). Shyness, friendship quality, and adjustment during middle childhood. *Journal of Child Psychology and Psychiatry, 40,* 757–768.

French, S. A., Story, M., Downes, B., Resnick, M. D., & Blum, R. W. (1995). Frequent dieting among adolescents: Psychosocial and health behavior correlates. *American Journal of Public Health, 85,* 695–701.

Freud, S. (1950). *Beyond the pleasure principle.* New York: Liveright.

Friedman, P. G. (1980). *Shyness and reticence in students.* Washington, DC: National Education Association.

Furby, L., & Beyth-Marom, R. (1992). Risk taking in adolescence: A decision-making perspective. *Developmental Review, 12,* 1–44.

Furnham, A., & Manning, R. (1997). Young people's theories of anorexia nervosa and obesity. *Counselling Psychology Quarterly, 10,* 389–414.

Galanter, M. (1980). Psychological induction into the large group: Findings from a modern religious sect. *American Journal of Psychiatry, 137,* 1574–1579.

Galanter, M. (1982). Charismatic religious sects and psychiatry: An overview. *American Journal of Psychiatry, 139,* 1538–1542.

Galanter, M. (1983). Unification Church ("Moonie") dropouts: Psychological readjustment after leaving a charismatic religious group. *American Journal of Psychiatry, 140,* 984–989.

Galanter, M. (1989). *Cults: Faith, healing, and coercion.* New York: Oxford University Press.

Galanter, M. (1996). Cults and charismatic group psychology. In E. Shafranske (Ed.), *Religion and the clinical practice of psychology* (pp. 269–296). Washington, DC: American Psychological Association.

Galanter, M., Rabkin, R., Rabkin, J. G., Deutsch, A. (1979). The "Moonies": A psychological study of conversion and membership in a contemporary religious sect. *American Journal of Psychiatry, 136*, 165–170.

Gallup Organization (1991). *Teenage suicide study: Executive summary.* (Available from the Gallup Organization, Inc., Princeton, NJ.)

Gambrill, E. (1996). Loneliness, social isolation, and social anxiety. In M. Mattaini & B. Thyer (Eds.), *Finding solutions to social problems: Behavioral strategies for change* (pp. 345–371). Washington, DC: American Psychological Association.

Garbarino, J. (1999). The effects of community violence on children. In L. Balter & C. Tamis-LeMonda (Eds.), *Child Psychology: A handbook of contemporary issues* (pp. 412–425). Philadelphia: Psychology Press/Taylor & Francis.

Garber, J., Weiss, B., & Shanley, N. (1993). Cognitions, depressive symptoms, and development in adolescence. *Journal of Abnormal Psychology, 102*, 47–57.

Gardner, W. (1993). A life-span rational-choice theory of risk taking. In N. Bell & R. Bell (Eds.), *Adolescent risk taking* (pp. 66–83). Newbury Park, CA: Sage.

Garland, A. F., & Zigler, E. (1993). Adolescent suicide prevention. *American Psychologist, 48*, 169–182.

Garrison, C. Z., Lewinsohn, P. M., Marsteller, F., Langhinrichsen, J., & Lann, I. (1991). The assessment of suicidal behavior in adolescents. *Suicide and Life-Threatening Behavior, 21*, 217–228.

Garrison, C. Z., Schoenbach, V. S., Schluchter, M. D., & Kaplan, B. H. (1987). Life events in early adolescence. *Journal of the American Academy of Child and Adolescent Psychiatry, 26*, 865–872.

Geller, B., Reising, D., Leonard, H. L., Riddle, M. A., & Walsh, B. T. (1999). Critical review of tricyclic antidepressant use in children and adolescents. *Journal of the American Academy of Child and Adolescent Psychiatry, 38*, 513–516.

Geller, B., et al. (1990). Double-blind placebo-controlled study of nortiptyline in depressed adolescents using a fixed plasma level design. *Psychopharmacology Bulletin, 26*, 85–90.

Gilbert, N. (1992). Realities and mythologies of rape. *Society, 29*, 4–10.

Gjerde, P. F., & Block, J. (1996). A developmental perspective on depressive symptoms in adolescence: Gender differences in autocentric-allocentric modes of impulse regulation. In D. Cicchetti & S. Toth (Eds.), *Adolescence: Opportunities and challenges* (pp. 167–196). Rochester, NY: University of Rochester Press.

Gladstone, T. R., & Kaslow, N. J. (1995). Depression and attributions in children and adolescents: A meta-analytic review. *Journal of Abnormal Child Psychology, 23*, 597–606.

Glaser, K. (1968). Masked depression in children and adolescents. *Annual Progress in Child Psychiatry and Child Development, 1*, 345–355.

Glass, C. R., & Shea, C. A. (1986). Cognitive therapy for shyness and social anxiety. In W. Jones, J. Cheek, & S. Briggs (Eds.), *Shyness: Perspectives on research and treatment* (pp. 315–327). New York: Plenum Press.

Goldsmith, H. H., & Gottesman, I. I. (1996). Heritable variability and variable heritability in developmental psychopathology. In M. Lenzenweger & J. Haugaard (Eds.), *Frontiers of developmental psychopathology* (pp. 5–43). New York: Oxford University Press.

Goldstein, A. (1991). *Delinquent gangs: A psychological perspective.* Champaign, IL: Research Press.

Goldstein, A. P. (1994). Delinquent gangs. In L. Huesmann (Ed.), *Aggressive behavior: Current perspectives* (pp. 255–273). New York: Plenum Press.

Goldstein, A. P., & Soriano, F. I. (1994). Juvenile gangs. In L. Eron, J. Gentry, & P. Schlegel (Eds.), *Reason to hope: A psychosocial perspective on violence and youth* (pp. 315–333). Washington, DC: American Psychological Association.

Golub, A. L., & Johnson, B. D. (1998). Alcohol is not the gateway to hard drug abuse. *Journal of Drug Issues, 28,* 971–984.

Goodyer, I. M. (1995). The epidemiology of depression in childhood and adolescence. In F. Verhulst & H. Koot (Eds.), *The epidemiology of child and adolescent psychopathology* (pp. 210–226). Oxford, England: Oxford University Press.

Gooren, L J. (1987). Androgen levels and sex functions in testosterone-treated hypogonadal men. *Archives of Sexual Behavior, 16,* 463–473.

Gould, M. S., Fisher, P., Parides, M., Flory, M., & Shaffer, D. (1996). Psychosocial risk factors of child and adolescent completed suicide. *Archives of General Psychiatry, 53,* 1155–1162.

Graber, J. A., Brooks-Gunn, J., Paikoff, R. L., & Warren, M. P. (1994). Prediction of eating problems: An 8-year study of adolescent girls. *Developmental Psychology, 30,* 823–834.

Graham, S., Hudley, C., & Williams, E. (1992). Attributional and emotional determinants of aggression among African-American and Latino young adolescents. *Developmental Psychology, 28,* 731–740.

Gross, R. T. (1984). Patterns of maturation: Their effects on behavior and development. In M. Levine & P Satz (Eds.), *Middle childhood: Development and dysfunction.* Baltimore: University Park Press.

Grossman, M., Coate, D., & Arluck, G. M. (1987). Proce sensitivity of alcoholic beverages in the United States. In H. Holder (Ed.), *Control issues in alcohol abuse prevention* (pp. 169–198). Greenwich, CT: JAI Press.

Groth, A. N. (1979). *Men who rape.* New York: Plenum Press.

Group for the Advancement of Psychiatry (GAP) (1992). *Leaders and followers: A psychiatric perspective on religious cults.* Washington, DC: American Psychiatric Press.

Group for the Advancement of Psychiatry (GAP). (1996). *Adolescent suicide.* Washington, DC: American Psychiatric Press.

Halmi, K. A., Casper, R. C., Eckert, E., Goldberg, S., & Davis, J. (1979). Unique features associated with age of onset of anorexia nervosa. *Psychiatry Research, 1,* 209–215.

Harris, M. G. (1994). Cholas, Mexican-American girls, and gangs. *Sex Roles, 30,* 289–301.

Hausenblas, H. A., & Carron, A. V. (1999). Eating disorder indices and athletes: An integration. *Journal of Sport and Exercise Psychology, 21,* 230–258.

Hazan, C., & Zeifman, D. (1999). Pair bonds as attachments: Evaluating the evidence. In J. Cassidy & P. Shaver (Eds.), *Handbook of attachment: Theory, research, and clinical applications* (pp. 336–354). New York: Guilford Press.

Heatherton, T. F., Herman, C. P., & Polivy, J. (1991). Effects of physical threat and ego threat on eating behavior. *Journal of Personality and Social Psychology, 60,* 138–143.

Heiserman, A., & Cook, H. (1998). Narcissism, affect, and gender. *Psychoanalytic Psychology, 15,* 74–92.

Henggeler, S. W., & Borduin, C. M. (1995). Multisystemic treatment of serious juvenile offenders and their families. In I. Schwartz & P. AuClaire (Eds.), *Home-based services for troubled children* (pp. 113–130). Lincoln: University of Nebraska Press.

Henggeler, S. W., Melton, G. B., & Smith, L. A. (1992). Family preservation using multisystemic therapy. *Journal of Consulting and Clinical Psychology, 60,* 953–961.

Henry, B., Caspi, A., Moffitt, T. E., & Silva, P. A. (1996). Temperamental and familial predictors of violent and nonviolent criminal convictions: Age 3 to age 18. *Developmental Psychology 32,* 614–623.

Henry, C. S., Stephenson, A. L., Hanson, M. F., & Hargett, W. (1994). Adolescent suicide and families: An ecological approach. *Family Therapy, 21,* 63–80.

Herman, J. L. (1990). Sex offenders: A feminist perspective. In W. L. Marshall, D. R. Laws, & H. E. Barbaree (Eds.), *Handbook of sexual assault: Issues, theories, and treatment of the offender* (pp. 177–193). New York: Plenum Press.

Herrmann, D. S., & McWhirter, J. J. (1997). Refusal and resistance skills for children and adolescents: A selected review. *Journal of Counseling and Development, 75,* 177–187.

Herzog, D. B., Dorer, D. J., Keel, P. K., Selwyn, S. E., Ekeblad, E. R., Flores, A. T., Greenwood, D. N., Burwell, R. A., & Keller, M. B. (1999). Recovery and relapse in anorexia and bulimia nervosa: A 7.5-year follow-up study. *Journal of the American Academy of Child and Adolescent Psychiatry, 38,* 829–837.

Herzog, D. B., Sacks, N., Keller, M., Lavori, P., von Ranson, K., & Gray, H. (1993). Patterns and predictors of recovery in anorexia nervosa and bulimia nervosa. *Journal of the American Academy of Child and Adolescent Psychiatry, 32,* 835–842.

Hewitt, P. L., Flett, G. L., & Ediger, E. (1995). Perfectionism traits and perfectionistic self-presentation in eating disorder attitudes, characteristics, and symptoms. *International Journal of Eating Disorders, 18,* 317–326.

Hexham, I., & Poewe, K. (1997). *New religions as global cultures.* New York: Westview Press.

Higgins, S., Budney, A., Bickel, W., Hughes, J., Foerg, F., & Bader, G. (1993). Achieving cocaine abstinence with a behavioral approach. *American Journal of Psychiatry, 150,* 763–769.

Higgins, S. T. (1997). Applying learning and conditioning theory to the treatment of alcohol and cocaine abuse. In B. Johnson & J. Roache (Eds.), *Drug addiction and its treatment* (pp. 367–386). Philadelphia: Lippincott-Raven.

Hill, J. P., & Lynch, M. E. (1983). The intensification of gender-related role expectations during early adolescence. In J. Brooks-Gunn & A. Petersen (Eds.), *Girls at puberty: Biological and psychological perspectives* (pp. 83–102). New York: Plenum Press.

Hokanson, J. E., Rubert, M. P., Welker, R. A., Hollander, G. R., & Hedeen, C. (1989). Interpersonal concomitants and antecedents of depression among college students. *Journal of Abnormal Psychology, 98,* 209–217.

Holinger, P. C., Offer, D., Barter, J. T., & Bell, C. C. (1994). *Suicide and homicide among adolescents.* New York: Guilford Press.

Hops, H., Davis, B., & Lewin, L. M. (1999). The development of alcohol and other substance use: A gender study of family and peer context. *Journal of Studies on Alcohol, 13,* 22–31.

Horesh, N., Gothelf, D., Ofek, H., Weizman, T., & Apter, A. (1999). Impulsivity as a correlate of suicidal behavior in adolescent psychiatric inpatients. *Crisis, 20,* 8–14.

Horne, L. R., Van Vactor, J. C., & Emerson, S. (1991). Disturbed body image in patients with eating disorders. *American Journal of Psychiatry, 148,* 211–215.

Horowitz, R. (1987). Community tolerance of gang violence. *Social Problems, 34,* 437–450.

Howell, J. C. (1999). Youth gang homicides: A literature review. *Crime and Delinquency, 45,* 208–241.

Huesmann, L. R., Eton, L. D., Lefkowitz, M. M., & Walder, L. O. (1984). Stability of aggression over time and generations. *Developmental Psychology, 20,* 1120–1134.

Huff, C. O. (1999). Source, recency, and degree of stress in adolescence and suicide ideation. *Adolescence, 34,* 81–89.

Huff, C. R. (1992). The new youth gangs: Social policy and malignant neglect. In I. Schwartz (Ed.), *Juvenile justice and public policy* (pp. 20–44). New York: Lexington.

Huff, C. R. (1996). The criminal behavior of gang members and non-gang at-risk youth. In C. R. Hoff (Ed.), *Gangs in America* (2nd ed., pp. 75–102). Thousand Oaks, CA: Sage.

Huizinga, D. A., & Elliott, D. S. (1987). Juvenile offenders: Prevalence, offender incidence, and arrest rates by race. *Crime and Delinquency, 33,* 206–233.

Hulbert, D. F., Apt, C., Gtasar, S., Wilson, N., & Murphy, Y. (1994). Sexual narcissism: A validation study. *Journal of Sex and Marital Therapy, 20,* 24–34.

Hunter, E. (1998). Adolescent attraction to cults. *Adolescence, 33,* 709–713.

Igra, V., & Irwin, C. E. (1996). Theories of adolescent risk-taking behavior. In R. J. DiCliemente, W. B. Hansen, & L. E. Ponton (Eds.), *Handbook of adolescent health risk behavior* (pp. 35–51). New York: Plenum Press.

Institute of Medicine (IM). (1994). *Growing up tobacco free.* Washington DC: National Academy Press.

Institute of Medicine (IM). (1997). *Dispelling the myths about addiction.* Washington, DC: National Academy Press.

Ishiyama, F. I. (1984). Shyness: Anxious social sensitivity and self-isolating tendency. *Adolescence, 19,* 903–911.

Jackson, T., Towson, S., & Narduzzi, K. (1997). Predictors of shyness: A test of variables associated with self-presentational models. *Social Behavior and Personality, 25,* 149–154.

Jacobson, K. C., & Rowe, D. C. (1999). Genetic and environmental influences on the relationships between family connectedness, school connectedness, and adolescent depressed mood: Sex differences. *Developmental Psychology, 35,* 926–939.

Jacoby, M. (1990). *Individuation and narcissism.* London: Routledge.

Jaffe, J. H. (1992). Current concepts of addiction. In C. O'Brien & J. Jaffe (Eds.), *Addictive states* (pp. 1–21). New York: Raven Press.

Jankowski, M. S. (1990). *Islands in the street: Gangs and American urban society.* Berkeley: University of California Press.

Jarman, M., & Walsh, S. (1999). Evaluating recovery from anorexia nervosa and bulimia nervosa: Integrating lessons learned from research and clinical practice. *Clinical Psychology Review, 19,* 773–788.

Jessor, R. (1991). Risk behavior in adolescence. *Journal of Adolescent Health Care, 12,* 597–605.

Joe, K. A., & Chesney-Lind, M. (1995). *Gender and Society, 9,* 408–431.

Johnson, I. M., & Sigler, R. T. (1997). *Forced sexual intercourse in intimate relationships.* Aldershot, England: Ashgate.

Johnson, R., & Kaplan, H. B. (1990). Stability of psychological symptoms: Drug use consequences and intervening processes. *Journal of Health and Social Behavior, 3,* 277–291.

Johnston, L.D., O'Malley, P.M., & Bachman, J.G. (1999). National survey results on drug use from the Monitoring the Future study, 1975–1998. Volume I: Secondary school students. (NIH Publication No., 99-4660.) Rockville, MD: National Institute on Drug Abuse.

Jones, W. H., Briggs, S. R., & Smith, T. G. (1986). Shyness: Conceptualization and measurement. *Journal of Personality and Social Psychology, 51,* 629–639.

Journal of School Health. (1995). Suicide among children, adolescents, and young adults, United States, 1980–1992. *Journal of School Health, 65,* 272–273.

Jurich, A. P., & Collins, O. P. (1996). Adolescents, suicide, and death. In C. Corr & D. Balk (Eds.), *Handbook of adolescent death and bereavement* (pp. 65–84). New York: Springer.

Kagan, J., & Reznick, J. S. (1986). In W. Jones, J. Cheek, & S. Briggs (Eds.), *Shyness: Perspectives on research and treatment* (pp. 81–90). New York: Plenum Press.

Kales, E. F. (1989). A laboratory study of cognitive factors in bulimia. *Annals of the New York Academy of Science, 575,* 535–537.

Kaminer, Y. (1994). *Adolescent substance abuse.* New York: Plenum Press.

Kandel, D. B. (1982). Epidemiological and psychosocial perspectives on adolescent drug use. *Journal of the American Academy of Child Psychiatry, 20,* 328–347.

Kanin, E. J. (1957). Male aggression in dating-courtship relations. *American Journal of Sociology, 63,* 197–204.

Kanin, E. J. (1967). An examination of sexual aggression as a response to sexual frustration. *Journal of Marriage and the Family, 24,* 428–433.

Kanin, E. J. (1985). Date rapists: Differential sexual socialization and relative deprivation. *Archives of Sexual Behavior, 14,* 219–231.

Kanin, E. J., & Parcell, S. (1977). Sexual aggression: A second look at the offended female. *Archives of Sexual Behavior, 8,* 67–76.

Kaplan, A. S., & Woodside, D. B. (1987). Biological aspects of anorexia nervosa and bulimia nervosa. *Journal of Consulting and Clinical Psychology, 55,* 645–653.

Karusu, T. B. (1990). Toward a clinical model of psychotherapy for depression. I: Systematic comparison of three psychotherapies. *American Journal of Psychiatry, 147,* 133–147.

Kashani, J. H., Dandoy, A. C., & Reid, J. C. (1992). Hopelessness in children and adolescents. *Acta Paedopsychiatrica, 55,* 33–39.

Kashden, J., Fremouw, W. J., Callahan, T. S., & Franzen, M. D. (1993). Impulsivity in suicidal and nonsuicidal adolescents. *Journal of Abnormal Child Psychology, 21,* 339–353.

Kaslow, N. J., Brown, R. T., & Mee, L. L. (1994). Cognitive and behavioral correlates of childhood depression: A developmental perspective. In W. Reynolds & H. Johnston (Eds.), *Handbook of depression in children and adolescents* (pp. 97–121). New York: Plenum Press.

Kegeles, S. M., Adler, N. E., & Irwin, C. E. (1988). Sexually active adolescents and condoms: Changes over one year in knowledge, attitudes, and use. *American Journal of Public Health, 78,* 460–461.

Keller, M. B., et al. (1988). Course of major depression in nonreferred adolescents. *Journal of Affective Disorders, 15,* 235–243.

Kernberg, O. F. (1975). Further contributions to the treatment of narcissistic personalities: A reply to the discussion by Paul H. Orstein. *International Journal of Psychoanalysis, 56,* 245–247.

Kernberg, O. F. (1998b). Pathological narcissism and narcissistic personality disorder. In E. F. Ronningstam (Ed.), *Disorders of narcissism* (pp. 29–51). Washington, DC: American Psychiatric Press.

Khantzian, E. J. (1985). The self-medication theory of addictive disorders: Focus on heroin and cocaine dependence. *American Journal of Psychiatry, 142,* 1259–1264.

Killen, J., Taylor, C. B., Hammer, L. D., & Litt, J. (1993). An attempt to modify unhealthy eating attitudes and weight reduction practices of young adolescent girls. *International Journal of Eating Disorders, 13,* 369–384.

King, C. A., Raskin, A., Gdowski, C. L., Butkus, M., & Opipari, L. (1990). Psychosocial factors associated with urban adolescent female suicide attempts. *Journal of the American Academy of Child and Adolescent Psychiatry, 29,* 289–294.

Kirk, W. G. (1993). *Adolescent suicide: A school-based approach to assessment and intervention.* Champaign, IL: Research Press.

Kirkpatrick, C., & Kanin, E. J. (1957). Male sex aggression on a university campus. *American Sociological Review, 22,* 52–58.

Klein, M. W. (1995). *The American street gang.* New York: Oxford University Press.

Klein, M. W. (1995). *The American street gang: Its nature, prevalence, and control.* New York: Oxford University Press.

Koss, M. P., Gidycz, C. A., & Wisniewski, N. (1987). The scope of rape: Incidence and prevalence of sexual aggression and victimization in a national sample of higher education students. *Journal of Consulting and Clinical Psychology, 55,* 162–170.

Koss, M. P., Leonard, K., Beezley, D., & Oros, C. (1985). Nonstranger sexual aggression. *Sex Roles, 12,* 981–992.

Koss, M. P., & Oros, C. (1982). Sexual experiences survey. *Journal of Consulting and Clinical Psychology, 50*, 455–457.

Kovacs, M., & Beck, A. T. (1978). Maladaptive cognitive structures in depression. *American Journal of Psychiatry, 135*, 525–533.

Kreipe, R. E., & Harris, J. P. (1992). Myocardial impairment resulting from eating disorders. *Pediatric Annals, 21*, 760–768.

Kulbartz-Klatt, Y. J., Florin, I., & Pook, M. (1999). Bulimia nervosa: Mood changes do have an impact on body width estimation. *British Journal of Clinical Psychology, 38*, 279–287.

Kurcher, S., & Sokolov, S. (1995). Adolescent depression: Neuroendocrine aspects. In I. Goodyer (Ed.), *The depressed child and adolescent: Developmental and clinical perspectives* (pp. 195–224). Cambridge, England: Cambridge University Press.

Laederach, J., Fischer, W., Bowen, P., & Ladame, F. (1999). Common risk factors in adolescent suicide attempters revisited. *Crisis, 20*, 15–22.

Lahey, B. B., Gordon, R. A., Loeber, R., Stouthamer-Loeber, M., & Farrington, D. P. (1999). Boys who join gangs: A prospective study of predictors of first gang entry. *Journal of Abnormal Child Psychology, 27*, 261–276.

Laliberté, M., Boland, F. J., & Leichner, P. (1999). Family climates: Family factors specific to disturbed eating and bulimia nervosa. *Journal of Clinical Psychology, 55*, 1021–1040.

Langone, M. D. (1993). Helping cult victims. In M. D. Langone (Ed.), *Recovery from cults*. New York: Norton.

Lazarus, P. J. (1982). Incidence of shyness in elementary-school children. *Psychological Reports, 51*, 904–906.

Leenaars, A. A., & Lester, D. (1995). Assessment and prediction of suicide risk in adolescents. In J. Zimmerman & G. Asnis (Eds.), *Treatment approaches with suicidal adolescents* (pp. 47–70). New York: John Wiley & Sons.

Lehnert, K. L., Overholser, J. C., & Spirito, A. (1994). Internalized and externalized anger in adolescent suicide attempters. *Journal of Adolescent Research, 9*, 105–119.

Leitenberg, H., Yost, L. W., & Carroll-Wilson, M. (1986). Negative cognitive errors in children: Questionnaire development, normative data, and comparisons between children with and without self-reported symptoms of depression, low self-esteem, and evaluation anxiety. *Journal of Consulting and Clinical Psychology, 54*, 528–536.

Leshner, A. I. (1997). Addiction is a brain disease, and it matters. *Science, 278*, 45–70.

Levy, J. C., & Deykin, E. Y. (1989). Suicidality, depression, and substance abuse in adolescence. *American Journal of Psychiatry, 146*, 1462–1467.

Lewin, L. M., Davis, B., & Hops, H. (1999). Childhood social predictors of adolescent antisocial behavior: Gender differences in predictive accuracy and efficacy. *Journal of Abnormal Child Development, 27*, 277–292.

Lewinsohn, P. M., & Clarke, G. N. (1999). Psychosocial treatments for adolescent depression. *Clinical Psychology Review, 19*, 329–342.

Lewinsohn, P. M., Rohde, P., & Seeley, J. R. (1993). Psychosocial characteristics of adolescents with a history of suicide attempt. *Journal of the American Academy of Child and Adolescent Psychiatry, 32*, 60–68.

Lewinsohn, P. M., Rohde, P., & Seeley, J. R. (1996). Adolescent suicidal ideation and attempts: Prevalence, risk factors, and clinical implications. *Clinical Psychology: Science and Practice, 3*, 25–46.

Liddle, H. A., & Dakof, G. A. (1995). Efficacy of family therapy for drug abuse: Promising but not definitive. *Journal of Marital and Family Therapy, 21*, 511–544.

Loeber, R., & Hay, D. (1997). Key issues in the development of aggression and violence from childhood to early adulthood. *Annual Review of Psychology, 48*, 371–410.

Loeber, R., & Stouthammer-Loeber, M. (1998). Development of juvenile aggression and violence. *American Psychologist, 53,* 242–259.

Lonsway, K. A. (1996). Prevention of acquaintance rape through education: What do we know? *Psychology of Women Quarterly, 20,* 229–265.

Lore, R. K., & Schultz, L. A. (1993). Control of human aggression: A comparative perspective. *American Psychologist, 48,* 16–25.

Lorenz, K. (1966). *On aggression.* New York: Harcourt, Brace, & World.

LoSciuto, L., Hilbert, S. M., Fox, M. M., Porcellini, L., & Lanphear, A. (1999). A two-year evaluation of the Woodrock Youth Development Project. *The Journal of Early Adolescence, 19,* 488–507.

Lowe, M. R. (1993). The effects of dieting on eating behavior: A three-factor model. *Psychological Bulletin, 114,* 100–121.

Lucas, A. R. (1992). The eating disorder "epidemic": More apparent than real? *Pediatric Annals, 21,* 746–751.

Lueger, R. J., & Gill, K. J. (1990). Frontal-lobe cognitive dysfunction in conduct disorder adolescents. *Journal of Clinical Psychology, 46,* 696–706.

Lyng, S. (1990). Edgework: A social psychological analysis of risk taking. *American Journal of Sociology, 95,* 851–886.

Lyubomirsky, S., & Nolen-Hoeksema, S. (1993). Self-perpetuating properties of dysphoric rumination. *Journal of Personality and Social Psychology, 65,* 339–349.

Maccoby, E. E. (1988). Gender as a social category. *Developmental Psychology, 24,* 755–765.

Madge, N., & Harvey, J. G. (1999). Suicide among the young: The size of the problem. *Journal of Adolescence, 22,* 145–155.

Malamuth, N. (1986). Predictors of naturalistic sexual aggression. *Journal of Personality and Social Psychology, 50,* 953–962.

Malamuth, N., & Check, J. (1985). The effects of aggressive pornography on beliefs in rape myths: Individual differences. *Journal of Research in Personality, 19,* 299–320.

Malamuth, N. M., Heavey, C. L., & Linz, D. (1993). Predicting men's antisocial behavior against women: The interaction model of sexual aggression. In G. Hall, R. Hirshman, J. Graham, & M. Zaragoza (Eds.), *Sexual aggression: Issues in etiology, assessment, and treatment* (pp. 63–97). Washington, DC: Taylor & Francis.

Malamuth, N. M., Sockloskie, R. J., Koss, M. P., & Tanaka, J. S. (1991). Characteristics of aggressors against women: Testing a model using a national sample of college students. *Journal of Consulting and Clinical Psychology, 59,* 670–681.

Mann, T., et al. (1997). Are two interventions worse than one? Joint primary and secondary prevention of eating disorders in college females. *Health Psychology, 16,* 215–225.

Marshall, W. L., & Eccles, A. (1993). Pavlovian conditioning processes in adolescent sex offenders. In H. Barbaree & W. Marshall (Eds.), *The juvenile sex offender* (pp. 118–142). New York: Guilford Press.

Marton, P., Connolly, J., Kutcher, S., & Korenblum, M. (1993). Cognitive social skills and social self-appraisal in depressed adolescents. *Journal of the American Academy of Child and Adolescent Psychiatry, 32,* 739–744.

Masterson, J. F. (1990). Psychotherapy of borderline and narcissistic disorders: Establishing a therapeutic alliance. *Journal of Personality Disorders, 4,* 182–191.

Maxson, C. L., & Klein, M. W. (1990). Street gang violence: Twice as great or half as great? In C. R. Huff (Ed.), *Gangs in America* (pp. 71–100). Newbury Park, CA: Sage.

Maxson, C. L., Woods, K. J., & Klein, M. W. (1996, February). Street gang migration: How big a threat? *National Institute of Justice Journal, 24–31.*

McCaul, K., Gladue, B. A., & Joppa, M. (1992). Winning, losing, mood, and testosterone. *Hormones and Behavior, 26*, 486–504.

McCauley, E., et al. (1993). Depression in young people. *Journal of the American Academy of Child and Adolescent Psychiatry, 32*, 714–722.

McCracken, J. T., Poland, R. E., & Tondo, L. et al. (1991). Cholinergic dysregulation in adolescent depression: Preliminary comparisons with adult depression. *Proceedings of the 144th Annual Meeting of the American Psychiatric Association,* New Orleans.

McFarlane, A. H., Bellissimo, A., & Normal, G. R. (1995). The role of family and peers in social self-efficacy: Links to depression in adolescence. *American Journal of Orthopsychiatry, 65*, 402–410.

Meilman, P. W., von Hippel, F. A., & Gaylor, M. (1991). Self-induced vomiting in college women: Its relations to eating, alcohol use, and Greek life. *Journal of American College Health, 40*, 39–41.

Mezzich, A. C., Tarter, R. E., Giancola, P. R., Lu, S., Kirisci, L., & Parks, S. (1997). Substance use and risky sexual behavior in female adolescents. *Drug and Alcohol Dependence, 14*, 157–166.

Miller, I. J. (1992). Interpersonal vulnerability and narcissism: A conceptual continuum for understanding and treating narcissistic psychopathology. *Psychotherapy, 29*, 216–224.

Miller, J. (1998). Gender and victimization risk among young women in gangs. *Journal of Research in Crime and Delinquency, 35*, 429–453.

Miller, R. S. (1995). On the nature of embarrassability: Shyness, social evaluation, and social skill. *Journal of Personality, 63*, 315–339.

Miller, T. W., Veltkamp, L. J., Kraus, R. F., Lane, T., & Heister, T. (1999). An adolescent vampire cult in rural America: Clinical issues and case study. *Child Psychiatry and Human Development, 29*, 209–219.

Millon, T. (1998). DSM narcissistic personality disorder. In E. F. Ronningstam (Ed.), *Disorders of narcissism* (pp. 75–101). Washington, DC: American Psychiatric Press.

Mills, R. S., & Rubin, K. H. (1993). Socialization factors in the development of social withdrawal. In K. H. Rubin & J. B. Asendorpf (Eds.), *Social withdrawal, inhibition, and shyness in childhood* (pp. 117–148). Hillsdale, NJ: Lawrence Erlbaum Associates.

Minnesota Department of Education (MDE). (1989). *Minnesota student survey report.* St. Paul: Learner Support Systems.

Minuchin, S., Rosman, D. L., & Baker, L. (1978). *Psychsomatic families: Anorexia nervosa in context.* Cambridge, MA: Harvard University Press.

Minuchin, S., et al. (1975). A conceptual model of psychosomatic illness in children. *Archives of General Psychiatry, 32*, 1031–1038.

Mitchell, J. E., & Mussell, M. P. (1995). Comorbidity and binge eating disorder. *Addictive Behaviors, 20*, 725–732.

Molidor, C. E. (1996). Female gang members: A profile of aggression and victimization. *Social Work, 41*, 251–257.

Montgomery, R. L., & Haemmerlie, F. M. (1986). Self-perception theory and re-education of heterosocial anxiety. *Journal of Social and Clinical Psychology, 4*, 503–512.

Moore, C. D., & Waterman, C. K. (1999). Predicting self-protection against sexual assault in dating relationships among heterosexual men and women, gay men, lesbians, and bisexuals. *Journal of College Student Development, 40*, 132–140.

Moore, J. P. (1997). *Highlights of the 1995 national youth gang survey.* Washington, DC: Office of Juvenile Justice and Delinquency Prevention.

Moore, J. W. (1991). *Going down to the barrio: Homeboys and homegirls in change.* Philadelphia: Temple University Press.

Moreno, A. M., & Thelan, H. (1993). A preliminary prevention program for eating disorders in a junior high school population. *Journal of Youth and Adolescence, 22,* 109–124.

Morrongiello, B. A., & Rennie, H. (1998). Why do boys engage in more risk taking than girls? The role of attributions, beliefs, and risk appraisals. *Journal of Pediatric Psychology, 23,* 33–43.

Muehlenhard, C. (1998). The importance and danger of studying sexually aggressive women. In P. Anderson & C. Struckman-Johnson (Eds.), *Sexually aggressive women: Current perspectives and controversies* (pp. 19–48). NY: Guilford.

Muehlenhard, C., & Hollabaugh, L. (1988). Do women sometimes say no when they mean yes? The prevalence and correlates of women's token resistance to sex. *Journal of Personality and Social Psychology, 54,* 872–879.

Muehlenhard, C., & Linton, M. (1987). Date rape and sexual aggression in dating situations: Incidence and risk factors. *Journal of Counseling Psychology, 34,* 186–196.

Muelenhard, C. L., Powch, I. G., Phelps, J. L., & Giusti, L. M. (1992). Definitions of rape: Scientific and political implications. *Journal of Social Issues, 48,* 23–44.

Munroe, R. (1955). *Schools of psychoanalytic thought.* New York: Holt, Rinehart & Winston.

National Institute on Drug Abuse (NIDA). (1997a). *Monitoring the future study—High school and youth trends.* Washington, DC: Author.

National Institute on Drug Abuse (NIDA). (1997b). *Monitoring the future study—Trends in drug use among college students.* Washington, DC: Author.

Nestler, E. J., & Aghajanian, G. K. (1997). Molecular and cellular basis of addiction. *Science, 278,* 58–63.

Nolen-Hoeksema, S. (1987). Sex differences in unipolar depression: Evidence and theory. *Psychological Bulletin, 101,* 259–283.

Nolen-Hoeksema, S., & Girgus, J. S. (1994). The emergence of gender differences in depression during adolescence. *Psychological Bulletin, 115,* 424–443.

North, C., Gowers, S., & Byram, V. (1997). Family functioning and life events in the outcome of adolescent anorexia nervosa. *British Journal of Psychiatry, 171,* 545–549.

Novacek, J., Raskin, R., & Hogan, R. (1991). Why do adolescents use drugs? Age, sex, and user differences. *Journal of Youth and Adolescence, 20,* 475–492.

Nowinski, J. (1990). *Substance abuse in adolescents and young adults.* New York: Norton.

Nucci, L., Guerra, N., & Lee, J. (1991). Adolescent judgements of the personal, prudential, and normative aspects of drug usage. *Developmental Psychology, 27,* 841–848.

Nurcombe, B. (1994). The validity of the diagnosis of major depression in childhood and adolescence. In W. Reynolds & H. Johnston (Eds.), *Handbook of depression in children and adolescents* (pp. 61–77). New York: Plenum Press.

Nutt, D. J. (1997). Neuropharmacological basis for tolerance and dependence. In B. Johnson & J. Roache (Eds.), *Drug addiction and its treatment* (pp. 171–186). Philadelphia: Lippincott-Raven.

O'Brien, C. P. (1996). Recent developments in the pharmacotherapy of substance abuse. *Journal of Consulting and Clinical Psychology, 64,* 677–685.

O'Brien, C. P. (1997a). A range of research-based pharmacotherapies for addiction. *Science, 278,* 66–70.

O'Brien, C. P., Childress, A. R., McLellan, A. T., & Ehrman, R. (1992). A learning model of addiction. In C. O'Brien & J. Jaffe (Eds.), *Addictive states* (pp. 157–177). New York: Raven Press.

Olweus, D. (1980). Familial and temperamental determinants of aggressive behavior in adolescent boys: A causal analysis. *Developmental Psychology, 16,* 644–662.

Palumbo, D. J., & Ferguson, J. L. (1995). Evaluating gang resistance education and training (GREAT). *Evaluation Review, 19,* 597–619.

Parks, C. P. (1995). Gang behavior in the schools: Reality or myth? *Educational Psychology Review, 7,* 41–68.

Parry-Jones, W. (1995). Historical aspects of mood and its disorders in young people. In I. Goodyer (Ed.), *The depressed child and adolescent: Developmental and clinical perspectives* (pp. 1–26). Cambridge, England: Cambridge University Press.

Patros, P. G., & Shamoo, T. K. (1989). *Depression and suicide in children and adolescents.* Boston: Allyn & Bacon.

Patterson, G. R. (1996). Some characteristics of a developmental theory for early-onset delinquency. In M. Lenzenweger & J. Haugaard (Eds.), *Frontiers of developmental psychopathology* (pp. 81–124). New York: Oxford University Press.

Patterson, G. R., Littman, R. A., & Bricker, W. (1967). Assertive behavior in children: A step toward a theory of aggression. *Monographs of the Society for Research in Child Development, 32* (5, Serial No. 113).

Patton, G. C. (1988). Mortality in eating disorders. *Psychological Medicine, 18,* 947–951.

Patton, P. L. (1998). The gangstas in our midst. *The Urban Review, 30,* 49–76.

Pepler, D. J., & Carig, W. M. (1995). A peek behind the fence: Naturalistic observations of aggressive children with remote audiovisual recording. *Developmental Psychology, 31,* 348–353.

Pepler, D. J., King, G., Byrd, W. (1991). A social-cognitively based social skills training program for aggressive children. In D. Pepler & K. Rubin (Eds.), *The development and treatment of childhood aggression* (pp. 361–379). Hillsdale, NJ: Lawrence Erlbaum Associates.

Pepler, D. J., & Slaby, R. G. (1994). Theoretical and developmental perspectives on youth and violence. In L. Eron & J. Gentry (Eds.), *Reason to hope: A psychosocial perspective on violence and youth* (pp. 27–58). Washington, DC: American Psychological Association.

Perry, B. D., Pollard, R. A., Blakley, T. L., Baker, W. L., & Vigilante, D. (1995). Childhood trauma, the neurobiology of adaptation, and "use-dependent" development of the brain: How "states" become "traits." *Infant Mental Health Journal, 16,* 271–291.

Petersen, A. C., Sarigiani, P. A., & Kennedy, R. E. (1991). Adolescent depression: Why more girls? *Journal of Youth and Adolescence, 20,* 247–271.

Peterson, C. B., & Mitchell, J. E. (1999). Psychosocial and pharmacological treatment of eating disorders: A review of research findings. *Psychotherapy in Practice, 55,* 685–697.

Pfeffer, C. R., Normandin, L., & Kakuma, T. (1994). Suicidal children grow up: Suicidal behavior and psychiatric disorders among relatives. *Journal of the American Academy of Child and Adolescent Psychiatry, 33,* 1087–1097.

Pfefferbaum, B., & Wood, P. B. (1994). Self-report study of impulsive and delinquent behavior in college students. *Journal of Adolescent Health, 15,* 295–302.

Phillips, D. P., & Carstensen, L. O. (1986). Clustering of teenage suicides after television news stories about suicide. *New England Journal of Medicine, 315,* 685–689.

Pike, K. M, & Rodin, J. (1991). Mothers, daughters, and disordered eating. *Journal of Abnormal Psychology, 100,* 198–204.

Piran, N. (1998). Prevention of eating disorders: The struggle to chart new territories. *Eating Disorders: The Journal of Treatment and Prevention, 6,* 365–371.

Plomin, R., & Daniels, D. (1986). Genetics and shyness. In W. H. Jones, J. M. Cheek, & S. R. Briggs (Eds.), *Shyness: Perspectives on research and treatment* (pp. 63–80). New York: Plenum Press.

Plomin, R., & Rowe, D. C. (1979). Genetic and environmental etiology of social behavior in infancy. *Developmental Psychology, 15,* 62–72.

Polivy, J., & Herman, C. P. (1985). Dieting and bingeing: A causal analysis. *American Psychologist, 40*, 193–201.

Polivy, J., & Herman, C. P. (1987). Diagnosis and treatment of normal eating. *Journal of Consulting and Clinical Psychology, 55*, 635–644.

Polivy, J., & Herman, C. P. (1993). Etiology of binge eating: Psychological mechanisms. In C. G. Fairburn & G. T. Wilson (Eds.), *Binge eating: Nature, assessment and treatment* (pp. 144–172). New York: Guilford Press.

Ponton, L. E. (1996). Disordered eating. In R. DiClemente, W. Hansen, & L. Ponton (Eds.), *Handbook of adolescent health risk behavior* (pp. 83–113). New York: Plenum Press.

Porteus, M. (1979). Survey of the problems of normal 15-year-olds. *Journal of Adolescence, 2*, 307–323.

Poznanski, E. O., & Mokros, H. B. (1994). Phenomenology and epidemiology of mood disorders in children and adolescents. In W. Reynolds & H. Johnston (Eds.), *Handbook of depression in children and adolescents* (pp. 19–39). New York: Plenum Press.

Probst, M., Vandereycken, W., Van Coppenole, H., & Pieters, G. (1998). Body size estimation in anorexia nervosa patients: The significance of overestimation. *Journal of Psychosomatic Research, 44*, 451–456.

Pulver, S. E. (1986). Narcissism: The term and the concept. In A. P. Morrison (Ed.), *Essential papers on narcissism* (pp. 91–111). New York: New York University Press.

Quadrel, M. J., Fischhoff, B., & Davis, W. (1993). Adolescent (in)vulnerability. *American Psychologist, 48*, 102–116.

Quinsey, V., Chaplin, T. C., & Upfold, D. (1984). Sexual arousal to nonsexual violence and sadomasochistic themes among rapists and non-sex-offenders. *Journal of Consulting and Clinical Psychology, 52*, 651–657.

Rao, U., Hammen, C., & Daley, S. E. (1999). Continuity of depression during the transition to adulthood: A 5-year longitudinal study of young women. *Journal of the American Academy of Child and Adolescent Psychiatry, 38*, 908–915.

Rao, U., et al. (1995). Unipolar depression in adolescents: Clinical outcome in adulthood. *Journal of the American Academy of Child and Adolescent Psychiatry, 34*, 566–578.

Raskin, R., Novacek, J., & Hogan, R. (1991). Narcissistic self-esteem management. *Journal of Personality and Social Psychology, 60*, 911–918.

Reiner, I. (1992). *Gangs, crime and violence in Los Angeles.* Arlington, VA: National Youth Gang Information Center.

Reinherz, H. Z., et al. (1995). Early psychosocial risks for adolescent suicide ideation and attempts. *Journal of the American Academy of Child and Adolescent Psychiatry, 34*, 599–611.

Rende, R. D., Plomin, R., Reiss, D., & Hetherington, E. M. (1993). Genetic and environmental influences on depressive symptomatology in adolescence: Individual differences and extreme scores. *Journal of Child Psychology and Psychiatry, 34*, 1387–1398.

Reynolds, W. M., & Mazza, J. J. (1994). Suicide and suicidal behaviors in children and adolescents. In W. Reynolds & H. Johnston (Eds.), *Handbook of depression in children and adolescents* (pp. 525–580). New York: Plenum Press.

Rhodewalt, F., & Morf, C. C. (1998). On self-aggrandizement and anger: A temporal analysis of narcissism and affective reactions to success and failure. *Journal of Personality and Social Psychology, 74*, 672–685.

Rickgarn, R. L. (1994). *Perspectives on college student suicide.* Amityville, NY: Baywood.

Robin, A. L., Gilroy, M., & Dennis, A. B. (1998). Treatment of eating disorders in children and adolescents. *Clinical Psychology Review, 18*, 421–446.

Robinson, B., Frye, E. M., & Bradley, L. J. (1997). Cult affiliation and disaffiliation: Implications for counseling. *Counseling and Values, 41*, 166–173.

Robinson, J. L., Kagan, J., Reznick, J. S., & Corley, R. (1992). The heritability of inhibited and uninhibited behavior: A twin study. *Developmental Psychology, 28*, 1030–1037.

Romney, T. M. (1991). Prosecuting mothers of drug-exposed babies: The state's interest in protecting the rights of a fetus versus the mother's constitutional rights to due process, privacy, and equal protection. *Journal of Contemporary Law, 17*, 325–344.

Rowe, D. C. (1994). Genetic and cultural explanations of adolescent risk taking and problem behavior. In R. D. Ketterlinus & M. E. Lamb (Eds.), *Adolescent problem behaviors: Issues and research* (pp. 109–126). Hillsdale, NJ: Lawrence Erlbaum Associates.

Rubin, C., et al. (1992). Depressive affect in normal adolescents: Relationship to life stress, family, and friends. *American Journal of Orthopsychiatry, 62*, 430–441.

Ruderman, A. J., & Besbeas, M. (1992). Psychological characteristics of dieters and bulimics. *Journal of Abnormal Psychology, 101*, 383–390.

Russell, D. E. H. (1984). *Sexual exploitation, child sexual abuse, and workplace harassment.* Beverly Hills, CA: Sage.

Russell, G., Szmukler, G., Dare, C., & Eisler, I. (1987). An evaluation of family therapy in anorexia nervosa and bulimia nervosa. *Archives of General Psychiatry, 44*, 1047–1056.

Saliba, J. A. (1996). *Understanding new religious movements.* Grand Rapids, MI: Eerdmans.

Santrock, J. W. (1999). *Adolescence.* New York: McGraw-Hill.

Schachter, S., & Singer, J. (1962). Cognitive, social, and physiological determinants of emotional state. *Psychological Review, 69*, 379–399.

Schraedley, P. K., Gotlib, I. H., & Hayward, C. (1999). Gender differences in correlates of depressive symptoms in adolescents. *Journal of Adolescent Health, 25*, 98–108.

Segal, B. M., & Stewart, J. C. (1996). Substance use and abuse in adolescence: An overview. *Child Psychiatry and Human Development, 26*, 193–210.

Seligman, M. E. (1975). *Helplessness: On depression, development, and death.* San Francisco: Freeman.

Shaffer, D., & Craft, L. (1999). Methods of adolescent suicide prevention. *Journal of Clinical Psychiatry, 60*, 70–74.

Shaffer, D., Garland, A., Gould, M., Fisher, P., & Trautman, P. (1988). Preventing teenage suicide: A critical review. *Journal of the American Academy of Child and Adolescent Psychiatry, 27*, 675–687.

Shaw, J. A., & Campo-Bowen, A. (1995). Aggression. In D. Sholevar (Ed.), *Conduct disorders in children and adolescents* (pp. 45–57). Washington, DC: American Psychiatric Press.

Shea, M. E. (1998). When the tables are turned: Verbal sexual coercion among college women. In P. Anderson & C. Struckman-Johnson (Eds.), *Sexually aggressive women: Current perspectives and controversies* (pp. 94–104). New York: Guilford Press.

Sheehan, W., & Garfinkel, B. D. (1988). Adolescent autoerotic deaths. *Journal of the American Academy of Child and Adolescent Psychiatry, 27*, 367–370.

Shelden, R. G., Tracy, S. K., & Brown, W. B. (1997). *Youth gangs in American society.* New York: Wadsworth.

Shelder, J., & Block, J. (1990). Adolescent drug use and psychological health. *American Psychologist, 45*, 612–630.

Sheley, J. F., Zhang, J., Brody, C. J., & Wright, J. D. (1995). Gang organization, gang criminal activity, and individual gang members' criminal behavior. *Social Science Quarterly, 76*, 53–68.

Shepperd, J. A., & Arkin, R. M. (1990). Shyness and self-presentation. In W. Crozier (Ed.), *Shyness and embarrassment* (pp. 286–314). Cambridge, England: Cambridge University Press.

Shneidman, E. S. (1991). The commonalities of suicide across the life span. In A. Leenaars (Ed.), *Life perspectives of suicide* (pp. 39–52). New York: Plenum Press.

Shneidman, E. S. (1993). Commentary: Suicide as psychache. *The Journal of Nervous and Mental Disease, 181*, 145–147.

Shotland, R. L., & Goodstein, L. (1983). Just because she doesn't want to doesn't mean it's rape: An experimentally based causal model of the perception of rape in a dating situation. *Social Psychology Quarterly, 46*, 220–232.

Siegel, S. J., & Alloy, L. B. (1990). Interpersonal perceptions and consequences of depressive-significant other relationships: A naturalistic study of college roommates. *Journal of Abnormal Psychology, 99*, 361–373.

Smith, C., Feldman, S. S., Nasserbakht, A., & Steiner, H. (1993). Psychological characteristics and DSM-III-R diagnoses at 6-year follow-up of adolescent anorexia nervosa. *Journal of the American Academy of Child and Adolescent Psychiatry, 32*, 1237–1245.

Smolak, L., & Levine, M. P. (1996). Adolescent transitions and the development of eating problems. In L. Smolak, M. Levine, & R. Striegel-Moore (Eds.), *The developmental psychopathology of eating disorders: Implications for research, prevention, and treatment* (pp. 207–233). Mahwah, NJ: Lawrence Erlbaum Associates.

Smoller, J. W., Wadden, T. A., & Stunkard, A. J. (1987). Dieting and depression: A critical review. *Journal of Psychosomatic Research, 31*, 429–440.

Sommers-Flanagan, J. (1996). The efficacy of antidepressant medication with depressed youth. *Professional Psychology: Research and Practice, 27*, 145–153.

Spergel, I., Ross, R. E., Curry, G. D., & Chance, R. (1989). *Youth gangs: Problem and response*. Washington, DC: Office of Juvenile Justice and Delinquency Prevention.

Spirito, A., Overholser, J., & Hart, K. (1991). Cognitive characteristics of adolescent suicide attempters. *Journal of the American Academy of Child and Adolescent Psychiatry, 30*, 604–608.

Spirito, A., & Overholser, J. C. (1993). Primary and secondary prevention strategies for reducing suicide among youth. *Child and Adolescent Mental Health Care, 3*, 205–217.

Spitz, R. A. (1949a). Anxiety in infancy: A study of its phenomenology. *International Journal of Psychoanalysis, 30*, 201.

Spoth, R., Redmond, C., & Lepper, H. (1999). Alcohol initiation outcomes of universal family-focused preventive interventions: One- and two-year follow-ups of a controlled study. *Journal of Studies on Alcohol, 13*, 103–111.

Stark, K. D., Rouse, L. W., & Kurowski, C. (1994). Psychological treatment approaches for depression in children. In W. Reynolds and H. Johnston (Eds.), *Handbook of depression in children and adolescents* (pp. 275–307). New York: Plenum Press.

Stark, R., & Bainbridge, W. S. (1987). *A theory of religion*. New York: Peter Lang.

Steinberg, L., & Belsky, J. (1996). An evolutionary perspective on psychopathology in adolescence. In D. Cicchetti & S. Toth (Eds.), *Adolescence: Opportunities and challenges* (pp. 93–124). Rochester, NY: University of Rochester Press.

Steinberg, L. D. (1999). *Adolescence*. New York: McGraw-Hill.

Steiner, H., & Lock, J. (1998). Anorexia nervosa and bulimia nervosa in children and adolescents: A review of the past 10 years. *Journal of the American Academy of Child and Adolescent Psychiatry, 37*, 352–359.

Stevens, M. M., Mott., L. A., & Youells, F. (1996). Rural adolescent drinking behavior: Three year follow-up in the New Hampshire substance abuse prevention study. *Adolescence, 31*, 159–166.

Stoil, M. J., & Hill, G. (1996). *Preventing substance abuse: Interventions that work*. New York: Plenum Press.

Stone, M. H. (1998). Normal narcissism. In E. F. Ronningstam (Ed.), *Disorders of narcissism* (pp. 7–28). Washington, DC: American Psychiatric Press.

Stoppard, J. M., & Paisley, K. (1987). Masculinity, femininity, life stress, and depression. *Sex Roles, 16,* 489–496.

Striegel-Moore, R. H. (1993). Etiology of binge eating: A developmental perspective. In C. G. Fairburn & G. T. Wilson (Eds.), *Binge eating: Nature, assessment and treatment* (pp. 144–172). New York: Guilford Press.

Strober, M., Lampert, C., Schmidt, S., Morrel, W. (1993). The course of major depressive disorder in adolescents. *Journal of the American Academy of Child and Adolescent Psychiatry, 32,* 34–42.

Strong, K. G., & Huon, G. F. (1998). An evaluation of a structural model for studies of the initiation of dieting among adolescent girls. *Journal of Psychosomatic Research, 44,* 315–326.

Struckman-Johnson, C., & Anderson, P. (1998). "Men do and women don't": Difficulties in researching sexually aggressive women. In P. Anderson & C. Struckman-Johnson (Eds.), *Sexually aggressive women: Current perspectives and controversies* (pp. 9–18). New York: Guilford Press.

Swaim, R. C., Beauvais, F., Chavez, E. L., & Oetting, E. R. (1997). The effect of school dropout rates on estimates of adolescent substance use among three racial/ethnic groups. *American Journal of Public Health, 87,* 51–55.

Synovitz, L. B., & Byrne, T. J. (1998). Antecedents of sexual victimization: Factors discriminating victims from nonvictims.

Tabish, K. R., & Orell, L. H. (1996). Respect: Gang mediation at Albuquerque, New Mexico's Washington Middle School. *The School Counselor, 44,* 65–70.

Taylor, C. S. (1993). *Girls, gangs, women, and drugs.* East Lansing: Michigan State University Press.

Thiessen, D. (1990). Hormonal correlates of sexual aggression. In L. Ellis & H. Hoffman (Eds.), *Crime in biological, social and moral contexts* (pp. 153–161). New York: Praeger.

Thompson, J. K., & Heinberg, L. (1993). Preliminary test of two hypotheses of body image disturbance. *International Journal of Eating Disorders, 14,* 59–63.

Thornberry, T. P. (1998). Membership in gangs and involvement in serious and violent offending. In R. Roeber & D. P. Farrington (Eds.), *Serious and violent juvenile offenders* (pp. 147–166). Beverly Hills, CA: Sage.

Thornberry, T. P., & Burch, J. H. (1997). *Gang members and delinquent behaviors.* Washington, DC: Office of Juvenile Justice and Delinquency Prevention.

Thornberry, T. P., Krohn, M. D., Lizotte, A. J., & Chard-Wierschem, D. (1993). The role of juvenile gangs in facilitating delinquent behavior. *Journal of Research in Crime and Delinquency, 30,* 55–87.

Toolan, J. M. (1962). Depression in children and adolescents. *American Journal of Orthopsychiatry, 32,* 404–415.

Tate, D. C., Reppucci, N. D., & Mulvey, E. P. (1995). Violent juvenile delinquents: Treatment effectiveness and implications for future action. *American Psychologist, 50,* 777–781.

Udry, J. R., Billy, J. O., Morris, N. M., Groff, T. R., & Raj, M. (1985). Serum androgenic hormones motivate sexual behavior in adolescent boys. *Fertility and Sterility, 43,* 90–94.

U.S. Department of Health and Human Services. (1998). *Child maltreatment 1996: Reports from the states to the National Child Abuse and Neglect Data System.* Washington, DC: Government Printing Office.

Van der Molen, H. T. (1990). A definition of shyness and its implications for clinical practice. In W. Crozier (Ed.), *Shyness and embarrassment* (pp. 286–314). Cambridge: Cambridge University Press.

Vannatta, R. A. (1996). Risk factors related to suicidal behavior among male and female adolescents. *Journal of Youth and Adolescence, 25,* 149–159.

Vieland, V., et al. (1991). The impact of curriculum-based suicide prevention programs for teenagers. *Journal of the American Academy of Child and Adolescent Psychiatry, 30,* 811–815.

Vigil, J. D. (1988). *Barrio gangs.* Austin: University of Texas Press.

Vitiello, B., & Stoff D. M. (1997). Subtypes of aggression and their relevance to child psychiatry. *Journal of the American Academy of Child and Adolescent Psychiatry, 36,* 307–315.

Waldron, H. B. (1997). Adolescent substance abuse and family therapy outcome. *Advances in Clinical Child Psychology, 19,* 199–234.

Walsh, J. F., & Foshee, V. (1998). Self-efficacy, self-determination, and victim blaming as predictors of adolescent sexual victimization. *Health Education Research, 13,* 139–144.

Warner, V., Mufson, L., & Weissman, M. M. (1995). Offspring at high and low risk for depression and anxiety: Mechanisms of psychiatric disorder. *Journal of the American Academy of Child and Adolescent Psychiatry, 34,* 786–797.

Watson, P. J., Hickman, S. E., & Morris, R. J. (1996). Self-reported narcissism and shame: Testing the defensive self-esteem and continuum hypotheses. *Personality and Individual Differences, 21,* 253–259.

Webster. (1999). *Webster's college dictionary.* New York: Random House.

Weinberg, N. Z., Rahdert, E., Colliver, J. D., & Glantz, M. D. (1998). Adolescent substance abuse: A review of the past 10 years. *Journal of the American Academy of Child and Adolescent Psychiatry, 37,* 252–261.

Weiss, J. M., Simson, P. G., & Simson, P. E. (1989). Neurochemical basis of stress-induced depression. In H. Weiner & I. Florin (Eds.), *Frontiers of stress research* (pp. 37–50). Stuttgart, Germany: Hans Huber.

Weissman, M. M., Wolk, S., Goldstein, R. B., Moreau, D., Adams, P., Greenwald, S., Klier, C. M., Ryan, N. D., Dahl, R. E., & Wickramaratne, P. (1999). Depressed adolescents grown up. *Journal of the American Medical Association, 281,* 1707–1713.

Whitaker, A., Johnson, J., Shaffer, D., Rapoport, J., Kalikow, K., Walsh, B., Davies, M., Braiman, S., & Dolinsky, A. (1990). Uncommon troubles in young people: Prevalence estimates of selected psychiatric disorders in a nonreferred adolescent population. *Archives of General Psychiatry, 47,* 487–496.

Whitaker, A. H. (1992). An epidemiological study of anorectic and bulimic symptoms in adolescent girls: Implications for pediatricians. *Pediatric Annals, 21,* 752–759.

Wiehe, V. R., & Richards, A. L. (1995). *Intimate betrayal.* Thousand Oaks, CA: Sage.

Wilens, T. E., Biederman, J., Abrantes, A. M., & Spencer, T. J. (1997). Clinical characteristics of psychiatrically referred adolescent outpatients with substance use disorder. *Journal of the American Academy of Child and Adolescent Psychiatry, 36,* 941–947.

Wilkinson, R. B., & Walford, W. A. (1998). The measurement of adolescent psychological health: One or two dimensions? *Journal of Youth and Adolescence, 27,* 443–455.

Wilson, M., & Daly, M. (1985). Competitiveness, risk-taking, and violence: The young male syndrome. *Ethnology and Sociobiology, 6,* 59–73.

Windle, M., Miller-Tutzauer, C., & Domenico, D. (1992). Alcohol use, suicidal behavior, and risky activities among adolescents. *Journal of Research on Adolescence, 2,* 317–330.

Wink, P. (1991). Two faces of narcissism. *Journal of Personality and Social Psychology, 61,* 590–597.

Winkel, F. W., & de Kleuver, E. (1997). Communication aimed at changing cognitions about sexual intimidation: Comparing the impact of a perpetrator-focused versus a victim-focused persuasive strategy. *Journal of Interpersonal Violence, 12,* 513–529.

Woodside, D. B. (1995). A review of anorexia nervosa and bulimia nervosa. *Current Problems in Pediatrics, 25,* 67–89.

Wright, S. A. (1987). *Leaving cults: The dynamics of defection.* Storrs, CT: Society for the Scientific Study of Religion.

Young, J. G., Brasic, J. R., Sheitman, B., & Studnick, M. (1994). Brain mechanisms mediating aggression and violence. In C. Chiland & J. Young (Eds.), *Children and violence* (pp. 13–48). Northvale, NJ: Jason Aronson.

Zimbardo, P. G. (1977). *Shyness: What it is, what to do about it.* Reading, MA: Addison-Wesley.

Zimbardo, P. G., Pilkonis, P., & Norwood, R. (1975). The social disease called shyness. *Psychology Today, 8,* 69–72.

Zuckerman, M. (1979). *Sensation seeking: Beyond the optimal level of arousal.* Hillsdale, NJ: Lawrence Erlbaum Associates.

Zuckerman, M. (1990). The psychophysiology of sensation seeking. *Journal of Personality, 58,* 313–345.

NAME INDEX

SUBJECT INDEX

A

Active consent, 180
Adjustment disorder, 68
Adolescence
  ages, 14
  increased vulnerability to
    narcissism, 61
Affective aggression, 159
Aggression
  anger control, 173
  biological influences, 162–164
  cognitive therapy, 173
  family therapy, 172
  positive aspects, 157
  stability, 160
  television and other media,
    166–167
  testosterone, 163–164, 171
Aggressive instinct, 169–170
Alcohol and other drugs
  aggression, 164, 171
  risk taking, 47, 49
  sexual assault, 186
  suicide, 100
Alcoholics Anonymous, 130
Anaclitic depression, 69
Anorexia nervosa
  characteristics, 134
Antidepressant medications, 82–83
Atypical binge eating, 135

B

Behavioral inhibition, 28
Binge-purge cycle, 134, 147, 148
Brainwashing, 217, 218
Bulimia nervosa
  characteristics, 134–135
Bullying, 161

C

Charismatic leader, 214
Children of depressed mothers, 76
Classical conditioning
  shyness, 38
Cognitions
  aggression, 168
  biased perception, 98
  constriction, 98–99, 146
  depression, 74–75
  drug use, 119, 120, 121, 122, 127
  eating disorders, 144, 146
  risk taking, 45, 48, 52
  shyness, 35, 38
  suicide, 98, 104–105
Completed suicide, 89
Conditioned withdrawal, 124, 129
Context of behavior, 19
Continuum of behaviors, 6, 16
Cults
  behavioral expectations, 214
  characteristics, 213–215
  deprogramming, 222
  isolation, 213, 214, 217
  joining, 215–216
  leaving, 218–220

D

D.A.R.E., 126–127, 206
Decisions about behaviors, 7
Depression
  attachment, 76
  characteristics, 68
  cognitive therapy, 83, 85–86
  medications, 82–83
  puberty, 78
  relapse, 72
  stress, 76, 79–80